CHILD EXPLOITATION AND TRAFFICKING

CHILD EXPLOITATION AND TRAFFICKING

Examining the Global Challenges and U.S. Responses

Virginia M. Kendall and T. Markus Funk

ROWMAN & LITTLEFIELD PUBLISHERS, INC.
Lanham • Boulder • New York • Toronto • Plymouth, UK

Published by Rowman & Littlefield Publishers, Inc.
A wholly owned subsidiary of The Rowman & Littlefield Publishing Group, Inc.
4501 Forbes Boulevard, Suite 200, Lanham, Maryland 20706
http://www.rowmanlittlefield.com

Estover Road, Plymouth PL6 7PY, United Kingdom

British Library Cataloguing in Publication Information Available

Library of Congress Cataloging-in-Publication Data

Kendall, Virginia M., 1962–
  Child exploitation and trafficking : examining the global challenges and U.S. responses / Virginia M. Kendall and T. Markus Funk.
    p. cm.
  Includes index.
  ISBN 978-1-4422-0980-0 (cloth : alk. paper) — ISBN 978-1-4422-0982-4 (electronic)
  1. Child trafficking victims—Legal status, laws, etc.—United States. 2. Human trafficking—United States. 3. Human trafficking—Investigation—United States. I. Funk, T. Markus. II. Title.
  KF9449.K46 2012
  345.73'0253—dc23   2011033711

∞™ The paper used in this publication meets the minimum requirements of American National Standard for Information Sciences—Permanence of Paper for Printed Library Materials, ANSI/NISO Z39.48-1992.

Printed in the United States of America

Contents

Foreword

Richard A. Posner *

C*HILD EXPLOITATION AND TRAFFICKING* by Virginia M. Kendall and T. Markus Funk is a detailed, lucid, and comprehensive legal treatise on a major global crime wave—the sexual abuse of children—and on the efforts of the United States and other nations to combat it. The authors are admirably equipped to tackle this difficult and important subject. Kendall is a federal district judge and former federal prosecutor; Funk is a formal federal prosecutor and present practicing lawyer. Kendall has prosecuted criminals and now tries and sentences them; Funk has both prosecuted and defended criminals. Together, as federal prosecutors in Chicago, they litigated a major child pornography case recounted in fascinating detail in the book.

The book describes the varieties of sexual abuse of children, the legal tools available to cope with them with particular emphasis on U.S. and international law, the methods of investigating and proving child sexual abuse, and (overlapping the methodologies of investigation and proof) the legal rules (including constitutional and statutory constraints) that come into play when a child sexual abuser is charged, tried, convicted, and sentenced. The book is fair-minded, with attention being paid to defending against accusations of child sexual abuse as well as prosecuting. It will be an invaluable resource to judges, prosecutors, police, criminologists, and the defense bar; not the least of its merits is simply unpacking the many layers of America's complex

---

*Judge, U.S. Court of Appeals for the Seventh Circuit; senior lecturer, University of Chicago Law School; and author of *Sex and Reason* (1992) and coauthor (with Katherine Sillbaugh) of *A Guide to America's Sex Laws* (1996).

and redundant set of federal criminal prohibitions of child sexual abuse. Sex crimes involving children are a major focus of federal law enforcement and a major subject of federal criminal litigation; participants in that litigation, whether as judges, prosecutors, investigators, or defense lawyers, will find this treatise indispensable. I know that it will be of great value to me in dealing with the many appeals that my court receives from convictions and sentences in cases of sex crimes against children.

There is nothing new about the sexual abuse of children, and, as the authors note, some observers think that the United States has an unhealthy, prurient, and perhaps even hysterical obsession with the problem. We do seem to take it a good deal more seriously than other nations, and the authors are persuasive that it deserves to be taken seriously. But what is true and concerning is the definition of "child" in our laws relating to sexual abuse: generally it is anyone under the age of eighteen, and the authors suggest that it be made the international norm. Yet the age of consent even in countries that we consider to be peers is generally lower. Given contemporary sexual mores, there is an argument for reducing it in the United States to sixteen, which would automatically reduce the amplitude of the sexual abuse crime wave. That issue aside, there is a strong argument for making it uniform across the states of the United States, and for reconsidering the paradox that minors well below the age of consent are considered mature enough to be punished as adults for most crimes, including murder. These are issues that would repay consideration by the authors in future work.

Consideration might also be given to the desirability and feasibility of legalizing prostitution, though not, of course, child prostitution. If adult prostitution were legal, as it is to a greater or lesser extent in many European countries, the ugly practice described by the authors of recruiting pre-adult girls as prostitutes because they are more easily inveigled and controlled would probably diminish as the supply of adult women willing to work as prostitutes increased.

But these are details. Even with reforms such as I have just been discussing, the nation will continue to be beset by a child sexual abuse crime wave, which has undoubtedly grown, and may still be growing, as a result of the electronic revolution. This is most obvious with regard to child pornography, and only a little less so with regard to child seduction or molestation; sexual predators enter chat rooms to arrange meetings with underage children, a method of recruitment that is more effective than accosting youngsters on the street or in other public places. (One reason for the prevalence of child molestation by priests is that they have innocent-appearing opportunities to meet in private with children.)

The greatest impact of the electronic revolution on sexual crime has been on child pornography. The production, distribution, and consumption of such pornography must have been uncommon offenses before the advent of the Internet; the logistics were complicated, and the risk of detection of pornography sent through the mail must have been high. Just difficulty in identifying other pedophiles must have been a formidable impediment to trafficking in child pornography. The Internet has changed all that. It has enabled the creation of a global network of pedophiles (and of producers of pornography who may be actuated by strictly financial motives, and have no personal interest in the stuff) who download, upload, sell, swap, and store photographic images of children (many very young) engaged in sexual activity (often sadistic) or shown nude.

Online child pornography is the major target of sex crime law enforcement, because it is so immense. Questions are sometimes raised about the criminal gravity of merely downloading child pornography, as distinct from producing or distributing it. There is, however, an invasion of the child's privacy, and any increase in the consumption of pornography increases the supply of it (increased demand increasing supply) and therefore the number of children who are victimized by it. Whether it also stimulates the consumers to molest children, operates as a substitute for molestation, or has both effects, which may or may not cancel out either in the individual or across individuals, is (so far as I am aware) unknown. But the other harms that consuming pornography causes are sufficient to justify treating it as serious criminal activity, as indeed it is (at least in this country). Nevertheless, reducing the age of consent might enable a sharper focus on the most harmful forms of child pornography.

There are three major, related, and unresolved issues concerning criminal sexual abuse of children. The first is how widespread it is despite the efforts made to combat it; the second is whether massively greater efforts to deter or otherwise prevent it should be made; and the third is what can be done to make law enforcement in this area more effective short of a major increase in law enforcement resources allocated to it.

Sexual abuse of children is undoubtedly very widespread. Sexual interest in children is widespread (although almost all the offenders are men) and, among men who harbor such an interest, it is compulsive. It is true that pedophiles, in the sense of men sexually attracted to prepubescent children, are only a small fraction of all men (for rather obvious evolutionary reasons—males who are attracted, even if not exclusively, to females who are too young to be fertile tend to have fewer descendants on average). I have read somewhere that it is only a tenth of 1 percent. But many normal men are attracted to pubescent girls, who are young teenagers highly vulnerable to seduction and abuse by men and therefore deserving of legal protection.

So potential sexual predators are very numerous, and, as the authors point out, sex crimes are greatly underreported. In this they resemble "victimless" crimes like gambling and the sale and consumption of illegal drugs. Sexual crimes against children are, of course, not victimless (nor are some of the other "victimless" crimes), but the victims may be too young to report a crime (or even realize that they have been victims of a crime), or may be embarrassed to do so, or easily intimidated. Moreover, even if the percentage of sexual predators among the male population is small, a small percentage of the world's entire male population translates into a very large absolute number: one thousandth of the world's adult male population is more than two million men.

There is no question of driving the rate of child sexual abuse to zero. Crime rates can be driven to zero only by decriminalizing conduct classified as criminal. In 2010, there were almost fifteen thousand reported murders in the United States (the actual number must have been higher, because not all murders are detected). The number is deemed tolerable in the sense that there is no great push to allocate more law enforcement resources to murders in order to push down the rate; one reason there is no such push is that the murder rate has declined considerably in recent years.

There is not the same complacent feeling about sex crimes involving children; the number is not known but the sense is that it is intolerably high. This is reflected in the very large number of overlapping sex crime laws that Congress has enacted in recent years, a trend well documented in the book. The authors make a number of suggestions for improving law enforcement in the area of child sexual abuse but do not recommend a massive increase in resources. The present fiscal crisis would make such a recommendation quixotic. But it is an issue that will have to be faced eventually.

Short of a massive expansion in resources devoted to the prevention and punishment of sex crimes involving children, the most promising avenue of improved law enforcement is greater surveillance. The Internet is not only the key enabler of the widespread dissemination and consumption of child pornography but also an important enabler of the seduction, kidnapping, rape, and occasional murder of children. The Internet thus plays a role in sexual abuse of children that is similar to the role it plays in international terrorism. But the Internet as a crime enabler is vulnerable to surveillance by law enforcement authorities—not only passive surveillance but also using the Internet to disrupt criminal planning, as when police officers enter Internet chat rooms pretending to be teenage girls in order to lawfully entrap men using the chat rooms to try to meet girls whom they might seduce (or worse).

But Internet surveillance—wiretapping writ large—raises issues of privacy and civil liberty. Modern technology enables the government to vacuum almost the world's entire electronic communications and use digitized search technology to identify suspicious messages which can then be read by police or intelligence analysts. The search techniques are not perfect and government personnel may not be entirely trustworthy. Some balance has to be struck between the justified desire to reduce criminal activity and the protection of privacy and civil liberties.

As with terrorism, so with sexual abuse of children—the response of governments is in flux. This treatise is a milestone on the road to improved policy in this difficult and important area.

Acknowledgments

The authors wish to acknowledge the tremendous help and support provided by Jeffrey Baltruzak, Thomas Weber, Omar Alam, Krista Stone-Manista, Antonio Haines, and Elliot Curry, without which this work would never have been completed.

To our amazing spouses, Preston and Kate, who have patiently suffered through the late-night editing sessions and constant discussion about topics that were not always dinner-table talk but that were generally had around meals. Thank you for your generosity in allowing us to follow our passion.

Lastly, to the victims we have worked with over the years, who have taught us that strength, determination, and courage can conquer all pains. You are the ones who have instilled in us the passion to commit to this project and see it through. We are indebted to you all for allowing us to walk with you during your journey.

1

Introduction

EACH YEAR, MORE THAN TWO MILLION CHILDREN around the world fall victim to commercial sexual exploitation.[1] The numbers of children sexually abused for noncommercial purposes are even higher.

The abuse does not end with the act of exploitation. Today's commercial and preferential abusers[2] routinely memorialize millions of sexually abusive acts through digital media devices, granting even "average" child pornography collectors the means to amass vast collections of pictures and videos unimaginable twenty years ago, and perpetuating the victims' sexual exploitation for generations.

Compounding the damaging impact of such pervasive and graphic chronicling of exploitation, the Internet now offers virtually instantaneous and anonymous dissemination of the images of abuse to all corners of the globe through online file-sharing networks, listservs, and more than 1,500 websites exclusively featuring child pornography. The cumulative effect of these paradigm-shifting developments is a drastic acceleration of the traditional supply-and-demand dynamics. The once dark, isolated, and secretive world of child sexual exploitation is now, put simply, a global commercial reality.

Trade through barter is one of the constant drivers of both the commercial and preferential markets for child pornography. In the world of the child-pornography trader, graphic depictions, particularly those that are "new" or otherwise not widely available, function as highly prized "chits." Such unique images permit pornography traders, through swapping, to continually expand their personal hoards. With modern communication technologies changing the way child pornographers produce, obtain, possess, and distribute their illicit collections, the Internet has created a true global bazaar of child pornography.

Organized crime's entry into the commercial child sexual exploitation arena explains why, from the perspective of law enforcement, the last fifteen to twenty years have produced the perfect storm of factors for this new world order of child sexual exploitation. While the child sex trade was once the *terra familiaris* of secluded clusters of socially isolated pedophiles, present-day organized crime groups, because of their trademark adaptability, have recognized the tremendous financial potential of feeding the dark desires of the world's millions of potential child pornography consumers, standing ready and willing to pay handsomely for fresh images of children being sexually abused. Capitalizing on their pre-existing criminal resources and supply chains put in place to serve "traditional" illicit activities, such as the global narcotics and arms trade, today's organized crime groups rely on child trafficking, as well as mobile child pornography production facilities, to flood the Internet with record volumes of new material. Child Exploitation, Inc., now sits on top of a multibillion-dollar annual cash stream that shows no signs of abating.

Although virtually every nation provides, at least in terms of legislation, criminal punishment for those who engage in such structured child exploitation, organized crime continues to tip the risk-reward calculus in its favor by operating out of developing world regions—areas where the rule of law has yet to fully take hold. Organized crime has unceremoniously seized the immensely lucrative commercial aspects of child exploitation, expanded it into one of its most vital and rapidly expanding profit centers, and has done so with remarkably little resistance from the world community.

Even in the United States, the victims are becoming younger, and the nature of the exploitation more violent. According to recent estimates, one in seven children, age ten and older, has received a sexual solicitation or has been approached over the Internet. The sexual exploitation of children, both in the United States and abroad, has, to put it bluntly, reached a tragic crisis point.

What sets this species of predatory crime apart from other crimes is that law enforcement and citizens alike almost universally revile its perpetrators. Society's challenge is to translate this deep-seated, global antipathy toward the exploiters into serious substantive action. Recently, there has been some good news to report as the internationally coordinated fight against child sexual exploitation has chalked up some impressive gains. Examples include the following: "Operation Cathedral," in which the British National Crime Squad and police forces from 13 other nations arrested 107 suspects and seized some 750,000 Internet-traded images containing 1,200 uniquely identifiable child victims[3]; "Operation Amethyst," a U.S./Republic of Ireland investigation leading to one of the Republic of Ireland's largest police operations[4]; "Operation Auxin," an Australian Federal Police operation leading to the arrest of some four hundred individuals involved in the transnational manufacturing and sharing of child pornography[5]; and, perhaps most notably, "Operation Rescue," a three-year Europol investigation culminating in the March 2011 arrests of 184 suspects[6] and the rescue of 230 children.[7]

While the world's police forces, through such operations, demonstrate their growing commitment to working cooperatively to crack down on child sexual exploitation, the U.S. government continues to carry the torch, expending the greatest resources in its quest to pursue high-level exploiters wherever they may be found. By drafting, promoting, and signing international treaties and conventions aimed at fighting child exploitation, boosting funding for U.S. and international anti-exploitation efforts, and passing proactive domestic legislation, including criminal statutes with extraterritorial reach and enhanced criminal penalties, the federal government has signaled its unequivocal commitment to making significant inroads in the global war against child exploitation.

That said, to the eyes of many critics of U.S. enforcement policy, the contemporary crucible has swung too far. Critics view U.S. efforts as a "witch hunt" for those who merely possess images of child pornography, and rue the draconian sentences for conduct, such as the simple possession of a few images viewed on the Internet—all of which they consider relatively *de minimus* criminal conduct.

Whatever one's political or moral view on the efficacy of recent U.S. and foreign law enforcement successes, enforcement efforts continue to target the ongoing battle against the corrosive combined impact of prejudices, flawed assumptions, and archaic misperceptions of the crime. These mordant influences interfere with both the effectiveness and the fairness of how politicians, law enforcement, judicial officials, victim advocates, and defense counsel approach the issues of domestic and international child exploitation.

Prosecutors and investigators assigned to handle child pornography cases, for example, may not be familiar with the complex legal and psychological nuances characterizing the investigations and, therefore, treat them as little more than unpleasant "kiddie porn"[8] matters that are to be disposed of as quickly as possible. Judges may also find dealing with these matters unpalatable and, as a result, may not be conversant on what the extensive academic literature teaches on key issues such as recidivism rates for the different categories of child exploitation offenses. Worse, they may feel inclined to "even a playing field" that they believe is being unfairly slanted against defendants as a result of overly emotional responses to this category of crime, thereby negating the body of academic, penological, and medical evidence supporting that response. Additionally, while a victim advocate may understand the difficulty of protecting the physical and psychological well-being of an abused child, the advocate may not appreciate her own impact on the victim's well-being, such as how the elicited victim's statement made to the advocate can subsequently be used in court to impeach the victim's version of events, or how it may expose the victim or her family[9] to retaliation at the hands of the victimizer. Likewise, defense counsel, confronted with the uniquely challenging task of advocating on behalf of an individual accused of child sexual exploitation, has his own set of distinct challenges, such as (1) not knowing where to look for potentially mitigating evidence, and (2) not recognizing the legal arguments that are most promising for persuading the prosecutor to drop certain charges or agree to leniency at sentencing, or for convincing the jury of his client's innocence. The upshot of this lack of familiarity is that victims are not treated appropriately, and cases are not properly investigated, with some defendants receiving inappropriately light sentences, while others are punished too severely. In short, historically, the roles played within the criminal justice system have become one-dimensional caricatures, limiting a comprehensive and thoughtful approach to the issues. Rather than embrace the intricacies of the problem, the players fall comfortably back into simplistic stereotypes. True social change, however, demands a thorough analysis of the offense, the offenders, and the treatment. It is time to embrace the discussion with the same vigor that academics and practitioners have used to address less emotionally volatile issues.

Our immediate aim, therefore, is to bring some fresh, practical thinking to this oft-uncomfortable area of the law, and to help erase some of its counterproductive mythology. This book provides the first comprehensive, practical introduction to the history and present-day reality of child sexual exploitation and trafficking, as well as to the interconnected web of domestic and transnational federal laws and law enforcement efforts launched in response thereto.

This book is no mere "academic" treatise. Rather, it is written from the distinctive perspective of those who have spent their careers in the trenches investigating, prosecuting, and adjudicating these intricate and commonly emotional cases. We have attempted to steer clear of purely psychological, legal, and academic terms, and have embraced a diction intended to make the issues more accessible to the trained practitioner, the curious academic or public official, and the educated layperson. We hope to open the debate about child sexual abuse by stripping it of its unhelpful, constricted definitions, and by candidly discussing the state of the law, the criminal justice process, and the treatment of offenders and victims.

This book, in short, will examine today's system of federal anti-exploitation laws; the Bermuda Triangle of family dynamics most likely to promote exploitation; the connection between modern communications technologies, such as the Internet, and the rise in U.S. and foreign child exploitation; the unique challenges posed by transnational investigations; organized crime's increasing domination over the commercial sexual exploitation of children; the current state of the U.S. government's transnational anti-trafficking efforts; the myriad of international legal instruments designed to enhance transnational enforcement efforts; how, during investigations, to avoid re-injuring the child victims; the hallmarks of an effective trial strategy; the most promising investigative and trial avenues for the defense; and what contemporary research tells us about charging- and sentencing-related issues, including victimization and recidivism rates.

Despite the descriptive aspects of this book, our deeper goal is to help untangle the complex maze of economic, social, and psychological factors that, by necessity, must inform any sound legal (as well as moral and clinical) analysis, and to build on these insights by suggesting best practices and legislative fixes. The book is proscriptive, as well as descriptive, in the sense that it relies on real-world examples to serve up practical advice and reform proposals aimed at those involved at all levels in this challenging area. Our hope is to provide laymen and experts alike a true practitioner's treatise, serving as a "first-line" resource for clear, practical thinking on the range of complex, and oft-misunderstood, investigative, prosecutorial, and rehabilitative issues surrounding child exploitation cases.

Additional firepower in the global war against exploitation is emphatically welcomed; today, we find ourselves at historic crossroads in the fight against the sexual exploitation of children. Such abuse, after all, presents true human rights issues, and if we accept the status quo ante, then the twin effects of almost-daily advances in modern communications technology and the stranglehold of organized crime promise to permanently outpace domestic and international enforcement efforts. Because this outcome is not acceptable, creative new thinking is required. It will be up to today's lawyers, legislators, politicians, prosecutors, investigators, judges, and concerned citizens to rise to the challenge, and to harness global resources and collective fresh thinking to stamp out the scourge of child sexual exploitation. We look forward to the discussion.

Notes

1. See Office to Monitor and Combat Trafficking in Persons, U.S. Department of State, Trafficking in Persons Report 13 (June 2010), available at www.state.gov/documents/organization/142979.pdf (hereafter 2010 TIP Report); see also Office to Monitor and Combat Trafficking in Persons, U.S. Department of State, Trafficking in Persons Report 24 (2008), available at www.state.gov/documents/organization/105501.pdf (hereafter 2008 TIP Report).

2. We use the term *preferential abuser* throughout this book to describe those who are sexually drawn to child pornography and children, and to distinguish them from those who sexually abuse children for commercial gain as their primary objective. In the real world, these lines of demarcation are, of course, not quite as sharply drawn; a large number of pornographers who are sexually attracted to children also decide to earn money from selling the child pornography they produce. Yet the distinction between preferential and commercial abusers is a useful one, and we, therefore, employ it throughout.

3. See generally Elaine Shannon, *Main Street Monsters*, TIME MAGAZINE, Sept. 14, 1998 (discussing the global sting relating to the criminal activities of the "Wonderland Club"), available at www.time.com/time/magazine/article/0,9171,989082,00.html (last visited on June 12, 2011).

4. See generally Conor Lally, *Garda Investigated over Child Porn on Internet*, IRISH TIMES, Dec. 19, 2002, at 3; Operation Amethyst, http://en.wikipedia.org/wiki/Operation_Amethyst (last visited on June 12, 2011).

5. See generally *More Arrests in Operation Auxin*, CANTERBURY EXPRESS, Nov. 12, 2004, at 2; *see also* Operation Auxin, http://en.wikipedia.org/wiki/Operation_Auxin (last visited on June 12, 2011).

6. The website at the center of the investigation was operated out of the Netherlands and had more than 70,000 worldwide members. *See Massive Online Pedophile Ring Busted by Cops*, MSNBC, available at www.msnbc.msn.com/id/42108748/ns/us_news-crime_and_courts/t/massive-online-pedophile-ring-busted-cops/ (last visited on June 12, 2011).

7. See generally Karen McVeigh, *Police Shut Down Global Paedophile Network in Operation Rescue*, THE GUARDIAN UK, March 16, 2011.

8. This common term is one that unjustifiably diminishes the seriousness of the offense and, therefore, is rarely uttered by experienced child exploitation prosecutors and investigators.

9. We, as a general matter, have tried to employ phraseology that eliminates the need for a pronoun. Because strict adherence to gender-neutral language can make for awkward reading, however, please forgive the default use of epicene masculine or feminine antecedents.

2

Surveying the Scope of the Problem

THE SEXUAL EXPLOITATION OF CHILDREN takes various forms, all of which bring to the fore complex and connected—but not always readily apparent—moral, legal, psychological, medical, sociological, and even geopolitical concerns. In terms of the spectrum of substantive criminal conduct, cases can range from the individual who possesses a few digital images of child pornography downloaded from the Internet, to transnational organizations that smuggle minors across national boundaries for purposes of forced prostitution and the commercial manufacture of highly lucrative child pornography. Though investigations may share some superficial similarities, each case and each accused is animated by a complex set of subsurface, but associated, factual and situational variables. The result is that no two cases are alike.

A. The Pros and Cons of Ramped-Up Media Attention

Popular media accounts in recent years have provided broad, often sensationalized, coverage of the high-profile cases, frequently involving either extreme facts (such as in the case of seventy-three-year-old Austrian Josef Fritzl, who locked his daughter beneath the family home for twenty-four years, fathered seven children with her, and raped her some three thousand times),[1] or defendants who occupied community positions of trust and influence (such as priests, doctors, Boy Scout leaders, coaches, and teachers). Headlines, however, tend to either bombastically scream with populist rage that a "Child Pornography Beast

Had the Book Thrown at Him" or somewhat ruefully note, "Man Subjected to Harsh Two-Hundred-Year Sentence for Kiddie Porn."

Setting aside for the moment matters of tone and accuracy, the popular attention brought to this emotionally charged topic unquestionably raises the profile of, and to some extent mainstreams the discussion of, the victimizers, the crime, and the victims. The largely positive upshot of this is that ramped-up media attention pulls the topic from the uncomfortable, and often hidden, recesses of the victims' very private narrative, placing it squarely within the popular mainstream and academic discourse.

B. Why Practitioners and the Public Must Understand "the Bigger (Exploitation) Picture"

While removing the social taboo that historically inhibited the open and honest discussion of child sexual exploitation has led to significant offender/victim treatment and law enforcement gains, the reality remains that judges, prosecutors, criminal investigators, defense lawyers, social workers, and victim advocates often operate in personal experiential and ideological silos. Stated bluntly, they are too frequently unaware of—and, worse, uninterested in—what animates those with perspectives or professional backgrounds differing from theirs.

The predictable result of such professional myopia is that judges all too frequently conceive of these extremely sensitive and difficult cases as little more than distasteful "kiddie porn" matters, which they wish would just disappear from their dockets. Prosecutors, on the other hand, can be tempted to steadfastly forge ahead in their effort to achieve convictions and maximize sentences, often with little sensitivity toward the re-victimization that results, or to the fact that child exploitation cases and defendants are not "one size fits all." Academics, social scientists, and civil libertarians, for their part, routinely author articles critical of current investigatory, prosecutorial, and sentencing approaches, even though their ruminations fail to encompass the benefit of a comprehensive understanding of the realities of today's criminal justice system, the serious harm inflicted on the victims, or the danger the defendants pose to their community. Meanwhile, the press provides continuing coverage of these cases from the above-described polarizing extremes, generally either vilifying the offender or disparaging the judiciary's attempts to deal with these intricate and challenging cases.

What is too often missing from the contemporary discourse on child exploitation is an accurate and comprehensive understanding of the interconnected investigative, legal, and psychological issues these cases involve. The ensuing knowledge vacuum is too frequently filled with brute intuition and bias.

C. Differing Perspectives on Child Sexual Exploitation

The topic of proscribing and punishing child exploitation triggers intense emotions. While there is general consensus that child sexual exploitation, whether through the Internet, forced prostitution, the international or domestic trafficking of children for sex, or molestation, is on the rise, observers in the United States and elsewhere find little common ground on the questions of how serious such conduct actually is, or what, if anything, must be done to address it.

There are, at bottom, fundamental moral and philosophical differences of opinion cleaving those who view "child sexual exploitation" as one of man's gravest sins from those who are supportive of "intergenerational relationships" and who hold the notion of child sexual "exploitation" to be little more than a social construct of recent vintage that is deployed by puritanical fanatics.

1. Advocates for, and Defenders of, Child-Adult Sexual Relationships

Those who advocate for the societal acceptance of adult/child sexual relationships find support in historical literature. Literal—not legal—"consent" is all that the law should require, argue those who support the decriminalization of most forms of "voluntary"[2] sexual contact between adults and minors:

- "A man . . . is at any rate born to be a lover of boys." (Plato, *Symposium*)
- "Some of the more experienced students of juvenile problems have come to believe that the emotional reactions of the parents, police officers, and other adults who discover that the child has had such a contact, may disturb the child more seriously than the sexual contacts themselves. The current hysteria over sex offenders may very well have serious effects on the ability of many of these children to work out sexual adjustments some years later. . . . The fact that there is a body of sex laws which is apart from the laws protecting persons is evidence of their distinct function, namely that of protecting custom." (Alfred Kinsey, et al., *Sexual Behavior in the Human Female* [1953])
- "Even at the age of four or five, this [female] seductiveness may be so powerful as to overwhelm the adult into committing the offense. The affair is therefore not always the result of the adult's aggression; often the young female is the initiator and seducer." (Ralph Slovenko and C. Phillips, "Psychosexuality and the Criminal Law," 15 *Vanderbilt L. Rev.* 809 [1962])
- "[Child molestation is a] relatively minor crime. . . . [The] absurdity of enforcing most of our sex laws . . . should be obvious, even to the most prudish

Neo-Puritans." (E. C. B. Jr., "Pedophilia, Exhibitionism, and Voyeurism: Legal Problems in the Deviant Society," 4 *Georgia L. Rev.* 150 [1969])

- "It makes about as much sense to leave children's sexual nourishment to their peers as it would to assume that the mud pies they make for each other are an adequate lunch. . . . A child's need for physical contact is as sexual as our own. . . . If we accepted sexual behaviour between children and adults, we would be far more able to protect our children from abuse and exploitation than we are now. . . . Children are sexual, and it is up to us to take responsibility for their real education." (Jane Rule, *Teaching Sexuality* [1979])
- "The threat to make all pedophile acts punishable by law can barely be labeled civilized. . . . It implies discrimination and persecution of a minority and should be abolished." (Dr. Gunter Schmidt, "Male Intergenerational Intimacy," 20 *J. of Homosexuality* [1990])
- "People seem to think that any (sexual) contact between children and adults has a bad effect on the child. I say this can be a loving and thoughtful, responsible sexual activity." (Michael Ebert, "Pedophilia Steps into the Daylight," *Focus on the Family Citizen* [November 16, 1992])
- "Naked kids have been a staple of delight for centuries, for both parents and onlookers. So to label pedophilia as criminal is ridiculous." (Allen Ginsburg, "The Liberation Is the Word," *Harv. Gay and Lesbian Rev.* [Summer 1997])

2. Critics of Prevailing Sentencing Practices

On the other end of the spectrum are those who do not subscribe to the moral relativists' "legalize it" positions, or to their view that adult-child sexual contact should be decriminalized, but instead take the position that the (increasingly harsh) punishment no longer fits the crime. Many in this group feel that, although child exploitation may be at its core morally wrong, jail is not the answer (or, perhaps, not the only answer), and that prevention and counseling should be given a more prominent role in a holistic approach directed at rehabilitation through the "treatment" of those afflicted with the "disease" of sexual desires relating to children. They, in short, advocate law reform:

- "These changes [to the federal child exploitation sentencing guidelines were] largely the consequence of numerous morality earmarks, slipped into larger bills over the last fifteen years, often without notice, debate, or study of any kind." (Troy Stabenow, "Deconstructing the Myth of Careful Study: A Primer on the Flawed Progression of the Child Pornography Guidelines" [2008])

- "Sentences are routinely more harsh and punitive than they need to be, especially in run-of-the-mill . . . child pornography cases." (Chief Judge Robert W. Pratt [S.D. Iowa], 2009 Sentencing Commission Testimony)
- "[The Federal Sentencing Guidelines] enhancements are often disconnected from any studied assessment of whether or why harsher sentences are warranted for defendants with certain characteristics." (Jelani Jefferson Exum, "Making the Punishment Fit the (Computer) Crime: Rebooting Notions of Possession for the Federal Sentencing of Child Pornography Offenses," 3 *Rich. J. L. & Tech.* 1 [2010])
- "Congress' appetite for expanding the scope of child pornography laws and increasing the length of prison sentences for child pornography offenders is blatant and unrelenting. . . . Despite strong Congressional belief, a growing number of federal judges . . . view most offenders who possess or trade child pornography as mostly harmless to others." (Melissa Hamilton, "The Efficacy of Severe Child Pornography Sentencing: Empirical Validity or Political Rhetoric" [2010])

3. The Proponents of Even Tougher Enforcement and Punishment

In notable contrast to the first two categories of critics are those who reject decriminalization and increased lenience, instead favoring even more "get-tough" measures, including mandatory incarceration for life and chemical castration for convicted child sex offenders. This group has concluded that rehabilitative efforts are largely futile because it is impossible to "reprogram" a person's sexual needs and desires; incapacitation through incarceration is, therefore, the most prudent response.

- "Penalties for sex offenses against children have been increased several times in recent years and are quite severe. Nevertheless, the Commission's analysis indicates that some amendments may be appropriate to increase sentences for the most dangerous offenders." (U.S. Sentencing Commission Report, "Sex Offenses against Children—Findings and Recommendations Regarding Federal Penalties" [June 1996])
- "[T]hese offenders have committed a sex crime and as a result have demonstrated a lack of mastery over their fantasies. . . . Castration is justified to help control their behavior. . . . Sex crimes are a significant public health problem, and efforts to deter offenders and protect the community [including chemical castration] are worthy." (Charles L. Scott, MD, and Trent Holmberg, MD, "Castration of Sex Offenders: Prisoners' Rights versus Public Safety," *31 J. Am. Acad. Psychiatry Law* 502 [2003])

- "Attorneys Generals, prosecutors, state legislatures should review and rectify the criminal law reforms brought in during the sexual revolution. We have a right to civility, to a return to relative safety and security for law-abiding citizens." (Dr. Judith A. Reisman, "Where Have We Been? Where Are We Going?" [November 2, 2005, speech to the Utah Council for Crime Prevention])
- "Child pornography harms and debases the most defenseless of our citizens." (*United States v. Williams*, 553 U.S. 285, 307 [2008])
- "We are on the right path, but I still say this is still not enough punishment for people who commit these despicable crimes. There is still a lot of work that needs to be done on this serious issue." (Senator Chuck Grassley, introducing the Prevention and Deterrence of Crimes against Children Act of 2008 [May 14, 2008])
- "Sexual exploitation of children causes irreparable harm to the youngest and most vulnerable members of our society." (Rob Nicholson, Minister of Justice and Attorney General of Canada, introducing the Protecting Children from Sexual Predators Act [November 4, 2010])
- "I want the message to the monsters that prey on our innocent children to be very clear: We will track you down, we will root you out, we will find you online—and when we do we will punish you with every tool we have. We will take away your freedom, your possessions, we will label you as a sex offender and we will do everything we can to keep you away from children." (Louisiana Governor Bobby Jindal, Press Conference [February 18, 2010])
- "[The Department of Justice] is focused on waging an aggressive battle to protect children from individuals who use computers or the United States mails to sexually abuse and exploit them." (USDOJ Child Exploitation and Obscenity Section's Mission Statement [2010])
- "A treatment regimen of [chemical castration] is not excessive when balanced against the harm the repeat child pornography offender has committed against children and society. Studies have revealed that chemical castration is the most effective and least intrusive method of treating criminal pedophiles." (Kristin Carlson, "Strong Medicine: Toward Effective Sentencing of Child Pornography Offenders," *Mich. L. Rev. First Impressions* [2010])

In the wake of these significantly divergent positions, observers can certainly be forgiven for being left unsure of the wisdom and fairness of today's coordinated law enforcement assault on those involved with manufacturing, distributing, trading, receiving, or possessing child pornography, or involved in child trafficking and forced prostitution.

D. What the Statistics Say about Predation and Rehabilitation

"Child Exploitation, Inc.," fuels a multibillion-dollar industry. Child pornography cartels produce and ship their "product" transnationally. Keeping the supply chain stocked and moving routinely involves the serial re-victimization of the same group of children, and the anonymity and relative safety of the Internet allows the illicit product to be efficiently shipped to paying customers around the globe, twenty-four hours a day, seven days a week.

And although it, as touched on above, in some circles is fashionable to minimize, or even deny, the actual danger posed to children, or to assert that the collective law enforcement response to child exploitation is disproportionately harsh, the statistical realities discussed below reveal that those who are sexually attracted to children pose a serious, and generally lifelong, danger to living, breathing minors. Even in the context of those who simply possess child pornography, the numbers demonstrate that the world of sexualized fantasies concerning children rarely remains purely the stuff of imagination. In the long run, actual sexual contact between the adult and minors is the norm and expected outcome. But to what extent?

The first of its kind, a 1988 study for which sex offenders were guaranteed anonymity provided a sobering insight into the reality of the criminal acts of sexual offenders. The study revealed that adult sex offenders in treatment admitted to having committed a staggering *average* of 533 sex offenses over the 12-year period predating their detection.[3]

Similarly, Dr. Andres E. Hernandez, director of the Sex Offender Treatment Program, Federal Bureau of Prisons, FCI Butner, in 2000 presented the results of his study of child pornography offenders, titled "Self-Reported Contact Sexual Offenses by Participants in the Federal Bureau of Prisons' Sex Offender Treatment Program: Implications for Internet Sex Offenders."[4] In this study, Dr. Hernandez, among other things, explored the correlation between child pornography offenses and actual child molestation. The study results were that a majority of the persons convicted of child pornography offenses actually molested significant numbers of children without detection by the criminal justice system:

> These offenders target children in Cyberspace in a similar manner as offenders who prey on children in their neighborhood or nearby park. They seek vulnerable children, gradually groom them, and eventually contact them to perpetrate sexual abuse.... These findings suggest that the majority of offenders convicted of Internet sexual crimes share similar behavioral characteristics as many child molesters. While these Internet sex offenders have unique patterns of sexual deviance, it appears that many can be equally [as] predatory and dangerous as extra-familial child molesters.[5]

More specifically, Dr. Hernandez found that 76 percent of the child pornographers or travelers (those who travel or intend to travel interstate for the purpose of having sex with a minor) who participated in his study admitted to having committed contact sex crimes that went undetected by the criminal justice system. Indeed, these offenders had an average of 30.5 child sex victims each, and, as a group, the study participants admitted to having molested a combined total of 1,433 victims without detection. And this number does not simply represent 1,433 undetected *offenses*; rather, it represents 1,433 undetected *victims* (many of whom were victimized multiple times).

Another prominent study echoed these findings; the average convicted child molester who in that study was interviewed under condition of anonymity admitted to having hundreds of previously unknown (and unreported) sexual contacts with children. The authors of this study were left to conclude that there is an "iceberg of undocumented offenses beneath the tip of the official records."[6]

Indeed, a number of studies similarly note that the "typical" sex offender's cold criminal record yields little useful information. The record, after all, in almost all cases drastically *under*states the actual rate of victimization, because most offenders are caught, prosecuted, and convicted on only a tiny fraction of the offenses they commit during their lives. That an average of ten to sixteen years pass between a sex offender's first sex offense and his arrest[7] serves to further underscore this concerning reality.

Moreover, even those who get caught continue to victimize. When tracked for twenty-five years, 88 percent of *convicted* offenders either reported criminal sexual contact with a minor or were re-arrested for such contact.[8]

These statistics, in short, lend weight to the claims of those who call for enhanced enforcement and long-term incapacitation through imprisonment. Today, all U.S. Attorney's Offices, and almost all larger state prosecutor offices, have prosecutors specifically designated to handle these cases, and the corresponding law enforcement agencies likewise have dedicated child exploitation investigators and agents. The Department of Justice (DOJ), moreover, provides daily advice and training to the nation's federal prosecutors through its Child Exploitation and Obscenity Section (CEOS), and on August 2, 2010, Attorney General Eric Holder announced DOJ's first-ever National Strategy for Child Exploitation Prevention and Interdiction.

But despite these advances, investigating and prosecuting offenders continues to be challenging, and the nature of this criminal activity frequently makes it difficult to gain the victims' trust and cooperation, and to arrest those involved. The U.S. Congress has responded to this challenge by incrementally passing extensive legislation aimed at severely punishing those involved in the exploitation of children and at promoting international anti-exploitation efforts, and has enacted a comprehensive set of victim protection laws.

Although this complex and interrelated legislative framework is now the firmly established law of the land, its theoretical and practical nuances are often misunderstood, and strategic opportunities are lost. The key to success, as we shall discover, is that the laws must be pursued in an integrated, holistic manner that involves not only investigators, prosecutors, and judges, but also child welfare advocates, social workers, state-federal task forces, the schools, foreign service officers, and others who provide critical support in the fight against child exploitation. It is true that the statistical realities touched on above paint a very different, and sadly more disheartening, picture than even practitioners working within the system generally realize. Understanding the laws' promises and limitations, and becoming more sensitive to the vulnerabilities of the victims and their family members, can advance a more nuanced and complete sense of how to justly deal with those who perpetrate sexual crimes against minors, as well as with their victims.

Notes

1. *See generally* Fritzl Case, http://en.wikipedia.org/wiki/Fritzl_case (last visited June 6, 2011).
2. Note that these advocates assume a minor is capable of providing such voluntary consent—an issue that certainly is not free from doubt, certainly as a matter of law.
3. G. G. Abel, et al., *Multiple Paraphilic Diagnoses among Sex Offenders*, 16 BULL. OF THE AM. ACAD. OF PSYCHIATRY AND THE L. 153 (1988) (concluding that "arrest records of paraphiliacs do not provide a reliable indication of the true scope of paraphilic acts," and noting that "most paraphilic acts are not reported").
4. Andres E. Hernandez, SELF-REPORTED CONTACT SEXUAL OFFENSES BY PARTICIPANTS IN THE FEDERAL BUREAU OF PRISONS' SEX OFFENDER TREATMENT PROGRAM: IMPLICATIONS FOR INTERNET SEX OFFENDERS (2000), available at www.kardasz.org/HernandezPrisonStudy.pdf.
5. Ibid.
6. M. P. Weinrott and M. Saylor, *Self-Report of Crimes Committed by Sex Offenders*, 6 J. OF INTERPERSONAL VIOLENCE 286 (1991).
7. See Abel, supra note 3.
8. R. Langevin, et al., *Lifetime Sex Offender Recidivism: A 24-Year Follow-Up Study*, 46 CANADIAN J. OF CRIMINOLOGY AND CRIM. JUST. 531 (2004).

3

The Broad Descriptive Challenge

CHILD EXPLOITATION IS A FEDERAL CRIME based on Congress's power to regulate interstate commerce. Consequently, each statute criminalizing aspects of child exploitation (pornography, etc.) has a jurisdictional "hook" to interstate commerce.[1] The dramatic growth of the Internet, social networking, and electronic means of communication, and the digitalization of the international community have significantly impacted the manner in which sexual offenders commit crimes. Definitions that applied to offenders two decades ago no longer accurately describe their behavior patterns. Although the underlying motivation remains the same, offenders employ a variety of electronic tools to validate their behavior through communication with other offenders, to share and store their contraband, to obtain financial benefits from commercial child sexual exploitation and to lure victims.

Researchers, as we discuss in more detail below, have, indeed, come to understand sexual offending behavior to be a process, rather than simply as an individual act. Understanding that process enables law enforcement to effectively investigate and prosecute, provides probation officers with valuable insights for effective monitoring and sentencing approaches, strengthens the sentencing judge's understanding of the behavior, and provides the defense bar with valuable insights critical to counsel's effective representation of individuals accused of child sexual exploitation. The following accounts, moreover, are largely descriptive, rather than "legal" (for a summary of the legal definitions of the different offenses, including the various elements that must be established to achieve a conviction, see chapter 7). These descriptions were developed from a combination of behavioral research and law enforcement

investigation, and sketch out for the practitioner a comprehensive overview
of each of the offending behaviors.

A. The Possessor of Child Pornography

Child pornography, under federal law, is defined as material depicting a
"minor engaging in sexually explicit conduct."[2] "Sexually explicit conduct,"
in turn, is defined as "actual or simulated: (i) sexual intercourse, including
genital-genital, oral-genital, anal-genital, or oral-anal, whether between persons of the same or opposite sex; (ii) bestiality; (iii) masturbation; (iv) sadistic
or masochistic abuse; or (v) lascivious exhibition of the genitals or pubic area
of any person."[3]

1. The Fundamentals of Possession

The possession of child pornography is a crime on the outset. Gone are the
days of magazines hidden in brown paper envelopes stored in the basement
of a socially isolated offender's home. Today, child pornography is possessed
in terms of gigabytes and terabytes. It is not uncommon for today's possessor
to have hundreds of thousands of images stored on his computer, flash drives,
external hard drives, and in off-site electronic storage.[4] The images are often
stored in elaborate electronic libraries organized by the offender using his
preferences, such as, say, ten-year-olds, blondes, boys, and sports.[5]

Offenders encrypt their prized collections to prevent law enforcement access. In one criminal case, for example, the encryption was so effective that
neither NSA nor NASA computers were able to crack the encryption to access
the potential treasure trove of the offender.[6] Instead, he was prosecuted based
on a live video "snag" (a short video recording of a live webcam display) of a
molestation of a boy that he had broadcast to other offenders, and that was
stored on another offender's computer.[7]

Aside from images, the offenders possess videos, some lasting only a matter
of seconds, others lasting minutes to hours long.[8] The videos depict everything from minors posing with various objects or playing with each other, to
minors being molested by an adult.

The federal statutes criminalize the possession of material that depicts the
"lewd and lascivious" exhibition of the genitalia of a minor under the age of
eighteen.[9] Yet federal laws also prohibit the receipt and distribution of the
same material. In *United States v. Malik*, the Seventh Circuit distinguished
between receipt of child pornography, which requires proof that the defen-

dant knew the subjects were minors, and possession, which lacks a scienter requirement.[10] Statutory penalties are significantly higher for the receipt and distribution of such images and videos.[11]

A forensic analysis of the media upon which the images are stored can usually provide insights into how and when the offender came to possess the images. In the prior example, a made-to-order video may be stored in the offender's electronic library as "ten-year-old girl on bed," but the computer will contain other electronic footprints that may link it to being a purchase from an overseas manufacturer. E-mail order forms, electronic bank records, and metadata of the image may reveal the information necessary to transform a mere possessor into a receiver or even into an aider and abettor of manufacturing.

Analysis of the offender's child pornography can also provide valuable insights into the offender's mental processes. Some offenders will be focused solely on man/boy images, will store details about victims in their grooming pipeline near the images, and will collect information to use to lure the child to them.[12] The methods an offender uses to catalog his contraband can offer priceless insights to law enforcement when it comes to determining the identities of the victims depicted in the seized materials, and can shed light on how best to monitor the offender.

Possession of certain types of material, moreover, can raise significant red flags. Sadomasochistic images, molestation images of infants or toddlers, and depictions of bestiality are seen less often in law enforcement operations, but raise serious concerns about the degree of sexual deviance exhibited by the offender. One circuit court upheld sentencing enhancements for an offender who had pictures of very young children (including a newborn), calling the pictures "horrific" and noting that the case was "not the run-of-the-mill child pornography case."[13]

2. Is There a Link between Child Pornography Possession and "Hands-On" Sexual Abuse?

The link between "hands-on" sexual offending and child pornography has been debated for decades. Generally, the debate plays out before the sentencing judge, who is presented with starkly competing versions of what it means when the defendant standing before her possessed thousands of images of child pornography. Is the offender a danger to the community? Should he be detained? Does evidence that a person was "addicted" to viewing and collecting images of child sexual abuse translate into evidence that this individual has "lived out" his sexual fantasies, or will?

Often the defense presents evidence of a law-abiding citizen who is respected in the community, remains employed, is socially and civically conscious, and has no criminal history. The link between the case-specific *nature* of the possession of child pornography, and what that says about the risk that the defendant will reoffend (or engage in even more serious offenses), becomes a critical piece of evidence for any judge to consider.

In recent years, numerous studies exploring these issues have been conducted. We start first with the now-accepted understanding that when compared to non-offenders, "hands-on" sexual offenders consume pornography at a higher rate,[14] and that many use pornography to reduce inhibitions and reinforce their sexually deviant arousal.[15] In regard to child "erotica," the reinforcement of the sexually deviant behavior is even more insidious because child pornographers frequently pose their child victims in such a manner that they appear at ease. By presenting smiling children being victimized, the exploiter justifies his distorted belief that he is helping the child, bringing pleasure to the child, and that the child is an eager participant in his own molestation.[16] When coupled with the offender's communication with other offenders via the Internet in chat rooms or through e-mails—including providing accolades for each incident of exploitation—this unique characteristic of child pornography reinforces the distorted fantasy that the deviant sexual behavior has some social merit.

In a particular criminal case involving the serial molestation of boys, for example, law enforcement recovered dozens of stories of molestation that depicted adult men "helping" young boys by showing them "love" that was allegedly greater than they would receive in their own homes and by providing them with monetary support and gifts that supposedly made their lives more enjoyable.[17] These stories included graphic depictions of man/boy sexual contact, but each depiction was framed in such a manner as to show that the child was receiving pleasure and was grateful to the offender. These stories and the offender's vast collection of child pornography constituted this particular offender's collection of materials, which he accessed regularly before going online to lure boys to his home.[18]

3. Using Possessed Images as a Luring Tool

The offender's collection of child pornography serves another purpose in the offending process—it aids in the "grooming process" whereby the offenders serve doses of the pornography to the minor to acclimate him to the idea of engaging in adult/child sexual contact.[19] The offender uses the pornography as a tool to lower the inhibitions of the minor and to prepare the minor for future sexual contact. By showing the child that others have engaged in sexual contact, that they are seemingly enjoying the sexual contact, and that it has been captured for viewing, the adult offender grooms his victim by "educating" him that such contact is normal and acceptable.

4. Types of Child Pornography and the Role of Erotica in the Offender's Library

Nearly all child pornography charged in federal courts is digitally saved in some type of electronic format. Whether images stored on flash drives, videos stored on DVDs, or files sent as attachments to e-mails, the significant volume of child pornography recovered in federal law enforcement investigations is obtained only after a search warrant for the offender's computers is typically secured and a forensic analysis of the hard drives is performed.

Often possessors of child pornography will also have a collection of images that do not fit within the statutory definition of "child pornography" because they do not depict the lewd and lascivious exhibition of the genitals.[20] Some courts call these materials "child erotica," and have cited government affidavits defining them as "depict[ing] young girls as sexual objects or in a sexually suggestive way, but . . . not sufficiently lascivious to meet the legal definition of sexually explicit conduct under 18 U.S.C. § 2256" or as "images that are not themselves child pornography but still fuel sexual fantasies involving children."[21] These images can be as banal as a child swinging on a swing, playing baseball, or smiling at the camera. For the pornography possessor, these images can be as provocative and stimulating as an image of child pornography.

In one criminal prosecution, the offender was known for his skill at producing these types of child erotica.[22] Using the screen name "Excel," the offender amassed a broad Internet audience of like-minded exploiters who admired his work and would pay handsomely to purchase an image of one of Excel's boys smiling at the camera. When interviewing one such admirer, one of the authors was informed that the picture was erotic because of the playful way the boy was posed near an adult, the manner in which the child smiled— which revealed "both innocence and devilishness"—and the suggestion that more was about to happen.

To the casual viewer, the image may well seem like any other holiday photo depicting an adult relative and a small boy. To this pedophile, the image was worth at least $5,000. "Excel" also sold similar child erotica through mainstream outlets such as eBay. For example, one series of images depicted fully clothed seven- to nine-year-old boys playing in wrestling suits. The wrestling suits were then sold on eBay for hundreds of dollars.

The connection between this erotica and the child pornography is a critical key to the process of offending. The manner in which an offender places these nonpornographic images side by side with pornographic images also serves as a window into the mind of the offender who does not differentiate the sexual and nonsexual aspects of his victim. Although not chargeable by the federal authorities, the erotica often reveals the offender's preferences, potential other victims, and the compulsion of the offender to maintain a library of images of the children he has exploited.

B. The Manufacturer of Child Pornography

The term *manufacturing* conjures up images of production factories, assembly lines, and elaborate distribution systems. Any perpetrator who "employs, uses, persuades, induces, entices, or coerces" a minor for "the purpose of producing any visual depiction of such [sexually explicit conduct] or for the purpose of transmitting a live visual depiction of such conduct" may be charged with manufacturing child pornography.[23] In the child pornography setting, an exploiter armed with a digital camera that he uses to take a picture of a naked minor displaying genitalia in a lewd and lascivious way is sufficient to qualify for a manufacture of child pornography charge.

This is not to say that manufacturers are solely engaged in this simplistic mode of manufacturing. Some offenders have elaborate studios where minors can be posed and can take instruction from camera holders off set and follow the instructions much like a movie actor.[24] Others employ cameras perched on their desktop computers or contained within their laptop computers to record discreet acts and broadcast them live for other sex offenders to view.[25] Some videos are self-made, while others are purchased from manufacturers who will create a "custom-made" video for the purchaser for a cost.[26] The purchaser can order up the age and gender of the minor, even specific characteristics that he wants displayed, and can create his own fantasy scene in his order. These made-to-order videos are then shipped electronically to the purchaser, and a money order is sent to the manufacturer.

Virtually any electronic camera can capture a minor in an image that can be charged as manufacturing on the federal level. Cell phones and iPods generally have cameras that can take both still images and record shorter segments of live video. Many of these cameras are compact and easily hidden, making surreptitious recording even easier. Federal real-world criminal case scenarios include offenders who hid cameras in clock radios and smoke detectors.[27] Indeed, it is this relative ease of manufacturing that accounts in significant part for the contemporary proliferation of child pornography.

C. The Interstate Traveler

1. Public Awareness of the Sex Traveler

Probably the most notorious of the sexual offenders in recent history is the so-called "sex traveler." A "sex traveler," under federal law, is a person who "travels in interstate commerce or . . . who travels in foreign commerce, for the purpose of engaging in any illicit sexual conduct with another person" under the age of eighteen.[28] Made popular by such television shows as NBC's *To Catch a Predator*, the general public began to gain an appreciation for this unique offender type when their online chats and telephone conversations were played for a national audience. The popular media has also detailed the practice of American men traveling to countries like Thailand as child exploitation tourists. The federal statute criminalizes both interstate and transnational travel for such purposes.

The rise of sex-traveler prosecutions began in the mid-1990s, when a handful of law enforcement officers recognized that minor victims in their communities were being lured from their homes to meet adult offenders in parking lots, shopping malls, and parks. These offenders had, indeed, typically groomed their victims over weeks and months, often spending countless hours in chat rooms to gather information about the victim's interests. If the child was interested in motocross racing, for example, the offender would learn every detail about the sport, learn the child's racing schedule, travel to the races, show support at each event, and purchase gifts that would nurture the child's interest in order to gain special access to the child. Specifically, in *United States v. Robinette*, the defendant groomed his victim by purchasing him racing gear and bikes, eventually becoming so close to the victim's family that the divorced mother of the victim allowed the defendant to live in her home because she believed that he was nurturing her child's efforts in racing.[29] In *United States v. Mallon*, however, a member of the Northern Ireland government told an agent posing as a fourteen-year-old girl that he would provide both financial and psychological support to her and serve as a "father substitute."[30]

2. How the Traveler Lures His Victims

Evidence gathered during these cases reveals savvy offenders who can manipulate their victims by mimicking their childhood interests. In one case, for example, the offender adopted numerous identities throughout the course of a year, all of which involved grooming various carefully selected and targeted child victims: the offender held himself out to be an avid video game player, a follower of the Wiccan religion, a believer in UFOs and extraterrestrials, and a wealthy playboy with high-end toys such as jet skis.[31] In that case, the offender was in the process of luring at least seven different boys to his home in Florida when he was finally arrested and charged with kidnapping. On the occasion of his arrest, the defendant had convinced his intended victim that he (the defendant) was the uncle of a boy who had become close friends with the victim. In truth, the defendant was both the boy and the uncle on the Internet. The victim was told by the boy persona that the uncle would come and take care of him. Based on this deception, the victim agreed to travel to the defendant.

The complexity of the luring process is often reflected on the defendant's computer, where the communications showing the defendant's efforts in learning about his victim's interests and family are frequently captured and stored. Often preying on child victims who are experiencing other challenges in their lives, such as learning disabilities, a fractured family life, or a period of depression, exacerbated by the already-complex insecurities of preteen years, the defendants in these cases have an uncanny ability to identify fragile victims. Trafficking and child pornography victims in fact share these characteristics.

Generally, travelers focus on one gender and age group.[32] This type of preferential sexual offending requires significant time and effort on the exploiter's part. As a consequence, prosecutions of such individuals frequently involve computers brimming with evidence, and this evidence is as likely to be on the exploiter's work computer as on his home computer. Depending on the fictitious persona the offender has created for his victim(s), communication with the victims may be necessary throughout the day in the form of text messages, chats, and e-mails. The common practice of grooming more than one victim within the preferential age and gender group at one time, moreover, requires the exploiter to maintain detailed logs of his communications in order to maintain the communication at the level necessary to keep the victim on the line and to, in a very basic sense, ensure that the exploiter does not simply get confused. Evidence obtained in traveler cases often shows how the offender provided elaborate excuses for a break in communication for one victim while he traveled to have sex with another child victim. Recognizing that the victim may lose interest if the communication grows cold, the offender often promises gifts upon return from travel or a period where he is engaged with other victims.

D. The Kidnapper

Probably the popular imagination's most feared offender is the kidnapper, who removes his victim from the security of her home and family and keeps her for his own sexual pleasure. The kidnapper may be charged under federal law when he "seizes, confines, inveigles, decoys, kidnaps, abducts, or carries away and holds . . . any person."[33]

1. The Captivity Kidnapper

Recently, a number of high-profile kidnapping cases have been brought to light: the kidnappings of Jaycee Dugard and Elizabeth Smart are, perhaps, the most notorious. Both cases shocked the public due to the bold seizure of the girls from their families—one girl taken from her school bus corner, the other pulled from her bed directly in front of her sister. Both girls were kept captive by the offenders for an extended period (Smart for ten months, Dugard for eighteen years), and were repeatedly sexually abused. In the case of Dugard, defendant Phillip Garrido impregnated the child victim at the age of fourteen, and she raised two children fathered by her kidnapper.

These kidnappers used fear to maintain their control over the girls, and threatened them with harm if they attempted to escape and with harm to their families if they revealed their plight to outsiders. In both cases, an astute outsider discovered the servitude by, respectively, recognizing the victim and recognizing the odd behavior of the victim in public. Kidnapping victims are typically habituated and desensitized to their "new lives" in much the same way that human trafficking victims forced into prostitution are.

The sexual kidnapper's asset is the age differential, which enables him to maintain psychological control over his minor victims. By kidnapping the children at an early enough age, before the child is able to be self-supportive or aware of her surroundings, the kidnapper maintains control over his victim by monitoring her environment and not allowing her to have access to the outside world, where her normal human instincts might change her perspective. Dugard, for example, was locked inside a backyard studio without being allowed to leave for an entire year during her first year of captivity.[34] In both cases, the male defendants were also supported by females who aided the capture and captivity knowing that the child victims would be used to satiate the sexual desires of their spouses.

2. The Opportunity Kidnapper

The final category of kidnapping defendants includes those who kidnap, molest, and then murder their victims. Indeed, the statistics for such "stereotypical kidnappings," which in over 70 percent of cases are committed by strangers, are shocking; in 40 percent of the cases, the child victims are killed, and in 4 percent they are never found.[35] These typically male[36] offenders are perhaps best described as situational offenders who act out and attack a child when the situation arises. Yet some share qualities with the captivity kidnappers in that they also seek out their victims, often monitoring their comings and goings for months, and then act when the moment is right. What distinguishes this type of kidnapper from the captivity kidnapper, however, is that once the molestation is complete, the offender must hide all evidence of the act, which is what leads to the murder of the victim.

E. The Situational v. Preferential v. Commercial Offender

The situational offender remains what the common public might label the "stranger danger." This is the offender who acts out on his sexual urges by grabbing a child at an opportune time, molesting the child, and then escaping. There is no long-term grooming involved, no long-term captivity, and the event often takes place where the offender can have easy access and escape. In this category of offenders we find sexually indiscriminate persons who lack a "true" sexual preference for children, but will simply sexually abuse children if and when the opportunity should arise.[35]

In contrast, we use the term *preferential* child exploiter to refer to the category of individuals who have an inherent sexual drive to gain sexual pleasure from, or through, children (that is, they have a sexual preference for children).

"Commercial" child exploiters, however, are primarily financially motivated, and include those operating individually and in syndicates who run commercial online pornography websites and engage in organized child trafficking, forced prostitution, and other forms of child exploitation that are primarily—though not necessarily exclusively—motivated by a desire for financial gain.

Of course, in the real-world context of preferential, situational, and commercial exploitation, these hard distinctions can often be considerably blurred (generally by preferential exploiters who turn their proclivities to cash by selling the images of the children they exploit). Nevertheless, the distinction between primarily commercial and primarily preferential sexual abusers is important and adds some nuance to the discussion.

Notes

1. See, e.g., 18 U.S.C. § 2252 (criminalizing transporting or shipping "using any means or facility of interstate or foreign commerce or in or affecting interstate or foreign commerce").

2. Ibid.

3. See 18 U.S.C. § 2256(2).

4. See, e.g., *United States v. Koch*, 625 F.3d 470, 475 (8th Cir. 2010) (flash drive and computer).

5. See *United States v. Mellies*, 329 Fed. Appx. 592, 607 (6th Cir. 2009) (noting the defendant "created an elaborate system of directories to organize the fruits of his addiction").

6. *United States v. Burt*, 04 CR 273 (N.D. Ill.); *United States v. Watzman*, 03 CR 1032 (N.D. Ill.).

7. *Burt*, 04 CR 273.

8. *United States v. Martin*, 04 CR 40 (E.D. Wisc.).

9. See 18 U.S.C. §§ 2252, 2256(2)(A)(v).

10. *United States v. Malik*, 385 F.3d 758, 760 (7th Cir. 2004).

11. See 18 U.S.C. § 2252 et seq.

12. *United States v. Romero*, 189 F.3d 576, 579 (7th Cir. 1999).

13. See *United States v. Maier*, 639 F.3d 927, 935 (9th Cir. 2011).

14. See generally W. L. Marshall, *The Use of Sexually Explicit Stimuli by Rapists, Child Molesters, and Non-Offenders*, 25 J. SEX. RESEARCH 267, 279–80 (1988).

15. See generally Ray Wyre, *Pornography and Sexual Violence: Working with Sex Offenders*, in PORNOGRAPHY: WOMEN, VIOLENCE AND CIVIL LIBERTIES 236, 237 (Catherine Itzen, ed., 1992).

16. See generally W. L. Marshall, *Revisiting the Use of Pornography by Sexual Offenders: Implications for Theory and Practice*, 6 J. SEXUAL AGGRESSION 67, 72–73 (2000); Ethel Quayle and Max Taylor, *Child Pornography and the Internet: Perpetuating a Cycle of Abuse*, 23 DEVIANT BEHAVIOR: AN INTERDISCIPLINARY J. 331, 340 (2002).

17. *Romero*, 96 CR 167.

18. Ibid.

19. Ibid.; *United States v. Selseth*, No. 03 CR 1043 (N.D. Ill.).

20. See *United States v. Burt*, 495 F.3d 733, 736 (7th Cir. 2007) (citing 18 U.S.C. §§ 2256(2)(A)(v)).

21. *United States v. Vosburgh*, 602 F.3d 512, 520 (3d Cir. 2010) (internal citations and quotations omitted).

22. *Burt*, 04 CR 273.

23. 18 U.S.C. § 2251(a).

24. *Watzman*, 03 CR 1032.

25. *Martin*, 04 CR 40; *Burt*, 04 CR 273.

26. *Watzman*, 03 CR 1032.

27. *United States v. Poulin*, 631 F.3d 17, 19 (1st Cir. 2011) (hidden camera concealed in a clock radio); *United States v. Harris*, 291 Fed. Appx. 300, 301 (11th Cir. 2008) (camera hidden in a smoke detector).

28. 18 U.S.C. § 2423(b).

29. *United States v. Robinette*, 02 CR 928 (N.D. Ill.).

30. *United States v. Mallon*, 345 F.3d 943, 944 (7th Cir. 2003).

31. *Romero*, 189 F.3d at 578–79.

32. Kenneth V. Lanning, SEX OFFENDER CONTINUUM (2002), available at www.cac-kent.org/pdfs/Lanning_-_Suspect_Typology.pdf.

33. 18 U.S.C. § 1201(a)(1).

34. See Lisa Leff, *Transcripts Reveal Details about Dugard Kidnapping,* Newark Star-Ledger, June 4, 2011, at 3.

35. See Dep't of Just., Office of Juvenile Justice and Delinquency Prevention, National Incidence Studies of Missing, Abducted, Runaway, and Thrownaway Children (October 2002).

36. Ibid.

37. See, e.g., Blaine D. McIlwaine, Fed. Bureau of Investigation, Interrogating Child Molesters, available at http://investigationshelpdesk.com/html/training/le_articles/94JUN001.TXT ("Situational child molesters do not have a true sexual preference for children, but instead, engage in sex with the young for varied and sometimes complex reasons. For such molesters, sexual contact with children may range from a 'once-in-a-lifetime' act to a long-term pattern of behavior. However, situational child molesters generally have a very limited number of victims. . . . Preferential child molesters have a definite sexual preference for children. Their sexual fantasies and erotic imagery focus on children. They engage in sexual acts with the young not because of some situational stress or insecurity, but because they are sexually attracted to, and prefer, children.") (last visited June 1, 2011).

4

Appreciating the Human Trafficking Problem and Its Enforcement Challenges

HUMAN TRAFFICKING, AND MOST NOTABLY the trafficking of minor children for the purposes of sexual exploitation or servitude, is one of today's stand-out "hot button" issues—and for good reason.[1] Not only a serious domestic crime—whether for purposes of sexual or labor exploitation—human trafficking is, in this era of rapid globalization and a borderless Internet, increasingly a significant international human rights challenge.

According to the United Nations:

- Human trafficking affects every continent and every type of economy.
- 161 countries are reported to be either source, transition, or destination countries for human trafficking.
- An estimated 1.2 million children are trafficked each year.
- 95 percent of victims experience physical or sexual violence during trafficking.
- 2.45 million people are estimated to be suffering currently from conditions of forced physical and sex-industry labor as a result of trafficking.
- 43 percent of trafficking victims are used for forced commercial sexual exploitation, and 98 percent of these victims are women and girls.[2]

Despite the crime's growing public profile and its near-universal reach across the world, most citizens, and even many in the law enforcement community, remain unaware of the true nature and extent of the problem.[3]

A. The Need for a Practical Definition of Human Trafficking

Though disagreements concerning the precise means and objectives of traffickers are unlikely to diminish, one thing most groups can agree on is that a sound, realistic, and, perhaps most importantly, *practical* (that is, reflecting the realities of how trafficking is organized and executed both domestically and across borders) model-law definition of human trafficking is the much-needed cornerstone to law enforcement's transnational enforcement efforts. The ability to enforce the laws and to hold accountable what is often a multitude of individuals who play a role in organizing, sustaining, and profiting from trafficking is critical. All of the idealistic preambles in the world will not change the fact that law enforcers must have a straightforward—and, where possible, internationally uniform—anti-trafficking law in their arsenal. Otherwise, they will be unable to appropriately staunch the problem. This would be a result welcomed by none, except the traffickers.

B. Definitional Problems and the Search for Common Ground

How to most effectively combat human trafficking remains a difficult challenge for the diverse group of stakeholders confronting it. These stakeholders include law enforcement, prosecutors, judges, victim advocates, social service providers, legislators, immigrant advocacy organizations, and non-governmental organizations worldwide, including faith-based groups. At the risk of oversimplifying the debate, the broad lines of disagreement run along the issues of (1) whether human trafficking victims must always be treated as such, or whether they should, as appropriate, be held criminally liable and treated as co-conspirators (e.g., for crimes such as prostitution or illegal entry into the country); (2) whether the problem of human trafficking is truly a global problem or, instead, a regional issue; and (3) whether developed countries, which fuel much of the demand, act hypocritically when complaining about developing countries and their role in trafficking, while exhibiting reluctance to provide these under-funded regions with the resources necessary to win the fight.

C. Who Are the Victims of Trafficking?

Because most trafficking victims are hidden from the view of law enforcement and society-at-large, identifying them poses a significant challenge. For one, many transnational trafficking victims in the United States are brought to the country illegally.[4] More importantly, once the victims are taken out of their home town, region, or country, the traffickers skillfully exploit the fact that these displaced victims often have no sense of their legal rights, do not understand the language, commonly have had their ties to their families and "old life" severed, and come from countries with weak and corrupt governments and law enforcement.[5]

The hallmark of human trafficking is that those who engage in it—which, as discussed in more detail below, are increasingly organized crime groups—prey on young and largely defenseless victims. The victims do not consent to their situations, are too young to be able to make any legally binding decisions, and/or are duped into consenting through the use of false promises.

While contemporary stereotypes portray trafficking victims as young girls from foreign countries who are manipulated, lied to, and often kidnapped and forced into prostitution (a stereotype certainly based in cold, hard reality), male and female children of all ages, both from the United States ("domestic trafficking") and abroad ("transnational trafficking"), make up the unfortunate demographic of trafficking victims.

Experience teaches that traffickers highly prize young girls age twelve and below, because young girls are malleable and thus more easily "trained" into their prospective roles as prostitutes, and because sexual virginity (or assumed virginity based on youth) is highly prized by certain "consumers" willing to pay a premium. For this reason, the traffickers often need the girls to appear older in order to appeal to a broader customer base—while hiding obvious "red flags" from law enforcement. By tapping into the fertile underground of false identification document manufacturing, the trafficker can make his victim any age he wants her to be. He knows her true age and understands that bringing younger girls into "the life" makes them less likely to struggle against their captors and more likely to become highly compliant, loyal, and dependent, viewing their captors as their new family unit. It is a brutal calculus, but one which has served traffickers well.

An additional virtual constant is that trafficking victims tend to share common characteristics, including that they hail from communities suffering high rates of crime, lack education or family support, and have histories of physical and sexual abuse. All of these characteristics leave them particularly vulnerable to traffickers.

On this point, consider the Congressional findings accompanying the Trafficking Victims Protection Act:

(2)   Many of these persons are trafficked into the international sex trade, often by force, fraud, or coercion. The sex industry has rapidly expanded over

the past several decades. It involves sexual exploitation of persons, predominantly women and girls, involving activities related to prostitution, pornography, sex tourism, and other commercial sexual services. The low status of women in many parts of the world has contributed to a burgeoning of the trafficking industry. . . .

(4)   Traffickers primarily target women and girls, who are disproportionately affected by poverty, the lack of access to education, chronic unemployment, discrimination, and the lack of economic opportunities in countries of origin. Traffickers lure women and girls into their networks through false promises of decent working conditions at relatively good pay as nannies, maids, dancers, factory workers, restaurant workers, sales clerks, or models. Traffickers also buy children from poor families and sell them into prostitution or into various types of forced or bonded labor.

(5)   Traffickers often transport victims from their home communities to unfamiliar destinations, including foreign countries away from family and friends, religious institutions, and other sources of protection and support, leaving the victims defenseless and vulnerable.

(6)   Victims are often forced through physical violence to engage in sex acts or perform slavery-like labor. Such force includes rape and other forms of sexual abuse, torture, starvation, imprisonment, threats, psychological abuse, and coercion.

(7)   Traffickers often make representations to their victims that physical harm may occur to them or others should the victim escape or attempt to escape. Such representations can have the same coercive effects on victims as direct threats to inflict such harm.

(8)   Trafficking in persons is increasingly perpetrated by organized, sophisticated criminal enterprises. Such trafficking is the fastest growing source of profits for organized criminal enterprises worldwide. Profits from the trafficking industry contribute to the expansion of organized crime in the United States and worldwide. Trafficking in persons is often aided by official corruption in countries of origin, transit, and destination, thereby threatening the rule of law.

(9)   Trafficking includes all the elements of the crime of forcible rape when it involves the involuntary participation of another person in sex acts by means of fraud, force, or coercion.

(10) Trafficking also involves violations of other laws, including labor and immigration codes and laws against kidnapping, slavery, false imprisonment, assault, battery, pandering, fraud, and extortion.

(11) Trafficking exposes victims to serious health risks. Women and children trafficked in the sex industry are exposed to deadly diseases, including HIV and AIDS. Trafficking victims are sometimes worked or physically brutalized to death. . . .

(16) In some countries, enforcement against traffickers is also hindered by official indifference, by corruption, and sometimes even by official participation in trafficking.

(17) Existing laws often fail to protect victims of trafficking, and because victims are often illegal immigrants in the destination country, they are repeatedly punished more harshly than the traffickers themselves.

(18) Additionally, adequate services and facilities do not exist to meet victims' needs regarding health care, housing, education, and legal assistance, which safely reintegrate trafficking victims into their home countries.

(19) Victims of severe forms of trafficking should not be inappropriately incarcerated, fined, or otherwise penalized solely for unlawful acts committed as a direct result of being trafficked, such as using false documents, entering the country without documentation, or working without documentation.

(20) Because victims of trafficking are frequently unfamiliar with the laws, cultures, and languages of the countries into which they have been trafficked, because they are often subjected to coercion and intimidation including physical detention and debt bondage, and because they often fear retribution and forcible removal to countries in which they will face retribution or other hardship, these victims often find it difficult or impossible to report the crimes committed against them or to assist in the investigation and prosecution of such crimes.

(21) Trafficking of persons is an evil requiring concerted and vigorous action by countries of origin, transit or destination, and by international organizations.

(22) One of the founding documents of the United States, the Declaration of Independence, recognizes the inherent dignity and worth of all people. It states that all men are created equal and that they are endowed by their Creator with certain unalienable rights. The right to be free from slavery and involuntary servitude is among those unalienable rights. Acknowledging this fact, the United States outlawed slavery and involuntary servitude in 1865, recognizing them as evil institutions that must be abolished. Current practices of sexual slavery and trafficking of women and children are similarly abhorrent to the principles upon which the United States was founded.

(23) The United States and the international community agree that trafficking in persons involves grave violations of human rights and is a matter of pressing international concern. The international community has repeatedly condemned slavery and involuntary servitude, violence against women, and other elements of trafficking, through declarations, treaties, and United Nations resolutions and reports, including the Universal Declaration of Human Rights; the 1956 Supplementary Convention on the Abolition of Slavery, the Slave Trade, and Institutions and Practices Similar to Slavery; the 1948 American Declaration on the Rights and Duties of Man; the 1957 Abolition of Forced Labor Convention; the International Covenant on Civil and Political Rights; the Convention Against Torture and Other Cruel, Inhuman or Degrading Treatment or Punishment;

United Nations General Assembly Resolutions 50/167, 51/66, and 52/98; the Final Report of the World Congress against Sexual Exploitation of Children (Stockholm, 1996); the Fourth World Conference on Women (Beijing, 1995); and the 1991 Moscow Document of the Organization for Security and Cooperation in Europe.

(24) Trafficking in persons is a transnational crime with national implications. To deter international trafficking and bring its perpetrators to justice, nations including the United States must recognize that trafficking is a serious offense. This is done by prescribing appropriate punishment, giving priority to the prosecution of trafficking offenses, and protecting rather than punishing the victims of such offenses. The United States must work bilaterally and multilaterally to abolish the trafficking industry by taking steps to promote cooperation among countries linked together by international trafficking routes. The United States must also urge the international community to take strong action in multilateral form to engage recalcitrant countries in serious and sustained efforts to eliminate trafficking and protect trafficking victims.[6]

Some of these characteristics of the abused amplify the challenges facing those responsible for "freeing" them from their captors. As a result of their isolation, and often due to the corrupt state of law enforcement within their home countries, the victims frequently come to view law enforcement as the enemy, and their captors as protectors. In short, out of necessity, they become habituated to the reality of their new life and circumstances. The victim can feel "helplessness, shame and humiliation, shock, denial and disbelief, disorientation and confusion, and anxiety disorders including post-traumatic stress disorder (PTSD), phobias, panic attacks, and depression . . . [and] Traumatic Bonding."[7]

In this regard, trafficking victims are frequently observed to suffer from a species of Stockholm Syndrome. This term describes a paradoxical psychological phenomenon wherein hostages over time develop positive feelings toward their captors. Captives who exhibit the syndrome tend to sympathize with and think highly of their captors, and eventually develop a strong bond with them. These feelings appear irrational in light of the danger or risk endured by the victims, but they stem from a coping mechanism by which the victims mistake a lack of abuse from their captors as an act of kindness.[8] Essentially, the victims begin to lose the sense that they have been victimized, and slowly begin to adopt a view of themselves as being involved in a pitched struggle between "us" (their pimp or trafficker) and "them" (the law enforcement and social services community). Once the victims have crossed this threshold, it becomes virtually impossible for service providers to break through, gain their trust, and obtain their assistance in bringing their traffickers to justice.

D. Trafficking Is Terrible . . . But It Could Never Happen Where I Live

Experience in the field teaches that victims, as well as their victimization, are generally carefully obscured from public view. The signs of abuse may not be obvious to the neighbors, because their captors go to great lengths to keep them hidden. Additionally, neighbors unfamiliar with the means and methods of human trafficking may not recognize the tell-tale signs of captivity and control—the tools of the trafficker's trade.

Because of the psychological phenomena discussed above, physical shackles, locks, and fences are not required to keep someone in de facto bondage. To many in the public, this absence of obvious physical restraints results in the trafficking victim—even very young ones—being moved to the "prostitute" side of the collective public perception ledger.

Most American communities consider human trafficking an undeniably terrible phenomenon, but one that exists elsewhere—perhaps in the "big city" or overseas in Southeast Asia—but not in their rural county or town. This false perspective permits traffickers to thrive, not only in major U.S. cities but also in more rural areas and border towns. After all, not unlike other criminals who operate in an organized fashion, traffickers will go where their cost-benefit analysis tells them the demand for the sexual services of their victims is high, and where, due to the absence of a law enforcement and community understanding of human trafficking's nuances and modus operandi, the chances of their detection, apprehension, and conviction are low. As a result, rural communities have, somewhat counter-intuitively, provided a real boon to the traffickers.[9]

E. Existing Federal Anti-trafficking Efforts

The federal government has enacted a number of relatively nuanced statutory schemes directed at the fight against domestic and international human trafficking. Those efforts include the following:

- The William Wilberforce Trafficking Victims Protection Reauthorization Act of 2008—Enhancing federal efforts to combat both international and domestic traffic in human beings.
- The Trafficking Victims Protection Reauthorization Act of 2005—Providing federal courts with jurisdiction over federal government employees and contractors for trafficking offenses committed abroad.
- The Trafficking Victims Protection Reauthorization Act of 2003—Creating an anti-trafficking watch list to keep pressure on countries of various

tiers in the trafficking report; transforming trafficking into a RICO predicate offense; permitting victims to sue their traffickers in U.S. courts; and requiring that U.S. government contracts, relating to international affairs, contain clauses authorizing the United States to terminate governmental contracts if the contractor engages in human trafficking or procures commercial sexual services while the contract is in force.

• The Trafficking Victims Protection Act of 2000 ("TVPA")—Providing a two-tiered definition of trafficking that includes several forms of trafficking in persons and sex trafficking; transforming 18 U.S.C. § 1591 and 18 U.S.C. §§ 2421–2423 into the four primary statutes criminalizing prostituting minors in interstate commerce; and ensuring that foreign national victims are able to receive benefits and services to the same extent as refugees, following certification/eligibility determinations by the Department of Health and Human Services, Office of Refugee Resettlement (HHS/ORR).

F. A Closer Look at the Trafficking Victims Protection Act of 2000

The TVPA, which supplements existing laws, primarily 18 U.S.C. § 1584 (proscribing involuntary servitude), also provides new tools to combat trafficking. Although occasionally criticized for being too narrow,[10] the TVPA is today's standout anti-trafficking provision. As already indicated, after years of significant debates on how human trafficking should be defined, the legal definition provided by the TVPA has, for good reason, become the accepted norm. This broad, though not universal, acceptance is true even for such disparate stakeholder groups as law enforcement, prosecutors, judges, victim advocates, social service providers, legislators, immigrant advocacy organizations, legal advocates, faith-based organizations, and service providers.

Moving from the general to the specific, the TVPA's Section 1591 criminalizes "sex trafficking," which, broadly speaking, is defined as causing a person to engage in a commercial sex act under certain statutorily enumerated conditions. A "commercial sex act," moreover, describes any sex act on account of which *anything* of value is given to or received by *any* person. The punishment for conduct that either (1) involves a victim who is under the age of fourteen or (2) involves force, fraud, or coercion is a mandatory term of imprisonment of fifteen years and a maximum sentence of life (Adam Walsh Act's amendment of Section 1591). The punishment for conduct that involves a victim between the ages of fourteen and eighteen, and in which force, fraud, or coercion is used, is a mandatory minimum sentence of ten years and a maximum term of life—these are considerable penalties.

Both the Adam Walsh Act and the William Wilberforce Trafficking Victims Protection Reauthorization Act of 2008, thus, made significant changes to 1591. The William Wilberforce Act also added "reckless disregard" language, gave 1591 a conspiracy provision, and included Section 1591(d), which criminalizes the obstruction or attempted obstruction of enforcement of any of the chapter 77 statutes, including 1591.

The TVPA's key provisions follow:

Whoever knowingly—
  (1) in or affecting interstate or foreign commerce, or within the special maritime and territorial jurisdiction of the United States, *recruits, entices, harbors, transports, provides, or obtains by any means a person;* or
  (2) *benefits, financially or by receiving anything of value,* from *participation in a venture* which has engaged in an act described in violation of paragraph (1),

Knowing or in reckless disregard that *force, fraud, or coercion* described in subsection (c)(2) will be used to cause the person to engage in a commercial sex act, *or that the person has not attained the age of 18 years and will be caused to engage in a commercial sex act,* shall be punished as provided in subsection (b).[11]

Subsection (c) then goes on to provide, rather exceptionally, strict liability for accused who had "a reasonable opportunity to observe" the putative trafficking victim; in those cases, "the Government need not prove that the defendant knew that the person had not attained the age of 18 years." (Note, however, that this section has not yet been tested, and may well be met with substantive constitutional challenges focusing in on the *mens rea* change.) Arguably, Congress intended for the strict liability standard to apply even if the defendant did not have an opportunity to observe the victims, but a safe reading of the statute is that the government should only rely on the "reckless disregard" language when the defendant had an opportunity to observe his victims.

Section 1593, in turn, mandates victim restitution:

(a) The court shall order restitution for any offense under this chapter.
(b) (1) The order of restitution under this section shall direct the defendant to pay the victim (through the appropriate court mechanism) the *full amount of the victim's losses,* as determined by the court under paragraph (3) of this subsection. . . .
      (3) As used in this subsection, the term "full amount of the victim's losses" has the same meaning as provided in section 2259 (b)(3) and shall in addition include the greater of the gross income or value to the defendant of the victim's services or labor or the value of the victim's labor as guaranteed under the minimum wage and overtime guarantees of the Fair Labor Standards Act (29 U.S.C. 201 et seq.). . . .

Chapter 4

(c) As used in this section, the term "victim" means the individual harmed as a
     result of a crime under this chapter, including, in the case of a victim who
     is under 18 years of age, incompetent, incapacitated, or deceased, the legal
     guardian of the victim or a representative of the victim's estate, or another
     family member, or any other person appointed as suitable by the court, but
     in no event shall the defendant be named such representative or guardian.[12]

G. A Brief Primer on the Definitional Challenges

One of the remaining misconceptions in human trafficking circles is that the
term *trafficking*, which implies some sort of movement from point A to point
B, in fact should require, as the term implies, some sort of travel or transport.
Not far behind is the question of whether *sex trafficking* should apply to situations where women are brought ("smuggled") to point B for no particular
pre-agreed purpose, and are then kept there to perform sexual services.

Trafficking by its very nature frequently involves the transport of people
from their own communities/countries and across borders or within a nation.
The reality of trafficking suggests that a victim need not be physically transported *by the accused* in order for the conduct to qualify as human trafficking,
provided the trafficker had reason to believe the victim *was* transported and,
thereafter, *continued* the exploitation.

Indeed, under both international law and the law of the United States,
human trafficking is defined as the "recruitment, transportation, transfer, *harboring* or receipt of persons, by means of threat or use of force or other forms of
coercion, of abduction, of fraud, of deception, of the abuse of power or of a position of vulnerability . . . for the purpose of exploitation"[13]; here, too, transport
of humans is not a necessary precondition for a human trafficking prosecutor,
including prosecution of the "recipient"/"harborer" of the trafficking victim.

18 U.S.C. § 1591, for example, penalizes not just the transportation of minors for the purpose of prostitution, but also threatens criminal punishment to
anyone who recruits, entices, harbors, provides, obtains, or maintains trafficked
minors. (18 U.S.C. § 2423(a), in contrast, requires interstate travel.)

It is our view that keeping a victim, *post*-transport, at a place through the
following means should qualify as trafficking under all domestic and international anti-trafficking laws (though such conduct may well also run afoul
of other criminal proscriptions, such as unlawful restraint and kidnapping):

- Threat
- Use of force
- Abduction

- Fraud
- Deception
- Abuse of power or of a position of vulnerability
- Giving or receiving of payments or benefits to achieve the consent of a person having control over another person
- Other forms of coercion

Additionally, we believe that there should be no requirement for force, fraud, or coercion when the commercial sex act involves a minor or someone under the age of eighteen.

H. Drafting a Model Child Trafficking Law

We, based on the above, believe that a "vertical integration" model of trafficking prosecution is the most appropriate approach because it best encompasses all of the actors within the crime. That is, in order to effectively combat both the supply and demand side of the problem, a sound trafficking law must allow for the prosecution of all individuals involved, from those (1) "recruiting" victims in the source country and (2) facilitating the travel or transport to those (3) receiving the victims and (4) who use a victim's services, knowing or having reason to believe the victim had been trafficked.

Although complex in their motivation and their long-term impact, child trafficking for sexual purposes can, as a general matter, be broken down into three fairly straightforward parts:

1. Criminal *acts*—The recruitment, transportation, transfer, harboring, or receipt of persons;
2. Criminal *means*—The trafficking victim was physically moved, or caused to be moved, or kept in a place, by threat or use of force or other forms of coercion, abduction, fraud, deception, the abuse of power or a position of vulnerability, or the giving or receiving of payments or benefits to achieve the consent of a person having control over another person[14]; and
3. Criminal *state of mind*—The foregoing acts occurred for the purpose of sexual exploitation.

Our proposed statute attempts to combine these fundamental acts, means, and state of mind elements into a cohesive whole that is not overreaching, but that also does not leave out critical trafficking-related conduct.

1. Proposed "Model" Child Trafficking Law

The following straightforward model law is proposed for use in other countries (particularly those that at present have no such anti-trafficking enactments).

- a. Prohibited Conduct:
  - (1) Trafficking. Whoever knowingly engages in trafficking in persons, or facilitates the trafficking in persons, shall be punished by a term of imprisonment of at least 5 years.
  - (2) Involvement of a Minor. When the offense provided for in paragraph 1 of the present Section is committed against a person under the age of 18 years, the perpetrator shall be punished by a term of imprisonment of at least 15 years.
  - (3) Organized Conduct. Whoever organizes, directly or indirectly, a group of three or more persons to commit the offense in paragraph 1 of the present Section shall be punished by a fine of up to $2 million or twice the gross profits of the offense, whichever is higher, and by a term of imprisonment of at least 10 years, and, if a minor was involved, by a term of imprisonment of at least 20 years.
  - (4) Procuring Sexual Services. Whoever uses or procures the sexual services of a person with the knowledge that such person is a victim of trafficking shall be punished by a term of imprisonment of at least 2 years.
  - (5) Procuring Sexual Services from a Minor. When the offense provided for in paragraph 4 of the present Section is committed against a person under the age of 18 years, the perpetrator shall be punished by a term of imprisonment of at least 10 years.
  - (6) Attempt and Conspiracy. Any person who attempts or conspires to commit any offense defined in this Section shall be subject to the same penalties as those prescribed for the offense, the commission of which was the object of the attempt or conspiracy.
  - (7) Obstruction. Whoever obstructs, attempts to obstruct, or in any way interferes with or prevents the enforcement of this Section, or conspires to do so, shall be punished as if that person committed the substantive offense which he sought to obstruct, attempt to obstruct, interfere with, or prevent the enforcement of.
  - (8) Aiding and Abetting. Whoever aids, abets, or assists in the conduct proscribed in this Section shall be treated as having committed the offense he aided, abetted, or assisted.
  - (9) No Dual Prosecutions. No prosecution may be commenced against a person under this section if a foreign government, in accordance

with jurisdiction recognized by the United States, has in good faith prosecuted or is prosecuting such person for the conduct constituting such offense, except upon the approval of the U.S. Attorney General or his/her designee.

b. Definitions:

For the purposes of the present Section,

(1) "Trafficking in persons." The term "trafficking in persons" means recruitment, transportation, transfer, harboring or receipt of persons, by means of threat or use of force or other forms of coercion, abduction, fraud, deception, the abuse of power or a position of vulnerability or the giving or receiving of payments or benefits to achieve consent of a person having control over another person, for the purpose of exploitation. A finding of guilt under this Section does not require the physical movement of a person, but must entail the exploitation of the person for labor or commercial sex.

The recruitment, transportation, transfer, harboring, or receipt of a minor under the age of 18 for the purpose of exploitation shall be considered "trafficking in persons," even if this does not involve any of the means set forth immediately above in this paragraph.

(2) "Exploitation." The term "exploitation" as used in subparagraph 1 of the present paragraph means using the person for the purposes of prostitution or other forms of sexual exploitation, forced labor or services, and slavery or similar practices involving servitude.

(3) "Consent." The ultimate consent of a victim of trafficking in persons to the intended exploitation shall be irrelevant where any of the means set forth in subparagraph 1 of the present paragraph were used against such victim.

c. Penalties

When the offense provided for in the present Section is committed by an official person in the exercise of his or her duties, the perpetrator shall be punished by a term of imprisonment of at least 7 years in the case of the offense provided for in paragraph (a)(1); by a term of imprisonment of at least 17 years in the case of the offense provided for in paragraph (a)(2); by a term of imprisonment of at least 12 years in the case of the offense provided for in paragraph (a)(3), except that, if the offense involved a minor, by a term of imprisonment of at least 22 years; by a term of imprisonment of at least 4 years in the case of the offense provided for in paragraph (a)(4); and by a term of imprisonment of at least 12 years in the case of the offense provided for in paragraph (a)(5).[15]

While changing circumstances may require that this developing definition of human trafficking be amended, we believe this definition of human trafficking spreads the net wide enough to include the most culpable individuals, while also ensuring fairness and proportionality to the accused.

Notes

1. Few law enforcement issues have garnered as much media attention.

2. See U.N. OFF. ON DRUGS AND CRIME, HUMAN TRAFFICKING: EVERYBODY'S BUSINESS, available at www.unglobalcompact.org/docs/news_events/Bulletin/HumanTraffic_Info.pdf.

3. See, for example, LexisNexis and the Polaris Project, U.S. AWARENESS OF HUMAN TRAFFICKING: EXECUTIVE SUMMARY OF SURVEY FINDINGS (2010), available at www .lexisnexis.com/redlight/lexisnexis-human-trafficking-survey.pdf ("A new survey of Americans' awareness of human trafficking reveals that the majority of Americans do not realize the severity and scope of this crime that affects nearly every country in the world, including the United States"), cited in Jonathan Todres, *Moving Upstream: The Merits of a Public Health Law Approach to Human Trafficking*, 89 N.C. L. REV. 447, 489 (2011) ("Today, there is increased attention on the problem of human trafficking, but still significant portions of the U.S. population are either unaware of the problem or unaware that it is an issue in the United States").

4. See also Kathy Kerr, *Returning Home: The Challenge of Repatriating Foreign Born Child*, 16 BUFF. H. RTS. L. REV. 155, 158 (2010):

> Some countries offer foreign-born victims an opportunity to remain in the country and exempt them from penalties of illegal entry. In the United States, for instance, victims of human trafficking, including victims smuggled into the United States and imprisoned in forced labor, can choose to remain in the United States or return home. If the trafficked victim desires to stay in the United States, she can qualify for continued presence or a T-Visa, a special non-immigrant visa, as an alternative to repatriation. To qualify she must be identified as having been subjected to "severe trafficking in persons," must assist in the investigation and prosecution of accused traffickers and must demonstrate that if returned to her home country she "would suffer extreme hardship involving unusual and severe harm." A child under the age of eighteen, however, does not need to be a witness in a legal case against her exploiter. The minor can still obtain the special immigration status as long as she can prove she was a victim.
>
> If victims choose to remain in the United States, they also qualify for a number of housing, training, employment and food benefits. For example, the Office of Victims of Crime and the Office of Refugee Resettlement provides grants to organizations offering services to victims of human trafficking, including case management, legal assistance, medical, psychological and dental services, shelter, clothing, daily sustenance, transportation, English language training and job skills training. Additionally, the Department of Labor provides career centers with job search assistance, general education diploma assistance, career counseling and occupational skills training. Survivors can live in the United States

on the T-Visa for up to four years. They are eligible to apply for adjustment of their status to lawful permanent residence or an extension on their T-Visa if they meet certain qualifications. Therefore, under U.S. law, the victim escapes penalty for violating immigration laws. Instead, the victim qualifies to receive a visa and other benefits.

5. Traffickers often transport victims from their home communities to unfamiliar destinations, away from family and friends, religious institutions, and other sources of protection and support, leaving the victims defenseless and vulnerable.

6. 22 U.S.C. § 7101(b) (2000).

7. U.S. Dep't of Health and Human Services, FACT SHEET: LABOR TRAFFICKING, available at www.acf.hhs.gov/trafficking/about/fact_labor.html (last visited June 3, 2011).

8. See generally Colin Feltham and Windy Dryden, DICTIONARY OF COUNSELING, at 109, 223 (2004).

9. See generally Wisconsin Office of Justice Assistance, HIDDEN IN PLAIN SIGHT: A BASELINE SURVEY OF HUMAN TRAFFICKING IN WISCONSIN (2008), available at ftp://doaftp04 .doa.state.wi.us/doadocs/Human_Trafficking_Report_Final.pdf, cited in Jessica E. Ozalp, Comment, *Halting Modern Slavery in the Midwest: The Potential of Wisconsin Act 116 to Improve the State and Federal Response to Human Trafficking*, 2009 WIS. L. REV. 1391, 1394 (2009).

10. See, for example, Jennifer M. Chacón, *Misery and Myopia: Understanding The Failures of U.S. Efforts to Stop Human Trafficking*, 74 FORDHAM L. R. 2977, 2986–87 (2006) ("Trafficking victims also include individuals who are not a subset of the group of 'voluntary migrants' previously identified, for it also encompasses those who are forcibly taken from their homes or sold by their own families and placed in positions of forced labor. The latter group is typically evoked in discussions of human trafficking, but the former—voluntary migrants who later become subject to coerced labor, including sex work—is actually the larger category. This disconnect between perception and reality has resulted in a law that is too narrow to reach a significant portion of the domestic trafficking problem").

11. 18 U.S.C. § 1591 (2000), emphasis added.

12. 18 U.S.C. § 1593 (2000).

13. Convention against Transnational Organized Crime, G.A. 55/25, U.N. Doc. A/ RES/55/25 (Nov. 15, 2000), available at www.unodc.org/documents/treaties/UNTOC/ Publications/TOC%20Convention/TOCebook-e.pdf (hereafter "TOC Convention").

14. Note, however, that such coercive means are not universally required. The UK's Sexual Offenses Act of 2003, for example, incorporated trafficking for sexual exploitation, but did not require those committing the offence to use coercion, deception, or force; as a result, it encompasses any person who enters the UK to carry out sex work, even with consent, as having been trafficked.

15. This model law is part of an ongoing ABA and Uniform Law Commission reform effort involving one of the authors. There are, of course, other model laws addressing many of the issues addressed in our model law. See, for example, FREEDOM NETWORK, STATE MODEL LAW ON PROTECTION FOR VICTIMS OF HUMAN TRAFFICKING, available at www.sexworkersproject.org/downloads/FN2005StateModelLaw.pdf.

5

Synchronized Abuse

The Impact of International Organized Crime Groups on Child Trafficking and Other Forms of Sexual Exploitation

> Trafficking in persons is increasingly perpetrated by organized, sophisticated criminal enterprises. Such trafficking is the fastest growing source of profits for organized criminal enterprises worldwide. Profits from the trafficking industry contribute to the expansion of organized crime in the United States and worldwide. Trafficking in persons is often aided by official corruption in countries of origin, transit, and destination, thereby threatening the rule of law. . . . Trafficking includes all the elements of the crime of forcible rape when it involves the involuntary participation of another person in sex acts by means of fraud, force, or coercion.[1]

THE TRANSNATIONAL MOVEMENT of children for purposes of sexual exploitation through human trafficking and the related forced prostitution, as well as global distribution of child pornography through, among other outlets, the Internet, share one constant—they are all commercial criminal enterprises substantially controlled by organized crime.[2] Indeed, various international organizations have formally reported what law enforcement already knew—namely, that organized crime groups operating in the United States and abroad, including the Italian, Russian, and Balkan Mafias, South American cartels, Chinese and Vietnamese Triads, and the Japanese Yakuza have used modern communications technology to forge highly profitable transnational alliances to more efficiently and safely facilitate their human trafficking and related child exploitation activities.[3]

And the trade in children and depictions of their abuse is far from a niche market. The latest studies estimate that criminal organizations earn as much from the manufacture and distribution of child pornography and the transfer of children domestically and internationally for purposes of sexual exploitation as they do from drug and arms trafficking. While guns, heroin, and cocaine were once the "commodity of choice," today children and child pornography vie for the distinction of being organized crime's top profit center.[4]

The Internet is the key to this shift, making it faster, easier, cheaper, and less risky for criminal groups worldwide to engage in this high-profit activity by satisfying the never-slackening thirst for "fresh" product. Low transaction and communication costs, coupled with immense profits, has, after all, always been organized crime's winning combination.

A. Organized Crime and the Trafficking of Minors

As noted above, organized crime groups large and small have worked hard to forge transnational alliances. These well-organized groups now rely on local contacts to provide safe houses, coordinate transportation, and obtain illegal immigration, residency, and identification documents.

But affiliating with organized crime has benefits even for "independent" traffickers, as larger groups can provide a steady flow of child victims through their networks of recruiters, transporters, and corrupt law enforcement and public officials. Having such a broad geographic sweep also permits the traffickers to coerce, intimidate, and effectively control the victims, the victims' parents, and anyone else who may threaten the organization. Purely local or regional traffickers simply do not have these capacities.

1. Yakuza and Child Trafficking

One of Japan's most infamous, enduring, and powerful organized crime groups is the Yakuza. The Yakuza, like virtually every organized crime group around the world, is involved in a myriad of different criminal enterprises. But human and child trafficking has, increasingly, become a major source of their illicit income. In particular, the Yakuza has established a significant pipeline of minor girls trafficked from child exploitation hotspot Thailand to prime child pornography consumer Japan. (Thailand is, of course, not the only country where women are recruited into Japan's sex industry; Japan's powerful organized crime figures also feed the demand through the trafficking of minor girls and young women from the Balkans and Eastern Europe, Asia, and Latin America.)

To keep the pipeline flowing, the Yakuza use the familiar network of recruiters, transporters, and safe houses. After the girls are brought through force, coercion, or fraud to Japan, they are typically sold to brothels or "snack bars," where the girls provide food and drink—as well as sexual services—to their Japanese and international patrons. The managers of these snack bars are typically women known as "mamas" or "mamasans."[5] These women ensure that the girls perform as expected and do not "cause trouble" by going to law enforcement or by attempting to flee. In exchange for a substantial cut of the profits, the Yakuza, for their part, provide protection from local law enforcement. The Yakuza, like the Mafia and other organized crime groups, uses its political clout and wealth to ensure that the local police conveniently ignore this illegal conduct.[6] Human Rights Watch reported that many of the Thai trafficking victims working in Japan who they interviewed stated that they thought any attempts to escape would be punished with death.[7]

2. Organized Crime in the Balkans and Elsewhere

Globalization has intensified the trafficking of both women and children around the world, particularly in such communities unsettled by conflict. The Balkans are in many ways the perfect illustration of this phenomenon. During the postwar turmoil, and against a backdrop of frail law enforcement systems that continue to characterize this region, Balkan political and legal leaders remained mired in struggles over control and ideology. Balkan organized crime groups, in contrast, were free of similar historic or political grudges. Instead, they remained united and focused on one goal—to make money.[8] This shared objective allowed them to overcome hundreds of years of regional and ethnic differences.

Years of war left this part of the world with weakened borders and a frail and corruption-ridden law enforcement system, creating an environment where organized criminals and traffickers flourished; hundreds of women and girls from the region were introduced into the sex worker "pipeline" in the mid-1990s with little chance of detection, but at great profit. As "normalcy" has slowly returned to this war-plagued part of the world, this pipeline only expanded. Every day, boys and girls are forced to work in the Balkan sex industry, while others are "exported" to Western Europe and other parts of the world for the purpose of coerced prostitution.[9]

Thus, while law enforcement and political leaders still refuse to work with each other, young girls and boys from Kosovo, Albania, Macedonia, Serbia, Croatia, Romania, and Bosnia are left unprotected at the mercy of organized crime groups who see them as nothing more than a means of making money.

But the Balkans and Western Europe are certainly not the only regions plagued by human trafficking. Trafficking in children is also on the rise in

Latin America, Africa, South Asia, and elsewhere. According to estimates, for example, as many as 9,000 girls are trafficked each year from Nepal and Bangladesh to India and Pakistan. Traffickers in these countries no longer fit the stereotype of uneducated, "paan-chewing" men.[10] Instead, they are equipped with cell phones and video cameras, and speak cultured English, allowing them to exploit women and children more efficiently and effectively than ever before.

Another persistent factor further exacerbates trafficking: in many countries, female children still are considered a financial burden to their families, are left largely uneducated (when compared to their brothers), and, therefore, have few employable skills. Combined with social and religious mores, these factors conspire to leave women financially and emotionally dependent on the male head of the household (i.e., either their father or husband).

For traffickers, this combination of extreme poverty, ingrained sexism, and the mistreatment of women is fertile ground. Disguising payments by calling them dowries, traffickers will, for all intents and purposes, buy minor girls from their families. Regardless of whether these parents knowingly sold their daughters or simply turned a blind eye to the blatant realities of the agreement in order to gain cash for a poverty-stricken family, what these parents may be less aware of is that they have sold them into the organized crime–controlled commercial sex industry.

Once in the grasp of organized crime, there is little chance of escape. Regardless of whether the girls land in organized crime's web through false job offers or false marriage claims, the habituation or "seasoning" process is largely the same the world over. Targeted abuse is used to break the women down physically and emotionally. Rape, assaults, and degrading treatment, combined with acts of false kindness and compassion, are used to "break" the woman and to remove any lingering defiance or resistance.[11]

Even those young boys and girls who are liberated from their captors may, from their families' perspective, be "beyond repairs," because they are now viewed as prostitutes who have shamefully dishonored the entire family and who, therefore, cannot be accepted back in the family. Ingrained social and religious conventions further exacerbate the abuse. Organized crime is, of course, fully aware of these pernicious factors, which (1) make it easier to separate a child from his or her parents, (2) allow them to, through force, break the child's will and make her compliant and habituated to her new "work" environment, and (3) virtually eliminate the chance that the child will ever be received back into the family. Insidiously, the child victim also understands these dynamics, and will be even more reluctant to talk to, or otherwise cooperate with, law enforcement, lest she be left completely unprotected and alone. The child also sees how the traffickers have law enforcement in their pockets and so they view law enforcement officers as another link in the chain.

The global community has been—and, frankly, remains—slow to respond, and is now well behind in the war against organized crime's domination over commercial child exploitation. Yet international instruments such as the 2000 U.N. Convention against Transnational Organized Crime, and its Optional Protocol to Prevent, Suppress, and Punish the Trafficking in Persons, are at least steps in the right direction.

One remarkable aspect of international efforts to stem human trafficking is the repeated establishment of a comprehensive legal structure without an apparent ability or desire by the signatory parties to effectuate the provisions both regionally and transnationally. In the United States, the development of criminal law often occurs as the result of a socially significant problem to which Congress reacts. An example of this in the U.S. domestic context is the federal kidnapping statute, which was, in significant part, enacted due to the Lindberg baby kidnapping.

In the area of human trafficking, by contrast, the legislators created a comprehensive piece of legislation prior to seeing law enforcement act to combat the crime, and have failed to mainstream these changes. The public eagerness to sign on to international instruments with soothing, positive titles, while doing little or nothing domestically to combat the problem, can be seen in virtually every corner of the globe. Consider, for example, that in India only West Bengal has enacted anti-trafficking legislation. West Bengal's Immoral Trafficking Prevention Act (ITPA), moreover, only addresses victims trafficked into sexual exploitation (ignoring the related crime of trafficking for labor purposes).[12]

National and regional anti-trafficking plans often overlook that the multifaceted nature of organized crimes' trafficking activity demands a sophisticated and coordinated approach:

- Public information campaigns must make families aware of the methods employed by traffickers to separate children from their caregivers.
- Families and law enforcement must view child trafficking victims as true victims, and not as prostitutes.
- Young persons and their families must understand that fraudulent job and marriage offers are a common organized crime tool.
- Law enforcement must be able to recognize child trafficking, whether organized or not.

- Transnational sharing of information and collaboration must be encouraged in order to identify and prosecute traffickers.
- Trafficking in women and children proliferates in countries with police corruption because traffickers realize that the likelihood of their actions being detected and punished is extremely low. Organized crime's primary ally—namely, police and judicial corruption—must, therefore, be purged from law enforcement.
- Legislators should enact appropriate legislation that outlaws all forms of child and human trafficking, and that imposes appropriately enhanced sentences for those defendants involved in organized schemes to traffic in children.
- Governments must be held accountable for their efforts aimed at stopping organized crime's child exploitation activities within their borders. International pressure, including sanctions and official condemnation, must be aimed at those nations who ignore organized child exploitation occurring within their borders.

Accurately identifying and treating trafficking victims is, of course, central, but efforts must also be made to more directly curb the escalating intensity and volume of the trafficking activity. As we know, advances in modern communications technology foster child exploitation. These advances make it easier, faster, and more profitable for organized traffickers to communicate and conduct transactions, regardless of their location around the world.

It is, of course, not feasible to restrict access to, or halt development in, technology. However, fortified law enforcement and immigration control increase the transaction costs and make trafficking less profitable. Critical is enhanced information-sharing and collaboration among the world's law enforcement agencies. After all, the more difficult it is for organized crime to coordinate activities in different countries without being monitored or disrupted by law enforcement, the less attractive this species of criminal activity becomes.

3. Examining the Trafficking Victims Protection Act's Tier System

The United States, through the Trafficking Victims Protection Act of 2000 (TVPA), has provided a general model for nations to follow. The TVPA provides useful standards calculated to eradicate human trafficking, including by providing legislative and sentencing benchmarks.[13] That said, although this Tier system has had some success, as we shall see in chapter 7, public corruption continues to undermine efforts to eradicate trafficking and serves to make trafficking lucrative.

The TVPA segregates countries into three different lists ("Tiers" 1–3), according to government compliance with the standards to counter trafficking activity.[14] Providing the concrete adverse consequences often missing from international proclamations, the TVPA punishes those countries failing to meet the TVPA's minimum standards. These punishments include penalties such as "withhold[ing] non-humanitarian, non-trade-related assistance [and] funding for participation in educational and cultural exchange programs . . . [as well as] U.S. opposition to assistance . . . from international financial institutions . . . and multilateral development banks." And, as those active in international relations know, these are particularly toothy international sanctions.

The threat of such penalties has not gone unheeded: the governments of Bangladesh, Ecuador, Guyana, and Sierra Leone, for example, have, in direct response to the TVPA, taken significant steps to fight trafficking in persons. For example, not only has Ecuador—a Tier 2 country, according to the 2010 U.S. State Department Trafficking in Persons Report's assessment of the country[15]—through its domestic legislation prohibited all forms of trafficking, but its enforcement efforts have also been ramped up in order to render these proscriptions substantively meaningful.[16] Moreover, the government of Ecuador has also fortified prevention efforts:

> The Government of Ecuador increased trafficking prevention efforts last year, particularly through vigorous public awareness campaigns against child forced labor and prostitution. The government forged partnerships with private telecommunications companies and a bank to combat child labor, in part through a network of schools for former child laborers. During the holidays, the government launched a national campaign against child begging and a radio soap opera series about the dangers of forced labor, which was broadcast on provincial radio stations in Spanish and Kichwa, a local language. State-owned radio stations also donated airtime to an NGO in the highlands to broadcast messages on how to identify and avoid human trafficking situations. The Ministry of Tourism launched a nationwide campaign to prevent the commercial sexual exploitation of children in the tourism industry, and the government continued a multimedia campaign in 20 departments to encourage citizens to identify and report trafficking cases.[17]

The combination of increased public awareness, strengthened law enforcement, and international pressure is the only way to put the brakes on organized crime's expansionist objectives in the realm of global child exploitation, to provide millions of victims a new voice against the injustice they are forced to suffer, and to generate an environment where traffickers, especially those associated with organized crime, will find it increasingly difficult to profit from their involvement in this modern-day slavery of women and children.

Notes

1. 22 U.S.C. § 7101(b) (2000) (Trafficking Victim Protection Act's Congressional findings).

2. See generally Richard J. Estes and Neil Alan Weiner, *The Commercial Sexual Exploitation of Children in the U.S., Canada and Mexico*, PENN SCHOOL OF SOC. POL'Y & PRAC. 8 (2003), available at www.sp2.upenn.edu/restes/CSEC_Files/Exec_ Sum_020220.pdf; see also Martti Lehti and Kauko Aromaa, *Trafficking for Sexual Exploitation*, 34 CRIME & JUST. 133, 218 (2006) (noting that the role of children is underestimated in the profitable enterprise of trafficking for sexual exploitation).

3. See generally James R. Richards, TRANSNATIONAL CRIMINAL ORGANIZATIONS, CYBERCRIME, AND MONEY LAUNDERING (1999); Claire Sterling, CRIME WITHOUT FRONTIERS: THE WORLDWIDE EXPANSION OF ORGANISED CRIME AND THE PAX MAFIOSA (1994); Carol Hallett, *The International Black Market: Coping with Drugs, Thugs, and Fissile Materials*, in GLOBAL ORGANIZED CRIME: THE NEW EMPIRE OF EVIL, 74, 76 (Linnea P. Raine and Frank J. Ciluffo, eds., 1994).

4. For an early example of this recognition, see *Child Pornography Prevention Act of 1995: Hearing before the Senate Comm. on the Judiciary*, 104th Cong., 2nd Sess. 12 (1996) ("It has been estimated that pornography, including child pornography, is an $8 to $10 billion a year business, and is said to be organized crime's third biggest money maker, after drugs and gambling").

5. See generally Kerry E. Yun, *How Japan's Recent Efforts to Reduce Sex Trafficking Can Be Improved through International Human Rights Enforcement Mechanisms: Fulfilling Japan's Global Legal Obligations*, 13 BUFF. HUM. RTS. L. REV. 205, 225–26 (2007) ("The Law on Control and Improvement of Amusement Entertainment Businesses regulates all other sexual services where there is no vaginal penetration. This has been described as the 'ejaculation business' and includes more than 21,000 businesses in 2001 including bath houses with 'private rooms,' strip clubs, sex hotels, 'snack bars,' pornographic theaters and peep shows. These services are not illegal, but are restricted to certain areas and require special licenses from the government and are evidence of the high demand for a diversity of sexual services by Japanese men. In many cases, women work as hostesses at 'snack bars' and 'date' clients by leaving the bar with the client to have sex in a nearby sex hotel to get around the law prohibiting prostitution").

6. Jake Adelstein, *This Mob Is Big in Japan*, WASH. POST, May 11, 2008 ("There's talk in Japan of criminalizing simple possession [of child pornography], but some political parties (and publishers, who are raking in millions) oppose the idea. U.S. law enforcement officers want to stop the flow of yakuza-produced child porn into the United States and would support such a law. But they can't even keep the yakuza themselves out of the country. Why? Because the national police refuse to share intelligence. Last year, a former FBI agent told me that, in a decade of conferences, the NPA had turned over the names and birthdates of about 50 yakuza members. 'Fifty out of 80,000,' he said"), available at www.washingtonpost.com/wp-dyn/content/article/2008/05/09/ AR2008050902544.html (last visited June 5, 2011).

7. See Human Rights Watch, Owed Justice: Thai Women Trafficked into Debt Bondage in Japan (2000), available at www.hrw.org/reports/2000/japan/ (last visited June 4, 2011).

8. See generally Economist Intelligence Unit, European Policy Analyst 4th Quarter 2006 (2006).

9. The traffickers sometimes use violence and remove the children from their homes; in other cases, they use "false advertisements" promising well-paying jobs (e.g., as domestic workers or waitresses) in Western Europe to persuade minors and their parents to let them go.

10. See Robyn Skinner and Catherine Maher, Child Trafficking and Organized Crime: Where Have All the Children Gone, 2 (undated), available at www.yapi.org/rpchildtrafficking.pdf ("Like guns and drugs, women and children are traded as commodities in the global black market. Because of the Internet and computer technology, it is faster, easier, and cheaper than ever before for groups around the world to conduct illicit economic transactions while evading government detection. Low transaction and communication costs are a major reason why the trafficking of women and children (especially into the commercial sex industry) is so profitable: in Russia alone, the trafficking of women and children is estimated to earn six-billion dollars per year. Given the extremely lucrative nature of this business, it is not surprising that organized criminals are also major players in the human trafficking industry").

11. See generally Eva J. Kane, Prostitution of Children and Child-Sex Tourism: An Analysis of Domestic and International Responses (1999) ("Once a [minor] girl has been 'turned out,' the pimp may 'season' her for life as a prostitute with physical and verbal abuse. Seasoning is meant to break her will and separate her from her previous life so that she does not know where to turn for help. He may change her identity and move her around because constant mobility breaks any personal ties she may have developed and ensures new ties are only temporary. The demoralizing and dehumanizing experience of prostitution confirms the child's poor self-image and provides another tool for manipulation by the pimp. The pimp may withhold love and affection, or use verbal abuse, fear, and violence to control her. By that time, the girl is completely under his control").

12. See Robyn Skinner and Catherine Maher, supra note 10, at 3 ("Moreover, the provisions of the ITPA only address victims trafficked into sexual exploitation, while neglecting other forms of human trafficking such as into forced labor. In 1997, the Supreme Court of India established a committee and a national plan of action to examine trafficking activity in the country's commercial sex industry. However, NGOs in the country report that, in fact, the government continues to pursue a misguided approach in its anti-trafficking efforts, including arresting victims for prostitution rather than arresting traffickers who are actually responsible for the exploitation").

13. For a criticism of the TVPA, see Jonathan Todres, *Law, Otherness, and Human Trafficking*, 49 Santa Clara L. Rev. 605, 650–51 (2009):

Developments in federal law—most notably, the Trafficking Victims Protection Act of 2000 and its subsequent reauthorizations in 2003, 2005, and 2008 (TVPA)—have followed a law enforcement model. While law enforcement is a necessary component of combating human trafficking, the belief in a heavy emphasis on law enforcement as a means to eliminating human trafficking is rooted in otherness-shaped beliefs that the cause is just a few "bad" actors that need to be caught. Similar to the international framework, developments in U.S. law have accorded more weight to the prosecution component than to protection or prevention. Thus, a major emphasis of the federal legislation was increased penalties for trafficking and commercial sexual exploitation of adults and children. Although the heavier sanctions represent a positive step toward recognizing the grave nature of these crimes, and have an expressive function, these measures alone are insufficient. Thus the strong emphasis on law enforcement as the answer has done little to reduce the incidence of trafficking, in part because a very small percentage of traffickers have been prosecuted and because tougher criminal sanctions do not address root causes of vulnerability of particular populations.

14. See Jonathan Todres, *Moving Upstream: The Merits of a Public Health Law Approach to Human Trafficking,* 89 N.C. L. Rev. 447, 457n32 (2011) ("The U.S. Department of State categorizes most countries as at least Tier 2, meaning their governments 'are making significant efforts to bring themselves into compliance with those standards' set by the United States in the Trafficking Victims Protection Act (TVPA), which incorporates the three-pronged approach to human trafficking").

15. Available at www.state.gov/g/tip/rls/tiprpt/2010/ (last visited August 21, 2011).

16. Ibid.

17. Ibid.

6

Public Corruption as the Silent Partner to Child Sexual Exploitation

ALTHOUGH THERE HAVE BEEN significant strides in prosecuting human traffickers and in assisting the victims of human trafficking, most efforts
have overlooked one critical piece[1]: the key roles corrupt public officials play
in source countries, along trafficking routes, and in destination countries.
Although a comprehensive discussion of this complex topic is outside of this
book's scope, we will cover some of the highlights to give the reader a sense of
the interconnectedness of these areas.

A. Human Traffickers and Other Exploiters' Reliance on Corrupt Officials

Public corruption facilitates the unwilling exits and unlawful entries of trafficking victims,[2] enables the development of complex multinational transit
routes,[3] and helps traffickers procure falsified passports, visas, and entry
documents at each step of the way.[4] The damage such pervasive public corruption wreaks upon the reputation of the organs of democratic society and
the morale of the wider public servant class generally—and of course on the
direct and indirect human trafficking victims, specifically—is incalculable.
To safeguard both the rule of law, as well as the dignity of those humans who
fall into the vicious grip of the organized criminal groups dominating transnational human trafficking, increased focus must, therefore, be placed on,
and resources directed to, the critical fight against public corruption in aid of
human trafficking.

Public corruption facilitates trafficking in a number of ways, often as a result of the complicity of law enforcement officials in trafficking.[5] Public corruption is implicated not only in the direct activities of human traffickers, but also in the criminal justice system—where corrupt officials may passively or actively impede efforts to bring traffickers to justice—and in the victim protection system, where corruption may limit efforts to provide victims with services and support.[6]

Researchers relying on the annual Trafficking in Persons (TIP) reports, produced by the United States Department of State under the authority of the Trafficking Victims Protection Act (TVPA), classify countries according to the three-tier approach set forth in the TVPA: countries are classified as "Tier 1"—those whose governments fully comply with the TVPA's minimum standards; "Tier 2"—those whose governments do not yet fully comply with the TVPA's standards, but are making significant efforts to come into compliance; and "Tier 3"—those whose governments do not fully comply and are not making significant efforts to do so.[7] Governments of Tier 3 countries may be subject to U.S. government sanctions in the form of the withdrawal of "nonhumanitarian, non-trade-related foreign assistance."[8] Although the TVPA "provides for a waiver of sanctions if necessary to avoid significant adverse effects on vulnerable populations, including women and children,"[9] some have criticized the sanctions system as being likely to harm the victims of trafficking, rather than the governments which tolerate it.[10]

A review of the TIP reports reveals that governments with significant levels of public corruption also have significant human trafficking numbers.[11] For example, Cambodia has pervasive corruption,[12] and has also been classified as either a Tier 2 or a Tier 3 Watchlist country in recent TIP reports.[13] In 2008, Cambodia enacted the Law on the Suppression of Human Trafficking and Commercial Sexual Exploitation, which prohibits and severely penalizes all forms of trafficking.[14] The 2010 TIP report section on Cambodia, nevertheless, concludes that "impunity, corruption, and related rent-seeking behavior continue to impede anti-trafficking efforts."[15] The report also notes the direct and indirect involvement of police and judicial officials in trafficking.[16] Most notably, Cambodian authorities failed to prosecute the former president of Cambodia's appeals court for allegedly accepting $30,000 in exchange for the release of brothel owners who were convicted of trafficking.[17]

Public corruption, therefore, increases human trafficking not only by facilitating the transport of victims because of public officials who accept bribes to turn a blind eye to the illegal conduct, but also by otherwise directly and indirectly cultivating a climate fertile for the rapid growth of human trafficking.[18] Economic decline due to government mismanagement of public resources, for example, impacts women and children by keeping them in a weakened condition through poverty, hunger, and lack of education, thereby making them prime targets of the trafficker.[19] Corruption in Nigeria has been labeled "endemic" and "systemic," and the overall level of trafficking has been characterized as staggering.[20]

Commentators caution, however, that an increase in law enforcement activity does not always equate to a reduction in human trafficking.[21] Governments focused narrowly on criminal enforcement measures often fail to provide victims with adequate remedies; this not only deprives victims of their rights, but it also fails to deter trafficking by not holding the traffickers monetarily accountable.[22]

B. Going Global: An International Focus on Public Corruption and Trafficking

A number of international reporting mechanisms focus on collecting both qualitative and quantitative data on human trafficking, as well as on the forms of public corruption that make such trafficking possible. As discussed in greater detail in chapter 8, many of these reporting mechanisms are embedded in international protocols and agreements, such as the Convention on the Elimination of All Forms of Discrimination against Women (CEDAW),[23] the United Nations Convention on the Rights of the Child (UNCRC),[24] and the U.N. Protocol to Prevent, Suppress, and Punish Trafficking in Persons, Especially Women and Children, supplementing the United Nations Convention against Transnational Organized Crime.[25] Both the CEDAW and the UNCRC, for example, require state parties to submit periodic reports documenting their compliance with provisions of the conventions, including their anti-trafficking articles.[26] The United Nations, for its part, has appointed a special rapporteur on trafficking in persons, especially women and children, who "has the power to investigate the scope of the problem, monitor and report on government actions, receive and inquire into complaints, and make recommendations for policy change."[27] Not surprisingly, public corruption continues to loom large in the special rapporteur's investigations and reporting.

In addition, regional state organizations have encouraged their members to collect internal, and related public corruption, human trafficking data. For example, the Organization for Security and Co-operation in Europe (OSCE), in its 2003 Action Plan, recommended that, in addition to addressing public corruption, state parties focus on research "related to victims of trafficking, the character and scale of trafficking in persons, the role of organized criminal groups, identification of the most vulnerable segments of the population, and an analysis of the root causes of trafficking in persons."[28]

Some countries also compile their own reports regarding human trafficking. These national reports are usually self-assessments of the government's response to human trafficking. For example, Sweden has appointed a government ministry, the National Police Board, to serve as the National Rapporteur on Trafficking in Women in Sweden; the national rapporteur assists the police in recording cases of trafficking, and proposes measures that the government can take to combat trafficking within Sweden and to stem any ill effects of public corruption.[29] The Netherlands, by contrast, relies on an independent, extra-governmental rapporteur to report annually on trafficking in all persons and other forms of exploitation.[30] The United States, like Sweden, assigns responsibility to an agency of the government, the Department of Justice, to report on the status of trafficking and the government's efforts to combat it.[31]

Although many countries thus commission such reports and fund them liberally to send the message they are supporting anti-trafficking initiatives, it must be noted that the reports routinely fail to mention the link between public corruption and human trafficking. Moreover, they rarely, if ever, address the role of illegal enterprises in perpetuating that trafficking.

C. Recommendations and Best Practices

What follows are some modest proposals for enhancing existing enforcement schemes so that they also take into account the central role public corruption plays in child sexual exploitation generally, and in human trafficking specifically.

1. Recommended Legislative Actions

First, states should amend their respective national statutes to incorporate the "3P Paradigm" of trafficking ("prevention, prosecution, and victim prevention") to include language specifically recognizing the critical role public corruption plays in facilitating and enabling human trafficking. The 2010 U.S. State Department TIP report proposes that the following elements be included in a "good anti-trafficking law":

- *An Expanded Understanding of Coercion.* A broad definition of the concept of *coercion* is recommended so that the term is understood to cover its many manifestations in modern forms of slavery, including the threat of physical, financial, or reputational harm sufficiently serious to compel a reasonable person to perform or to continue performing labor or services in order to avoid incurring that harm.

- *A Broad Definition for Trafficking.* A well-articulated definition of *trafficking* is needed which facilitates effective law enforcement and prosecutorial responses, and allows for the collection of meaningful data. The definition should incorporate all forms of compelled service in addition to forced prostitution. The definition should not simply criminalize the recruitment or transportation of prostituted persons. The definition should *not* include related but distinct crimes, such as alien smuggling or prostitution.
- *Expanded Victim Services.* What is needed are mechanisms to provide appropriate care to all suspected victims of trafficking so that they have the opportunity to access basic services—including shelter, food, medical care, psycho-social counseling, legal aid, and work authorization.
- *Immigration Relief.* Counties should provide explicit immigration relief for trafficking victims, regardless of their past legal status, and relief from any legal penalties for unlawful activities committed by victims as a direct result of their trafficking.
- *Protections for Child Victims.* The law should provide specific protections for child victims of trafficking ensuring the best interests of the child in all decisions made in providing services to them.
- *Victim Restitution.* The law should also contain explicit provisions ensuring identified victims have access to legal redress to obtain financial compensation for the trafficking crimes committed against them. In order to be meaningful, such access must be accompanied by options to obtain immigration relief. Trafficking victims should not be excluded from legal services providers who can assist with these efforts, whether nongovernmental organizations or government programs.[32]

Anti-trafficking statutes should, additionally, contain a specific anticorruption provision focusing on the need to research and monitor the role that public corruption plays in a country's human trafficking activities,[33] and that allows for a powerful and flexible prosecutorial scheme under which corrupt public officials who benefit from allowing human traffic to flow will be brought to justice. Monitoring the role public corruption plays in different prosecutions can educate law enforcement regarding the unique methods used by traffickers in different countries, which in turn provides insights on how to effectively close corrupt loopholes along the trafficker's route.[34] In turn, knowledge of such corrupt practices allows lawmakers to enact legislation targeting those specific practices.[35]

2. Recommended Systemic Changes

Some specific systemic recommendations include:

- Develop a comprehensive anticorruption strategy built around the existing public corruption laws and focused on identifying where the laws could be improved. The strategy should build on an analysis of the patterns of corruption in the country and be developed in a participatory process. It should propose focused anticorruption measures tailored for specific institutions. The strategy must also include effective monitoring and reporting mechanisms.
- Establish a national multi-stakeholder anticorruption council to facilitate the development and implementation of a comprehensive anticorruption strategy. Stakeholders of the body should include the representatives of all the branches of government, as well as civil society, as equal partners.
- Create a special anticorruption department empowered to detect, investigate, and prosecute public corruption offenses. The department could function as an autonomous department with a special status integrated in the prosecutor's office, with officers seconded from the main law enforcement agencies, and should have investigative, administrative, and analytical specialists, as well as specialized/dedicated prosecutors. The department would, thus, not only work on actual corruption cases and raise public awareness of the problem, but would also facilitate interagency cooperation (including security, law enforcement, and financial/bank bodies), and would also maintain and disseminate statistical findings enabling comparisons among the institutions.
- Adopt a protocol for enhanced cooperation, information exchange, and resource sharing between agencies responsible for the fight against organized crime and transborder trafficking *and* smuggling (including drugs, counterfeit items, humans, etc.—all part of the same universe of criminality).
- Organize corruption-specific joint trainings for police, prosecutors, judges, and other law enforcement officials; provide adequate resources for the enforcement of anticorruption legislation; ensure the possibility of effective search and seizure of financial records.
- Conduct public awareness campaigns and organize trainings for the public, state officials, and the private sector employees focused on the sources and the impact of corruption, on the tools to fight against and prevent corruption, and on the rights of citizens.

3. Some Suggested Amendments to the TVPA and the TIP Reporting Scheme

The extent to which a country's government is actively working to address and minimize public corruption in general, and particularly the enabling effect of public corruption for human trafficking, should be added to the TVPA's list of minimum standards for the elimination of trafficking, and should be included in the standard TIP reporting produced under the TVPA and under similar national and international protocols.[36] The TVPA currently provides for the following minimum standards:

(1) The government of the country should prohibit severe forms of trafficking in persons and punish acts of such trafficking.

(2) For the knowing commission of any act of sex trafficking involving force, fraud, coercion, or in which the victim of sex trafficking is a child incapable of giving meaningful consent, or of trafficking which includes rape or kidnapping or which causes a death, the government of the country should prescribe punishment commensurate with that for grave crimes, such as forcible sexual assault.

(3) For the knowing commission of any act of a severe form of trafficking in persons, the government of the country should prescribe punishment that is sufficiently stringent to deter and that adequately reflects the heinous nature of the offense.

(4) The government of the country should make serious and sustained efforts to eliminate severe forms of trafficking in persons.[37]

Although the 2010 Global TIP Report notes a correlation between levels of public corruption in a given country and its performance under the TVPA's tier system,[38] the explicit degree of connection between public corruption in a country and the prevalence of human trafficking within that country is not specifically included within the TIP reports[39] or made part of a country's placement within the TVPA's three-tier system.[40] This is an oversight that should be remedied.

4. Holding OECD Countries to Account

Currently some thirty-eight countries are members of the Organization for Economic Cooperation and Development (OECD) Anti-bribery Convention,[41] and have adopted various pieces of legislation to enforce the Convention's goals of combating bribery.[42] The signatory countries' performance, however, leaves much to be desired.

The Anti-bribery Convention became effective on February 15, 1999.[43] The member countries agreed to take action to ensure that their national governments pass legislation to ratify and implement the convention.[44] Specifically, the convention directs its members to adopt domestic legislation criminalizing bribery of foreign public officials.[45] In addition, member countries agree to (1) appropriately sanction offenders and (2) share information relevant to criminal investigations.[46] The OECD has also implemented a peer review system, whereby the OECD monitors and publishes an assessment of each member nation's efforts to implement the convention's goals.[47]

On December 9, 2009, the OECD released the OECD Recommendation for Further Combating Bribery of Foreign Public Officials.[48] The recommendation elucidates how the convention can more effectively investigate and deter foreign bribery.[49] The OECD Working Group on Bribery, composed of representatives from each member nation, is responsible for implementing the goals set forth in the recommendation.[50] Specifically, the recommendation calls on the state parties to improve the cooperation and sharing of information between member nations, shield whistle blowers from retaliation, and interact more closely with the private sector to adopt ethics programs.[51]

For the first time since the Working Group convened, in June 2010 it published its findings concerning the signatory countries' enforcement of the provisions of the convention.[52] Although a significant number of prosecutions occurred,[53] a more careful review of the individual countries' enforcement procedures reveals that only eleven of the thirty-eight signatory countries have sanctioned an individual or entity under anti-bribery laws they enacted pursuant to the provisions of the convention.[54] Such low enforcement numbers indicate that anticorruption efforts are not taken sufficiently seriously by many signatory countries.

As of now, under the 2009 recommendation, a member nation that fails to comply with the Convention is subject to "strong pressure" from the OECD to fix the problem,[55] which may take the form of dispatching a high-level mission to the noncompliant country, sending a letter to the country's officials, or issuing a formal public statement.[56] The convention should explore using more robust methods to hold its members accountable.

Moreover, countries should be encouraged to adopt—and enforce—the 2009 recommendation because public corruption affects illegal businesses as well as legal ones. By placing human trafficking bribes on the same level as any other corrupt business practice, countries will demonstrate their awareness that public corruption acts as the grease that moves this extremely profitable financial enterprise. Given that human trafficking is connected with the illegal arms industry as the second-largest criminal industry behind only drug trafficking,[57] it clearly qualifies as a corrupt business whose shareholders reap huge financial benefits. Moreover, human trafficking is the fastest-growing criminal industry, so attention to the public-corruption aspect of the crime is long overdue.[58]

5. Encouraging the Transnational Fight against Corruption through MLATs

Further, as detailed in chapter 11, in order to add teeth to the enforcement provisions so sorely lacking in this first review of the OECD convention signatories' enforcement actions, countries should be encouraged to adopt Mutual Legal Assistance Treaties (MLATs) as part of their anti–human trafficking statutes and protocols. These MLATs would provide for the sharing of evidence across borders in order to effectively prosecute corrupt officials along the entire chain of the trafficking and child exploitation enterprise.

In February 2010, for example, the United States and the European Union entered into an MLAT. This multi-party MLAT "enhances and modernizes law enforcement and judicial cooperation by, among other things: allowing prompt identification of financial account information in criminal investigations; permitting the acquisition of evidence, including testimony, by means of video conferencing; and authorizing the participation of U.S. criminal investigators and prosecutors in joint investigative teams in the EU."[59] Currently, the United States has bilateral mutual legal assistance treaties in force with every EU Member State,[60] many of the Organization of American States member states,[61] and other countries around the world.[62] These MLATs are an innovative and vital resource for U.S. enforcement authorities and prosecutors.

D. Keeping the Eye on the Public Corruption Ball

The role of public corruption in the creation, facilitation, and continuation of international child trafficking and other forms of child sexual exploitation cannot be underestimated. Although academics, world leaders, and nongovernmental organizations have focused their efforts on the protection of the victim and the prosecution of the offenders, those efforts will, in the end, be fruitless unless an equal focus is paid to combating the interconnected problem of official corruption. Awareness of the role that public corruption plays in aiding and abetting the lucrative business of child sexual exploitation through commercial pornography and human trafficking will aid law enforcement's efforts to investigate and prosecute offenders. The collection of data showing the specific methods of trafficking within a particular country will, moreover, provide lawmakers with the information necessary to more effectively combat the crime through effective legislation. By following some of the suggestions set forth above, countries and law enforcement agencies can work together to reduce the amplified harm public corruption causes in the area of child sexual exploitation and human trafficking.

Notes

1. See 2010 TIP REPORT, supra chapter 1, note 1 (omitting reference to public corruption in its suggestions for "a good anti-trafficking law"); ibid. at 28 (noting a correlation between the performance of countries on the TIP Report ranking system and those countries' rankings on scales of perceived corruption and lack of protection of civil liberties, but failing to examine the ways in which public corruption directly facilitates human trafficking).

2. See U.N. Global Initiative to Fight Human Trafficking, THE VIENNA REPORT: A WAY FORWARD TO COMBAT HUMAN TRAFFICKING, at 11 (2008), available at www.ungift .org/gifts/ungift/pdf/vf/ebook2.pdf (hereafter VIENNA FORUM REPORT).

3. See ibid. at 11, 25–26.

4. See U.N. Office on Drugs and Crime, THE ROLE OF CORRUPTION IN TRAFFICKING IN PERSONS, at 11 (Nov. 11, 2009) (Background Paper for the Side Event "The Role of Corruption in Trafficking in Persons" at the Third Session of the Conference of State Parties to the United Nations Convention against Corruption, Doha, Qatar), available at www.unodc.org/documents/human-trafficking/Corruption_and_trafficking_Doha_final.pdf (hereafter Doha Background Paper).

5. See 2010 TIP REPORT, supra chapter 1, note 1, at 31.

6. See Doha Background Paper, supra note 4, at 7–8, 11.

7. See 2010 TIP REPORT, supra chapter 1, note 1, at 22.

8. 2010 TIP REPORT, supra chapter 1, note 1, at 25. In addition to these direct sanctions, the TVPA also allows the U.S. government to oppose IMF and World Bank assistance that would otherwise flow to Tier 3 countries.

9. 2010 TIP REPORT, supra chapter 1, note 1, at 28.

10. See Janie Chuang, *The United States as Global Sheriff: Using Unilateral Sanctions to Combat Human Trafficking*, 27 MICH. J. INT'L L. 437, 457–59 (2006).

11. See, for example, Sheldon X. Zhang and Samuel L. Pineda, *Corruption as a Causal Factor in Human Trafficking*, in ORGANIZED CRIME: CULTURE, MARKETS, AND POLICIES, at 53 (Dina Siegel and Hans Nelson eds., 2008). This study concludes that although most of the examined predictor variables—including poverty, infant mortality, and life expectancy—are significantly correlated with the ranking in the TIP Report, only corruption comes close to statistical significance. Ibid. at 52. Based on this assessment the authors conclude that "countries that make the least effort to fight human trafficking also tend to be those with high levels of official corruption." Ibid. at 53.

12. See 2010 TIP REPORT, supra chapter 1, note 1.

13. See ibid. at 48, 50; 2008 TIP REPORT, supra chapter 1, note 1, at 44.

14. 2010 TIP REPORT, supra chapter 1, note 1, at 101.

15. Ibid. at 102.

16. Ibid.

17. Ibid. According to the report, the official remains employed with the Cambodian government.

18. See Osita Agbu, *Corruption and Human Trafficking: The Nigerian Case*, 4 W. AFR. REV. 1, 4 (2003).

19. Ibid. at 4–5.

20. Ibid. at 3.

21. See, for example, Mindy M. Willman, *Human Trafficking in Asia: Increasing Individual and State Accountability through Expanded Victims' Rights*, 22 COLUM. J. ASIAN J. 283, 304 (2009).

22. See ibid.

23. G.A. Res. 34/180, art. 17, U.N. Doc. A/34/46 (Dec. 18, 1979) (hereafter CEDAW).

24. G.A. Res. 44/25, art. 43, U.N. Doc. A/44/49 (Nov. 20, 1989) (hereafter UNCRC).

25. G.A. Res. 55/25, Annex II, U.N. Doc. A/RES/55/383 (Nov. 15, 2000).

26. See CEDAW, supra note 23, art. 18; UNCRC, supra note 24, art. 44(1); see also Mohamed Y. Mattar, *Comparative Models of Reporting Mechanisms on the Status of Trafficking in Human Beings*, 41 VAND. J. TRANSNAT'L L. 1355, 1392–95 (2008).

27. Mattar, supra note 26, at 1359; Commission on Human Rights, Special Rapporteur on Trafficking in Persons, Especially Women and Children, 60th Sess., E/CN.4/2004/L62 (Apr. 19, 2004).

28. Mattar, supra note 26, at 1362, citing OSCE Action Plan to Combat Trafficking in Human Beings, Annex, 462nd Plenary Meeting, PC.DEC/557 (July 24, 2003).

29. Ibid. at 1365–66, citing Government Offices of Sweden, *Prostitution and Trafficking in Human Beings*, available at http://regeringen.se/sb/d/7119 (last visited October 18, 2010).

30. See Mattar, supra note 26, at 1368, citing Press Release, Dutch Ministry of Justice, *Appointment of National Rapporteur on Trafficking in Human Beings* (Jan. 27, 2000), available at http://english.justitie.nl/currenttopics/pressreleases/archives2000/-appointment-of-national-rapporteur-on-trafficking-in-human-beings.aspx (last visited June 15, 2011).

31. See 22 U.S.C. § 7103(d)(7) (2006) (defining the requirements of the Justice Department report).

32. 2010 TIP REPORT, supra chapter 1, note 1, at 13.

33. See Doha Background Paper, supra note 4, at 32 ("A vital step in addressing trafficking related corruption is the collection of relevant information in order to get a better insight into the problem, which would allow customize[d] knowledge-based responses").

34. See ibid. at 32 ("States need to start collecting data on investigations and prosecutions of officials in connection with trafficking which in turn would also put an obligation on the criminal justice system to collect data and ensure that these types of crime are investigated").

35. See ibid. at 29 ("In most countries, there are already anticorruption measures for public officials in place. Trafficking in persons, however, may require specific prevention measures to address particular risks and vulnerabilities. With regard to special anticorruption measures for relevant public officials, it would be useful to identify and address the sectors of law enforcement, criminal justice and other public officials whose tasks could be linked to the identification, investigation, prosecution, adjudication and referral, as well as the facilitation of human trafficking cases. Such actors would include but not be limited to border control, customs and immigration authorities, law enforcement and criminal justice actors specialized in trafficking in persons, etc.").

36. See, for example, ibid. at 32 ("There is hardly any official report that points out how the corruption of public officials has made trafficking from, through or to their country possible. If reference is made to reported cases, such cases are treated as exceptions, but not collected systematically, to examine patterns of corruption in trafficking in persons and to be used as evidence or indicator for the existence or nonexistence of systemic corruption of public officials in this context").

37. 22 U.S.C. § 7106(a).

38. See 2010 TIP REPORT, supra chapter 1, note 1, at 28 ("It appears governments ranked Tier 3 and Tier 2 Watch List more closely track Freedom House's low-performing civil liberties scale than do those countries ranked Tier 2 and Tier 1. These poor-performing governments, on average, rank significantly "higher" on this scale, reflecting lower freedoms").

39. See 2010 TIP REPORT, supra chapter 1, note 1, at 20–21 (listing the factors reflected by the tier rankings and country narratives, but making no mention of public corruption or government complicity in human trafficking).

40. See ibid. at 20, 22. Because tier placement is "based on the extent of governments' efforts to reach compliance with the TVPA's minimum standards for the elimination of human trafficking" and the standards themselves do not include corruption as a factor, tier placement would not necessarily take into account the impact of corruption on human trafficking. Ibid. at 20.

41. Convention on Combating Bribery of Foreign Public Officials in International Business Transactions, Dec. 17, 1997, S. Treaty Doc. No. 105-43, 37 I.L.M. 1, available at www.oecd.org/dataoecd/4/18/38028044.pdf (hereafter OECD Convention); OECD, RATIFICATION STATUS AS OF MARCH 2009, available at www.oecd.org/dataoecd/59/13/40272933.pdf. The thirty-eight parties to the OECD Convention are the thirty OECD member countries and the following non-OECD countries: Argentina, Brazil, Bulgaria, Chile, Estonia, Israel, Slovenia, and South Africa. OECD, ABOUT THE NEW RECOMMENDATION FOR FURTHER COMBATING BRIBERY OF FOREIGN PUBLIC OFFICIALS IN INTERNATIONAL BUSINESS, at 2, available at www.oecd.org/dataoecd/34/15/44281002 .pdf (hereafter RECOMMENDATION EXPLANATION).

42. OECD, OECD ANTI-BRIBERY CONVENTION: NATIONAL IMPLEMENTING LEGISLATION, available at www.oecd.org/document/30/0,3343,en_2649_34859_2027102_1_1_1_1,00 .html (last visited June 13, 2011).

43. OECD, OECD ANTI-BRIBERY CONVENTION: ENTRY INTO FORCE OF THE CONVENTION, available at www.oecd.org/document/12/0,3343,en_2649_34859_2057484_1_1_1_1,00 .html (last visited June 13, 2011).

44. Ibid.

45. See OECD Convention, supra note 41, art. 1. Under the OECD Convention, the offence of "bribery of a foreign public official" is defined as (1) "intentionally to offer, promise or give any undue pecuniary or other advantage, whether directly or through intermediaries, to a foreign public official, for that official or for a third party, in order that the official act or refrain from acting in relation to the performance of official duties, in order to obtain or retain business or other improper advantage in the conduct of international business"; and (2) "complicity in, including incitement, aiding and abetting, or authorisation of an act of bribery of a foreign public official."

46. Ibid., art. 3, art. 9.

47. Ibid., art. 12 ("The Parties shall co-operate in carrying out a programme of systematic follow-up to monitor and promote the full implementation of this Convention. Unless otherwise decided by consensus of the Parties, this shall be done in the framework of the OECD Working Group on Bribery in International Business Transactions and according to its terms of reference, or within the framework and terms of reference of any successor to its functions"); OECD, COUNTRY REPORTS ON THE IMPLEMENTATION OF THE OECD ANTI-BRIBERY CONVENTION, available at www.oecd.org/document/24/0,3343,en_2649_34859_1933144_1_1_1_1,00.html (last visited June 13, 2011).

48. OECD, RECOMMENDATION OF THE COUNCIL FOR FURTHER COMBATING BRIBERY OF FOREIGN PUBLIC OFFICIALS IN INTERNATIONAL BUSINESS TRANSACTIONS, available at www.oecd.org/dataoecd/11/40/44176910.pdf (hereafter OECD RECOMMENDATION); RECOMMENDATION EXPLANATION, supra note 41, at 1.

49. See, for example, OECD RECOMMENDATION, supra note 48, at para. 4 ("Recommends, in order to ensure the vigorous and comprehensive implementation of the OECD Anti-Bribery Convention, that Member countries should take fully into account the Good Practice Guidance on Implementing Specific Articles of the Convention on Combating Bribery of Foreign Public Officials in International Business Transactions, set forth in Annex I hereto, which is an integral part of this Recommendation"); ibid. at para. 5 ("Recommends that Member countries undertake to periodically review their laws implementing the OECD Anti-Bribery Convention and their approach to enforcement in order to effectively combat international bribery of foreign public officials"); see also RECOMMENDATION EXPLANATION, supra note 41, at 1.

50. OECD RECOMMENDATION, supra note 48, at para. 14.

51. Ibid. at para. 13, para. 9, para. 10(C); RECOMMENDATION EXPLANATION, supra note 41, at 1.

52. WORKING GROUP ON BRIBERY, DATA ON ENFORCEMENT OF THE ANTI-BRIBERY CONVENTION, available at www.oecd.org/dataoecd/11/15/45450341.pdf.

53. There were 138 total convictions of individuals, 49 total convictions of legal persons, 32 total acquittals of individuals, and 0 acquittals of legal persons. Ibid.

54. Ibid.

55. RECOMMENDATION EXPLANATION, supra note 41.

56. Ibid.

57. U.S. Department of Health and Human Services, Administration for Children and Families, HUMAN TRAFFICKING FACT SHEET (2010), available at www.acf.hhs.gov/trafficking/about/fact_human.html (last visited June 13, 2011).

58. Ibid.

59. Press Release, Department of Justice, *U.S./EU Agreements on Mutual Legal Assistance and Extradition Enter into Force* (Feb. 1, 2010), available at www.justice .gov/opa/pr/2010/February/10-opa-108.html (last visited June 13, 2011).

60. Special Committee on Foreign Relations, Mutual Legal Assistance Treaties with the European Union: Report, S. Exec. Rep. No. 110-13, at 3–4.

61. See, for example, Treaty on Mutual Legal Assistance in Criminal Matters, Oct. 12, 1997, U.S.-Venez., S. Treaty Doc. No. 105-38; Mutual Legal Assistance Cooperation Treaty with Mexico, Dec. 9, 1987, U.S.-Mex., S. Treaty Doc. No. 100-13; Treaty with Canada on Mutual Legal Assistance in Criminal Matters, Mar. 18, 1985, U.S.-Can., S. Treaty Doc. No. 100-14.

62. See, for example, Treaty on Mutual Legal Assistance in Criminal Matters, Oct. 17, 2001, U.S.-India, S. Treaty Doc. No. 107-3; Treaty on Mutual Legal Assistance in Criminal Matters, Sep. 16, 1999, U.S.-S. Afr., S. Treaty Doc. No. 106-36; Treaty on Mutual Legal Assistance in Criminal Matters, Jan. 26, 1998, U.S.-Isr., S. Treaty Doc. No. 105-40.

7

Federal Statutes Targeting
Child Exploitation

FEDERAL PROSCRIPTIONS ON child exploitation can be divided into three broad categories of criminality: the child pornography statutes, which prohibit the possession, distribution, and manufacturing of child pornography; the travel statutes, which prohibit the coercion, travel, and transportation of minors in interstate commerce for the purpose of sexual activity; and the human trafficking statutes, which prohibit the slavery and transportation of minors for purposes of labor or sexual activity.

A. The History of Federal Criminalization of Child Pornography

The prosecution of child pornography as a federal crime is a fairly recent development when compared to other areas of federal prosecution. Arising out of need to address a problem that was not adequately being addressed by the obscenity statute, Congress enacted the Protection of Children against Sexual Exploitation Act of 1977.[1] Prior to that enactment, child pornography was simply treated as "obscene speech" and regulated under the Supreme Court's analysis in *Miller v. California.*

In *Miller,* the Supreme Court held that the government acts within its rights to criminalize the possession, receipt, and distribution of "obscene" materials, provided that the trier of fact determine the following: (1) the average person, applying community standards, would find that the work as a whole appealed to the prurient interest; (2) the work depicts or describes sexual conduct in a patently offensive way; and (3) the work, taken as a whole, lacks serious literary, artistic, political, or scientific value.[2] The Protection of Children against Sexual Exploitation Act of 1977 took this scheme one step further by prohibiting the production, receipt, possession, transmission, and sale of visual depictions of minors engaged in sexually explicit conduct. Its actual reach and use, however, proved limited.

1. *New York v. Ferber*

In 1982, the Supreme Court held that the states have a compelling interest in safeguarding the physical and psychological well-being of minors and, therefore, upheld the constitutionality of a New York statute that prohibited child pornography by applying a stricter test than the one set forth in *Miller*.[3] In *Ferber*, the Court found that the state's interest in protecting children outweighed the need to protect child pornography. Differentiating child pornography from general pornography and other obscene speech, the *Ferber* Court held that child pornography is outside the protection of the First Amendment.[4] More significantly, the Court held that the "distribution of photographs and films depicting sexual activity by juveniles is intrinsically related to the sexual abuse of children."[5] As such, the Court ruled that a trier of fact "need not find that the material appeals to the prurient interest of the average person; it is not required that sexual conduct portrayed be done so in a patently offensive manner; and the material at issue need not be considered as a whole."[6]

Ferber also reaffirmed that criminal liability would only be imposed with a showing of scienter on the part of the defendant. In short, *Ferber* held that child pornography—using images of actual minors—may be banned without regard to whether it depicts works of value, because the images themselves are the product of child sexual abuse.[7] The Court, however, left open the possibility that adult actors who looked younger—or other forms of "simulation"—could be utilized to circumvent these restrictions.[8]

2. The Child Protection Act of 1984

Congress responded to the *Ferber* decision with the Child Protection Act of 1984, which amended the 1977 Act by removing the "obscenity test" and, in keeping with *Ferber*, prohibited material involving minors engaged in sexually explicit conduct.

In 1988, Congress, again faced with technological advances that were outpacing its statutes and facilitating an increase in production and distribution of child pornography, further amended the 1977 Act by passing the Child

TABLE 7.1
Statutory Overview

Statute (18 U.S.C.)	Offense
Section 2251	Sexual exploitation of children
Section 2251A	Selling or buying of children
Section 2252	Certain activities relating to material involving the sexual exploitation of minors
Section 2252A	Certain activity relating to material constituting or containing child pornography
Section 2252B	Misleading domain names on the Internet
Section 2252C	Misleading words or digital images on the Internet
Section 2253	Criminal forfeiture
Section 2254	Civil forfeiture
Section 2255	Civil remedy for personal injuries
Section 2256	Definitions of chapter
Section 2257	Recordkeeping requirements
Section 2257A	Recordkeeping requirements for simulated sexual conduct
Section 2258	Failure to report child abuse
Section 2258A	Reporting requirements for electronic communications service providers and remote computing service providers
Section 2258B	Limited liability for electronic communications service providers, remote computing providers, or domain name registrants
Section 2258C	Use to combat child pornography of technical elements relating to images reported to the CyberTipline
Section 2258D	Limited liability for the National Center for Missing and Exploited Children
Section 2258E	Definitions
Section 2259	Mandatory restitution
Section 2260	Production of sexually explicit depictions of a minor for importation into the United States
Section 2260A	Penalties for registered sex offenders

Protection and Obscenity Enforcement Act of 1988, which included computers as a prohibited means of transporting or moving child pornography. As part of the Child Protection Restoration and Penalties Enhancement Act of 1990, moreover, Congress added another amendment that prohibited child pornography containing "materials" that had previously moved in interstate or foreign commerce.[9]

Six years later, Congress enacted the Child Pornography Prevention Act of 1996 (CPPA), further expanding the reach of child protection statutes and broadening the definition of child pornography to include images that may not have even been made with actual minors.[10] While the CPPA also amended 18 U.S.C. § 2256 to criminalize the possession of electronically stored data and data stored on computer disks, its most notable impact was, as noted, to expand the definition of "child pornography" to include:

(8)   any visual depiction, including any photograph, film, video, picture, or computer or computer-generated image or picture, whether made or produced by electronic, mechanical, or other means, of sexually explicit conduct, where—

   (A)   the production of such visual depiction involves the use of a minor engaging in sexually explicit conduct;
   (B)   such visual depiction is, or appears to be, of a minor engaging in sexually explicit conduct;
   (C)   such visual depiction has been created, adapted, or modified to appear that an identifiable minor is engaging in sexually explicit conduct; or
   (D)   such visual depiction is advertised, promoted, presented, described, or distributed in such a manner that conveys the impression that the material is or contains a visual depiction of a minor engaging in sexually explicit conduct.

The expanded definitions—specifically (1) the prohibition on images that "appear to be" of minors, and (2) the prohibition on promoting or advertising a product as containing visual depictions of minors engaging in sexually explicit conduct—brought into the definition of child pornography images that may have been created without the use of actual minors. These images became known as "virtual child pornography," and were a direct outgrowth of the rapidly developing computer and imaging industries.

These legislative "fixes" were challenged as overbroad, and the appellate courts split on the issue of whether the CPPA was invalid—the Ninth Circuit held the CPPA invalid on its face, while four other Courts of Appeal upheld the statute.[11]

3. *Ashcroft v. Free Speech Coalition*

In 2002, the Supreme Court, in *Ashcroft v. Free Speech Coalition*,[12] resolved the "virtual child pornography" dispute. The Supreme Court in *Ashcroft* invalidated §§ 2256(8)(B) and (D) of the CPPA, holding that Congress's attempt to ban virtual child pornography violated a producer's freedom to engage in lawful speech.[13]

The *Ashcroft* Court was faced with a challenge to the CPPA from a California trade association for the adult entertainment industry, a publisher of a book advocating the nudist lifestyle, a painter of nudes, and a photographer specializing in erotic images. These parties challenged the CPPA as overbroad in the Northern District of California. The district court disagreed, upheld the statute, and the parties appealed. The Ninth Circuit reversed the district court, finding that "the Government could not prohibit speech because of its tendency to persuade viewers to commit illegal acts."[14] The Ninth Circuit ruled the CPPA overbroad and distinct from *Ferber*, because the CPPA banned materials that were "neither obscene nor produced by the exploitation of real children."[15] Justice Kennedy, writing for the majority, affirmed the Ninth Circuit.

The *Ashcroft* Court distinguished virtual child pornography from actual child pornography, and found that the CPPA ran afoul of the First Amendment because it sought to ban images "appearing to be" child pornography that may not actually involve minors. Similarly, the Court found that the provision barring advertisement or marketing that "conveys the impression that the material is" child pornography would unfairly include mainstream Hollywood movies and falsely marked products. Indeed, the Court questioned whether, under the CPPA, *Romeo and Juliet* would be considered child pornography, noting that Juliet was only thirteen years old. Moreover, the Court worried that under Congress's amendments, a person could face prosecution for possessing unobjectionable material that someone else along the distribution chain had pandered or advertised as objectionable material.

The Court rationalized that under these circumstances—involving virtual child pornography or misleadingly marked products—minors were not actually injured in the manufacture or distribution, and, as such, *Ferber*'s more stringent restrictions did not apply.[16] Whereas in *Ferber*, the "speech" itself "is the record of sexual abuse, the CPPA prohibits speech that records no crime and creates no victims by its production" because virtual child pornography is not "intrinsically related to the sexual abuse of children."[17]

Courts interpreting *Ashcroft* have made clear that the Supreme Court did not invalidate the entire CPPA, only the two statutory provisions before it.[18] Nonetheless, Congress swiftly responded to the Court's decision.

4. PROTECT Act

In 2003, Congress enacted the Prosecutorial Remedies and Other Tools to End the Exploitation of Children Today Act (PROTECT Act).[19] Section 503 of the PROTECT Act amended 18 U.S.C. § 2252A to add a new pandering and solicitation provision, creating liability for:

(a) Any person who—
   (3) knowingly—
      (A) reproduces any child pornography for distribution through the mails, or using any means or facility of interstate or foreign commerce or in or affecting interstate or foreign commerce by any means, including by computer; or

    (B) advertises, promotes, presents, distributes, or solicits through the mails, or using any means or facility of interstate or foreign commerce or in or affecting interstate or foreign commerce by any means, including by computer, any material or purported material in a manner that reflects the belief, or that is intended to cause another to believe, that the material or purported material is, or contains—

       (i) an obscene visual depiction of a minor engaging in sexually explicit conduct; or

      (ii) a visual depiction of an actual minor engaging in sexually explicit conduct.

The PROTECT Act also increased the penalties associated with child pornography violations. In addition, it defined sexually explicit conduct as "actual or simulated" sexual intercourse, bestiality, masturbation, sadistic or masochistic abuse, or lascivious exhibition of the genitals or pubic area of any person.[20] The PROTECT Act also addressed the concerns raised in *Ashcroft*—that "downstream" consumers may be penalized for possessing material that was marketed as child pornography by someone earlier in the distribution chain—by removing subparagraph (D), which the *Ashcroft* Court had found invalid.

a. Congressional Findings

The PROTECT Act's findings "indicate that Congress was concerned that limiting the child-pornography prohibition to material that could be *proved* to feature actual children, as [the] decision in [*Ashcroft*] required, would enable many child pornographers to evade conviction."[21] Moreover, the "emergence of new technology and the repeated retransmission of picture files over the Internet could make it nearly impossible to prove that a particular image was produced using real children."[22] Congress also noted that there is "no substantial evidence that any of the child pornography images being trafficked today were made other than by the abuse of real children, virtual imaging being prohibitively expensive."[23]

5. *United States v. Williams*

In 2008, the Supreme Court upheld several of the PROTECT Act's amendments to § 2252A in *United States v. Williams*.[24]

Williams used a sexually explicit screen name in a publicly accessible Internet chat room advertising pictures of toddlers. Williams stated that he had pictures of men molesting his four-year-old daughter, and linked seven pictures of actual children, approximately five to fifteen years in age, engaging in sexually explicit conduct and displaying their genitals.

Officials seized two hard drives containing at least twenty-two images. Prosecutors later charged Williams with pandering child pornography pursuant to § 2252A(a)(3)(B), and with possessing child pornography pursuant to § 2252A(a)(5)(B). Williams challenged his pandering conviction, arguing that the PROTECT Act was unconstitutionally overbroad. The Eleventh Circuit agreed with Williams, finding the statute overbroad and impermissibly vague. The Supreme Court reversed, however, holding that offers to provide or requests to obtain child pornography are categorically excluded from the First Amendment.[25]

In doing so, the Supreme Court reiterated that offers to give or receive what it is unlawful to possess have no social value and enjoy no First Amendment protection. It also noted the PROTECT Act's scienter requirement, its definition of sexually explicit conduct, and § 2252A(a)(3)(B)(ii)'s requirement of a visual depiction of an actual minor (unless it is obscene) as key factors weighing against a finding that it is overbroad or impermissibly vague. Also finding that the PROTECT Act does not criminalize a substantial amount of protected expressive activity, the Supreme Court upheld the charges against Williams.

Specifically, the Court distinguished a proposal to engage in illegal activity and the abstract advocacy of illegality, finding the PROTECT Act's use of the word "promote" to refer to the recommendation of a particular piece of child pornography, not the general advocacy of the genre. It found that the PROTECT Act does not prohibit advocacy of child pornography, but does prohibit offers to provide or requests to obtain it. It also noted that offers to deal in illegal products do not acquire First Amendment protection when the offeror is mistaken about the factual predicate of his offer. As such, the impossibility of completing the crime because the facts were not as the offeror believed is not a defense. Therefore, the Supreme Court clarified that a defendant must believe that the picture contains certain prohibited material. The PROTECT Act, however, is not applicable where the material is a harmless picture of a nude child, but the defendant erroneously believes that the materials constitute a lascivious exhibition of the genitals.

In short, the PROTECT Act holds that a crime is committed when a speaker believes or intends the listener to believe that the subject of the proposed transaction depicts *real children*. Therefore, while simulated child pornography remains "as available as ever," provided it is offered and sought as simulated pornography and not real child pornography, *Williams* effectively held that child pornography may still be proscribed even if no actual children were harmed in the production of the material. As Justice Souter noted in dissent, the Court upheld a prohibition on virtual child pornography by prohibiting proposals to transact in such images, and, in doing so, the Court silently overruled its prior precedent of *Ferber* and *Ashcroft*, which declined to criminalize child pornography that did not include actual children.

B. Current Statutes

1. 18 U.S.C. § 2256—Defining Child Pornography

Section 2256, as modified by the PROTECT Act in light of the Supreme Court's ruling in *Ashcroft*, sets forth the definitions used in the child pornography statutes, defining "child pornography" as any visual depiction, including computer-generated images and pictures, whether made or produced by electronic, mechanical, or other means, of sexually explicit conduct, where—

(A) the production of such visual depiction involves the use of a minor engaging in sexually explicit conduct;

(B) such visual depiction is a digital image, computer image, or computer-generated image that is or is indistinguishable from that of a minor engaging in sexually explicit conduct; or

(C) such visual depiction has been created, adapted, or modified to appear that an identifiable minor is engaging in sexually explicit conduct.

A *minor* is any person under the age of eighteen years. *Identifiable minors* are those who were minors at the time the depiction was created, whose image was used, and who are recognizable as an actual person by their face, likeness, or other distinguishing characteristics.

The statute defines *producing* as directing, manufacturing, issuing, publishing, or advertising. *Visual depiction*, in turn, includes undeveloped film and videotape, data stored on computers or electronically which is capable of conversion into a visual image, and data capable of conversion to a visual format that has been transmitted by any means, whether or not stored in a permanent format. The statute uses the term *indistinguishable* to mean virtually indistinguishable, such that an ordinary person would conclude that the depiction is of an actual minor engaged in sexually explicit conduct; it does not apply to drawings, cartoons, sculptures, or paintings depicting minors or adults.[26]

Sexually explicit conduct means actual or simulated sexual intercourse, bestiality, masturbation, sadistic or masochistic abuse, or lascivious exhibition of the genitals or pubic area.

a. Lascivious Exhibition

One of the terms challenged most frequently by offenders is the definition of what constitutes "lascivious exhibition of the genitals or pubic area," such that the material depicts sexually explicit conduct. The First Circuit noted that "the absence of a sexual come-on . . . does not mean that an image is not lascivious."[27] Yet, as this statement indicates, what does constitute lascivious exhibition is not easily defined.

Appellate and district courts have utilized the nonexhaustive list of factors put forth in *United States v. Dost* to help clarify whether images are "lascivious"—

1. whether the focal point of the visual depiction is on the child's genitalia or pubic area;
2. whether the setting of the visual depiction is sexually suggestive;
3. whether the child is depicted in an unnatural pose or in inappropriate attire given the child's age;
4. whether the child is fully or partially clothed, or nude;
5. whether the visual depiction suggests sexual coyness or a willingness to engage in sexual activity; and
6. whether the visual depiction is intended or designed to elicit a sexual response in the viewer.[28]

Note that not all six factors need be present for a depiction to be proscribed by the statute.[29]

Though the Supreme Court has held that the term *lascivious* in the statute is not unconstitutionally vague, the *Dost* factors are certainly not without criticism.[30] The First Circuit, for example, has suggested that the six-factor test invites more questions than it answers because it leaves open whether a subjective or objective standard applies.[31]

Nevertheless, the majority of circuits continue to apply the *Dost* factors as a starting point to determine whether a depiction contains sexually explicit conduct. Indeed, the Second Circuit has clarified that the sixth *Dost* factor is more appropriately applied in cases involving the production of child pornography, not in cases involving the possession of child pornography.[32]

An illustrative example of *Dost*'s application is *United States v. Overton*.[33] In *Overton*, the Ninth Circuit affirmed the district court's finding, after a bench trial, that three of five images of a seventeen-year-old girl depicted lascivious exhibition of the genitals or pubic area. One of the images was of a child whose partially covered genitals were not the focal point of the picture, though the child's breasts were visible. The district court found the image suggestive because the child was sitting on a bed, "a place generally associated with sexual activity." The district court also found that the arrangement of the victim's hair—covering parts of her face—suggested sexual coyness and reluctance. Significantly, the victim testified that the offender directed her regarding where to place her hands, thus demonstrating that the sexual coyness was intended and was "likely designed to elicit a sexual response."[34]

b. Morphed Images

Morphed images implicate the definitions of both child pornography and identifiable minors. The Second Circuit upheld a district court's decision that morphed child pornography—which used the faces of known minors and the bodies of adult females—is not protected expressive speech under the First Amendment.[35] Citing dicta from the Supreme Court's decision in *Williams*, the Second Circuit stated that although morphed images may fall within the definition of virtual child pornography, they implicate the interests of real children, bringing them closer to the images in *Ferber*. Here, as discussed above, the offender labeled the images with the actual names of the minors whose pictures were used, marked them with a URL, and then indexed and encoded them in HTML. The Second Circuit referenced *United States v. Bach*, in which the Eighth Circuit held that an offender's morphing of the face of an unknown minor onto a lasciviously posed body of another minor was not protected expressive speech.[36] The Second Circuit agreed, finding that the interests of actual minors are implicated when their faces are used to create morphed images. Adding the actual names of the minors only further bolstered the connection between the minor and the depicted sexually explicit conduct. The court distinguished this case from *Ashcroft*, because this dealt with six identifiable minor victims who were at risk of reputational harm and had already suffered psychological harm knowing that their images and likenesses were exploited by a trusted adult.

2. 18 U.S.C. § 2251—Production and Distribution of Child Pornography

Section 2251 penalizes those who are directly involved in the production and distribution of visual depictions of minors engaged in sexually explicit conduct. The October 2008 amendments to the statute expanded its scope to also prohibit the transmission of live images of sexually explicit conduct. Because several subparagraphs of the statute deal with the criminalization of the production of child pornography, appellate courts have found the sixth *Dost* factor—whether the visual depiction is intended to elicit a sexual response in the viewer—particularly useful in determining whether materials contain sexually explicit conduct.[37] To that end, courts may look to the intended effect on the viewer, not the actual effect, to determine whether the conduct is sexually explicit. Significantly, courts have held that knowledge of a performer's age is not an element of a prosecution for production under § 2251(a).[38] Indeed, producers of child pornography have been analogized to statutory rapists who are not entitled to any *mens rea* safeguards, because producers, unlike distributors and downstream consumers, are more conveniently able to ascertain the age of the performers.[39]

Section 2251 also prohibits the distribution and dissemination of child pornography. Specifically, the statute holds liable any person who knowingly makes or causes to be made any notice or advertisement seeking or offering to receive, exchange, buy, produce, display, or reproduce any visual depiction involving a minor engaging in sexually explicit conduct. Courts have read this portion of the statute broadly, and include as dissemination a live video feed that caused a visual image to appear on a remote computer screen, descriptive folders in peer-to-peer file-sharing networks, and links posted in chat rooms.[40] Circuit courts, however, have split as to whether the First Amendment requires reading a "reasonable mistake of age defense" into the statute.[41]

Offenders who violate or attempt to violate § 2251 are fined and imprisoned between fifteen and thirty years. If the offender has a prior conviction relating to sexual abuse, sex trafficking of children, or the production, possession, receipt, mailing, sale, distribution, or transport of child pornography, the offender will be imprisoned for between twenty-five and fifty years. For an offender with two or more relevant prior convictions, the term of imprisonment is thirty-five years to life.

a. Congressional Findings

In 2008, Congress found that child pornography is a global, multibillion-dollar industry that provides a "product" that is readily available through the Internet, e-mail, instant messaging, online groups, bulletin boards, and peer-to-peer file sharing. To that end, the transmission of child pornography over the Internet constitutes transportation in interstate commerce.

Earlier, in 2006, Congress found that intrastate incidents of the production, transportation, distribution, receipt, advertising, and possession of child pornography, and the transfer of custody of children for the production of child pornography, had a substantial and direct effect upon interstate commerce, bringing these actions within the purview of the Commerce Clause. Congress's interest in protecting children from those who sexually exploit them extends not just to child molesters and child pornographers, but to all levels in the distribution chain.

b. Constitutionality and Current Application of Prohibitions on the Production of Child Pornography

Courts have consistently affirmed the constitutionality of the statute as applied to producers of child pornography.

i. Commerce Clause Challenges

One common challenge, for example, is that the statute violates the Commerce Clause in its criminalization of the production of child pornography because not all actions taken toward the manufacture of child pornography affect interstate commerce. Appellate courts facing this issue, however, have routinely held that Congress has broad authority to regulate interstate child pornography, and this authority has been upheld in the prosecution of intrastate child pornography as well.[42] Indeed, Commerce Clause challenges to any of the child pornography statutes face a higher hurdle since their amendment in 2007 to expand jurisdictional coverage. Specifically, the amendments replaced all instances of "in interstate" commerce with "in or affecting interstate" commerce.[43]

For example, in *United States v. Culver,* the Eleventh Circuit found that § 2251 did not violate the Commerce Clause. The court compared the statute with another provision of the CPPA, § 2251A, which it had previously found did not violate the Commerce Clause because "there is nothing irrational about Congress' conclusion that pornography begets pornography, regardless of its origin. Nor is it irrational for Congress to conclude that its inability to regulate the intrastate incidence of child pornography would undermine its broader regulatory scheme designed to eliminate the [child pornography] market in its entirety."[44]

Similarly, the Eighth Circuit in *United States v. McCloud* found meritless the claim that the statute violates the Commerce Clause because, in that case, the offender utilized physical materials that actually traveled in interstate commerce to produce the child pornography. The Eighth Circuit has also held that mere transportation across state lines of a camera used in the manufacture of child pornography constitutes a sufficient impact on interstate commerce for Congress to intervene under the Commerce Clause.[45] The Third Circuit, in *United States v. Gallo,* held that the offender's camera, film, and photographic paper used to make the child pornographic pictures all traveled in interstate commerce, and that Congress's actions were therefore appropriate under the Commerce Clause.[46]

The Seventh Circuit, in *United States v. Blum,* held that the statute was appropriately applied to an offender who manufactured child pornography in his home for his own private viewing.[47] The court stated that intrastate manufacture of child pornography, taken in aggregation with others engaged in similar activities, substantially affected interstate commerce such that the statute, as applied to the offender, did not violate the Commerce Clause.

The Tenth Circuit held that the statute validly regulates intrastate child pornography because Congress has made the rational determination that local activities—such as the local or household manufacture of child pornography—constituted an essential element of the interstate market for child pornography.[48]

The First Circuit, moreover, recently held that § 2251 does not violate the Commerce Clause when applied to an offender's child pornography that was produced for private use and never disseminated because, when taken in the aggregate, the production of child pornography had a substantial effect on interstate commerce.[49]

In sum, then, though they continue to be raised, arguments that provisions in § 2251 regulating the production of child pornography violate the Commerce Clause have consistently been held to be unavailing.

ii. Double Jeopardy Challenges

The Ninth Circuit has held that convictions for violations of §§ 2251(a) and (b) did not violate the Double Jeopardy Clause of the Fifth Amendment.[50] The Ninth Circuit found that the two statutory provisions constituted separate offenses, from which the court inferred that Congress intended to authorize multiple punishments for a single act or transaction. For example, a conviction under § 2251(a) requires that the offender employed, induced, or coerced a minor to engage or assist in sexually explicit conduct for the purpose of producing a visual depiction. Section 2251(b), on the other hand, requires that the offender, as a parent or guardian, knowingly permits a minor to engage in sexually explicit conduct for the purposes of producing a visual depiction. As such, the facts establishing a violation of one subsection were not necessarily sufficient to establish a violation of the other.

iii. Requirements for Attempted Production Conviction

The Eighth Circuit held that to convict an offender of attempted production of child pornography under the statute, the government must prove beyond a reasonable doubt that: (1) the defendant believed during the time period that the child was under eighteen; (2) the defendant attempted to use, persuade, induce, entice, or coerce that child to engage in sexually explicit conduct; (3) the defendant voluntarily and intentionally engaged in this behavior for the purpose of producing a visual depiction of such conduct; and (4) the materials used to attempt to produce the visual depiction were shipped or transported, including by computer, in interstate or foreign commerce.[51] In *Pierson*, the court upheld a jury's finding that the government proved these elements beyond a reasonable doubt by showing, in part, that the defendant requested naked pictures, asked if the undercover profile would perform sexually explicit acts in front of a webcam and transmit the images to him over the Internet, and offered to pay her if she could convince her underage friends to participate as well. The court also found reasonable the jury's determination that the defendant believed the undercover profile was a minor.

c. Distribution of Child Pornography Penalties Constitutional

Offenders have also challenged the validity of the statute's penalties for the distribution of child pornography. As more and more distribution charges involve various forms of online activity, the statute has successfully been applied to chat room postings and peer-to-peer file sharing. However, as with earlier iterations of the child pornography statutes, Congress and the courts are continually challenged by technological advancements.

Some courts have held that suggestive chat room postings relating to child pornography can qualify as a notice or advertisement under § 2251. The Second Circuit, for example, stated that this subsection is "not so narrow that it only captures those who state, 'I have child-pornographic images for trade.'"[52] In *Rowe*, the court found unavailing the offender's claims that his posting did not explicitly indicate that pornography was involved. Indeed, the court held that offering pictures of children in a chat room named "preteen00" that was peppered with queries such as "anybody with baby sex pics for trade?" was sufficient to constitute a "notice or advertisement" within the meaning of the statute, even though the offender's offering required a password to access the file server containing the images. The court agreed with the government's characterization that the sole purpose for the offender's decision to post his notice in the chat room that he was offering "preboys/girls pics" was to advise others that he had child pornography available to trade.

i. Peer-to-Peer File Sharing

In *United States v. Sewell*, the Eighth Circuit found an offender liable for offering to distribute child pornography by placing it in a peer-to-peer file-sharing system.[53] In this case, the offender admitted to using a peer-to-peer file-sharing system named "Kazaa" to share child pornography, but argued that his actions did not represent an offer to distribute the illicit files. The court disagreed, finding that Kazaa's purpose is to allow users to download each other's files, and the purpose of the descriptive fields are to alert other users to the content that the shareable file contains. Entering search terms in Kazaa creates a results list of downloadable files, but it does not download the files onto one's computer. The user has access to the descriptive fields of the files and can then choose which ones to download. The court found that placing a file in a shared folder with descriptive text was clearly an offer to distribute and, thus, satisfied the notice requirement of the statute.

In a similar case, *United States v. Shaffer*, the Tenth Circuit, applying § 2252A, found that an offender's use of Kazaa to freely allow others to access the child pornography on his computer constituted the distribution of child pornography.[54] In doing so, the court analogized the peer-to-peer file-sharing system to the owner of a self-serve gas station: the owner need not be present, and neither the owner nor his agents may ever pump gas, but the owner's roadside sign advertising his station lets all passersby know that they can obtain gas by stopping at his station. The gas station owner's passive position does not negate that he is in the business of delivering gasoline. Therefore, the court held, an offender cannot claim that passive file sharing does not also constitute delivery, transfer, or dispensation of materials in the same way that active transfer of possession through e-mail, or physically handing material to another, does.

A variation on the use of peer-to-peer file sharing arises when the validity of search warrants issued on the basis of undercover searches of an offender's computer are challenged in court as violations of the Fourth Amendment. The Eighth Circuit upheld a search warrant where an undercover agent, utilizing the peer-to-peer file-sharing program "LimeWire," searched for users accessing known child pornography sites.[55] The undercover agent used LimeWire to connect with IP addresses relevant to his search terms and viewed files that the owners of the IP addresses had made available for sharing. The undercover agent then downloaded files from a particular IP address. These files, with explicit and suggestive titles, formed the basis for the search warrant application. The Eighth Circuit, in accord with decisions from the Ninth and Tenth Circuits,[56] upheld the district court's finding that there is no reasonable expectation of privacy in computer files that are accessible to users of a computer network. Distinguishing the reasonable expectation of privacy in one's personal computer, the Eighth Circuit held that the decision to install and use file-sharing software opens an offender's computer to anyone else with the same freely available program, and limits any expectation of privacy that an offender might claim to have.

3. 18 U.S.C. § 2252—Possession, Receipt, and Distribution of Child Pornography

Section 2252 prohibits the knowing interstate transportation, shipping, receipt, distribution, sale, or reproduction of visual depictions of minors engaged in sexually explicit conduct and the knowing possession with intent to view one or more books, magazines, films, videos, or other matter containing minors engaged in sexually explicit conduct that have been transported by any means, including by computer. Effectively, in order to be convicted for knowing receipt and possession of child pornography pursuant to § 2252(a), an offender must know that the images depict actual minors engaged in sexually explicit conduct.

Penalties for violating the statute with regard to transport, sale, or distribution include imprisonment of between five and twenty years or, for repeat offenders, imprisonment of between fifteen and forty years. Penalties for violating the statute with regard to possession include imprisonment of up to ten years; repeat offenders face imprisonment of between ten and twenty years. The statute also provides affirmative defenses for a charge of possession if the offender possessed less than three matters containing a sexually explicit visual depiction and, promptly and in good faith, took reasonable steps to destroy the depictions or report the matter to a law enforcement agency.

a. Constitutionality and Current Application of Receipt and Possession Proscriptions

The Second Circuit has held that Congress intended to subject a person who simultaneously possesses multiple books, magazines, periodicals, films, video tapes, or other matter containing the visual depiction of child pornography to only one conviction under § 2252(a)(4)(B) because that statutory provision, unlike § 2252A(a)(5)(B), which prohibits knowing possession of *any* material containing an image of child pornography, prohibits knowing possession of *one* or more materials depicting child pornography.[57] In so holding, the Second Circuit found that a person possessing one or more materials violates § 2252(a)(4)(B) only once. Moreover, the court noted that an affirmative defense to § 2252 applies if an offender maintained fewer than three materials containing prohibited images and, as such, Congress contemplated that an offender with two obscene materials would only face a single charge.

i. Cache Files

Appellate courts are increasingly faced with the question of whether child pornography files stored in temporary Internet cache folders qualify as receipt or possession of explicit material. The Fifth Circuit addressed this issue directly in *United States v. Winkler*, noting that the contours of the crime of knowingly receiving electronic child pornography were murky, given the constantly shifting technological background.[58] In *Winkler*, the offender was convicted for knowingly receiving sexually explicit images of minors pursuant to § 2252(a)(2). On appeal, the offender claimed that the images he was convicted of receiving were merely images stored in temporary folders containing his Internet browsing history. The question before the court was not whether the files were received—that they were on his computer affirmatively answered that question. Rather, the question the court faced was whether the receipt was knowing.

The Fifth Circuit compared its case to *United States v. Dobbs*, where the Tenth Circuit reversed a conviction of knowing receipt of child pornography based on two electronic images found in the alleged offender's Internet cache.[59] In *Dobbs*, the Tenth Circuit found that there was no evidence the alleged offender had accessed the files stored in his computer's cache, or that he knew his computer kept such files. There was also no evidence that the images were in the defendant's possession as the result of a specific child pornography–related Internet search, or that the defendant had even seen the two images. While there was a general pattern of child pornography–related searches, the alleged offender did not belong to any pay-per-view child pornography websites. The *Dobbs* court held that these factors rendered irrational the jury's finding that he knowingly received the images.

In contrast, in *Winkler*, the Fifth Circuit found that the offender's files came from a members-only section of a child pornography website and that the offender routinely paid for access to these websites using a password. In addition, there was evidence that the files only ended up in his cache because he had actually watched the films associated with them. The offender also had a pattern of receiving, possessing, and hiding his child pornography. As such, the Fifth Circuit distinguished this case from *Dobbs* and others, and affirmed the offender's conviction.

The extent to which temporary Internet files and one's Internet browsing history may be used to demonstrate knowledge of possession of child pornography continues to be a fact-specific inquiry. For example, in *United States v. McNealy*, the Fifth Circuit affirmed the district court's examination of the search histories on the offender's computer, which included "preteen girls" and "preteen girls russian," his Internet browser bookmarks and his use of peer-to-peer file-sharing software to locate child pornography.[60] The court affirmed the jury's finding beyond a reasonable doubt that the offender knew that the images he downloaded depicted actual minors engaged in sexually explicit acts. The Sixth Circuit, in *United States v. Wagers*, noted that it, along with the Second and Fifth Circuits, had already held that evidence of an offender's visits or subscriptions to websites containing child pornography supports the conclusion that the offender likely downloaded, kept, and otherwise possessed child pornography.[61]

b. 18 U.S.C. § 2252A

Section 2252A, as discussed above, prohibits the knowing receipt and distribution of child pornography by any means of interstate or foreign commerce, including by computer.[62] It also makes unlawful the knowing possession of any book, magazine, periodical, film, videotape, computer disk, or any other material that contains an image of child pornography by any means of interstate or foreign commerce, including by computer. Unlike § 2251, § 2252A retains a scienter requirement. To determine whether an offender acted with the requisite knowledge, some courts allow juries to view images of the alleged child pornography. To that end, courts have allowed expert testimony to establish that the individuals depicted in the materials were, in fact, minors.

Offenders who violate or attempt to violate the statute face fines and imprisonment of at least five years, depending on the subsection violated. The statute, however, also allows for affirmative defenses if the alleged child pornography was produced without the use of any minors. Regarding possession, an affirmative defense exists if the offender possessed less than three images of child pornography and promptly took reasonable steps to destroy the image or reported the matter to a law enforcement agency.[63]

i. Constitutionality and Current Application of Receipt and Possession Proscription

The statute has been challenged on several fronts, including allegations that it is unconstitutionally vague and that it violates the Double Jeopardy Clause and the Commerce Clause.

In *United States v. Watzman,* for example, the offender challenged that certain subsections of the statute were unconstitutionally vague because they criminalized the receipt of child pornography without defining "receipt" and without distinguishing "receipt" from "possession."[64] The Seventh Circuit disagreed, noting a clear distinction between receipt and possession: to be convicted of receiving, an offender must have known that the material he was receiving depicted minors engaged in sexually explicit activity. As such, someone who receives child pornography by mistake is not guilty of knowingly receiving it, but may be guilty of knowingly possessing it if he retains it. In short, all receivers of child pornography are possessors, but not all possessors are receivers. Moreover, arguments that the child pornography was received for private use are unavailing because the statute contains no "personal use" exception. Other courts have similarly held that downloading child pornography constitutes both the act of possession and the act of receipt.

Courts have generally rejected Double Jeopardy challenges to § 2252A. For example, in *Overton*, the Ninth Circuit found that an offender's convictions for both possession and receipt of contraband images did not violate the Double Jeopardy Clause of the Fifth Amendment.[65] The court rejected the Double Jeopardy claim, noting, first, that the district court relied on different acts for possession and receipt crimes: the district court, after a bench trial, convicted the offender for receipt based on his Internet searches and downloading; it convicted the offender for possession based on the photographs that he took of his minor stepdaughter. Moreover, the appellate court noted that convictions could be premised on the same images, citing to earlier case law demonstrating that the receipt of child pornography onto a computer hard drive, and the subsequent transfer of those pictures to different physical media—for example, printing the images or transferring them to other electronic devices—constituted separate conduct.[66]

This analysis was in accord with the Fifth Circuit's treatment of a similar question: whether two of the three possession counts charged to an offender were multiplicitous. The court, in *United States v. Planck*, held that possession of child pornography on three separate types of devices at the same time and place resulted in three separate violations of § 2252A(a)(5)(B).[67] The court distinguished the offender's three different types of media from a book or magazine that contained multiple images, ruling that the government may charge multiple counts where the prohibited images on different devices were obtained through different transactions. The court also distinguished multiplicitous receipt from multiplicitous possession: for receipt pursuant to § 2252(a)(2), each separate receipt of child pornography violates the statute and each receipt must be charged and proved; for possession, however, the *actus reus* is the possession itself, and the government must only prove that the offender possessed the material at a single place and time to establish a single crime.

Conversely, in *United States v. Davenport*, the Ninth Circuit found that a judgment entered against an offender on separate counts for violating § 2252A(a)(2) and § 2252A(a)(5)(B), for the same underlying conduct, was inconsistent with the Double Jeopardy Clause.[68] The court held that the offense of possessing child pornography is a lesser included offense of the receipt of child pornography.

Commerce Clause challenges to § 2252A have, similar to Commerce Clause challenges to § 2251, been broadly rejected by the courts. For example, the

Third Circuit has held that the Internet is inexorably intertwined with interstate commerce and that, as such, regulating the downloading of child
pornography from the Internet was within Congress's power, even if specific
images did not travel across state lines.[69] The Eleventh Circuit, in *United States
v. Maxwell*, came to a similar conclusion, holding that "it is within Congress'
authority to regulate all intrastate possession of child pornography, not just
that which has traveled in interstate commerce or has been produced using
materials that have traveled in interstate commerce."[70]

Defendants in child pornography cases have also argued that a strict reading of § 2252A prevents them from receiving a fair trial because the statute
does not carve out an exception for defense counsel or defense experts who
view images of potential child pornography, tendered as discovery, as part of
their work representing a defendant. According to this line of reasoning, the
risk that a defendant's counsel or experts would be prosecuted renders the
ensuing trial a violation of due process and Sixth Amendment rights. The
Sixth Circuit, however, rejected this argument in *United States v. Paull*, noting that the offender made no allegations that the government utilized the
statute to disrupt his defense, or that any specific expert witness he sought
would not cooperate with him for fear of subsequent prosecution.[71] The Sixth
Circuit then cited an Ohio district court case where defense and government
counsel entered into joint protective orders allowing defense counsel to view
the alleged child pornography. Returning to its case at hand, and finding no
attempt by the offender to work with the district court to ensure his defense
would be uncompromised, the Sixth Circuit affirmed the conviction and held
that the offender's right to a fair trial was not violated.

c. 18 U.S.C. § 2252B: Deceptive Use of Internet Domain Names

Section 2252B prohibits people from using misleading Internet domain
names with the intent to deceive a person into viewing obscene material, or a
minor into viewing harmful materials. The section applies its own definition
of "material that is harmful to minors," providing that the term includes any
communication consisting of nudity, sex, or excretion that, taken as a whole
and with reference to its context, (1) predominantly appeals to a prurient
interest of minors; (2) is patently offensive according to prevailing standards
in the adult community regarding what is suitable for minors; *and* (3) lacks
serious literary, artistic, political, or scientific value for minors. The punishment for violations related to obscene materials is imprisonment of less than
two years and a fine; punishment for violations related to harmful materials
and minors is imprisonment up to ten years and a fine.

d. 18 U.S.C. §§ 2253, 2254, 2255: The Forfeiture Provisions

Section 2253 allows for criminal forfeiture of certain property of those convicted of offenses involving visual depictions described in §§ 2251, 2251A, 2252, 2252A, or 2260 (discussed below). Under the statute, the convicted offender forfeits to the United States his interest in (1) any visual depiction, book, film, video, or other matter that was produced, transported, or received in violation of the chapter ("instrumentalities of the crime") and (2) any property constituting or traceable to gross profits or other proceeds obtained, and any property used to commit, or promote the commission of, the offense ("proceeds of the offense").

The Eighth Circuit affirmed a criminal forfeiture order requiring an offender convicted of two counts of distributing child pornography in violation of § 2252(a)(1) to forfeit his nineteen acres of land.[72] The court held that the offender's commission of child pornography crimes involved his real property: specifically, he set up his computer in a room of his house, connected to the Internet, and distributed pornography from there. The house allowed the offender to store his images and facilitated his illegal behavior since he did not need to use public computers at a library or senior center. These substantial connections to the land were sufficient to find the order of forfeiture valid. That the area used to commit the offense was the house and not the entire acreage was unavailing; the court noted that the value of the entire property did not exceed the maximum fine recommended by the Sentencing Guidelines for his offenses. In the above-described *United States v. McCaffrey*, the United States similarly argued that the defrocked priest's house was used to house the defendant's computer (which he used to download and store his collection), and had an Internet connection that was through the wall, and provided him with the needed "privacy." The Chicago trial judge accepted the government's argument that defendant's house functioned similarly to the drug dealer's storage warehouse, in that both were instrumentalities of the crime used to further the offense.

Section 2254 states that any property subject to forfeiture in § 2253 may also be forfeited to the United States in a civil case. Though this statute has rarely been considered by the appellate courts, the Sixth Circuit, in an unpublished opinion, affirmed an order of civil forfeiture pursuant to § 2253 against an offender convicted of seven counts of pandering obscenity involving a minor under Ohio state law.[73]

Finally, Section 2255 authorizes victims who were minors at the time they suffered violations of the child pornography statutes to sue within six years for actual damages, the cost of suit, and a reasonable attorney's fee. Damages are deemed to be *at least* $150,000. The Sixth Circuit, in dealing with this statutory provision, noted that the sizeable damages threshold of $150,000 may have suggested that Congress's personal injury requirement was a "serious one."[74]

e. 18 U.S.C. §§ 2257, 2257A: Recordkeeping Requirements

These twin sections impose various recordkeeping, labeling, and inspection requirements on certain visual depictions of actual or simulated sexually explicit conduct. Section 2257 requires producers of pornography to determine, by examination of an identification document, the performer's name and date of birth.[75] The statute authorizes first-time offender penalties of up to five years imprisonment and fines; those violating the section a second time will be imprisoned for between two and ten years and fined. The D.C. Circuit has held that the recordkeeping required under this provision "can hardly be considered onerous" because similar records "are routinely required to facilitate the enforcement of our immigration, labor, and tax laws."[76]

Section 2257A, in turn, requires those producing images depicting simulated sexually explicit conduct that is produced with or placed in interstate or foreign commerce to maintain records regarding the name and date of birth of actual performers.[77] Violators are subject to imprisonment up to one year and fines. Those who violate this statutory provision in an effort to conceal a substantive offense involving a minor's engagement in sexually explicit conduct face up to five years imprisonment and a fine. Repeat offenders will be imprisoned between two and ten years and fined. A district court in Pennsylvania rejected the argument that this statutory provision was overbroad and unconstitutional.[78]

f. 18 U.S.C. §§ 2258A, 2258B, 2258C: Duties to Report and Limits on Liability

These statutes apply to electronic communication service providers, their duties to report, and their liabilities. Section 2258A, for one, requires that providers of electronic communication services let the CyberTipline of the National Center for Missing and Exploited Children know when they encounter suspected violations of the child pornography statutes.[79] Knowing and willful failure to report will result in a fine of not more than $150,000 for a first offense, and up to $300,000 for subsequent offenses. Pursuant to subsection (h), notifications from the CyberTipline to an electronic communications service provider are treated as requests to preserve.

Section 2258B, in contrast, grants limited liability for electronic communications service providers and their employees for their reporting or preserving responsibilities, provided they do not engage in intentional misconduct, act or fail to act with malice, reckless disregard, or for a purpose unrelated to the performance of any responsibility or function under the statutes.[80]

Finally, Section 2258C allows the National Center for Missing and Exploited Children to provide relevant information to electronic communications service providers and limits the way the electronic communications service providers may use that information.[81]

g. 18 U.S.C. § 2260: Production of Sexually Explicit Depictions of a Minor for Importation into the United States

Underused Section 2260(a) prohibits the inducement or coercion of a minor to engage in or assist in any sexually explicit conduct for the purpose of producing a visual depiction of such conduct or for the purpose of transmitting a live visual depiction of such conduct, intending that the visual depiction be imported or transmitted into the United States, or to within twelve miles of its coasts.[82] Section 2260(b) forbids persons outside the United States to knowingly receive, transport, distribute, or possess with intent to transport or distribute any visual depiction of a minor engaging in sexually explicit conduct, intending that the depiction be imported to the United States or to within twelve miles of its coasts. The penalties for violating § 2260(a) and § 2260(b) are the same as those outlined in § 2251 and § 2252, respectively. At bottom, these statutes are intended to extend the jurisdictional reach of the U.S. government to conduct occurring outside the United States, but that has an impact inside the United States.

C. The Travel Statutes

1. Section 2422—Coercion and Enticement (Communications with Minors)

The current formulation of 18 U.S.C. § 2422 criminalizes efforts to persuade or lure minors to engage in illegal sexual activity. While subsection (a) deals with general coercion efforts, such as in person, subsection (b) is a modern change designed to target sexual predators that use the Internet or other devices of communication to persuade minors to engage in illegal sexual activity. The most relevant portions of the statute read as follows:

(a) Whoever knowingly persuades, induces, entices, or coerces any individual to travel in interstate or foreign commerce, or in any Territory or Possession of the United States, to engage in prostitution, or in any sexual activity for which any person can be charged with a criminal offense, or attempts to do so, shall be fined under this title or imprisoned not more than 20 years, or both.

(b) Whoever, using the mail or any facility or means of interstate or foreign commerce, or within the special maritime and territorial jurisdiction of the United States knowingly persuades, induces, entices, or coerces any individual who has not attained the age of 18 years, to engage in prostitution or any sexual activity for which any person can be charged with a criminal offense, or attempts to do so, shall be fined under this title and imprisoned not less than 10 years or for life.[83]

Like § 2423, which deals with the transportation of minors for illegal sexual purposes, the unique aspect of § 2422(b) is that it is confined to protecting minor victims. There are other statutes that cover the use of the Internet to entice or coerce a victim over the age of 18 into prostitution or sex trafficking.[84] Section 2422(b) differs because of its emphasis on protecting *minor* victims.

To sustain a conviction under § 2422(b), a provision far more prominent in the technology age than § 2422(a), the government must prove beyond a reasonable doubt that the defendant "knowingly": (1) actually or attempt to (2) persuade, induce, entice, or coerce (3) a minor (4) to engage in criminal sexual conduct.[85]

a. Legislative History

Until the addition of subsection (b) in 1996, § 2422 was limited to subsection (a), which generically covered the persuasion of a minor to cross state or foreign lines to engage in illegal sexual conduct. Its origins from the Mann Act are clear, as the initial language prohibited persuasion of "any woman or girl" for "immoral purposes" or "debauchery."[86] Congress updated this text in 1998 to cover both male and female victims and took out the "immoral purposes" and "debauchery" language.[87] These minor changes, however, had little impact on the substance or scope of the law.

The groundbreaking amendment to § 2422 came in 1996, when Congress passed the Telecommunications Act of 1996, creating subsection (b).[88] The addition of subsection (b) resulted from a fundamental concern about predators misusing the Internet to manipulate minors into engaging in illegal sexual contact. The House Committee Report explains the problem of Internet stalking that § 2422(b) was intended to address:

With the advent of ever-growing computer technology, law enforcement officials are discovering that criminals roam the Internet just as they roam the streets. While parents strive to warn their children about the dangers outside the home, they are often unaware of the dangers within—on the World Wide Web. "Cyber-predators" often "cruise" the Internet in search of lonely, rebellious or trusting young people. The anonymous nature of the on-line relationship allows users to misrepresent their age, gender, or interests. Perfect strangers can reach into the home and befriend a child.

Recent, highly publicized news accounts in which pedophiles have used the Internet to seduce or persuade children to meet them to engage in sexual activities have sparked vigorous debate about the wonders and perils of the information superhighway. Youths who have agreed to such meetings have been kidnapped, photographed for child pornography, raped, beaten, robbed, and worse.[89]

Notably, Section 2422(b) covers not only the use of the Internet that results in illegal sexual conduct but also "attempt[s] to do so." This attempt provision allows prosecutors to pursue illegal online solicitation that fails to materialize into actual illegal sexual contact, and as will be discussed, has been aggressively used by law enforcement to detect and prosecute offenders.

Recent legislative activity has also increased the penalties of offenders targeting minors over the Internet. First, the Protection of Children from Sexual Predators Act in 1996 elevated the maximum sentence from ten to fifteen years.[90] Later, Congress passed the Adam Walsh Child Protection and Safety Act, which added a mandatory *minimum* sentence of ten years in prison and a maximum sentence of life for violations of 2422(b).[91]

b. Constitutionality

Section 2422 has withstood constitutional vagueness and First Amendment challenges. Defendants have argued that § 2422 is vague because it does not define a number of statutory terms, such as "attempt," "persuade," "induce," "entice," or "coerce." Defendants claim that, as a result, ordinary people are unable to understand exactly what kind of activity § 2422 prohibits.[92]

Courts have held that although these terms are not defined in § 2422, the ordinary meanings of the words are widely known so as to put the public on notice about the prohibited conduct.[93] Acknowledging that there may be some uncertainty about the distinction between "asking" and "persuading," courts have, nevertheless, held that such distinctions fail to render the statute unconstitutional.[94] Moreover, in looking to the second element in the vagueness analysis, there is no legitimate chance that it will be enforced in an arbitrary or discriminatory manner because § 2422(b) requires a *mens rea* of "knowingly."[95] Because the terms in § 2422(b) have plain and ordinary meanings, and enforcement is likely to be even-handed due to the scienter requirement, § 2422(b) has not been found to be unconstitutionally vague.

The argument that § 2422(b) is overly broad is linked to claims that it violates the First Amendment. The government cannot prohibit unprotected speech if doing so requires the government to also ban a significant amount of protected speech.[96] The defendant's argument in *United States v. Gagliardi* is representative of the type of argument that many defendants have raised. In *Gagliardi*, the defendant claimed that § 2422(b) barred "fantasy speech" by adults pretending to be minors.[97] The Second Circuit, like other circuits, squarely rejected this proposition. First, § 2422(b) applies to persuading or attempting to persuade minors to engage in prohibited sexual activity; it does not reach unintentional communications with minors or the posting of messages over the Internet for adults and minors alike to read.[98] In other words, any chilling effect on speech is incidental because § 2422(b) regulates the conduct of persuading minors, not speech. As one court noted, § 2422(b) prohibits persuading minors to engage in illegal sexual conduct, and such "speech" is "merely the vehicle through which a pedophile ensnares the victim."[99] Second, appellate courts have routinely applied the rule, somewhat circular in this context, that there is no First Amendment right to engage in criminal conduct.[100] In the context of § 2422(b), there is no First Amendment right to communication with minors for the purpose of persuading them to engage in illegal sexual conduct.[101]

c. Elements

i. Actual Minor/Intent

A feature of § 2422(b) that makes it unique is the emphasis on protecting minors. Without proving that the defendant's *actus reus* of attempting to persuade to engage in illegal sexual conduct was directed at a minor, it falls outside the enhanced penalties of § 2422(b). Often law enforcement efforts include having adult agents pose as minors over the Internet. Other times, parents pretend to be minors and obtain communications over the Internet from a defendant who believes he or she is talking with a minor. In situations like these, defendants have argued that they cannot be convicted under § 2422(b) because their criminal conduct was not directed to a victim under the age of eighteen.

Appellate courts have uniformly rejected such rather weak attempts to avoid § 2422(b). The general rule is that there need not actually be a minor victim "on the other end" to be convicted of attempt under § 2422(b).[102] Rather, the analysis centers on whether the defendant *believed* that the victim is actually a minor, even if he or she was not.[103] For example, in the typical sting operation, where an adult law enforcement agent poses as a minor, it is irrelevant that an actual minor was not involved. If during the course of the Internet communications between the agent and the defendant, there are sufficient statements to show an intent to entice or persuade a minor to engage in sexual conduct, there can be a conviction under § 2422(b).[104] The same result follows where a defendant tries to persuade a minor's guardian (whether it is the actual guardian or someone posing as the guardian) to engage in sexual conduct with the guardian's minor child.[105]

ii. Legal Impossibility Defense

Because § 2422(b) criminalizes knowingly trying to get a minor's consent to engage in sexual contact, it matters not whether the target of the persuasion is actually the minor. For this reason, defendants trying to assert the defense of legal impossibility have been unsuccessful. Once caught in a sting operation, whether as a result of conversations with a parent or undercover agent, defendants argue that, had they been successful in persuading the target to engage in sexual conduct, it would be legal, consensual sex between two adults. They contend that it is impossible to violate § 2422(b) without the victim being a minor, as § 2422(b) criminalizes the knowing persuasion of a minor to engage in illegal sexual contact.[106]

Courts have generally discarded this defense for two reasons. First, in this type of situation, courts have recast the legal impossibility defense as really being one of factual impossibility, which typically cannot defeat a crime involving attempt. This is because, for criminal attempt crimes, ultimately being "successful" in executing the crime is not a criminal element.[107] For example, in *United States v. Farner*, the defendant contacted an individual whom he thought was a fourteen-year-old girl over the Internet. The defendant tried to coerce and induce the victim to have sex with him, and eventually they made plans to meet to engage in sexual activity. The fourteen-year-old girl, however, was really an FBI agent and the defendant argued legal impossibility. The Fifth Circuit rejected his defense, finding that the defendant "unquestionably intended to engage in the conduct proscribed by law [§ 2422(b)] but failed only because of circumstances unknown to him."[108] This, the court noted, was a factual impossibility defense, not a legal impossibility one, and, as such, was an insufficient defense to the § 2422(b) charge.

Second, courts have found legal impossibility invalid based on the legislative intent of § 2422(b). *United States v. Tykarsky* involved communication between the defendant and an FBI agent posing as a fourteen-year-old girl. In rejecting the legal impossibility defense, the Third Circuit held that the text and purpose of § 2422(b) illustrated that Congress did not intend such a defense. The court found that, because the attempt provision does not require actual persuasion of the victim, it was the "subjective intent" of the defendant, not the age of the victim, that was important.[109] Moreover, because § 2422(b) was part of legislation that Congress intended to be a "comprehensive solution" to the harm posed by

sexual predators, allowing the legal impossibility defense would dilute government efforts to enforce the law.[110]

Similarly, appellate courts have interpreted § 2422(b) as not requiring an
intent to engage in the sexual act with the minor. It focuses solely on the intent to *persuade and entice* a minor to engage in such contact. In this way, for
the attempt to violate § 2422(b), the *mens rea* is linked to the *persuasion* and
coercion aspect of the statute, and *not* the final sexual act.[111]

iii. Attempt

The attempt provision provides an important tool for law enforcement because it can detect and punish offenders before the prohibited sexual act occurs. By definition, the final criminal act is not completed and, as such, the
government must prove that the defendant had the *intent* to complete the
crime, and took a substantial step toward completion.[112] In a § 2422(b) case, a
"substantial step" can include traveling, arranging a meeting by agreeing on a
time and place, making a hotel reservation, buying a bus ticket, or purchasing
a gift.[113] The facts of the case are, therefore, pivotal to this analysis.

For example, in *United States v. Gladish*, the defendant solicited "Abigail,"
an FBI agent, over the Internet to have sex with him. The two discussed the
possibility of meeting, but did not agree on any specific details. Because the
defendant's alleged criminal conduct only consisted of speech, without a
further step, the court acquitted him on the § 2422(b) count.[114] On the other
end of the spectrum, *United States v. Davey* involved a defendant who did take
substantial steps toward completion of the offense. He set a specific meeting
place and established how he would recognize the victim, traveled twenty-five
miles from his home to the place they had agreed to meet, and called her on
a payphone. These discrete actions amounted to "substantial steps" to complete the crime, and the court held this was different from *Gladish*, which only
involved "explicit sex talk."[115]

d. Section 2422(a)

Although the government brings far more charges under subsection (b)
because of its application to criminal enticing of minors over the Internet,
charges are still brought under subsection (a), which criminalizes knowingly
persuading an individual to travel through interstate or foreign commerce to
engage in prostitution or other illegal sexual conduct. While subsection (b)
deals with the Internet and other devices of communication, subsection (a)
covers communication with victims through other means, such as in-person
or through ads. In *United States v. Rashkovski*, the defendant held in-person
meetings in Russia to recruit the victims to move to the United States to

engage in prostitution. In the end, the defendant convinced the victims to come to the United States and made it possible for them to make such a trip by offering to pay for all of the travel arrangements. This conduct constitutes a violation of § 2422(a), and provides a prime example of its function as a general provision that catches criminal persuading and enticing that does not fall under § 2422(b).

2. Section 2423—Transportation

Traveling in interstate or foreign commerce to engage in illicit sexual conduct is illegal under the "Transportation of Minors" statute, 18 U.S.C. § 2423 ("Section 2423"). It generally covers two distinct criminal acts. First, as set forth in subsection (a), it addresses knowingly transporting a minor through interstate or foreign commerce for the purpose of having the minor engage in prostitution or other illicit sexual activity.[116] And second, as set forth in subsections (b) and (c), it addresses traveling in interstate or foreign commerce to engage in illicit sexual conduct.[117] So the transportation statute covers both (1) a defendant targeting and facilitating travel by a minor for illegal purposes, and (2) the defendant's own travel to engage in illegal sexual acts. The main provisions are:

(a) Transportation with intent to engage in criminal sexual activity.—A person who knowingly transports an individual who has not attained the age of 18 years in interstate or foreign commerce, or in any commonwealth, territory or possession of the United States, with intent that the individual engage in prostitution, or in any sexual activity for which any person can be charged with a criminal offense, shall be fined under this title and imprisoned not less than 10 years or for life.

(b) Travel with intent to engage in illicit sexual conduct.—A person who travels in interstate commerce or travels into the United States, or a United States citizen or an alien admitted for permanent residence in the United States who travels in foreign commerce, for the purpose of engaging in any illicit sexual conduct with another person shall be fined under this title or imprisoned not more than 30 years, or both.

(c) Engaging in illicit sexual conduct in foreign places.—Any United States citizen or alien admitted for permanent residence who travels in foreign commerce, and engages in any illicit sexual conduct with another person shall be fined under this title or imprisoned not more than 30 years, or both.

a. Legislative History

Congress passed the "White-Slave Traffic Act" ("Mann Act") in 1910. The Mann Act prohibited the transportation, in interstate or foreign commerce, of "any woman or girl for the purpose of prostitution or debauchery, or for any other immoral purpose." A 1986 amendment broadened the act to prohibit the transportation, in interstate or foreign commerce, of not just females but also males.[118] The modern formulation of the Mann Act is 18 U.S.C. § 2421, which criminalizes the knowing transportation of an individual in interstate or foreign commerce with the intent that the individual engage in prosecution or any criminal sexual activity.

Section 2423(a) covers the same general criminal conduct as Section 2421, but makes it a more serious crime if the victim being transported is a minor. This is a reflection of Congressional concern about the sexual exploitation of minors.[119]

Congress, thereafter, passed subsection (b) in 1994 through the Violent Crime Control and Law Enforcement Act of 1994, which made it illegal to travel for the purpose of committing an illicit sexual act with a minor.[120] The intent requirement of subsection (b), however, allowed some criminal conduct to escape prosecution. For example, under Section 2423(b), it was possible for a person to travel for a reason unrelated to engaging in illicit sexual conduct, such as business; if that person *then* engaged in sexual conduct with a child prostitute in another country, the person could escape the cramped intent requirement of subsection (b).[121] In other words, no statutory scheme covered "situational sex," where a U.S. citizen travels not for the purpose of engaging in sexually illicit conduct, but in the course of travel "happens to" engage in that conduct.[122]

Congress passed subsection (c) through the PROTECT Act of 2003 to fill this void.[123] It was passed to combat child sex tourism, where pedophiles travel outside the United States to foreign countries, most of which have more offender-friendly laws.[124] Subsection (c) prohibits engaging in illicit sexual conduct with a minor after traveling in foreign commerce.[125] As there is no intent for this crime, the government need only establish the relevant *actus reus*, which makes it a much more effective tool for law enforcement.

In sum, then, Section 2423 encompasses three related variations of criminal conduct involving interstate or foreign transportation and travel involving illegal sexual contact with minors. Subsection (a), a direct descendent of the original Mann Act, covers the defendant transporting a minor with the intent to have the minor engage in prostitution or illegal sexual conduct. Subsection (b) deals with U.S. citizens traveling in interstate or foreign commerce for the purpose of engaging in illicit sexual conduct. Finally, subsection (c) covers having sex with a minor during the course of traveling in foreign commerce, even if the defendant had no such illegal intent when embarking on the trip.[126]

b. Constitutionality

Section 2423 has withstood constitutional challenges based on the Commerce Clause, the fundamental right to travel, and the First Amendment.[127] First, in *United States v. Han*, the Second Circuit held that Section 2423 was an appropriate use of Congress's commerce power.[128] The court found that Section 2423 was similar to two other federal statutes that have been found to be valid uses of Congress's commerce power. Specifically, it pointed first to *United States v. Von Foelkel*,[129] where the Second Circuit upheld a statute criminalizing crossing a state line with the intent to violate an order of protection, and then violating it; and, along similar lines, in *United States v. Gluzman*,[130] the court upheld a statute criminalizing travel across state lines with the intent to harass or intimidate a spouse, and as a result of that travel, the eventual commission of a crime of violence against the spouse. Like *Foelkel* and *Gluzman*, the Second Circuit reasoned that Section 2423 involves Congress's regulation of the "channels of interstate commerce," and Congress has the ability to keep these channels "free from immoral and injurious uses."[131] The court rejected the application of *United States v. Lopez*,[132] which, unlike *Han*, answered the question of whether certain regulated activity "substantially affects" interstate commerce, not whether it involved the use of channels of interstate commerce. Accordingly, Section 2423 has proven itself impervious to challenges based on the Commerce Clause.

Defendants have also unsuccessfully claimed that Section 2423(b), which criminalizes travel with the purpose to engage in illicit sexual activity, impermissibly punishes "mere thought." For example, in *United States v. Tykarsky*, the defendant argued that he could not be charged under Section 2423(b) for "doing nothing more than traveling to another state with the intent prohibited by that section" and that, as such, the statute lacks a "meaningful *actus reus*" by punishing the act of "thinking while traveling."[133] Courts have declined to credit this argument because it is premised on a faulty understanding of the type of conduct that Section 2423(b) proscribes. That is, Section 2423(b) does not criminalize simply traveling with an immoral thought or an undeveloped intent to engage in sexual activity with a minor in another state; rather, "the travel must be *for the purpose* of engaging in the unlawful sexual act."[134] Because interstate travel must be "for the purpose of" engaging in illegal sexual activity, and Section 2423(b) applies only when "travel is a necessary step in the commission of a crime," it omits "preparation, thought or fantasy" from its scope.[135]

Finally, in *United States v. Brockdorff*, the defendant asserted that Section 2423(b) was an improper burden on his fundamental right to interstate travel, in violation of the Due Process Clauses of the Fifth and Fourteenth

Amendments.[136] The right to interstate travel is a fundamental right, he argued, and any government conduct that limits that right is analyzed under strict scrutiny. But there is no fundamental right to travel if the travel is for an illicit purpose.[137] The district court found that Section 2423(b), therefore, did not improperly burden this right.

c. Extraterritorial Jurisdiction

Section 2423(b) reaches the conduct of United States citizens traveling between two foreign countries to commit an illegal sex act with a minor, even if their travel does not directly involve the United States. There is, it must be said, a general presumption against the extraterritorial application of United States laws, but such a presumption can be surmounted by a "clear" and "affirmative indication" from Congress that the statute applies to certain criminal conduct that occurs in a foreign country.[138] The language of Section 2423 illustrates Congress's explicit intent to cover illegal conduct that occurs in foreign countries.

Subsection (b) and (c) both criminalize traveling in foreign commerce to engage in "illicit sexual conduct." This term is defined in subsection (f) to mean a sexual act that would be illegal "if the sexual act occurred in the special maritime and territorial jurisdiction of the United States."[139] Courts have found that Section 2423's extraterritorial provision applies to travel coupled with the requisite criminal intent, whether within the United States or abroad.[140]

d. Elements

i. Purpose of Travel

The cornerstone of Section 2423 is travel with the intent to engage in illegal sexual activity, so courts have had to clarify when defendants traveled for the *purpose* of committing these illegal acts, as opposed to the prohibited sexual conduct being a tangential or spontaneous event that happens to occur after interstate or foreign commerce. This often depends on whether a principal reason of the defendant's travel was to commit the illegal acts.[141]

The language of Section 2423(b) refers to travel for "the purpose" of engaging in illegal sexual conduct. It may, therefore, appear at first glance that, to sustain a conviction, the government must prove that the *primary* reason for travel was for illegal purposes. Appellate courts, however, have consistently rejected such a limited reading of Section 2423.

Defendants, for example, have argued that Section 2423 requires that "the dominant" reason for travel in interstate or foreign commerce was to commit the illegal sexual activity. This argument is premised on the Supreme Court's *Mortensen v. United States* decision. *Mortensen* was a Mann Act case and the Supreme Court commented, in dicta, that the prohibited sexual activity "must be the dominant purpose" of the interstate travel.[142] *Mortensen* involved a trip taken by prostitutes for one innocent purpose unrelated to their otherwise illegal activity: simply to give them a vacation.[143] Courts have found that, because there was only one purpose for the *Mortensen* trip, the case doesn't render Section 2423 inapplicable when there are *multiple* reasons for making a trip—both illegal and legal.[144]

Although the appellate courts have adopted different iterations of this reasoning, the prevailing consideration for the "purpose of travel" requirement is not whether the illegal sexual conduct is the sole reason for the conduct. Rather, when there are multiple purposes for the travel, the issue becomes whether one of the motivations for the trip was to have illicit sexual contact. Some courts, for instance, have employed a "dominant purpose" test, where the analysis centers around whether "a dominant purpose, as opposed to an incidental one" of the defendant's travel was to engage in criminal sexual conduct.[145] Courts have also phrased it as whether the illegal activity was an "efficient and compelling" reason for the travel,[146] a "significant or motivating" purpose for the travel,[147] or "one of the several motives . . . not a mere incident" of the travel.[148] While there is not an exact test that appellate courts have universally applied, each of these formulations indicate that the analysis depends on the unique facts of the case bearing on the reasons why the defendant traveled between states or in foreign commerce in the first place.

A few concrete examples illustrate how courts have applied Section 2423's "purpose of travel" requirement. A Jesuit priest recruiting boys to assist him in carrying his bags, helping him with his medications, and doing physical therapy at various religious retreats constituted travel for the purpose of committing illegal sexual acts.[149] Although he traveled in interstate and foreign commerce to lead the retreats, the Seventh Circuit found that he chose specific trips and made travel arrangements to "optimize his sexual activity."[150] The purpose of the priest choosing to travel with these particular boys was to have illegal sex.

Likewise, defendants have repeatedly tried to characterize their travel resulting in forbidden sexual activity as being motivated by a legitimate purpose, such as attending an out-of-state football game; they contended that the illegal sexual activity with minors occurred "spontaneously" upon arrival at the destination.[151] In such a circumstance, the court examines evidence of interactions between the defendant and victim *prior to* the trip resulting in the illegal conduct. So, any pre-travel activity that potentially makes the victim more comfortable with the later sexual advances, or steps taken to ensure that the victim is separated from his or her guardians, can be outcome-determinative.[152]

ii. Knowledge/Intent

Section 2423 implicates a number of issues bearing on the offender's intent. As an intent crime, it is not necessary for the underlying sexual act to ever actually occur; the defendant must simply take sufficient steps demonstrating his intent to bring out such illegal conduct.[153] The first principal issue is the timing of the defendant forming the necessary intent—the *mens rea* (the intent to have sexual contact) must match with the *actus reus* (the crossing of state lines).[154] A second issue is whether the defendant must have knowledge of the victim's age before the criminal sexual conduct.

Section 2423(a) makes it illegal to (1) knowingly transport a minor (or a child under the age of 18) across state lines, (2) with the intent to engage in criminal sexual activity with the minor.[155] Section 2423(a), however, does not reach illegal sexual conduct with a minor that occurs before the crossing of state lines; in such a case, there is no intent at the time of crossing state lines.[156] A similar principle applies to Section 2423(b), which involves the defendant traveling across state lines to engage in illicit sexual conduct in the visiting state or country. As the "purpose" for travel must be to engage in a sex act with a person under eighteen, the intent must be formed at the time that the defendant crosses the state line.[157] As a result, the critical timing elements of subsections (a) and (b) are similar.

One type of conduct Section 2423(a) criminalizes is the knowing transportation of a minor with the intent that the individual engage in prostitution. Generally, transportation of an individual for the purpose of prostitution is illegal under 18 U.S.C. § 2421. But Section 2423(a) is a more serious crime because Congress specifically intended to take extra measures to protect minors. It is the victim's minor status that exposes the defendant to an increased penalty. As a result, it is not a valid defense for the defendant to argue ignorance of the victim's age in an attempt to escape Section 2423(a)'s elevated penalties.[158] As one court aptly put it, "If someone knowingly transports a person for the purposes of prostitution or another sex offense, the transporter assumes the risk that the victim is a minor, regardless of what the victim says or how the victim appears."[159]

This rule extends to variations involving attempt and Section 2423(b). A defendant can be convicted of attempting to transport a minor across state lines to engage in illegal sexual conduct when law enforcement officers or parents pose as minors and the defendant incorrectly believes that he is corresponding with a minor.[160] For example, assume a mother poses as a minor and upon the defendant's request agrees to meet with him and have sex; the defendant, therefore, goes ahead and purchases a bus ticket for the purported minor. Such a defendant cannot claim that he was simply mistaken about the minor's age. Similarly, under Section 2423(b), if the defendant travels in interstate or foreign commerce with the intent to commit an illicit sex act with a minor, the defendant can be convicted if he believes the victim, regardless of whether the victim was actually a minor.[161]

3. 18 U.S.C. § 1201—Kidnapping

The federal kidnapping statute makes it unlawful to take control of a victim against his or her will and transport the victim in interstate or foreign commerce for "ransom or reward." The relevant portion of the statute states:

(a) Whoever unlawfully seizes, confines, inveigles, decoys, kidnaps, abducts, or carries away and holds for ransom or reward or otherwise any person, except in the case of a minor by the parent thereof, when—

(1) the person is willfully transported in interstate or foreign commerce, regardless of whether the person was alive when transported across a State boundary, or the offender travels in interstate or foreign commerce or uses the mail or any means, facility, or instrumentality of interstate or foreign commerce in committing or in furtherance of the commission of the offense.[162]

Section 1201(g) contains a unique subsection, with a mandatory minimum sentence of imprisonment of twenty years if the victim of the kidnapping is a minor.[163] If the victim is a minor, the offender is an adult, and the offender is not a parent, grandparent, brother, sister, aunt, uncle, or person with legal custody of the victim, this sentencing-enhancement provision applies.[164]

a. Elements/Application

The government must prove four elements to convict the defendant: (1) transportation in interstate or foreign commerce; (2) of a victim who does not give consent; (3) the victim is held for random, reward, or otherwise; and (4) the defendant acted knowingly and willingly.[165] The jurisdictional prerequisite to bringing a § 1201 charge in federal court is that the defendant crossed state lines as part of the crime.[166]

The third element, the purpose for which the victim is held, is the avenue through which child exploitation and other sex crimes can fall under the federal kidnapping statute. Section 1201 applies to kidnapping for "ransom or reward *or otherwise*," and appellate courts have interpreted the "otherwise" element broadly. In addition to holding the victim for the specific reason of ransom or pecuniary gain, if a defendant illegally holds a victim to gain *any benefit*, that defendant meets this element. The appellate courts have consistently applied this rule where the defendant kidnaps a victim for reasons other than for ransom or pecuniary gain.[167] Thus, where the defendant holds a victim, against his or her will, and travels across state lines for the purpose of committing a sexual assault, § 1201 can apply.[168]

For example, in *United States v. Brown,* the defendant, a truck driver, visited friends in Kansas, and during the visit offered to take the friend's daughter on an overnight trip to Texas; the daughter's parents consented. En route to Texas, the defendant sexually assaulted the victim at an Arkansas campground. The government charged him not only under the federal aggravated sexual abuse statute but also under § 1201's kidnapping statute. The defendant argued that, because he kidnapped the victim neither for random nor pecuniary gain, § 1201 did not apply. The Eighth Circuit, however, affirmed his conviction, holding that the federal kidnapping statute is violated where the defendant receives a nonpecuniary benefit (here, sex) as a result of the kidnapping, and focused in on Section 1201's extremely broad "otherwise" language.

United States v. Osborne also involves application of the kidnapping statute to a sexual assault crime committed while the victim was restrained. In *Osborne*, the defendants, during the course of a two-day crime spree, kidnapped a minor and sexually abused her multiple times. By taking the victim over two state lines and refusing her pleas to go home, the defendants seized her for the unlawful purpose of performing the sexual assaults. The Fifth Circuit, accordingly, affirmed the defendants' convictions.[169]

b. Sentencing Enhancement of 1201(g)

Until 2003, Section 1201(g) had a provision requiring enhancements in the sentencing guidelines based on certain specific offense characteristics. Subsection (g)(2) provided a three-level sentencing enhancement if the "victim was sexually exploited (i.e., abused, used involuntarily for pornographic purposes)" during the kidnapping.[170] By striking this provision, the PROTECT Act created in its place a mandatory minimum sentence of twenty years for kidnapping of a minor.

4. 18 U.S.C. §§ 2241–2248: Sexual Abuse Act of 1986

Until 1986, the operative federal statute covering sexual abuse on federal property prohibited "rape" on property "within the special maritime and territorial jurisdiction of the United States."[171] It was only in 1986 that Congress recognized that the preexisting law did not adequately define the "outer limits of the conduct proscribed by [the] statute."[172] The Sexual Abuse Act of 1986 ("Act") was Congress's solution to the previously unclear federal laws. The Act attempted to "modernize and reform" the federal rape laws by shifting the focus at trial to the defendant's conduct, not the victim's conduct or state of mind, widening the type of offenses to include all forms of sexual abuse, and expanding the jurisdiction of the federal courts to include all federal prisons.[173]

The Sexual Abuse Act of 1986 covers a number of sexual abuse offenses: (1) aggravated sexual abuse, 18 U.S.C. § 2241; (2) sexual abuse, 18 U.S.C. § 2242; (3) sexual abuse of a minor or ward, 18 U.S.C. § 2243; and (4) abusive sexual contact, 18 U.S.C. § 2244. It is, therefore, important to understand how the statute defines a "sexual act." Under the definitions provision, a sexual act means: (1) penetration of the vulva or anus by the penis; (2) contact between the mouth and penis, vulva, or anus; (3) penetration of the anal or other genital opening by the hand or finger "with an intent to abuse, humiliate, harass, degrade, or arouse or gratify the sexual desire of any person"; or (4) intentional touching (not through clothing) of the genitalia of the victim, who is under sixteen years, with the intent to "abuse, humiliate, harass, degrade, or arouse or gratify the sexual desire of any person."[174]

Turning to the jurisdictional hook, the provisions cover illegal sexual acts committed in the "special maritime and territorial jurisdiction of the United States or in a Federal prison, or in any prison, institution, or facility in which persons are held in custody by direction of or pursuant to a contract or agreement with the head of any Federal department or agency."[175]

a. Aggravated Sexual Abuse, § 2241

Aggravated sexual abuse, at its simplest form, is the use of force or threats of serious bodily injury to engage in a sexual act. According to the language of the statute, a defendant can be guilty of § 2241 for knowingly engaging in a sexual act "(1) by using force against that other person; or (2) by threatening or placing that other person in fear that any person will be subjected to death, serious bodily injury, or kidnapping."[176] Section 2241 also includes *attempts* to commit aggravated sexual abuse.

Defining "force," courts focus on whether the defendant physically prevented the victim from escaping, and left the victim no choice as to whether to consent to the sexual activity. This is usually a straightforward analysis to see if the defendant's physical actions were "sufficient to overcome, restrain, or injure a person."[177] Courts also examine whether the victim was able to escape the sexual contact.[178] Moreover, it is irrelevant to the analysis whether the defendant used a weapon or actually inflicted pain on the victim.[179] Aggravated sexual abuse, furthermore, does not require physical action by the defendant because simply *threatening* the victim with death, serious bodily injury, or kidnapping if the victim does not engage in sexual activity also falls under § 2241. But, as the wording of the statute suggests, only severe threats of death or very serious injury will qualify under § 2241(a)(2).[180]

Section 2241(c) also criminalizes aggravated sexual abuse of a child. Crossing state lines to engage in a sexual act with a child under the age of twelve is a violation of § 2241(c). It is also illegal, on federal land, to knowingly engage in a sexual act (or attempt to do so) under the following circumstances: (1) the victim is under the age of twelve; or (2) the victim is between twelve and sixteen and the defendant uses force or threats of serious bodily harm.[181] The statutory mandatory minimum for these violations is significant: the defendant must be imprisoned for *at least* thirty years. In proving a charge under § 2241(c), moreover, the government does not have to prove that the defendant knew the victim was actually under the age of twelve.[182]

The typical test for determining whether "attempt" applies to § 2241 is whether the defendant took a substantial step to complete the "sexual act," as defined by 18 U.S.C. § 2246(2). For example, if the defendant tries to restrain the victim and removes his or her clothes, but for whatever reason is unable to complete the sexual act, there is still a § 2241 violation.[183] In *United States v. Crowley*, the defendant was convicted of attempted aggravated sexual abuse where he physically pinned the victim against the wall or bed and put his hand inside her shorts, but, due to the victim's resistance, was unable to complete the sexual act.

b. Sexual Abuse, § 2242

If a defendant uses threats or fear to persuade a victim to engage in a sexual act, but the fear is not of the severity of § 2241, covering death and serious bodily harm, it falls under § 2242. For example, if the defendant's actions create some fear of bodily harm (but not serious bodily harm), § 2422 applies.[184] This level of fear, therefore, is of a lesser degree than that contemplated by § 2241.

United States v. Johns is a prime example of a defendant who creates fear in the victim to engage in the illegal conduct. In *Johns*, the defendant was a father figure to the victim. He controlled her life and used his position as a religious leader to tell her that the abuse was "ordained by the spirits"; he also warned that he would hurt her family if she "disrespected the spirits." Using this fear to engage in nonconsensual sexual acts with the victim violated § 2242(1).

c. Sexual Abuse of a Minor or Ward, § 2243

Abusive sexual acts that do not involve force or threats, but are prohibited because of the victim's young age, also fall under Section 2243. Under Section 2243(a), sexual abuse of a minor exists where a defendant engages in a sexual act with a victim who is between the ages of twelve and sixteen, and is at least four years younger than the defendant. It is also a crime to attempt to engage in the sexual act, and the punishment is a prison sentence of up to fifteen years. Section 2243(d) does not require the government to prove that the defendant was aware of the victim's age at the time of the crime.

The pivotal issue that emerges in these cases is whether the defendant "reasonably believed" that the victim was younger than seventeen years old. The defendant, in fact, has the burden to establish lack of knowledge about a victim's age.[185] Under §§ 2241 and 2242, the government must affirmatively prove lack of consent; therefore, one court has taken the position that Congress put in the mistake of an age affirmative defense, because, under § 2243, the government has no burden to prove that the defendant knew the victim's age or the age difference.[186] Accordingly, § 2243 cases will frequently turn on whether the defendant can sufficiently establish this affirmative defense.

d. Abusive Sexual Conduct, § 2244

Section 2244 encompasses sexual abuse crimes that are not as serious as those in §§ 2241–2243. As defined in § 2246, *sexual contact* means "the intentional touching, either directly or through the clothing, of the genitalia, anus, groin, breast, inner thigh, or buttocks of any person with an intent to abuse, humiliate, harass, degrade, or arouse or gratify the sexual desire of any person." Section 2244 is linked to the other crimes by the Sexual Abuse Act of 1986.

D. The Federal Human Trafficking Statutes

In chapter 4 we discussed the intersection of the legal, cultural, and logistical dynamics that drive *child* trafficking activity, and provided a model trafficking law that more fully takes these realities into account. Here, in contrast, we discuss the "nuts and bolts" of today's federal adult *and* child anti-trafficking laws. Read together, this section and chapter 4 will provide the reader with a comprehensive overview of today's trafficking problem, particularly as it relates to the sexual exploitation of minors.

1. Trafficking Victims Protection Act of 2000 (and Reauthorizations)

a. Passage of the TVPA

In the late 1990s, an international women's rights coalition teamed up with Christian groups to put the human trafficking problem before Congress.[187] As discussed in chapter 4, legislators from both parties began to introduce a series of progressively more comprehensive anti-trafficking bills in the House and Senate.[188] In late 2000, as part of the broader Victims of Trafficking and Violence Protection Act of 2000, Congress passed, almost unanimously, the Trafficking Victims Protection Act (TVPA) as the United States' first comprehensive legislation tackling human trafficking.[189] The TVPA has been reauthorized and tweaked in 2003, 2005, and 2008. In passing the TVPA, Congress specifically found that existing legislation failed to effectively put the brakes on human trafficking. "Even the most brutal instances of trafficking in the sex industry," Congress observed, "are often punished under laws that also apply to lesser offenses, so that traffickers typically escape deserved punishment."[190]

Congress also noted the cruel irony that trafficking victims, often illegal immigrants, were punished more harshly than the traffickers themselves, while at the same time being left without any protection or social services.[191] One of the TVPA's original sponsors pointed out during the debate that treating trafficking victims as criminals left no one to testify against the traffickers, and made other victims afraid to come forward.[192]

The TVPA, as amended, has three main lines of attack[193]: (1) prevention of human trafficking through international grants and awareness programs[194]; (2) new criminal statutes and harsher penalties aimed specifically at traffickers[195]; and (3) protection and assistance for victims.[196] The TVPA's prevention provisions are beyond the scope of this book; it will suffice to note that those provisions took a carrot-and-stick approach, providing various assistance to foreign countries who take steps to combat trafficking, while outlining procedures to withhold aid from countries that do not.[197]

b. The TVPA's Criminal Statute Enhancements

Before the TVPA, the closest the United States had to an anti-trafficking statute were the general anti-slavery statutes found at 18 U.S.C. §§ 1581, 1583, and 1584. Those sections, which proscribed holding, inducing, and selling others into slavery, were decades old and aimed at traditional slavery. For instance, when Congress passed § 1581 in 1948, the statute read simply, "Whoever holds or returns any person to a condition of peonage, or arrests any person with the intent of placing him in or returning him to a condition of peonage" could be fined or imprisoned.[198] By 2000, other than a minor tweak of more prison time for offenders, § 1581 stood surprisingly unchanged. The provision, as written, provided no assistance to a prosecutor faced with a trafficking ring that exploited young women as prostitutes, but still paid them something. Similarly, before the TVPA, § 1584 punished an offender who "knowingly and willfully holds to involuntary servitude or sells into any condition of involuntary servitude."[199] In 1988, the Supreme Court in *United States v. Kozminski* found that § 1584's term *involuntary servitude*, was borrowed from the Thirteenth Amendment, which banned slavery after the Civil War.[200] The Court walked through that § 1584's history, noting that it was the product of the 1948 reorganization of two much older statutes: (1) a statute originally passed in 1818, soon after the United States banned the African slave trade, and (2) an 1874 statute intended to curb "Padrones" that enslaved Italian children to beg on American streets. Relying on this history, the Court ruled § 1584 "should be limited to cases involving the compulsion of services by the use or threatened use of physical or legal coercion."

The Supreme Court's limitation of § 1584 to physical and legal coercion provided no help to prosecutors targeting trafficking rings, which used common psychological abuse, not their fists, to keep their victims in line. In response, the TVPA added a handful of overdue provisions explicitly designed to address the gaps created by *Kozminski*'s interpretation, as applied to modern human trafficking. In its report to the House of Representatives, the Judiciary Committee wrote that the TVPA's provisions "will provide federal prosecutors with the tools to combat severe forms of worker exploitation that do not rise to the level of involuntary servitude as defined in *Kozminski*."[201] The Committee gave examples:

> It is intended that prosecutors will be able to bring more cases in which individuals have been trafficked into domestic service, an increasingly common occurrence, not only where such victims are kept in service through overt beatings, but also where the traffickers use more subtle means designed to cause their victims to believe that serious harm will result to themselves or others if they leave, as when a nanny is led to believe that children in her care will be harmed if she leaves the home. In other cases, a scheme, plan or pattern intended to cause a belief of serious harm may refer to intentionally causing the victim to believe that her family will face harm, including banishment, starvation, or bankruptcy in their home country.[202]

c. TVPA—§ 1590

The first of the TVPA's new provisions, § 1590, is an overarching anti-trafficking statute banning recruiting, harboring, transporting, or "obtaining by any means" any person in violation of the more specific anti-slavery and anti-trafficking statutes.[203] The next three statutes are aimed at common trafficking scenarios. Section 1589 outlaws providing or obtaining someone's labor (1) using force or threats of force to the victim or someone else; (2) serious harm or threats of serious harm against the victim, or anyone else; (3) abusing or threatening to abuse the legal process; *or* (4) using a "scheme, plan or pattern" intended to make the victim think that if she does not work, the victim or someone else will be harmed.[204] The Committee, moreover, intended "harm" to refer to a "broad array" of harms, and § 1589's provisions to be interpreted in light of the "particular type or certain degree of harm or coercion is sufficient to maintain or obtain a victim's labor . . . including the age and background of the victims."[205]

The TVPA's amendments also define *serious harm* broadly (and appropriately) to include "any harm, whether physical or nonphysical, including psychological, financial, or reputational harm" serious enough "to compel a reasonable person of the same background and in the same circumstances to perform or continue performing labor or services in order to avoid incurring that harm." The amendments, furthermore, explicitly defined abuse of the legal process to mean "use or threatened use of a law or legal process, whether administrative, civil or criminal, in any manner or for any purpose for which the law was not designed, in order to exert pressure on another person to cause that person to take some action or refrain from taking some action." Finally, under § 1589, criminal liability extends to anyone who benefits, financially or by receiving anything of value, from participating in a trafficking "venture." The statute does not require that the offender know the venture has engaged in forced prostitution or other "labor"; reckless disregard will suffice for liability to attach.

Sections 1590 and 1589 provide penalties of up to twenty years in prison, with life sentences possible for certain aggravating factors, including, if the violation of the statute results in death, or includes kidnapping, sexual abuse, or attempts to kidnap, abuse, or kill.[206]

d. TVPA—§ 1591

The next section, § 1591, concerns forced prostitution.[207] Similar to the forced labor statute above, this provision expands possible criminal liability for forced prostitution to *everyone* in the trafficking ring, from the lowliest recruiter ("recruits, entices, harbors, provides" or "obtains by any means"), to its leadership ("benefits, financially or by receiving anything of value" from participation in a venture). Unlike the forced labor statute, this section defines "venture," calling it "any group of two or more individuals associated in fact, whether or not a legal entity."

Section 1591 applies criminal liability to two broadly defined scenarios. The first is if the offender knows, or recklessly disregards, that "force, fraud or coercion" will be used to "cause" the victim to engage in prostitution. The second is if the prostitute is under the age of eighteen, regardless of whether force or coercion is used.

Section 1591, moreover, defines abuse of the legal process, "coercion," and "serious harm" using the same language of § 1589. Punishments for violations of § 1591 differ slightly from other trafficking statutes. It mandates a minimum sentence of fifteen years, and up to life in prison, if the offense (1) involved the use of force, threats of force, fraud, or coercion, or if it (2) involved a child under fourteen. It applies a ten-year minimum sentence (and possible life sentence) if the victim was between fourteen and eighteen years old. Conspiracy to violate § 1591, likewise, makes an offender eligible for up to life in prison.[208]

e. TVPA—§ 1592

The fourth statute, § 1592, addresses the common practice of holding victims' passports and other immigration documents to keep them tied to their traffickers.[209] It provides for prison sentences of up to five years for destroying, concealing, removing, confiscating, or possessing another person's passport in the course of violating, or with intent to violate, the anti-slavery and anti-trafficking statutes discussed above. It also applies to any conduct designed to "prevent or restrict" a person's "liberty to move or travel . . . in order to maintain the labor or services of that person." Congress designed this statute to address, in part, situations where other trafficking crimes were not completed, but there is enough to show the trafficker has at least commenced the crime by holding the victim's passport.[210]

As expanded upon below in the discussion of the TVPA's victim protections, § 1592 exempts certain victims from liability under this statute. Consistent with its comprehensive approach, the TVPA, in § 1594, also criminalizes any attempts to violate these antislavery and anti-trafficking statutes.[211] The TVPA directs that attempted trafficking, and those who conspire to be sex traffickers, are to be punished with the same severity as those who actually traffic.[212] Setting the same prison sentence for attempted trafficking as actual trafficking is a boon for prosecutors, who need to prove less to subject an offender to a long prison sentence. Prosecutors no doubt can also use long prison sentences for attempted trafficking as "motivation" to help turn defendants into cooperating witnesses so that they can "flip upstream" and cooperate against those higher up in the trafficking network.

f. TVPA—§ 1594

The TVPA also makes restitution to trafficking victims mandatory. Section 1593 requires the court to enter an order directing the defendant to pay "the full amount of the victim's losses," as determined by the judge. The statute defines "full amount" by reference to 18 U.S.C. § 2259(b)(3), which allows restitution for lost income and medical costs, among other items. Section 1593 also directs the court to include in the restitution order, in addition to the amounts recoverable under § 2259(b)(3), the greater of the gross income or value to the offender of the victim's labor, or the value of the victim's labor under the minimum wage provisions of the Fair Labor Standards Act. In other words, if the victim was a prostitute, he or she would be entitled to all the money paid to the traffickers for his or her prostitution. Under § 1593, this restitution may also be paid to the victim's representative if the victim is a child, deceased, or otherwise incapacitated. In a similar vein, § 1593 requires forfeiture of any property under the same terms as the Controlled Substances Act. Section 1594 also has mandatory forfeiture of any property *used in* the trafficking operations or *proceeds* that the trafficker received from his or her crimes. The TVPA directs the Sentencing Commission to ensure that the TVPA's policies are applied when sentencing those who violate the anti-slavery and anti-trafficking statutes.[213]

Finally, with regard to the anti-slavery statutes, the TVPA doubled the maximum penalties to twenty years.[214] It also ameliorated the *Kozminski* problem by defining "involuntary servitude" as a "condition of servitude induced by" either "any scheme, plan, or pattern intended to cause a person to believe that, if the person did not enter into or continue in such condition, that person or another person would suffer serious harm or physical restraint," or "the abuse or threatened abuse of the legal process."[215] The TVPA and its amendment also impose possible life sentences if violations of the statutes result in death, or include kidnapping, sexual abuse, or attempts to kidnap, abuse, or kill.

g. Victim Protection

The TVPA also makes prosecuting traffickers easier by offering a number of protections for victims. One provision, § 1592, simply exempts victims from the normal five-year sentence for destroying or concealing immigration documents if the victims' conduct was "caused by, or incident to" their trafficking.[216] The TVPA's most important victim protection provisions for successful prosecution of traffickers, however, are found at 18 U.S.C. § 1594(f) and 22 U.S.C. § 7105(c). Section § 1594(f) makes violations of the anti-slavery and anti-trafficking statutes "organized criminal activity" for the purposes of 18 U.S.C. § 3521.[217] This allows trafficking victims to be eligible for witness relocation and protection. Section 7105(c), in contrast, protects victims of "a severe form of human trafficking." The TVPA defines "severe form of human trafficking" broadly to mean, among other things, sex trafficking where the victim is forced, tricked, or coerced into prostitution or is under the age of eighteen.[218] Section § 7105(c) requires that victims not be detained in jails or other "facilities inappropriate to their status as crime victims," and that they receive all appropriate medical care. The statute also directs that victims receive access to information about their rights, translators, and available benefits. The government, furthermore, must protect victims and their families if their safety is at risk.

Because victim testimony is critical to trafficking prosecutions, Section § 7105(c) also empowers federal agents and prosecutors to keep trafficking victims in the country to help in the prosecution of traffickers. To do so, a federal law enforcement official must apply to the Department of Homeland Security to allow the victim to stay in the United States to facilitate the investigation and prosecution of her trafficker(s).[219] The victim may also stay in the United States if he or she files a civil suit against her traffickers under 18 U.S.C. § 1595.

Under 22 U.S.C. § 7105(b)(1), regardless of whether they are in the United States illegally, some victims of a "severe form of human trafficking" may receive Federal and state benefits and services.[220] Victims are eligible for benefits and services under the TVPA if they are children, or if the Department of Health and Human Services (HHS) certifies them as eligible.[221] HHS will certify adult victims when: (1) they are willing to assist in the "investigation and prosecution" of traffickers, and (2) they have either applied for a "T-Visa" as a victim of trafficking (see below) or the Departments of Justice and Homeland Security have deemed them to be necessary to prosecute traffickers. Amendments to the TVPA have clarified that victims can still be eligible for benefits even if they cannot cooperate with the authorities due to physical or psychological trauma.[222] The statute defines "investigation and prosecution" to include identifying and locating human traffickers, testifying against the traffickers, and cooperating with requests for evidence and information. Section 7105, as amended, also directs HHS to consider statements from state and local law enforcement officials concerning whether a victim is cooperating fully. Children seeking benefits asserting they are qualified as victims of a "severe form of human trafficking" are eligible for interim assistance for up to 120 days while HHS sorts out if they are, in fact, victims of a "severe form of human trafficking."

Finally, the TVPA created a new visa category, the T-Visa, for up to 5,000 trafficking victims a year to remain, and work legally, in the United States for three years (since amended to four years).[223] The visa is available to victims of a "severe form of human trafficking," who are present in the United States and would suffer "extreme hardship involving unusual and severe harm" if deported. To qualify, the victim must also be either under 18 or must have complied with all "reasonable" law enforcement requests for assistance in prosecuting his or her trafficker.[224] The victim's family can stay in the United States by filing derivative applications linked to the victim's T-Visa. In addition to changes to the statutes above (described in their most recent form), the reauthorizations filled a hole in the TVPA and made violations of the anti-trafficking statutes (§§ 1589–1591) predicate offenses under the Racketeer Influenced and Corrupt Organizations Act.[225] The 2003 reauthorization also created a civil cause of action for victims of trafficking to sue their traffickers after criminal cases against their traffickers had ended.[226]

h. Current Interpretation and Use of TVPA Statutes

Though the TVPA's provisions are not frequently litigated, courts have consistently rejected attempts to narrow the application of the TVPA's new statutes. For instance, one defendant, a psychologist, was convicted under § 1589 after he had his mentally ill patients work on his farm in the nude, supposedly as "treatment."[227] He told the Tenth Circuit that his conviction should be overturned because the forced labor statute only covered labor that was "work in an economic sense." The court expressly declined to extend the *Kozminski* framework or otherwise water down § 1589, finding that the statute applied to "coerced acts other than 'work in an economic sense.'"

In *United States v. Evans*, another appellate court considered an instance where the pimp of an underage prostitute argued § 1591 was unconstitutional, when applied to him, because he limited his illegal activities to Florida, which, therefore, did not affect interstate commerce.[228] The court applied Commerce Clause precedent to find that the pimp's activities, in aggregate with other activities, contributed to the human trafficking market Congress wanted to stop with the TVPA. Several district courts have relied on *Evans* to reject similar Commerce Clause challenges.[229]

2. 18 U.S.C. § 2251A—Buying and Selling Children

As part of its comprehensive scheme to root out exploitation and child pornography, Congress passed the Child Protection and Obscenity Act in 1988, adding 18 U.S.C. § 2251A.[230] Section 2251A imposes stiff jail sentences—thirty years is mandatory and the minimum—on anyone who buys or sells, or offers to buy or sell, a child knowing that the child will be used in pornography.[231] The statute also criminalizes offering to buy or sell a child with the intent to promote sexual conduct by the child for use in pornography, or promoting the child to help another person engage in sexual conduct for the purpose of creating pornography. *Selling* under the statute is broad and does not require that the child be exchanged for money. Section 2251A only requires that a parent, guardian, or any other person having "custody or control" of a minor sell or "otherwise transfer custody of" the minor. Similarly, the statute only requires that the buyer "purchase or *otherwise obtain* custody or control of a minor" to impose liability. Finally, to satisfy the Commerce Clause, the statute has a broad jurisdictional hook requiring that either (1) the minor or one of the parties to the exchange traveled in, or affected, interstate or foreign commerce; or (2) the offer was sent through interstate or foreign commerce (including using a computer).

The few courts that have considered § 2251A over the past two decades have upheld its constitutionality and applied it broadly. After guidance from the Supreme Court, the Eleventh Circuit found that § 2251A passes muster under the Commerce Clause as a regulation aimed at eliminating the market for child pornography.[232] In *United States v. Frank*, the Eleventh Circuit confirmed that Congress intended § 2251A to have a broad sweep and that it applies outside the United States.[233] *Frank* also found that the offender does not need to purchase the child from a third party to be liable under § 2251A. A minor does not have the capacity to "separate her services from herself," reasoned *Frank*, so paying the child for sex directly, with the intent to create pornography, is enough. In short, under *Frank*, anyone who pays a child for sex intending to make pornography faces 30 years in prison. Other defendants have quibbled, unsuccessfully, with the meaning of "control" in the statute. Courts have rejected arguments that the defendant must have the same, or similar, control over the child that a parent has.[234] "Custody or control" is defined in 18 U.S.C. § 2256(7) to include "temporary supervision over or responsibility for a minor whether legally or illegally obtained." Using a day care center owner as an example, one appellate court found that the definition is broad enough to include instances where the defendant has supervision of the child for a brief period, and does not require the defendant to have the full "array of parental rights" during that period.[235] Similarly, the government does not need to show that the child's parents approved of—or even knew about—the offender's custody for the offender to run afoul of § 2251A.[236]

Notes

1. 18 U.S.C. §§ 2251, *et seq.*
2. 413 U.S. 15 (1973).
3. 458 U.S. 747 (1982).

4. Ibid. at 756 (noting that "the States are entitled to greater leeway in the regulation of pornographic depictions of children" than for other forms of obscene or pornographic material).

5. Ibid. at 756–59.

6. Ibid. at 764–65.

7. Ibid. at 761.

8. The idea of using young looking adult actors foreshadows the future debate over virtual child pornography, discussed below.

9. 18 U.S.C. § 2252.

10. 18 U.S.C. § 2252A.

11. See *Free Speech Coalition v. Reno*, 198 F.3d 1083 (9th Cir. 1999) (finding the CCPA invalid on its face); *United States v. Fox*, 248 F.3d 394 (5th Cir. 2001) (upholding the CCPA); *United States v. Mento*, 231 F.3d 912 (4th Cir. 2000) (same); *United States v. Acheson*, 195 F.3d 645 (11th Cir. 1999) (same); *United States v. Hilton*, 167 F.3d 61 (1st Cir. 1999).

12. 535 U.S. 234 (2002).

13. Ibid.

14. Ibid. at 243.

15. Ibid.

16. Ibid. at 242 (the Court explicitly withheld judgment on whether the CPPA's prohibition on computer morphing violated the First Amendment because the parties before the Court did not challenge that element of the CPPA. The Court, however, noted that morphed images "implicate the interests of real children and are in that sense closer to the images in *Ferber*").

17. Ibid. at 250.

18. See, for example, *United States v. Kimler*, 335 F.3d 1132 (10th Cir. 2003) (noting that *Ashcroft* invalidated two specific parts of the CCPA).

19. Pub. L. No. 108-21, 117 Stat 650 (2003).

20. 18 U.S.C. § 2256(2)(A).

21. *United States v. Williams*, 553 U.S. 285, 290 (2008).

22. Ibid.

23. Ibid. at 291.

24. 553 U.S. at 285.

25. Ibid.

26. 18 U.S.C. § 2256(11).

27. *United States v. Frabizio*, 459 F.3d 80, 89 (1st Cir. 2006).

28. 636 F. Supp. 828, 832 (S.D. Cal. 1986), *aff'd sub nom., United States v. Wiegand*, 812 F.2d 1239 (9th Cir. 1987), cert. denied, 484 U.S. 856 (1987); see also *United States v. Overton*, 573 F.3d 679, 686 (9th Cir. 2009) ("The *Dost* factors, as they are commonly referred, are neither exclusive nor conclusive, but operate as merely a starting point for determining whether a particular image is so presented by the photographer as to arouse or satisfy the sexual cravings of a voyeur") (internal quotations and citation omitted).

29. See, for example, *United States v. Wallenfang*, 568 F.3d 649, 657 (8th Cir. 2009); *United States v. Wolf*, 890 F.2d 241, 245 (10th Cir. 1989).

30. *United States v. X-Citement Video, Inc.* 513 U.S. 64, 78–79 (1994).

31. *United States v. Amirault*, 173 F.3d 28, 34 (1st Cir. 1999) (questioning whether the sixth *Dost* factor is "a subjective or objective standard, and should we be evaluating the response of an average viewer or the specific defendant. . . . Moreover, is the intent to elicit a sexual response analyzed from the perspective of the photograph's composition, or from extrinsic evidence?").

32. *United States v. Rivera*, 546 F.3d 245, 252 (2d Cir. 2008) (affirming district court's decision to recommend the *Dost* factors to jurors as considerations but also noting that the factors should not be relied on exclusively).

33. *United States v. Overton*, 573 F.3d 679, 687 (9th Cir. 2009).

34. Ibid.

35. *United States v. Hotaling*, 634 F.3d 725, 728 (2d Cir. 2011).

36. 400 F.3d 622 (8th Cir. 2005).

37. *Overton*, 573, F.3d at 688–89 (collecting cases).

38. *X-Citement Video*, 513 U.S. at 76 (noting in dicta that when Congress amended the statutes in 1977, it deleted the word *knowingly* from § 2251(a) but retained *knowingly* in § 2252); *United States v. Fletcher*, 634 F.3d 395, 401 (7th Cir. 2011) (noting that "every circuit to have considered the issue" has found that knowledge of a victim's age is not an element of § 2251(a)).

39. Ibid. at 72n2; see *United States v. Wilson*, 565 F.3d 1059, 1067–68 (8th Cir. 2009).

40. *United States v. Nichols*, 317 Fed. App'x 546 at 3 (5th Cir. 2010) (applying 2006 version of statute and finding the phrase "any visual depiction" to include live video transmissions even though Congress later explicitly amended the statute in 2008 to criminalize live video feeds of child pornography).

41. *Wilson*, 565 F.3d at 1068 (collecting cases and then determining that the district court's preclusion of a reasonable mistake of age defense did not violate due process).

42. See *United States v. Culver*, 598 F.3d 740 (11th Cir. 2010) (rejecting claim that § 2251 violates the Commerce Clause); *United States v. McCloud*, 590 F.3d 560 (8th Cir. 2009) (same); *United States v. Blum*, 534 F.3d 608 (7th Cir. 2008).

43. See *United States v. Lewis*, 554 F.3d 208, 216 (1st Cir. 2009).

44. *Culver*, 598 F.3d at 746–47.

45. *United States v. Betcher*, 534 F.3d 820, 824 (8th Cir. 2008).

46. 239 F.3d 572 (3d Cir. 2001).

47. *Blum*, 534 F.3d 608.

48. *United States v. Grimmett*, 439 F.3d 1263 (10th Cir. 2006).

49. *United States v. Poulin*, 631 F.3d 17 (1st Cir. 2011).

50. *Overton*, 573 F.3d at 690.

51. *United States v. Pierson*, 544 F.3d 933, 939 (8th Cir. 2008).

52. *United States v. Rowe*, 414 F.3d 271, 277 (2d Cir. 2005).

53. *United States v. Sewell*, 513 F.3d 820, 821–22 (8th Cir. 2008).

54. 472 F.3d 1219, 1223–24 (10th Cir. 2007).

55. See *United States v. Stults*, 575 F.3d 834, 838 (8th Cir. 2009).

56. See *United States v. Ganoe*, 538 F.3d 1117, 1127 (9th Cir. 2008); *United States v. Perrine*, 518 F.3d 1196, 1205 (10th Cir. 2008).

57. *United States v. Polouizzi*, 564 F.3d 142, 154 (2d Cir. 2009).

58. No. 11-1535237 at 4 (5th Cir. Apr. 25, 2011).

59. 629 F.3d 1199, 1201 (10th Cir. 2011).

60. 625 F.3d 858, 870 (5th Cir. 2010).

61. 452 F.3d 534, 540 (6th Cir. 2006), citing *United States v. Martin*, 426 F.3d 68, 77 (2d Cir. 2005) and *United States v. Froman*, 355 F.3d 882, 890–91 (5th Cir. 2004).

62. 18 U.S.C. § 2252A.

63. See 18 U.S.C. §§ 2252(c), 2252A(d).

64. 486 F.3d 1004, 1009 (7th Cir. 2007).

65. *Overton*, 573 F.3d at 697–99.

66. See ibid., citing *United States v. Schales*, 546 F.3d 965, 980 (9th Cir. 2008).

67. 493 F.3d 501, 503 (5th Cir. 2007).

68. 519 F.3d 940, 947 (9th Cir. 2008).

69. *United States v. MacEwan*, 445 F.3d 237 (3d Cir. 2006).

70. 446 F.3d 1210, 1218 (11th Cir. 2006).

71. 551 F.3d 516, 524–25 (6th Cir. 2009).

72. *United States v. Hull*, 606 F.3d 524, 527 (8th Cir. 2010).

73. *United States v. 7046 Park Vista Rd., Englewood, Montgomery County, Ohio*, 331 Fed. App'x 406 (6th Cir. Aug. 19, 2009).

74. *Doe v. Boland*, 630 F.3d 491, 499 (6th Cir. 2011).

75. 18 U.S.C. § 2257.

76. *Am. Library Ass'n v. Reno*, 33 F.3d 78, 91 (C.A.D.C. 1994).

77. 18 U.S.C. § 2257A.

78. *Free Speech Coal., Inc. v. Holder*, 729 F. Supp. 2d 691 (E.D. Pa. 2010).

79. 18 U.S.C. § 2258A.

80. 18 U.S.C. § 2258B.

81. 18 U.S.C. § 2258C.

82. 18 U.S.C. § 2260.

83. 18 U.S.C. § 2422.

84. See, for example, 18 U.S.C. §§ 2422(a) and 2251.

85. *United States v. Meek*, 366 F.3d 705, 718 (9th Cir. 2004).

86. Andriy Pazuniak, *A Better Way to Stop Online Predators: Encouraging a More Appealing Approach to § 2422(B)*, 40 SETON HALL L. REV. 691, 694 (2010).

87. H.R. REP. 99-110 (1986).

88. Telecommunications Act of 1996, Pub. L. No. 104-104, 110 Stat. 56.

89. H.R. REP. 105-557 (1998).

90. Protection of Children from Sexual Predators Act of 1998, Pub. L. No. 105-314, § 102(2), 112 Stat. 2974, 2975–76 (1998).

91. Adam Walsh Child Protection and Safety Act, Pub. L. No. 109-248, 120 Stat. 587 (2006).

92. *United States v. Gagliardi*, 506 F.3d 140, 147 (2d Cir. 2007).

93. Ibid.; *United States v. Tykarsky*, 446 F.3d 458, 473 (3d Cir. 2006).

94. *Gagliardi*, 506 F.3d at 147; *Tykarsky*, 446 F.3d at 473.

95. *Gagliardi*, 506 F.3d at 147; *United States v. Panfil*, 338 F.3d 1299, 1301 (11th Cir. 2003) (§ 2422[b]'s "scienter requirement discourages 'unscrupulous enforcement'").

96. *Free Speech Coalition*, 535 U.S. at 255.

97. *Gagliardi,* 506 F.3d at 148.

98. Ibid. at 148; *United States v. Bailey,* 228 F.3d 637, 639 (6th Cir. 2000).

99. *United States v. Meek,* 366 F.3d 705, 721 (9th Cir. 2004).

100. *Bailey,* 228 F.3d at 639; *Giboney v. Empire Storage & Ice Co.,* 336 U.S. 490, 498; *Tykarsky,* 446 F.3d at 473; *United States v. Hornaday,* 392 F.3d 1306, 1311 (11th Cir. 2004).

101. *Bailey,* 228 F.3d at 639; *Tykarsky,* 446 F.3d at 473; *Meek,* 336 F.3d at 721.

102. *United States v. Farley,* 607 F.3d 1294, 1325 (11th Cir. 2010).

103. *United States v. Helder,* 452 F.3d 751, 755 (8th Cir. 2006); *United States v. Spurlock,* 495 F.3d 1011, 1014 (8th Cir. 2007).

104. See, for example, *United States v. Douglas,* 626 F.3d 161, 164 (2d Cir. 2010).

105. Ibid. at 164–65.

106. *Tykarsky,* 446 F.3d at 465.

107. *United States v. Sims,* 428 F.3d 945, 959–60 (10th Cir. 2005).

108. *United States v. Farner,* 251 F.3d 510, 512–13 (5th Cir. 2001).

109. *Tykarsky,* 446 F.3d at 466.

110. Ibid. at 467.

111. *Douglas,* 626 F.3d at 164–65; *United States v. Murrell,* 368 F.3d 1283, 1286 (11th Cir. 2004).

112. *United States v. Gladish,* 536 F.3d 646, 649 (7th Cir. 2008).

113. Ibid.

114. Ibid. at 650.

115. *United States v. Davey,* 550 F.3d 653, 657 (7th Cir. 2008).

116. See 18 U.S.C. § 2423(a).

117. See 18 U.S.C. § 2423(b), (c).

118. Child Sexual Abuse and Pornography Act of 1986, Pub L. No. 99-628, § 5(c), 100 Stat. 2510 (1986).

119. See *United States v. Taylor,* 239 F.3d 994 (9th Cir. 2001).

120. Violent Crime Control and Law Enforcement Act of 1994, Pub. L. No. 103-222, Title XVI, § 160001(g), 108 Stat. 1796 (1994). This was codified at 18 U.S.C. § 2423(b).

121. Daniel Edelson, note, *The Prosecution of Persons Who Sexually Exploit Children in Countries Other Than Their Own: A Model for Amending Existing Legislation,* 25 FORDHAM INT'L L.J. 483, 537 (2001).

122. Ibid.

123. Prosecutorial Remedies and Other Tools to End the Exploitation of Children Today Act of 2003, Pub. L. No. 108-21, 117 Stat. 650 (2003).

124. James Asa High Jr., *The Basis for Jurisdiction over U.S. Sex Tourists: An Examination of the Case against Michael Lewis Clark,* 11 U.C. DAVIS J. INT'L L. & POL'Y 343, 347 (Spring 2005).

125. 18 U.S.C. § 2423(c).

126. For a concise summary of the scope of Section 2423, see *United States v. McGuire,* 624 F.3d 622, 624 (7th Cir. 2010).

127. It has also been unsuccessfully challenged as violating the *ex post facto* clause. *United States v. Hersh,* 297 F.3d 1233, 1244–45 (11th Cir. 2002).

128. 230 F.3d 560, 562–63 (2d Cir. 2000).

129. 136 F.3d 339 (2d Cir. 1998).

130. 154 F.3d 49 (2d Cir. 1998).

131. 230 F.3d at 560, quoting *Foelkel*, 136 F.3d at 341; see also *Tykarsky*, 446 F.3d at 470.

132. 514 U.S. 549 (1995).

133. *Tykarsky*, 446 F.3d at 471.

134. Ibid. (emphasis in original).

135. Ibid.; see, for example, 992 F. Supp. 22, 25 (D. D.C. 1997) (like the murder-for-hire statute, which was found to be a valid exercise of commerce power, Section 2423[b] is also permissible because it involves crossing a state line with the intent to commit a serious crime).

136. 992 F. Supp. at 25.

137. See, for example, *United States v. Burton*, 475 F.2d 469, 471 (8th Cir. 1973) ("The citizen's right to travel is subordinate to the Congressional right to regulate interstate commerce when the travel involves the use of an interstate facility for illicit purposes").

138. *United States v. Weingarten*, 632 F.3d 60, 65 (2d Cir. 2011).

139. 18 U.S.C. § 2423(f).

140. *Weingarten*, 632 F.3d at 65–66; *United States v. Clark*, 315 F. Supp. 2d 1127, 1131 (W.D. Wash. 2004).

141. *United States v. McGuire*, 627 F.3d 622, 625 (7th Cir. 2010).

142. *Mortensen v. United States*, 322 U.S. 369 (1944).

143. Ibid.

144. See, for example, *McGuire*, 627 F.3d at 622; *United States v. Sirois*, 87 F.3d 34, 39 (2d Cir. 1996).

145. See, for example, *United States v. Vang*, 128 F.3d 1065, 1068 (7th Cir. 1997); *United States v. Snow*, 507 F.2d 22, 24 (7th Cir. 1974).

146. *United States v. Hitt*, 473 F.3d 146, 152 (5th Cir. 2006).

147. *United States v. Hayward*, 359 F.3d 631, 638 (3d Cir. 2004).

148. *United States v. Ellis*, 935 F.2d 385, 390 (1st Cir. 1991).

149. *McGuire*, 627 F.3d at 626.

150. *McGuire*, 627 F.3d at 626.

151. *Hitt*, 473 F.3d at 152.

152. Ibid.

153. *United States v. Broxmeyer*, 616 F.3d 120, 130 n.8 (2d Cir. 2010).

154. Ibid. at 129.

155. *United States v. Chambers*, 441 F.3d 438, 450 (6th Cir. 2006).

156. *Broxmeyer*, 616 F.3d at 130.

157. *Hersh*, 297 F.3d at 1246.

158. *Taylor*, 239 F.3d at 997.

159. *Taylor*, 239 F.3d at 997; *United States v. Hamilton*, 456 F.2d 171, 173 (3d Cir. 1972); *United States v. Scisum*, 32 F.3d 1479, 1485 (10th Cir. 1994); *United States v. Cox*, 577 F.3d 833, 836 (7th Cir. 2009).

160. *United States v. Morris*, 549 F.3d 548, 550 (7th Cir. 2008).

161. *United States v. Hicks*, 457 F.3d 838, 841 (8th Cir. 2006).

162. 18 U.S.C. § 1201.

163. 18 U.S.C. § 1201(g).

164. Ibid.

165. *United States v. Osborne*, 68 F.3d 94, 100 (5th Cir. 1995); *United States v. Mc-Grady*, 191 F.2d 829, 830 (7th Cir. 1951).

166. *United States v. Jackson*, 978 F.2d 903, 910 (5th Cir. 1992); *United States v. Garcia*, 854 F.2d 340, 344 (9th Cir. 1988).

167. *United States v. Stands*, 105 F.3d 1565, 1576 (8th Cir. 1997); *United States v. Childress*, 26 F.3d 498, 503 (4th Cir. 1994); *United States v. McBryar*, 553 F.2d 433, 434 (5th Cir. 1977).

168. *United States v. Brown*, 330 F.3d 1073, 1078 (8th Cir. 2003); *McBryar*, 553 F.2d at 434.

169. *Osborne*, 68 F.3d at 100.

170. Pub. L. No. 108-21, § 104(b), 117 Stat. 650.

171. 18 U.S.C. § 2031.

172. H.R. Re. No. 594.

173. H.R. Re. No. 594; *United States v. Cherry*, 938 F.2d 748, 754 (7th Cir. 1991); Pub. L. No. 99-654, § 2, 100 Stat. 3660.

174. 18 U.S.C. § 2246(2).

175. 18 U.S.C. §§ 2241(a), 2242(a), 2243(a), 2243(a).

176. 18 U.S.C. § 2241.

177. *United States v. Fire Thunder*, 908 F.2d 272, 274 (8th Cir. 1990).

178. *Fire Thunder*, 908 F.2d at 274; *United States v. Lauck*, 905 F.2d 15, 18 (2d Cir. 1990).

179. *United States v. Denjen*, 258 F. Supp. 2d 194 (E.D. N.Y. 2003).

180. *Cherry*, 938 F.2d at 754.

181. 18 U.S.C. § 2241(c).

182. 18 U.S.C. § 2241(d).

183. *United States v. Wright*, 540 F.3d 833, 839 (8th Cir. 2008).

184. *Cherry*, 938 F.2d at 755.

185. *United States v. Jennings*, 438 F. Supp. 2d 637, 644 (E.D. Va. 2006).

186. Ibid.

187. See Melissa Lambert and Josh Meyer, *House OKs Crackdown on Trafficking in Sex*, L.A. TIMES, Oct. 7, 2000, at A1; Henry Yoder, *Civil Rights for Victims of Human Trafficking*, 12 U. PA. J. L & SOC. CHANGE 133, 143 (2008–2009).

188. See Kelly Hyland, *Protecting Human Victims of Trafficking: An American Framework*, 16 BERKELEY WOMEN'S L.J. 29, 61 (2001) (recounting previous legislative efforts).

189. Pub. L. No. 106-386 (2000).

190. Ibid. at § 102(b)(14).

191. Ibid.

192. 106 CONG. REC. H2684 (May 9, 2000) (statement of Rep. Smith).

193. See Hyland, supra note 188, at 61 (noting the three prong approach).

194. Pub. L. No. 106-386, § 106 (2000).

195. Ibid. at § 112.

196. Ibid. at § 107.

197. See ibid. at §§ 104, 105, 106 109, 110.

198. Pub. L. No. 80-772, § 1581 (1948).

199. See *United States v. Kozminski*, 487 U.S. 931, 944 (1988), quoting the statute as it existed in 1988.

200. See ibid. at 944–48.

201. H.R. REP. NO. 106-939 at 101 (2000).

202. Ibid.

203. 18 U.S.C. § 1590.

204. 18 U.S.C. § 1589.

205. H.R. REP. NO. 106-939 at 101 (2000).

206. 18 U.S.C. §§ 1589, 1590.

207. 18 U.S.C. § 1591.

208. 18 U.S.C. § 1594(b).

209. 18 U.S.C. § 1592.

210. H.R. REP. NO. 106-939 at 101 (2000).

211. 18 U.S.C. § 1594(a).

212. 18 U.S.C. § 1594(a).

213. See 18 U.S.C. § 1594(b).

214. See 18 U.S.C. §§ 1581, 1583, 1584.

215. 22 U.S.C. § 7102(5).

216. 18 U.S.C. § 1592.

217. 18 U.S.C. § 1594(f).

218. 22 U.S.C. § 7102(8).

219. 22 U.S.C. § 7105(c)(3).

220. 22 U.S.C. § 7105(b)(1)(a).

221. 22 U.S.C. § 7105(b)(1)(C).

222. 18 U.S.C. § 7105(b)(1)(E)(i)(I).

223. 8 U.S.C. § 1101(a)(15)(T).

224. See 8 U.S.C. § 1101(a)(15)(T).

225. See 18 U.S.C. § 1961(1)(A).

226. See 18 U.S.C. § 1595.

227. *United States v. Kaufman*, 546 F.3d 1242, 1260 (10th Cir. 2008).

228. *United States v. Evans*, 476 F.3d 1176, 1178 (11th Cir. 2007).

229. See *United States v. Chappell*, No. 09-139, 2010 U.S. Dist. LEXIS 27941, at 18–21 (D. Minn. Jan. 12, 2010); *United States v. Paris*, No. 06-64, 2007 U.S. Dist. LEXIS 78418, at 21–24 (D. Conn. Oct. 23, 2007).

230. Pub. L. No 100-690, § 7512 (1988); see also *United States v. Frank*, 599 F.3d 1221, 1231 (11th Cir. 2010).

231. 18 U.S.C. § 2251A.

232. See *United States v. Maxwell*, 446 F.3d 1210, 1218 (11th Cir. 2006).

233. See *Frank*, 599 F.3d at 1230–31.

234. See *United States v. Buculei*, 262 F.3d 322, 331–32 (4th Cir. 2001); *United States v. Block*, 635 F.3d 721, 723024 (5th Cir. 2011).

235. See *Block*, 635 F.3d at 723–24.

236. See *Buculei*, 262 F.3d at 332.

8

Finding the World's Voice

International Instruments Targeting the Sexual Exploitation of Children

A S WE DISCUSSED AT THE OUTSET, each year, millions of children are sexually exploited in brothels, by sex travelers, through online pornography syndicates, and at the hands of human traffickers.[1] And although such startling statistics concerning both preferential and commercial[2] child sex abusers have, quite rightly, elevated the issue into a top political and law enforcement priority, authorities in many countries continue to be either unequipped or, in some cases, unwilling to take the necessary measures to fight the problem.

Commercial child sex tourism continues to thrive as a multibillion-dollar industry, involving some two million children around the globe.[3] Indeed, the number of children forced into prostitution in India's metropolitan cities *alone* is somewhere between 270,000 and 400,000.[4]

On the demand side of the equation, every year tens of thousands of American men travel to the world's impoverished countries to have largely unfettered sexual contact with children. These exploiters target destination countries such as Thailand, Brazil, Mexico, and the Netherlands[5] precisely because these areas are infamous for being sexual playgrounds for pedophiles. Weak national law enforcement responses are, at least partially, to blame.

For an unvarnished account of the brutal cost-benefit calculus motivating these travelers, consider this excerpt from an article authored by a contributor to the North American Man/Boy Love Association (NAMBLA) bimonthly newsletter:

> Weigh the pros and cons of becoming involved yourself in sex tourism overseas. Seek and find love from American boys on a platonic, purely emotional level.

For sexual satisfaction, travel once or twice yearly overseas. You might get arrested overseas for patronizing a boy prostitute. But the legal consequences of being caught patronizing a boy prostitute in a friendly place overseas will be less severe.[6]

A similar moral relativist perspective is in evidence at "www.sextourism.org":

An Australian diplomat may pursue a posting in Cambodia because child sex is much easier arranged there than, for example, in Canada.

Men have a natural interest in parallel sexual relationships. And if the chances to achieve such a setting are slim in Europe or the U.S., or if such an undertaking requires undue effort, they will move to more favorable grounds. . . . North Americans and Europeans have an easy time setting up multiple sexual relationships in South America, in many countries in Asia, and in Africa. And they usually can pick the most attractive girls. . . . The anti-coalition, of course, is much stronger than the coalition of those who benefit from a sex tourism constellation. Therefore, we can see the conditions becoming worse for sex tourists anywhere in the world.[7]

Simply put, exploiters—from sex tourists to those who obtain their child pornography from overseas—disporportionately prey directly and indirectly on children from impoverished countries. They choose these distant victims primarily because they can largely live out their sexual fantasies with impunity. And the sad truth is, their gamble largely pays off. How the world community has, and *should*, unite in the fight against those who take advantage of the world's most defenseless victims is the subject of this chapter.

A. Defining the Problem

Starting at a fundamental level, one U.N. commission defines child sexual abuse as follows:

Contacts or interactions between a child and an older or more knowledgeable child or adult (a stranger, sibling or person in a position of authority, such as a parent or caretaker) when the child is being used as an object of gratification for an older child's or adult's sexual needs. These contacts or interactions are carried out against the child using force, trickery, bribes, threats or pressure.[8]

The Declaration from the First World Congress against Commercial Sexual Exploitation of Children, moreover, describes *commercial* child sexual exploitation as follows:

Sexual abuse by the adult and remuneration in cash or kind to the child or a third person or persons. The child is treated as a sexual object and as a commercial object. The commercial sexual exploitation of children constitutes a form of coercion and violence against children, amounts to forced labour and a contemporary form of slavery.

The UNICEF definition, in turn, directly links child sexual abuse to commercial sexual exploitation:

Child sexual abuse becomes sexual exploitation when a second party benefits— through a profit or through a *quid pro quo*—through sexual activity involving a child. This may include prostitution, brothel and street-based sexual exploitation, trafficking for sexual purposes and child pornography.[9]

Child prostitution, child pornography, and the sale and trafficking of minor boys and girls for sexual purposes are, indeed, so closely linked that, as a practical matter, they are often largely indistinguishable. Child prostitution, for example, while closely tied to the trafficking of the child prostitutes, is also routinely coupled with the production of pictures, videos, and other sexually explicit visual material involving the children (whether manufactured by a pimp, a pornography syndicate, or a preferential exploiter).[10]

Although the transnational commercial sexual exploitation of minors, including via human trafficking, pornography, and prostitution, is routinely described as a single offense by lawyers, the media, and politicians, in reality, it is best conceived as a bundle of crimes committed in pursuit of a common, unlawful purpose. Put another way, human trafficking and commercial child sexual exploitation are best considered a criminal *process*, rather than criminal *acts*. The process can encompass kidnapping (since a child victim is unable to legally consent to being removed from his or her family); human trafficking; assault and battery; sexual abuse; the creation, possession, and distribution of child pornography; and assorted immigration violations.

B. A Brief Refresher on the "Mechanics" of Transnational Child Exploitation

To gain a fuller understanding of the magnitude of the global challenge, we must turn from preliminary definitional issues to the day-to-day mechanics of transnational commercial child sexual abuse. Although the modalities are far from uniform, and vary considerably from culture to culture and exploiter to exploiter, child victims typically are, through a variety of means, (1) identified and targeted, and then (2) lured or abducted by recruiters operating at the front lines. Commercial recruiters and preferential abusers, regardless of geographic location, exhibit a keen ability to identify and exploit (or "source") children with vulnerabilities—giving the targeted child the attention, affection, and care that may be missing from his or her everyday household environment.[11] The typical recruitment, therefore, does not happen overnight, but is rather a multistage process through which the abuser engages the child in a relationship and desensitizes the child to increasingly abusive behavior:

- *Trust Building and Favoritism*: The recruiter takes deliberate steps to create a relationship of trust with the child, often by spending online or in-person time with the child and giving the child presents or other special treatment that may be missing from the home.[12]
- *Isolation/Secrecy*: Once the child trusts the recruiter, the recruiter begins to slowly isolate the child from family members and/or siblings or other caretakers. This process further alienates the child, and makes the child emotionally reliant on the recruiter.
- *Desensitization*: Using techniques such as grooming, the recruiter breaks down social taboos and the inherent discomfort the child has toward being intimate with a stranger. This desensitization gives the recruiter the ability to test the child's resistance, and to begin to blur the line between appropriate and inappropriate behavior, including sexual contact.[13]

Once the child victim is on the recruiter's "hook," the recruiter can easily manipulate the child victim, persuade the child to engage in sexual activities, or convince the child to leave his or her home. In the child trafficking context, for example, the compliant child, once removed from his or her caretakers, is given false documentation, harbored in secret holding areas, and instructed to lie to any immigration or law enforcement officers who might ask questions concerning the child's true home or the child's relationship with the recruiter.

Once the minor reaches the brothel, the abuse and desensitization continues. The child victim is introduced to his or her new "work" environment, and must face the harsh realities of this new existence. Over time, the child becomes habituated to an abusive environment. The exploiter maintains his control over his victims by making them completely dependent upon him for their daily needs—everything from toiletries to food—and by holding the purse strings so that there can be no independence. By the time the child reaches majority, she will have acclimated to the belief that the abusers are now her only real family and caregivers. By this point, in effect, the child will be past the point of potential rehabilitation—working in a brothel and being controlled by others will have become second nature and her reality. In fact, the ability to "train" young girls to a life of exploitation is one of the benefits traffickers see in recruiting minors. Once passed through this system of abuse, the girl will remain compliant and, therefore, be a better "earner" than one who is introduced to prostitution at an older age.

As we can see, integral to all exploitation schemes is the exploiter's control over the child, which systematically disempowers her through routine physical and psychological abuse. The child remains confined by her own fear of the negative consequences if she fails to comply with the demands of her exploiter. Insidiously, she will have been taught to crave the exploiter's approval. Although the means employed by preferential and commercial exploiters are far from uniform, case after case demonstrates that the broad elements of ingratiation, secrecy, isolation, and desensitization are seldom missing. We have prosecuted pediatric doctors, air traffic controllers, emergency room nurses, deacons, priests, police officers, salesmen, air force engineers, politicians, and construction workers—and the one thing they all have in common is that, without exception, they follow this same general script.

Understanding the abuse process is the only way to begin prevention, and for investigators and prosecutors it is the key to searching for physical evidence, identifying other victims and questioning witnesses. The preferential abuser, for example, in his e-mails or phone calls, discusses the child's fears and hopes, appears to show great concern for the child's emotional needs, characterizes himself as being uniquely positioned to understand and empathize with the child, and sends the child presents. This type of abuser is just a variant of the archetypal child predator who offers candy as a means of coaxing the child to his car or van. The difference is that the real child predator is far more patient, spends an inordinate amount of time on this process, and relishes the steps leading up to the exploitation.

C. The Daunting Challenge for Global Law Enforcement

As we have seen, domestic and transnational abuse both involve very similar criminal processes. However, disentangling the acts that are part of each process, determining who has jurisdiction over what offenses, and formulating the appropriate charges invariably present complex legal, investigative, political, and sociological challenges. And, as discussed in chapter 4, common experience with transnational crimes teaches that these challenges are only amplified when the victims and perpetrators of the offenses, or their "product" (such as child pornography, or the children themselves), cross national borders.[14]

Those involved in preferential or commercial exploitation of children are, as highlighted by the above-mentioned NAMBLA article, fully aware of these hurdles for law enforcement. As a consequence, these individuals routinely operate their criminal schemes in those countries least able—or willing—to collaborate with other nations in eradicating the abuse occurring in their proverbial back yards.

The challenges to law enforcement in these countries are precisely those one would imagine. Successful prosecution of transnational cases typically requires the prosecutor to obtain important (admissible) evidence from abroad. This evidence may come in the form of testimony from witnesses and victims with divergent cultural and socioeconomic backgrounds—individuals often unwilling or unable to cooperate or to travel in aid of a far-away prosecution.

Despite these challenges, letting the offenders live on in impunity is not an acceptable outcome. Human trafficking and the sexual exploitation of children are crimes with increasingly present international dimensions; there is an amplified need to rely on cross-border investigations and to pursue foreign targets. Such trans-border efforts, in turn, require ongoing and proactive cooperation at all levels within the law enforcement community. Effective strategies require not only informed victim-assistance services, but also stepped-up judicial collaboration and adequate protective measures for witnesses.[15]

D. International Instruments as Catalysts for Change

Because the will to push a "pro-child" agenda is sometimes lacking among the world's law enforcement, legal, and political classes, international instruments are often the only available means to begin to persuade recalcitrant countries to put these issues on their domestic agendas. The goals of such international efforts are as varied as their efficacy, but, at bottom, remains the desire to move source and destination countries toward proactive collaboration. This includes the sharing of model approaches, key exploitation-related data, and victim-focused innovations.

Best practices in the child trafficking context, for example, involve law enforcement from around the world:

- Encouraged to create checklists of "red flags" so their immigration officers are better able to determine whether a child is a trafficking victim;
- Educated on appropriate standards for determining whether "repatriating" the child victim to his or her country of origin or family is, in fact, in the child's best interests;

- Motivated to develop training materials and simple guidelines to help educate border officials and other law enforcement agents on the use of appropriate interview protocols for child victims (including factors interviewers should be aware of when interviewing children who may be traumatized);
- Given guidance on how to devise effective victim/witness security programs;
- Persuaded to enter into Memoranda of Understanding with other countries on issues such as how to respond to foreign information requests;
- Assisted in their efforts to proactively aggregate—and *share*—data concerning the age, travel route, destination, travel companion(s), and so forth of suspected child victims in order to tailor more effective detection and investigation programs and policies.

Recognizing the need for nation-to-nation collaboration, the international community—primarily through the United Nations—has implemented a number of legal instruments collectively forming an international framework. At least in principle, this framework obligates member states to establish domestic laws and regulations aimed at effectively addressing the problem of human trafficking and child sexual exploitation. The most significant include the following:

- United Nations Convention on the Rights of the Child (1989) and the follow-on Optional Protocol to the Convention on the Rights of the Child on the Sale of Children, Child Prostitution and Child Pornography (2000);
- Rome Statute of the International Criminal Court (1998);
- ILO Convention concerning the Prohibition and Immediate Action for the Elimination of the Worst Forms of Child Labour (1999);
- U.N. Convention on Transnational Organized Crime (2000) and its Optional Protocol to Prevent, Suppress and Punish Trafficking in Persons especially Women and Children.

At the risk of stating the obvious, the sexual exploitation of children and adolescents will obviously not be solved by any single nation or organization working alone, nor can it be solved by simple goodwill (or international declarations formally enshrining such goodwill).[16] To counter these violations against children, clear-eyed, goal-directed, coordinated, and substantive international action by governments and nongovernmental organizations (NGOs) from around the globe is required. And for every action-plan, coordination team, task force, or protocol, there must also be *tangible* and *objective* benchmarks so that success, failure, or desuetude can be readily identified.

E. The "Big Two" International Child Exploitation Instruments

If there is one truism when it comes to international efforts to combat child sexual abuse, it is that the most moving preamble or carefully crafted law will eventually fail if it is not conceived in light of those social, cultural, legal, and economic realities that facilitate the ongoing abuse. Local law enforcement that does not consider child sexual abuse to be a "real crime," like cynical regional attitudes that such crimes either do not exist or are problems caused by unspecified "foreigners," impede prevention and investigation. These views, moreover, create fear and shame in the victims.

Abject poverty, racism, sexism, homophobia, religious intolerance, and inadequate or nonexistent educational or vocational opportunities are just some of the hope-extinguishing factors making life easier for the "recruiter" relying on limited or nonexistent support structures to lure minors from their homes and herd them into the waiting hands of brothels, sex-tour operators, child pornography syndicates, or human traffickers. Indeed, post-conflict environments and post–natural disaster areas frequently serve up the perfect storm of these various destabilizing factors. When combined with an anemic appreciation for the rule of law, these environments provide a veritable feeding frenzy for opportunistic exploiters.

Once societal structures break down, whether through conflict or natural disaster, any vigilance that communities may have had regarding the monitoring of illegal behavior is typically replaced by concern about meeting the community's more basic needs: safety, shelter, food. Human traffickers move into the instability like bees to honey. And desperate people do desperate things both intentionally and unintentionally. Families broken by conflict and disaster are often exploited by those with malintent. International anti-exploitation treaties and protocols, though typically lacking meaningful remedies for noncompliance, can at least standardize the terms of the debate, and point recalcitrant nations in the right direction.

Although there has undoubtedly been a proliferation of such treaties, protocols, and resolutions touching on protecting the right of children to be free from, among other things, sexual exploitation, the two that gained the greatest traction are (1) the 1989 United Nations Convention on the Rights of the Child (UNCRC)[17] and (2) the follow-up 2000 Optional Protocol to the Convention on the Rights of the Child on the Sale of Children, Child Prostitution and Child Pornography (Optional Protocol).[18] The former human rights treaty sets out universally recognized norms and standards concerning the protection and promotion of the rights of children, whereas the Optional Protocol focuses primarily on prohibiting child pornography, child prostitution, and the sale of children.

The UNCRC went into force on September 2, 1990, and has been ratified by more than 190 countries (indeed, the only two countries in the U.N. not to have ratified it are the United States[19] and Somalia). The Optional Protocol went into force on January 18, 2002, and has been ratified by more than 140 nations.

1. 1989 United Nations Convention on the Rights of the Child (UNCRC)

World leaders in 1989 decided that children needed a special convention, just for them, to ensure that the world recognized that children also have human rights. The groundbreaking UNCRC, which, it should be noted, the United States played an active role in drafting[20] and signed in 1995 (though, to date, not ratified), is the most rapidly and widely ratified international human rights instrument in history.

a. Surveying the UNCRC

The UNCRC stands as the first international treaty placing a comprehensive, affirmative duty[21] on member states to take all available measures to guarantee the rights of children and to ensure their protection from all forms of abuse, exploitation, and violence. The Convention's four very broad "core principles" are (1) nondiscrimination; (2) devotion to the best interests of the child; (3) the right to life, survival, and development; and (4) respect for the child's views. The UNCRC's goal, therefore, is the protection of children's health and welfare, which includes their civil, political, economic, cultural, and social rights.

Turning from the general to the specific, the UNCRC, employing standard U.N. idealized terminology, spells out the basic human rights for children everywhere. These legally binding (but, in reality, little more than aspirational) rights include the right to the following:

- "Survival and development"[22]
- "Identity"[23]
- "Social security"[24]
- An appropriate "standard of living"[25]
- Protection from harmful influences[26]
- "Provision of appropriate and equal opportunities for cultural, artistic, recreational and leisure activities."[27]

Although most states parties to the UNCRC have little chance of delivering on most, if not all, of these rather generalized rights, the UNCRC contains cer-

tain impactful—and mandatory/"shall"—provisions setting forth clear-cut requirements that have seen application in the real world, including the following:

> Article 34: States Parties undertake to protect the child from all forms of sexual
> exploitation and sexual abuse. For these purposes States Parties shall in particu-
> lar take all appropriate national, bilateral and multilateral measures to prevent:
>
> a) The inducement or coercion of a child to engage in any unlawful sexual
>   activity;
> b) The exploitative use of children in prostitution or other unlawful sexual
>   practices;
> c) The exploitative use of children in pornographic performances and materials.
>
> Article 35: States Parties shall take all appropriate national, bilateral and mul-
> tilateral measures to prevent the abduction of, the sale or traffic in children for
> any purpose or in any form.
>
> Article 39: States Parties shall take all appropriate measures to promote physi-
> cal and psychological recovery and social reintegration of a child victim of: any
> form of neglect, exploitation, or abuse; torture or any other form of cruel, inhu-
> man or degrading treatment or punishment; or armed conflicts.
>
> Such recovery and reintegration shall take place in an environment which
> fosters the health, self-respect and dignity of the child.

In terms of interpretation and scope, although the UNCRC's fifty-four
individual articles are not short on the usual diplomatic "fluff," the UNCRC's
fundamental premise is that no single article or group of articles can be applied in isolation. Rather, the entire Convention must be read and interpreted
in an integrated, holistic manner.

b. Monitoring the UNCRC: The Committee on the Rights of the Child

Compliance with the UNCRC and its below-described Protocols is monitored
by the Committee on the Rights of the Child (UNCRC Committee).[28] The
UNCRC Committee is composed of eighteen independent experts who are
"persons of high moral character and recognized competence in the field of
human rights." States parties elect members of the UNCRC Committee for a
term of four years, and members serve in their personal capacity and may be
reelected if nominated.[29] The United Nations High Commissioner for Human
Rights (UNHCHR), moreover, provides key technical and substantive support to the committee, and seeks to foster the implementation of children's
rights at the national level by providing appropriate technical assistance and
advisory services programs.[30]

Governments of countries that have ratified the UNCRC are required to periodically report to, and appear before, the UNCRC Committee to be examined on their progress with regards to the advancement of the implementation of the convention. (Indeed, even the non-ratifying United States periodically submits extremely comprehensive reports to the committee in order to keep it updated on U.S. compliance with the Optional Protocol.)[31] The UNCRC Committee, thereafter, issues Concluding Observations concerning the Convention and the nation's existing level of compliance.[32]

The committee, for example, has rightly criticized various parties' lack of national criminal legislation proscribing all forms of child sexual abuse, including over the Internet, and the absence of a minimum age of consent of eighteen.[33] It has, moreover, recommended that parties develop an effective system of reporting and investigation, set up child-sensitive inquiry and judicial procedures, avoid unnecessarily repetitive interviews of child victims, and fortify children's privacy protections. Of course, because the committee has no power of enforcement, it can only make recommendations.

By agreeing to undertake the obligations of the convention, national governments in a very public way commit themselves to protecting and ensuring a host of specific children's rights, and consent to being held accountable before the international community. The political and moral dimensions of such promises can prove to be particularly useful when one nation seeks judicial assistance from another, or asks for the extradition of a wanted exploiter. Though the United States is only a signatory to the convention (that said, as a signatory, it is bound to avoid actions that would defeat the "object and purpose" of the convention), reference to the above provisions can help underscore that the assistance being sought is consistent with the state's international obligation to protect children from sexual exploitation.

2. Optional Protocol to the Convention on the Rights of the Child on the Sale of Children, Child Prostitution and Child Pornography

The lead universal treaty specifically addressing the sexual exploitation of children is the 2000 Optional Protocol to the UNCRC on the Sale of Children, Child Prostitution and Child Pornography. The Optional Protocol, drafted with the explicit goal of "achiev[ing] the purposes of the [UNCRC],"[34] requires states to criminalize various acts in relation to the sale of children, child prostitution, and child pornography, including attempt, complicity, and participation. Article 8 of the Optional Protocol, moreover, suggests seven sensible measures for protecting the rights and interests of child victims during all stages of the criminal justice process. Additional key provisions follow:

Article 2 (Definitions)
For the purpose of the present Protocol:
a)   Sale of children means any act or transaction whereby a child is transferred by any person or group of persons to another for remuneration or any other consideration;
b)   Child prostitution means the use of a child in sexual activities for remuneration or any other form of consideration;
c)   Child pornography means any representation, by whatever means, of a child engaged in real or simulated explicit sexual activities or any representation of the sexual parts of a child for primarily sexual purposes.[35]

Article 3 (Criminal Proscriptions)
1.   Each State Party shall ensure that, as a minimum, the following acts and activities are fully covered under its criminal or penal law, whether these offences are committed domestically or transnationally or on an individual or organised basis:
    (a)   In the context of sale of children as defined in article 2:
        (i)   The offering, delivering or accepting, by whatever means, a child for the purpose of:
            a)   Sexual exploitation of the child;
            b)   Transfer of organs of the child for profit;
            c)   Engagement of the child in forced labour;
        (ii)   Improperly inducing consent, as an intermediary, for the adoption of a child in violation of applicable international legal instruments on adoption;
    (b)   Offering, obtaining, procuring or providing a child for child prostitution, as defined in article 2;
    (c)   Producing, distributing, disseminating, importing, exporting, offering, selling or possessing for the above purposes child pornography as defined in article 2.

Readers should note that the prefatory language in subsection 1 ("whether these offences are committed domestically or transnationally") also rather exceptionally provides for *extraterritorial* jurisdiction.

Article 5 (Extradition)
1.   The offences referred to in article 3, paragraph 1, shall be deemed to be included as extraditable offences in any extradition treaty existing between States Parties and shall be included as extraditable offences in

every extradition treaty subsequently concluded between them, in accordance with the conditions set forth in such treaties.

2. If a State Party that makes extradition conditional on the existence of a treaty receives a request for extradition from another State Party with which it has no extradition treaty, it may consider the present Protocol to be a legal basis for extradition in respect of such offences. Extradition shall be subject to the conditions provided by the law of the requested State.

3. States Parties that do not make extradition conditional on the existence of a treaty shall recognize such offences as extraditable offences between themselves subject to the conditions provided by the law of the requested State.

4. Such offences shall be treated, for the purpose of extradition between States Parties, as if they had been committed not only in the place in which they occurred but also in the territories of the States required to establish their jurisdiction in accordance with article 4.

5. If an extradition request is made with respect to an offence described in article 3, paragraph 1, and the requested State Party does not or will not extradite on the basis of the nationality of the offender, that State shall take suitable measures to submit the case to its competent authorities for the purpose of prosecution.

Of particular note here is subsection 2, which invites states parties to refer to the Optional Protocol as "a legal basis for extradition" in those cases in which the parties have no existing extradition treaty. The Optional Protocol, as noted above, makes extraditable all offenses concerning the sale of children, child prostitution, and child pornography.

In terms of the Optional Protocol's mechanics, if State A receives an extradition request from State Y (a state with which State A has no existing extradition treaty), State Y can use the Optional Protocol as a legal basis for extraditing the individual. Again, a simple reference to this subsection can prove invaluable in nudging reluctant bureaucrats into action.

Although the Optional Protocol may leave some victim advocates wishing for a greater focus on child-friendly judicial procedures, it does, as discussed above, set forth minimum standards on the protection of the child victim in criminal justice processes.[36] The Optional Protocol, moreover, provides for the right of victims to seek compensation[37] and encourages the strengthening of international cooperation and assistance and the adoption of extraterritorial legislation.

This last point deserves some additional attention. The Optional Protocol, in pushing for extraterritorial jurisdiction for child sexual exploitation offenses, joins the legal vanguard by recognizing the importance of a state being able to criminally prosecute the acts of its citizens or residents who abuse children outside of that nation. Thus, a U.S. citizen who travels to Thailand for the purpose of having sexual encounters with minors and taking pictures of his child victims cannot escape punishment merely because local authorities may be unable to bring a case against him.[38] The Optional Protocol rather strictly confines the ability of abusers to escape prosecution, and, in so doing, recognizes the pervasively transnational nature of this specific species of criminality.

F. Other Important International Instruments

The UNCRC and its Optional Protocol are clearly the preeminent international anti-exploitation instruments. But they are not the only international instruments to have spread the pro-enforcement word.

1. 1990 Commission on Human Rights Appointment of Special Rapporteur on the Sale of Children, Child Prostitution and Child Pornography

The United Nations Commission on Human Rights in 1990 appointed a Special Rapporteur on the sale of children, child prostitution, and child pornography.[39] The Special Rapporteur's mandate was to collect and analyze relevant data, and to recommend measures aimed at eliminating the sale of children, child prostitution, and child pornography at the global, regional, and national levels.

In recent years, the Human Rights Council has expanded the Special Rapporteur's mandate in resolutions renewing his authority by, among other things, annually focusing on different themes, such as human trafficking, domestic violence, the role of the justice system, the influence of education and the media, and the impact of the private sector.

2. 1996 Hague Convention on the Protection of Children and Cooperation with Respect to Inter-Country Adoption

Designed to ensure that inter-country adoptions are arranged in the best interests of the child, and with respect for the child's fundamental human rights, the Hague Convention, now ratified by some seventy-five countries, was an early and symbolically important mechanism for restraining the international trafficking of children. (Arguably unwisely limiting the work of international adoption agencies, however, the Hague Convention prohibits "improper financial gain" from inter-country adoption; pursuant to article 32, only costs and expenses, including "reasonable professional fees of persons involved in the adoption," may be charged or paid.)[40]

3. 1998 Rome Statute of the International Criminal Court

The International Crime Court (ICC) has jurisdiction over war crimes, crimes against humanity, and genocide.[41] More specifically, ICC article 7's "crimes against humanity" encompasses sexual slavery, trafficking, and forced prostitution, knowingly committed as part of a widespread or systematic attack.[42] Rape, sexual slavery, and forced prostitution may, moreover, constitute Article 8 war crimes.[43]

Though the ICC's performance to date has left many skeptics doubting the institution's ability to deliver on its promise to bring to justice the world's greatest criminals, its recognition of sex crimes, including those committed against children, as some of society's most serious violations is quite clearly a positive development.

4. 1999 ILO Convention Concerning the Prohibition and Immediate Action for the Elimination of the Worst Forms of Child Labour

The International Labour Organization (ILO) Worst Forms of Child Labour Convention includes among the "worst forms of child labour" the trafficking of children; procuring, offering, or using children for purposes of prostitution; and using children to produce pornographic materials or in the context of sexually exploitive performances. The convention, moreover, in article 3 includes a catch-all proscription against all forms of work that are likely to harm the morals, safety, or health of children (including, presumably, work in brothels).

5. 1999 International Conference on Combating Child Pornography on the Internet

The 1999 International Conference on Combating Child Pornography on the Internet convened in Vienna and is the first international common commitment to tackle the distribution of child sexual exploitation material on the Internet. The conference participants recognized that child sexual exploitation through the Internet was a growing problem, and that, as more of the world comes online, this form of exploitation will continue to expand.[44]

6. Security Council Resolutions 1261 (1999) and 1314 (2000)

U.N. Security Council Resolutions 1261 and 1314 relate directly to the sexual exploitation of children in the context of armed conflict, and, significantly, are binding on all Member States of the United Nations. Resolutions 1261 and 1314, broadly stated, urge all parties in armed conflicts to ensure the protection of all children, and note the particular vulnerabilities of girls.

Resolution 1261 urges all parties in armed conflicts to "take special measures to protect children, in particular girls, from rape and other forms of sexual abuse and gender-based violence in situations of armed conflict and to take into account the special needs of the girl child throughout armed conflicts and their aftermath, including in the delivery of humanitarian assistance."

Resolution 1314, in turn, highlights how important it is to give special consideration to the unique needs and peculiar vulnerabilities of girls affected by armed conflict, including those sexually exploited.

7. 2000 United Nations Convention on Transnational Organized Crime

As discussed in chapter 5, the sexual exploitation of children is a vital source of lifeblood for contemporary organized criminal groups the world over. The U.N. Convention on Transnational Organized Crime (TOC Convention),[45] adopted by the General Assembly on November 15, 2000,[46] as well as its three supplemental protocols,[47] stands as the international community's primary instrument in the fight against international organized crime.

a. The Transnational Organized Crime Convention's Broad Sweep

The TOC Convention seeks to promote cooperation and to prevent and combat transnational organized criminal activity. More specifically, according to the U.N. Office on Drugs and Crime, the U.N. agency that supports states in implementing the Convention:

> The Convention represents a major step forward in the fight against transnational organized crime and signifies the recognition by Member States of the seriousness of the problems posed by it, as well as the need to foster and enhance close international cooperation in order to tackle those problems. States that ratify this instrument commit themselves to taking a series of measures against transnational organized crime, including the creation of domestic criminal offences (participation in an organized criminal group, money laundering, corruption and obstruction of justice); the adoption of new and sweeping frameworks for extradition, mutual legal assistance and law enforcement cooperation; and the promotion of training and technical assistance for building or upgrading the necessary capacity of national authorities.[48]

A major caveat, however, is that the TOC Convention only addresses offenses (1) carrying penalties of four or more years imprisonment,[49] or (2) involving obstruction offenses.[50] The criminal laws of many nations, however, have child exploitation penalties falling below these (relatively low) thresholds. To the extent that parties impose penalties falling under this bar, the TOC Convention will likely not apply to them.

On the upside, one of the TOC Convention's key features is a requirement of mutual legal assistance between and among parties.[51] Such mutual legal assistance, moreover, is broadly defined as including: (1) assistance in gathering evidence, (2) executing searches, (3) taking statements, (4) seizing and freezing assets, (5) serving judicial documents, and (6) engaging in *other collaborative conduct*, provided it is consistent with the requested state's domestic laws.[52]

The TOC Convention also requires parties to enact oft-absent domestic legislation criminalizing obstructive conduct, such as witness tampering and the threatening of, or interference with, law enforcement officials.[53] Continuing the theme of shoring up the rule of law against such obstructive threats, under the TOC Convention parties promise to protect witnesses and to permit the taking of their testimony by video link and other methods aimed at guarding witnesses' identities and safety, while at the same time ensuring the rights of the accused.[54]

b. U.N. Optional Protocol to Prevent, Suppress, and Punish Trafficking in Persons, Especially Women and Children

The Optional Protocol to Prevent, Suppress and Punish Trafficking in Persons, Especially Women and Children (also known as the "Palermo Protocol")[55] went into force on December 25, 2003, and by June 2011, 146 countries had ratified it. The Optional Protocol builds on the TOC Convention and seeks to further an inclusive, collaborative, and comprehensive international approach to prevention, protection, and punishment. The Protocol can well be considered the most important contemporary instrument dealing specifically with the complex issues of trafficking due to its comprehensive and liberal interpretation of trafficking.[56] It arguably is also the only one providing a generally agreed-upon international definition of trafficking in persons[57]:

Article 3
For the purposes of this Protocol:
  a) "Trafficking in persons" shall mean the recruitment, transportation, transfer, harbouring or receipt of persons, by means of the threat or use of force or other forms of coercion, of abduction, of fraud, of deception, of the abuse of power or of a position of vulnerability or of the giving or receiving of payments or benefits to achieve the consent of a

person having control over another person, for the purpose of exploitation. Exploitation shall include, at a minimum, the exploitation of the prostitution of others or other forms of sexual exploitation, forced labour or services, slavery or practices similar to slavery, servitude or the removal of organs;

b) The consent of a victim of trafficking in persons to the intended exploitation set forth in subparagraph (a) of this article shall be irrelevant where any of the means set forth in subparagraph (a) have been used;

c) The recruitment, transportation, transfer, harbouring or receipt of a child for the purpose of exploitation shall be considered "trafficking in persons" even if this does not involve any of the means set forth in subparagraph (a) of this article;

d) "Child" shall mean any person under eighteen years of age.

Notably, subsection (c) contains an expansive definition of trafficking, providing that "trafficking in persons" involves *any* kind of "recruitment, transportation, transfer, harbouring or receipt of a child for the purpose of exploitation."[58] Moreover, the "consent" of a child to trafficking is irrelevant, even if the specified "means" of trafficking are not involved.

The stated purpose of the Protocol is to facilitate national cooperation in investigating and prosecuting trafficking in persons cases. An additional objective of the Protocol is to protect and assist the victims of human trafficking, with full respect for their human rights.

The Optional Protocol applies equally to source, transit, and destination countries. Indeed, the Protocol is considered the first universal instrument addressing most, if not all, aspects of human trafficking. Signaling how important the fight against human trafficking has become, then–U.N. Secretary General Kofi Annan in the TOC Convention and Optional Protocols' Foreword wrote:

> I believe the trafficking of persons, particularly women and children, for forced and exploitative labour, including for sexual exploitation, is one of the most egregious violations of human rights that the United Nations now confronts. It is widespread and growing. It is rooted in social and economic conditions in the countries from which the victims come, facilitated by practices that discriminate against women and driven by cruel indifference to human suffering on the part of those who exploit the services that the victims are forced to provide.[59]

In terms of the highlights, the Protocol contains a well-reasoned definitional section. For example, in addition to the above-discussed definition of trafficking, it defines "exploitation" as encompassing "the exploitation of the prostitution of others or other forms of sexual exploitation, forced labour or services, slavery or practices similar to slavery."[60]

The Protocol's restorative agenda is set out in article 6. It provides, for example, that parties must consider implementing measures to provide child exploitation victims with the means to achieve at least some level of psychological, social, and physical recovery and reintegration.[61] The Protocol, critically, also mandates the establishment of procedures to provide victims with access to restitution.[62]

8. European Commission Directive on Combating Sexual Abuse, Sexual Exploitation of Children and Child Pornography

On March 29, 2010, the European Commission adopted a proposal for a new Directive on Combating Sexual Abuse, Sexual Exploitation of Children and Child Pornography.[63] The directive's uncharacteristically aggressive "U.S.-style" call for action—including the imposition of minimum terms of imprisonment, the criminalization of grooming-related offenses, and the enactment of extraterritorial provisions—is explicitly premised, in part at least, on the finding that between 10 and 20 percent of all children in Europe will be sexually assaulted during their childhood.[64] In the words of the proposal:

> Fighting these crimes is very difficult. Children are vulnerable, ashamed and afraid to report what has happened to them. The Internet makes it easier to groom (the on-line solicitation of children for sexual purposes) children or to produce and distribute child pornography. In some cases, such as sex tourism or child pornography, abuse happens in different countries, and this, together with national differences in legislation, makes it difficult for authorities to act. Some convicted offenders go on abusing children after their sentences. Furthermore organised crime can make a high profit from it with limited risk.
>
> National legislation covers some of these problems to varying degrees. However, it is not strong or consistent enough to provide a vigorous social response to this disturbing phenomenon.
>
> The main EU instrument to fight against child sexual exploitation, Council Framework Decision 2004/68/JHA, introduces a minimum of approximation of Member States' legislation. Due to the short existence of this legal framework, it has a number of shortcomings.[65]

The new directive, if approved, will build on the October 25, 2007, Council of Europe "Convention on the Protection of Children against Sexual Exploitation and Sexual Abuse," and is expected to address, *inter alia*, the following key areas[66]:

- *Criminal law*: The directive covers new ground for the EU, establishing provisions that punish all offenses related to child pornography already falling under the Europol mandate, as listed in the April 6, 2009, Council Decision establishing the Europol Police Office.

- *Criminal investigation*: Various provisions are designed to assist with investigating potential crimes and filing charges in the absence of reporting by the child victim.
- *Internet-specific changes*: All forms of sexual abuse and exploitation facilitated through the Internet are criminalized (including "grooming," as well as viewing child pornography online without purposefully downloading the files).
- *Extraterritoriality*: Rules on jurisdiction are to be amended to ensure that child sexual abusers or exploiters from the EU face prosecution, including if they commit their crimes in non-EU countries (specifically, in the context of "sex tourism").
- *Enhanced victim protections*: A number of provisions are designed to ensure that abused children have easy access to legal remedies and do not suffer as a result of participating in criminal proceedings.
- *Prevention*: In addition to rehabilitation programs, the task of developing methods of blocking access to websites featuring child pornography will be placed under the supervision of judicial services or the police.

G. There Has Been Progress, but There Is Much More Work to Do

These various international instruments, painstakingly drafted after seemingly endless negotiation, evidence a very real desire on the part of states to enter into binding legal obligations consistent with their self-image as modern, forward-leaning, proactive nations. By entering into treaties, the parties publicly promise to incorporate the above-described provisions directly into their respective domestic legislation, and pledge to the world that they will enforce these laws in their national courts. Such public commitments, legally binding as a matter of international law (and also as a matter of *domestic* law if the country's internal processes incorporate international law into domestic law), signify these nations as co-equals on the international stage, dedicated to strengthening their organs of democratic society and to promoting the rule of law and international standards of justice. Of course, as with individuals, actions speak louder than words, and, so far, many of these parties are truly talking with hushed, and, at times, almost inaudible voices.

1. Signing a Treaty Does Not Equate with Abiding by It

As we have seen, ratifying a treaty is not the same thing as actually living up to the treaty obligations—and therein lies the international rub. Seldom, indeed, are treaty promises kept. And this, even accounting for the symbolic and educative impact of treaty ratification or accession, undermines the legitimacy of such instruments.

Although the international community has made significant strides toward providing nations with the basic tools required to begin the transnational fight, state accountability and follow-through have continued to lag. For example, it is difficult to gain a meaningful sense of how effectively states have lived up to their obligations under the UNCRC. Moreover, legislative "best practices" are difficult to come by. Indeed, even basic information, such as when substantive legislation was passed, is far from readily available (ironically, the nonratifying United States, as noted above, has provided the most complete report on whether its domestic provisions are in line with the Optional Protocol's requirements). This, frankly, is nothing short of a tragic state of affairs.

It is high time that the international community draft substantive "best practices" and model legislation so that states have a yardstick against which to measure their own enforcement efforts. Requiring all parties to provide reliable statistical enforcement and assistance data, moreover, would provide a method of determining those states complying with their treaty obligations, those who are making good-faith efforts to comply, and those who have done little or nothing to protect children from sexual exploitation. Without this type of basic compliance information, the international community will continue to be unable to assess progress made, as well as impediments remaining.

2. The Pressing Need to Step Up National Efforts to Combat Child Sexual Exploitation

Although far from perfect, an encouraging development has been that the recognition of the importance of passing legislation specifically aimed at the commercial sexual exploitation of children continues to spread. An increasing number of states, moreover, have revised their penalties to more fully account for the serious and, often, irreparable harm such criminal conduct inflicts on its victims, specifically, and on the nation, generally. But far more needs to be done.

a. Expand Extradition

States should be discouraged from refusing extradition of their nationals. Extradition of those implicated in child sexual offenses is typically conditioned on a bilateral treaty or agreement between the requesting state and the requested state. Most nations, moreover, adopt a "double criminality" approach to extradition, requiring that the conduct of the alleged offense for which extradition sought be a crime in both the requesting and the requested nation. Thus, if a requested state has either no, or incomplete, legislation relating to, say, the exploitation of minors through simulated sexual conduct, extradition cannot take place. While some states have dropped the double criminality requirement and others are still reviewing it, this legal requirement continues to be a fixture of contemporary extradition practice.

Given that the double criminality requirement is, as discussed above, likely a permanent aspect of most contemporary treaties, the international community should encourage all nations to enact legislation proscribing all possible sexual offenses committed against children under the age of eighteen. The European Commission Directive on Combating Sexual Abuse, Sexual Exploitation of Children and Child Pornography, for example, provides a sound example of such an effort. After all, sexual exploitation is a universally recognized violation of children's rights. States will, therefore, be hard-pressed to contend that an individual charged with a child sex offense is being unfairly prosecuted.

b. Target Sex Tourism

Stopping the pernicious sex tourism business is an intensifying global law enforcement priority. Nations should be encouraged to build on this momentum by convening inter-agency commissions dedicated to preventing victimization and to caring for child and adolescent victims of prostitution in identified high-priority tourist centers. Moreover, representatives of various tourism- or child-related sectors (including hotel associations, restaurants, transportation companies, the media, the police, UNICEF, and other NGOs and agencies) should be urged to sign on to protocols and declarations aimed at stopping sex tourism, should be educated about sex tourism, and should have disincentives to aiding sex tourism.

c. Proscribe All Forms of Child Pornography and Child Prostitution

Countries are increasingly united in the conviction that child pornography generally—and the manufacture and distribution of child pornography via the Internet, specifically—pose major threats that must be aggressively dealt with. While some now proscribe all forms of sexual exploitation of children under the age of eighteen, others are more skeptical of such legislative steps (often citing freedom of expression concerns). This skepticism, however, results in ongoing victimization.

Nations should continue the trend of amending or augmenting their domestic legislation so that it distinguishes between the prostitution of women and of children, and recognizes that boys can also be victims of sexual exploitation through prostitution. Moreover, law enforcement authorities should, as a rule, treat prostituted children as crime *victims*, rather than as *perpetrators*.

d. Revise Age of Consent

National laws in many countries define children as being age fourteen or younger. Under Muslim Personal Law, moreover, a child, upon gaining puberty, is considered an adult. Protection against sexual exploitation should be extended to all minors under the age of eighteen, regardless of the age of consent. This definition of a minor should be incorporated into all national and extraterritorial legislation.

e. Devise National Action Plans

Countries such as Nepal, India, Pakistan, and Bangladesh, in partnership with civil-society, have developed much-needed national plans of action encompassing various dimensions of child sexual exploitation, including: protection, recovery and reintegration; awareness raising; and training and capacity building.[67]

Some countries have also set up task forces and committees at the local and district levels responsible for policy formulation, follow-up, and monitoring. For example, in 1998, India adopted its National Plan of Action to Combat Trafficking and Commercial Sexual Exploitation of Women and Children. The plan included efforts to institute legal and law enforcement reforms, to generate awareness generation and social mobilization, to provide health care services, and to provide a rescue and rehabilitation framework for children.[68] Such plans provide a roadmap so that countries can finally move toward compliance with their long-standing treaty obligations.

Law enforcement agencies, the private sector (and, specifically, the tourism and transportation sector), and NGOs should cooperate and collaborate to establish protocols and standards of conduct for interactions with child victims and the identification and reporting of suspected instances of child sexual abuse.

f. Provide for Repatriation

Countries and international organizations have begun to, where appropriate (and it often is not), incorporate repatriation of child victims into their prevention and rehabilitation programs. Children who immigration officials identify as having been sexually exploited, moreover, should not come under general immigration legislation, but, instead, should be protected under humanitarian provisions, in accordance with article 20 of the UNCRC.

g. Expand Extraterritoriality

As discussed in chapter 7, extraterritoriality at its core extends the jurisdiction of a state by allowing the prosecution of nationals for offenses committed abroad. As such, extraterritoriality is a critical component in the fight against the sexual exploitation of children. Nevertheless, commencing prosecutions in the state in which the offense occurred is, as a general matter, preferable for a host of reasons. For one, experienced prosecutors understand how difficult it can be to obtain admissible evidence—whether the results of forensic exams on computers, testimony from child witnesses, or documentary evidence—from another country.

h. End Inappropriate Offender Impunity Courtesy of Statutes of Limitations

A sensible approach adopted by many nations is that the period of limitation begins to run only once the victim reaches majority, thereby reducing impunity. The rationale for extending the statute of limitations in this manner is that many child victims are unable or unwilling to come forward with narratives of their abuse until years after the event. This reluctance can be explained by the child victim's relative immaturity, psychological trauma inflicted by the offender, or dependency on the offender. In our experience, many victims seek justice as they become teenagers and young adults. Bilateral and multilateral treaties, going forward, should, therefore, extend the statute of limitations in this manner.

i. Facilitate Child-Friendly Legal Procedures and Training

A fundamental truism of child exploitation prosecutions is that they are, *ab initio*, doomed to fail *if* the child witnesses are not viewed as credible. Divergent cultures, customs, and religious traditions not surprisingly produce legal systems with divergent institutional values. In many, the focus is on adults, and there is built-in unease about facing the reality that (1) adults can have sexual desires toward minors, and (2) that these desires, once acted upon, cause serious long-term harm to the child victims.

Child-centered proceedings, in which children are not expected to adopt adult patterns of reasoning, are rare. Officials, whether in the judiciary, law enforcement, or border patrol and immigration, are simply not used to crediting the testimony of children—which, naturally, inures to the direct benefit of the abusers.

Through training and experience, those in the law enforcement community must become sensitized to the special needs of children who are victims of, or witnesses to, sex crimes. For example, questioning must be simplified and open-ended, and complex questions should be avoided; the physical environment and questioning styles must be nonthreatening, and the children must be provided with appropriate social support. An emerging trend focused on achieving these ends, while also guaranteeing the rights of the accused, is to permit child testimony through closed-circuit television or from behind a screen.

All parties to the justice system, moreover, must be trained not only on the new legislation, but, more importantly, on the driving public policy rationale and on how it is most effectively implemented. Thus, if, say, a nation adopts new legislation concerning reparations for victims or the seizure of instrumentalities of, or proceeds from, child sexual exploitation, judges, prosecutors, police, and victim advocates must understand why such reparations and seizures are important, and how they are most effectively and fairly effectuated. Some attitudes may be difficult to shift, but by engaging in interactive trainings, provided by experienced practitioners, entire legal systems can over time be successfully transformed and modernized.

j. Encourage Appropriate Ratification

Formal and informal international pressures should be exerted on nations to sign, ratify, and implement the key international instruments addressing child sexual exploitation. Efforts must be focused on ensuring that parties enshrine in their national legislation the key provisions. (Of course, some skeptics may contend that, for nations such as the United States, which already have all major pro-child provisions in their national legislation, and in which there is a skepticism toward signing on to what in practice are largely aspirational treaties, ceding sovereignty is not in the nation's interest.)

k. Mandate Benchmarks, National Action Plans, and Evidence of Progress

States parties to the UNCRC should be encouraged to provide the committee with detailed information on legislation, case law, and enforcement policies concerning child sexual exploitation. It is critical that realistic timetables for implementation are set, and that implementation benchmarks for accountability are included.

l. Permit Proactive Litigation

National legal systems should explore the wisdom of permitting concerned citizens to draw the attention of courts to breaches of national and international human rights and child rights commitments.

m. Seize Assets

Routinely seizing the assets of those involved in the sexual exploitation of children—whether as proceeds or instrumentalities—must, as discussed above, become a primary international and national law enforcement priority.

n. Ensure Child-Sensitive Demobilization

Post-conflict demobilization agreements should include guarantees that monitors have access to children who may have been sexually exploited.

o. Enact Social Welfare Legislation

Countries should consider creating safety nets, and should provide opportunities for education, mentoring, and vocational training/sustainable livelihood training with the goal of encouraging self-reliance and meaningful reintegration.

p. Increase Public Awareness

As touched on above, local attitudes and prejudices are frequently the most significant impediment to effectively combating the sexual abuse of minors. Citizens in many countries at times feel that the whole idea of child sexual abuse is a figment of the international community's imagination. Or they claim that, while it is a problem, it is not a problem in their area. The reality, of course, is that child sexual abuse occurs in every region, and among every demographic group. Because protecting children against sexual exploitation is one of the fundamental duties of the state, effective law reform, which incorporates community participation, should be encouraged.

In turn, for such law reform to take root, citizens must become aware of the problems, as well as of the laws aimed at addressing them. In the Balkans, for example, 2005 television and billboard ads sent the message that the minor prostitute "Could Be Your Daughter." These advertisements pointed out that, as a matter of empirical fact, the vast majority of men paying for the services of prostitutes—who were frequently minors and trafficking victims—in the Balkans were citizens, not tourists or international NGO employees. Panel discussions and televised round-tables were used to further emphasize these points. Countries should also consider advocacy and training efforts to sensitize the media to the reality of the child exploitation problem and to the challenges this problem poses.

q. Develop Model Laws

The international community must develop a well-reasoned, but not unreasonably ambitious or unrealistic, set of model laws covering all aspects of the sexual exploitation of children. Such model laws could then be distributed to all states in a variety of formats, including online.

r. Provide Pro Bono Services for Victims

Local, regional, and national bar associations should encourage their members to provide free legal services to victims of child sexual abuse. For example, lawyers should be urged to file suits on behalf of putative child victims for reparations from their abusers.

Notes

1. See generally UNICEF, Child Protection from Violence, Exploitation and Abuse (2011), available at www.unicef.org/protection/index_childlabour.html (last visited June 15, 2011); see also Office to Monitor and Combat Trafficking in Persons, U.S. Department of State, Trafficking in Persons Report 2010 (2010), available at www .state.gov/g/tip/rls/tiprpt/2010/index.htm (last visited June 15, 2011); Martti Lehti and Kauko Aromaa, *Trafficking for Sexual Exploitation*, 34 Crime & Just 133, 186 (2006) ("According to the national and regional estimates . . . the annual volume of trafficking for sexual exploitation would be several millions. The number of minors engaged in organized child prostitution around the world according to these estimates is somewhere between 5 and 10 million"); UNICEF, Profiting from Abuse: An Investigation into Sexual Exploitation of Our Children, at 20 (2001) (estimating that one million children enter the global sex trade each year), available at www.unicef .org/publications/files/pub_profiting_en.pdf, cited in Geneva Brown, *Woman and Children Last: The Prosecution of Sex Traffickers as Sex Offenders and the Need for a Sex Trafficker Registry*, 31 B.C. Third World L.J. 1, 8 (2011); Aaron Sachs, *The Last Commodity: Child Prostitution in the Developing World*, World Watch, Jul./Aug. 1994, at 26 (arguing that child prostitution is a multibillion-dollar industry).

2. We use the term *preferential* child exploiter to refer to the category of individuals who have an inherent sexual drive to gain sexual pleasure from, or through, children (that is, they have a sexual preference for children). *Commercial* child exploiters, in contrast, are primarily financially motivated. Another commonly identified category of

sex offender is the "situational child molester," who is described as sexually indiscriminate persons who lack a "true" sexual preference for children, but will simply sexually
abuse children if and when the opportunity should arise. See, for example, Blaine D.
McIlwaine, INTERROGATING CHILD MOLESTERS, available at http://investigationshelpdesk
.com/html/training/le_articles/94JUN001.TXT (last visited June 15, 2011) ("Situational
child molesters do not have a true sexual preference for children, but instead, engage
in sex with the young for varied and sometimes complex reasons. For such molesters,
sexual contact with children may range from a 'once-in-a-lifetime' act to a long-term
pattern of behavior. However, situational child molesters generally have a very limited
number of victims. . . . Preferential child molesters have a definite sexual preference
for children. Their sexual fantasies and erotic imagery focus on children. They engage
in sexual acts with the young not because of some situational stress or insecurity, but
because they are sexually attracted to, and prefer, children"). Although the distinction
between situational and preferential molesters can be an important one, for present
purposes the value it adds is outweighed by the confusion and linguistic awkwardness
it adds. We will, therefore, generally distinguish between those who seek sexual contact
with children due to a personal sexual/emotional/psychological preference and those
who do so entirely, or largely, for financial gain. Of course, in the real-world context of
preferential v. commercial exploitation, these hard distinctions can often be considerably blurred (generally by preferential exploiters who turn their proclivities to cash by
selling the images of the children they exploit). Nevertheless, we feel that the distinction
between primarily commercial and primarily preferential sexual abusers is important
and adds some nuance to the discussion.

3. See generally Janet Bagnall, *Sex Trade Blights the Lives of 2 Million Children*,
MONTREAL GAZETTE, Oct. 24, 2007.

4. See UNICEF, COMMERCIAL SEXUAL EXPLOITATION AND SEXUAL ABUSE OF CHILDREN
IN SOUTH ASIA, at 12–16 (2001) ("Many factors, both modern and traditional, are
commonly cited for commercial sexual exploitation of children and trafficking, including trafficking for sexual purposes. Globalisation is a stimulus since it involves
increased trade across national borders, greater mobility of capital and workers,
increased urbanisation, and the incorporation of subsistence communities into the
market economy. Globalisation has also led to the growth of tourism, the expansion
of international organised crime, the profitability of trafficking and the consequent
commodification of children's bodies. Large profits lead to the well-known nexus between prostitution mafias, law enforcement agencies and others. Family members are
sometimes also involved in the trafficking of children as a means of earning money.
Communities along many borders also profit from trafficking by providing meals,
shelter and other support services").

5. See generally USDOJ, CHILD EXPLOITATION AND OBSCENITY SECTION, SEX TOURISM
(2011) ("While Asian countries, including Thailand, India, and the Philippines,
have long been prime destinations for child-sex tourists, in recent years, tourists
have increasingly traveled to Mexico and Central America for their sexual exploits
as well"), available at www.justice.gov/criminal/ceos/sextour.html (last visited June
15, 2011).

6. Anonymous, *Letter to a Young Boy-Lover*, N. Am. Man/Boy Love Ass'n Bull., Jan/Feb 1993, at 30, reprinted in Wendy Waldron and Michael Yoon, *Obtaining Foreign Evidence in Child Sex Tourism Cases*, U.S. Att'ys Bull., Nov. 2006.

7. Sam Zanahar, Why Sex Tourism (2010), available at http://sextourism.org/ (last visited June 15, 2011).

8. See U.N. ESCAP, Commercial Sexual Exploitation and Sexual Abuse of Children: Definitions of Terms (1998), available at www.escap-hrd.org/csec2.htm (last visited June 15, 2011).

9. See UNICEF, Commercial Sexual Exploitation and Sexual Abuse of Children in South Asia (2001), available at www.unicef.org/rosa/commercial.pdf, citing UNICEF Child Protection Programme Home Page, available at www.unicef.org/programme/cprotection (last visited June 13, 2011).

10. See, for example, *United States v. Dye*, 2010 WL 4146187, at 2 (3rd Cir. 2010) (defendant, who possessed child pornography, admitted that he traveled in interstate commerce for purposes of engaging in sexual contact with a minor and filming that encounter); *United States v. Mallon*, 345 F. 3rd 943 (7th Cir. 2003) (defendant, a high-ranking political official from the Republic of Ireland, traveled to the United States for the purpose of having sex with a minor and filming the encounter; search warrants issued in Ireland also uncovered child pornography on his personal computer).

11. See, for example, *Mallon*, 345 F. 3rd at 943 (7th Cir. 2003) (defendant spent considerable effort to give the putative child victim gifts and to otherwise play on her perceived insecurities).

12. See ibid.

13. See generally *United States v. McNerney*, 636 F.3d 772, 777 (6th Cir. 2011) (discussing Congressional "concerns that pedophiles, including those who use the Internet, are using child pornographic and obscene material to desensitize children to sexual activity, to convince children that sexual activity involving children is normal, and to entice children to engage in sexual activity") (citation and quotation omitted).

14. See generally Sally Stoecker and Louise Shelley, eds., Human Traffic and Transnational Crime: Eurasian and American Perspectives (2005).

15. For a more detailed discussion of the challenges facing U.S. prosecutors seeking to build a case using evidence from abroad, as well as tips for overcoming them, see chapter 11.

16. See generally T. Markus Funk, Victims' Rights and Advocacy at the International Court 3 (2010) ("Well-intentioned rhetoric, deployed by diplomats often possessing only the vaguest understanding of what it takes to achieve a criminal conviction, is, after all, not a substitute for professionally-conducted investigation and prosecution. . . . Indeed, threats and promises not followed up by concrete action can, in the long run, become justice's most devastating enemy").

17. See appendix 1.

18. See appendix 2.

19. U.S. opposition to this, as with many similar international instruments, is based on domestic concerns about ceding an undue amount of national sovereignty to international bodies. See generally Patrick Fagan, *How U.N. Conventions on Women's*

and Children's Rights Undermine Family, Religion, and Sovereignty, HERITAGE FOUND. BACKGROUNDER, Feb. 5, 2001 ("Rather than supporting how the U.N. committees are using the [UNCRC] . . . to push policy changes that would ultimately deconstruct the two-parent married family and counter traditional religious norms, the Bush Administration should examine the documents emanating from U.N. implementing committees, develop a plan to strengthen the voices of U.N. members that oppose this agenda, and take the lead in restoring the U.N.'s traditional approach of letting sovereign nations determine their own domestic policies on marriage, parenting, and religion"), available at www.heritage.org/library/backgrounder/bg1407.html (last visited June 15, 2011). On the issue of whether this, and similar treaties, can impact national sovereignty, consider the Supremacy Clause of Article VI of the U.S. Constitution ("This Constitution, and the Laws of the United States which shall be made in Pursuance thereof; and *all Treaties made*, or which shall be made, under the Authority of the United States, shall be the supreme Law of the Land; and the Judges in every State shall be bound thereby, *any Thing in the Constitution or Laws of any State to the Contrary notwithstanding*" [emphasis added]), as well as the Vienna Convention on the Law of Treaties, Art. 27 ("A party may not invoke the provisions of its internal law as justification for its failure to perform a treaty").

20. As with the Rome Statute of the International Criminal Court, the United States often is a key drafter of some of the most impactful international treaties (even though it may not in the end become a ratifying signatory). See generally Cynthia Price Cohen, *The Role of the United States in the Drafting of the Convention on the Rights of the Child*, 20 EMORY INT'L L. REV. 185, 190–92 (2006) ("The United States was the most active in the expansion process, proposing more articles than any other nation in the Working Group. In total, the United States initiated seven articles, including Article 10 (family reunification), Article 19 (protection from abuse), and Article 25 (review of placement). In addition, the United States influenced the textual editing of almost every article. Only five other States proposed entirely new articles for the Convention: Denmark (Article 5, parental guidance), India (Article 6, survival and development), Argentina (Article 8, identity), Norway (Article 29, recovery and reintegration), and China (Article 33, narcotics). U.S. influence was so strong that some people referred to the Convention as the 'U.S. child rights treaty'") (citations omitted).

21. See generally International Council of Voluntary Agencies, Inter-Agency Standing Committee Reference Group on Humanitarian Action and Human Rights, FREQUENTLY ASKED QUESTIONS ON INTERNATIONAL HUMANITARIAN, HUMAN RIGHTS, AND REFUGEE LAW (2002) ("Human rights law also contains provisions obliging states to implement its rules, whether immediately or progressively. States must adopt a variety of legislative, administrative, judicial and other measures that may be necessary to give effect to the rights provided for in the various treaties. This includes providing for a remedy before domestic courts for violations of specific rights and ensuring that the remedy is effective. The fact that a state has a federal or devolved system of government does not affect a state's obligation to implement human rights law"), available at www.icva.ch/doc00001023.html#24 (last visited June 5, 2011).

22. Article 6(2).

23. Ibid. at 8(1).

24. Ibid. at 26(1).

25. Ibid. at 27(a).

26. Ibid. at 32(1).

27. Ibid. at 31(2).

28. Convention on the Rights of the Child, G.A. Res. 44/25, at Art. 43, Annex, U.N. Doc. A/RES/44/25/Annex (Nov. 20, 1989).

29. Ibid.

30. In 1996, moreover, the U.N. High Commissioner for Human Rights launched a "Plan of Action" to strengthen the implementation of the UNCRC. The purpose of this plan is to provide substantive support to the committee's work with the States Parties reporting process and assist, where necessary, in transforming recommendations into reality through the provisions of adequate resources, coordination and follow-up. See generally Muireann O'Briain, CHILD SEXUAL EXPLOITATION AND THE LAW: A REPORT ON THE INTERNATIONAL LEGAL FRAMEWORK AND CURRENT NATIONAL LEGISLATIVE AND ENFORCEMENT RESPONSES, available at www.csecworldcongress.org/.../ Theme%20 paper%20CSEC%20and%20the%20Law.pdf.

31. See, for example, U.S., OPTIONAL PROTOCOL TO THE CONVENTION ON THE RIGHTS OF THE CHILD ON THE SALE OF CHILDREN, CHILD PROSTITUTION AND CHILD PORNOGRAPHY (Jan. 22, 2010), available at www.state.gov/documents/organization/136023.pdf ("The United States became party to the Optional Protocol pursuant to Article 13(2). . . . Although the United States signed the Convention in February 1995, it has not proceeded to ratify it. Therefore, the United States stated in its instrument of ratification of the Optional Protocol that it understands that the United States assumes no obligations under the Convention on the Rights of the Child by becoming a party to the Protocol. . . . In the spirit of cooperation, the United States has provided as much information as possible on other issues raised, not limited to those that directly relate to U.S. obligations arising under the Optional Protocol").

32. See G.A. Res. 44/25, at Art. 44.

33. See generally EUR. CONSULT. ASS., CONVENTION ON THE PROTECTION OF CHILDREN AGAINST SEXUAL EXPLOITATION AND SEXUAL ABUSE, Doc. No. 201, at para. 7 (2007) ("Compliance with the [UNCRC] and its Protocols is monitored by the Committee on the Rights of the Child, which has come to the conclusion that children in Europe are not sufficiently protected against sexual exploitation and abuse. In particular the Committee underlines the lack of exhaustive national criminal legislation in this field in the State Parties, especially as concerns trafficking of children, 'sex tourism' and child pornography, the lack of a clearly defined minimum age for consenting sexual relations and lack of protection for children against abuse on the Internet. It has, for example, recommended that States develop an effective system of reporting and investigation, within a child-sensitive inquiry and judicial procedure, avoiding repeated interviews of child victims, in order to ensure better protection of child victims, including the protection of their right to privacy").

34. United Nations, OPTION PROTOCOL TO THE CONVENTION ON THE RIGHTS OF THE CHILD: ON THE SALE OF THE CHILD, CHILD PROSTITUTION AND CHILD PORNOGRAPHY, G.A. 54/263, Preamble, U.N. Doc. A/RES/54/263 (May 25, 2000) ("Considering that, in

order further to achieve the purposes of the Convention on the Rights of the Child and the implementation of its provisions, especially articles 1, 11, 21, 32, 33, 34, 35 and 36, it would be appropriate to extend the measures that States Parties should undertake in order to guarantee the protection of the child from the sale of children, child prostitution and child pornography").

35. Note that, under article 2(c), any representation by any means of a child engaged in real, *or simulated*, explicit sexual activities or any representation of the sexual parts of a child for primarily sexual purposes are proscribed. Ibid. at Art. 2.

36. See ibid. at Art. 8.

37. Ibid. at Art. 9(4) ("States Parties shall ensure that all child victims of the offences described in the present Protocol have access to adequate procedures to seek, without discrimination, compensation for damages from those legally responsible").

38. It, indeed, is difficult to overstate the importance of functioning extradition provisions between nations in terms of prosecution, deterrence, and prevention. Extradition's centrality to the burgeoning global effort to fight child sexual abuse lies in the ability of law enforcement authorities in one country to obtain the arrest and removal of a suspect, accused, or fugitive found in another jurisdiction. The reality is that, as the universe of "safe havens" for exploiters becomes ever smaller, children become safer.

39. See Patrick J. Gibbons, *Redeeming Peacekeeping: Using the U.N. Security Council to Internationalize the U.S. Military Ban on Prostitution Patronage*, 200 MIL. L. REV. 1, 20 (2009) ("The High Commissioner created the Special Rapporteur on the Sale of Children, Child Prostitution and Child Pornography in 1990. The Children's Rapporteur's mandate is to investigate the exploitation of children around the world and report to the General Assembly and Commission on Human Rights, recommending means to protect children's rights"). Note that the U.N. Council on Human Rights has replaced U.N. Commission on Human Rights, and that the Special Rapporteur now reports to the council.

40. See generally Laura McKinney, *International Adoption and the Hague Convention: Does Implementation of the Convention Protect the Best Interests of Children?*, 6 WHITTIER J. CHILD & FAM. ADVOC. 361 (2007).

41. See Funk, supra note 16, at 46–49.

42. See ibid. at 48.

43. See ibid. at 49.

44. See Eric Holder, Deputy Attorney General, Department of Justice, *Remarks at the International Conference on Combating Child Pornography on the Internet* (Sept. 29, 1999) (stating that federal prosecutions of Internet child pornographers have increased 10 percent every year since 1995, and approximately four hundred Internet child pornographers are convicted each year), available at www.usdoj.gov/criminal/cybercrime/dagceos.html (last visited June 15, 2011).

45. TOC Convention, supra chapter 4, note 13.

46. The TOC Convention went into force on September 29, 2003.

47. The three protocols target specific substantive areas of organized crime—namely, human trafficking (The Protocol to Prevent, Suppress and Punish Trafficking in Persons, Especially Women and Children), smuggling (The Protocol to Prevent,

Suppress and Punish Trafficking in Persons, Especially Women and Children), and arms smuggling (The Protocol to Prevent, Suppress and Punish Trafficking in Persons, Especially Women and Children).

48. U.N. summary of the convention, available at www.unodc.org/unodc/en/treaties/CTOC/index.html (last visited June 15, 2011).

49. See TOC Convention, supra chapter 4, note 13, at Art. 2(a) and (b) (describing "organized criminal groups" as three or more individuals "acting in concert with the aim of committing one or more serious crimes or offences," and defining *serious crime* as "conduct constituting an offence punishable by a maximum deprivation of liberty of at least four years").

50. See ibid. at Arts. 3(1)(a) and 23.

51. See ibid. at Art. 18 ("Mutual legal assistance shall be afforded to the fullest extent possible under relevant laws, treaties, agreements and arrangements of the requested State Party with respect to investigations, prosecutions and judicial proceedings in relation to the offences for which a legal person may be held liable in accordance with article 10 of this Convention in the requesting State Party"); ibid. at Art. 29 ("States Parties shall promote training and technical assistance that will facilitate extradition and mutual legal assistance. Such training and technical assistance may include language training, secondments and exchanges between personnel in central authorities or agencies with relevant responsibilities").

52. See generally ibid. at Art. 29(3). The convention wisely does not limit the circumstances under which mutual legal assistance should be granted. See ibid. at Art. 29(3)(i) (the article's catch-all: mutual legal assistance includes "any other type of assistance that is not contrary to the domestic law of the requested State Party").

53. Ibid. at Art. 23.

54. Ibid. at Art. 24.

55. OPTIONAL PROTOCOL TO PREVENT, SUPPRESS AND PUNISH TRAFFICKING IN PERSONS, ESPECIALLY WOMEN AND CHILDREN, G.A. Res. 55/383, U.N. Doc. A/RES/55/383 (Dec. 25, 2003), available at www.unodc.org/documents/treaties/UNTOC/Publications/TOC%20Convention/TOCebook-e.pdf.

56. See Roza Pati, *States' Positive Obligations with Respect to Human Trafficking: The European Court of Human Rights Breaks New Ground in Rantsev v. Cyprus and Russia*, 29 B.U. INT'L L.J. 79, 115 (2011) ("[The Trafficking Protocol] provides a globally accepted definition of human trafficking, and it determines the scope of its application, as well as that of the United Nations Convention against Transnational Organized Crime, to trafficking activities. Namely, the . . . Protocol defines the scope of application to the prevention, investigation, and prosecution of the . . . Protocol offenses, and the protection of victims") (citation omitted).

57. Note, however, that some scholars have commented that there is no classification of the crime within the framework of international law. See Alison Cole, *Reconceptualizing Female Trafficking: The Inhumane Trade in Women*, 26 WOMEN'S RTS. L. REP. 97, 111–12 (2005).

58. G.A. Res. 55/383, supra note 55, at Art. 3(c).

59. Ibid. at iv (foreword).

60. Ibid. at Art. 3(a).

61. Ibid. at Art. 6(3)(a–d).

62. Ibid. at Art 6(6) ("Each State Party shall ensure that its domestic legal system contains measures that offer victims of trafficking in persons the possibility of obtaining compensation for damage suffered").

63. COMMISSION PROPOSAL FOR A DIRECTIVE OF THE EUROPEAN PARLIAMENT AND OF THE COUNCIL ON COMBATING THE SEXUAL ABUSE, SEXUAL EXPLOITATION OF CHILDREN AND CHILD PORNOGRAPHY, REPEALING FRAMEWORK DECISION 2004/68/JHA, COM (2010), available at www.europeanlawmonitor.org/legislation/2010/COM201094text.pdf.

64. See ibid.

65. Ibid.

66. EUR. CONSULT. ASS., PROTECTION OF CHILDREN AGAINST SEXUAL EXPLOITATION AND SEXUAL ABUSE, Doc. No. 201 (2007), available at http://conventions.coe.int/Treaty/EN/Treaties/Word/201.doc (last visited June 15, 2011).

67. See generally HUMAN TRAFFICK AND TRANSNATIONAL CRIME, supra chapter 11, section D.

68. INTEGRATED PLAN OF ACTION TO PREVENT AND COMBAT HUMAN TRAFFICKING WITH SPECIAL FOCUS ON CHILDREN AND WOMEN, available at http://webapps01.un.org/vawdatabase/uploads/Plan%20of%20ACtion%20to%20Combat%20Trafficking.doc (last visited June 15, 2011).

9

Investigating Child Exploitation Cases

A S WITH ALMOST ALL CRIMINAL CONDUCT, investigations in the child sexual exploitation context can be as simple as following up a tip from, say, a computer repair shop reporting that one of its customers has child pornography on his computer, and as involved as a lengthy undercover investigation of overseas child pornography syndicates. No matter how the case comes to law enforcement's attention, however, there are certain basic steps investigators must take in order to ensure that they build a strong case, while at the same time safeguarding the rights of the suspect(s).

A. The Benefits of Coordination—Adopting the Task Force Approach

The initial report of illegal sexual conduct with a minor is often made to local authorities. Yet the investigation of illegal conduct that involves interstate communications facilities, the dissemination of child pornography over the Internet, or the transportation of minors or child pornography across state lines requires federal involvement.

Local authorities are of course trained to respond, largely reactively, to crimes and to take all appropriate investigative steps. They, however, are also restricted in their ability to cross jurisdictional boundaries and, given these limitations, will often be unable to obtain search warrants outside of their jurisdiction, nor will they have access to the most well-trained computer analysts. Simply put, local authorities will generally be restricted by both budgetary limitations and by the authority given to them. Moreover, state laws and sentencing schemes are not as developed, nor do they provide for the most serious penalties, when compared to the federal system. It is, therefore, not uncommon for a local police department to gather significant evidence, put together a solid case against the suspected child exploiter, and to then leave the continuation of the investigation regarding the offender's contact with other offenders, or his international dissemination of contraband, for another day. This is not a negative reflection on local authorities; rather, it is a realistic understanding of the defined parameters of the typical local investigative authority's ability to investigate and pursue the most serious charges.

Yet the volume of activity in some local jurisdictions is staggering. The Cook County State's Attorney's Office in Chicago, as an example, prosecutes some 30,000 criminal felonies per year.[1] And Cook County is merely one county out of seventeen comprising the Northern District of Illinois. That volume includes some of the worst offenders.

Often when offenders are charged with the "hands-on" molestation of minors there is no federal jurisdiction, and the states are usually in the best position to address issues such as removal of a child from his family, the placement of the child into protective foster care, and the issuance of protective orders against offenders who have expressed the desire to harm potential victims and witnesses against them.

The federal authorities, for their part, have the ability to serve search warrants across the country (and, in fact, across the globe), and can recruit law enforcement partners to simultaneously work different "leads" in numerous domestic or international jurisdictions. Computer forensics resources, such as those possessed by the FBI's Computer Recovery and Response Teams (CART Teams), which have trained professionals who analyze seized hard drives and provide immediate details to an investigative team, are sparse in low-population areas and those localities with a limited tax base. Federal agencies such as the FBI, Bureau of Immigration and Customs Enforcement (ICE), and United States Postal Inspectors, moreover, have specified undercover agent training on how to legally and effectively record their contacts with, and investigations of, targets. These types of high-level resources are often unavailable to local authorities.

The role of a child exploitation task force, composed of both local *and* federal investigators and prosecutors, is, therefore, critical to the effective investigation and prosecution of child exploitation cases. The federal prosecutor's office must establish a network of contacts with local authorities in order to gather evidentiary leads that may uncover a network of child exploiters who either share their contraband over the Internet or share their "exploits" with other offenders in other jurisdictions.

A direct state-federal line of communication is, indeed, critical for a number of reasons. First, the federal sentencing guidelines, although advisory, offer criminal sanctions that are significantly more severe than those contained in most state sentencing schemes. More importantly, the federal statutes subsequent to the PROTECT Act provide a number of statutory mandatory minimum sentences not found in comparable state proscriptions. If, for example, a local authority has the ability to charge production of child pornography and can use the federal threat of a mandatory fifteen-year sentence for each produced image, the chances of law enforcement being able to use the threat of the comparatively severe sentence as a "bargaining chip" to motivate the defendant to "flip" and identify other exploiters with whom he had contact rise exponentially.

Second, federal law enforcement agents have access to the image libraries maintained by certain agencies, such as the FBI and ICE, reflecting evidence seized over decades in various federal and foreign cases. This enables the task force to identify the actual victims depicted in, say, traded images, and notify them, as required by federal victim notification laws. The libraries maintained by federal law enforcement agencies can also rebut some of the commonly presented defenses, such as a challenge to whether the image is that of a "real" child, or a claim that the pornography does not depict a juvenile. Finally, the ability of federal law enforcement to "cut leads" to other agents in other jurisdictions can result in the efficient and timely investigation of other worthwhile targets (and, significantly, allows such investigation prior to the other targets having a chance to destroy evidence, obstruct justice, and/or flee the jurisdiction after being "tipped off" online).[2]

That said, this ability to send investigative leads that result in separate prosecutions in separate jurisdictions is not without complications. In fact, it was the increasing number of multiple jurisdictional investigations and prosecutions that led to the creation of the Attorney General's Advisory Committee. Composed of experienced professionals, the committee can aid federal and local agents at the early stages of the investigation by reviewing the proposals of the law enforcement agency to ensure that (1) the victims' rights are protected, (2) discovery material can be uniformly shared and turned over to the defense as required by law, and (3) duplicative or cumulative efforts do not frustrate the efficient prosecution of groups of interconnected offenders.[3]

The need for a task force operation is perhaps greatest in the area of human trafficking investigations. The first responder to a human trafficking case is often a vice squad police officer who follows up a report of prostitution. On-scene investigation often results in the collection of false identification documents, or a distorted interview with the minor who is bound to protect her "pimp" due to fear and coercion. A trained local officer who can recognize the markings of a human trafficking situation can call on federal task force officers for a variety of resources that may be unavailable to him: surveillance of the location—whether in-state or elsewhere—where the victim resides; review of the identification or immigration documents for a determination of whether they were manufactured by a document mill; search warrants of the victim's e-mail accounts and/or the website where the victim was advertised for her "services"; and investigation into the property where the victim is being housed. Effective training and sharing of information among task force officers can, in short, be critical to the effective prosecution of human trafficking cases.

B. Evidence Collection

As earlier chapters of this book have described, the bulk of the evidence that will eventually be used to convict today's sexual offenders will be electronic. The investigator's main objective in child pornography cases will be to establish probable cause that the offender was knowingly storing, receiving, manufacturing, distributing, or selling child pornography. In traveler cases, this approach will be supplemented by evidence demonstrating the luring aspect of the offender's criminal activity, such as e-mails, tweets, text messages, phone messages, and stored chats, which establish the defendant's intent to travel to his victim or transport her in interstate commerce. In both types of cases, the investigator will also be seeking to establish the interstate connection applicable for the charge(s) being contemplated. Knowing where this evidence is stored is the critical first step in investigating a target's conduct. Knowing how third parties preserve and store data, moreover, is critical to the investigator's ability to obtain evidence that will support the probable cause necessary for a search warrant.

The Electronic Communication Privacy Act of 1986 and its subsequent amendments[4] provide an essential tool in combating child exploitation and human trafficking. Through the act, investigators can use both subpoenas and court orders to obtain information from Internet service providers and other online storage facilities where offenders maintain their vast collections of child pornography. Search warrants for computers and other electronic data storage media, after all, remain the primary tool for gathering an individual's personal cache of contraband, details of his communications with minors, and evidence of his travel and grooming tools in the form of receipts, images, and third-party documents.

1. Consent

Although certain investigators have had success with a "knock and talk" approach to entering a residence and subsequently obtaining consent to search an offender's computer, these consent searches can be challenged in pretrial motions to suppress where defendants may raise questions concerning the voluntariness of the consent.[5] The trial court will need to conduct a hearing in order to determine if the circumstances were such that the consent was freely given. Factors to consider in the analysis can include the education level of the defendant and the totality of the circumstances surrounding the agent's entry into the residence (How many investigators were there? How physically close were they to the defendant when he "voluntarily" consented? Were the investigators armed? Exactly what was said preceding the purported consent? What was the "tone" of the investigator's questioning and request for consent? Was the consent written or oral, and were there any witnesses?).[6]

In certain cases, another member of the residence may, if she has complete access to the computer, consent to the search of the computer, thereby allowing investigators to access a jointly held computer.[7] The Supreme Court, however, recently addressed a residential search where the defendant refused consent, but the spouse consented to the search when investigators sought both individuals' consent.[8] The investigators relied on the spouse's consent over the refusal of the defendant.[9] The Court concluded that the search could not be deemed reasonable because the defendant (1) shared the residence with his spouse and (2) had explicitly asserted his refusal for the search.[10] Put another way, defendant's wife's consent did not "override" or otherwise vitiate defendant's refusal.

Certain factors that may be taken into consideration in deciding whether there is sole or joint access are as follows:

- whether the computer is stored in a common area
- whether the computer is password protected
- whether both residents share the same password
- whether others are permitted access to the computer[11]

The consent doctrine is not limited to searches of the defendant's residence or computers. Investigators may use the consent of one side of a computer conversation ("one-party consent") as permission to enter that conversation either in an undercover capacity or merely to observe.[12] This form of consent has been used for years to allow law enforcement to record "consensual" conversations when one side to that conversation agrees.[13] The setting of a chat room or e-mail does not affect the constitutionality of this method of investigation.

Yet there are still some unique settings for consent searches of computers, specifically in the context of the employee/employer relationship, and when computer technicians are involved. As to the former, most employers provide a "banner" across the employee's computer screen when he logs in, reminding him that he has no expectation of privacy on his work computer. IT Departments generally have access to an employee's workstation, to his files, and to the materials stored on his work desktop. They may also have access to the sites he has visited by reviewing Internet logs. An employee is, therefore, hard-pressed to persuasively argue that he has a legitimate expectation of privacy in his work computer and work files. Moreover, well-grounded employer interests, such as ensuring work efficiency and protecting the integrity of the workplace, allow employers this access, and most employees are warned of this access either upon hiring, through the computer banner, and/or through an employee handbook. As such, it would be an uphill climb for most defendants to challenge an employer's search of his computer that revealed contraband.[14]

Similarly, when a defendant drops off his computer to have it repaired by a technician, he relinquishes his right to privacy by consenting to allow the technician to look through his machine.[15] As such, if the technician discovers contraband, the technician may turn that over to law enforcement for prosecution. The risk for law enforcement in this area occurs if the technician (not a state actor) reports the contraband, and *then* the law enforcement officer (a state actor) directs the technician to conduct a thorough search. This would constitute a state actor circumventing the Fourth Amendment requirement, and will likely result in the suppression of the evidence.[16]

2. Search Warrants

Obtaining a search warrant for a computer has become commonplace for investigators of child exploitation cases. The manner in which search warrants are obtained, however, varies significantly from jurisdiction to jurisdiction. Although it is clear that probable cause to believe that evidence of the crime will be found on the computer to be searched continues to be the applicable standard, some courts have required investigators to set forth a detailed protocol for searching computers that preserves the First Amendment rights of the property owner and ensures that the scope is not exceeded.[17] For example, magistrate judges in the Northern District of Illinois require law enforcement agents to return the computers and electronic storage devices within 30 days of seizure, unless contraband is discovered. The same judges, as well as others around the nation, have also defined the types of permissible searches.[18]

Establishing that certain evidence will be preserved on a computer is, however, not always as straightforward as one might assume. For example, if a sex traveler chats with his victim nightly and encourages her to travel to see him for a "romantic weekend," it is not a given that those chats will be found on the offender's computer. Those chats occur in real time, and unless the traveler has referenced in his chats that he is storing them or has mentioned previous chats as if he has a library of them, it may not be appropriate for the investigator to make the inferential leap to assume such chats will be stored. Similarly, evidence that an offender is a member of a particular website may not be sufficient to show probable cause that he downloaded images from that website and that those images will, therefore, be found on his personal computer.[19] Linking the offending behavior to what the agent believes will be found on the computer seems simple in theory, but often threatens to involve inferential steps that may be too much of a stretch. For example, probable cause that an individual molested a child does not naturally lead to the conclusion that there will be child pornography on that offender's computer.[20]

In such instances, the investigator, if he himself is not an expert, may need to rely on an expert's affidavit to establish probable cause. The expert will establish the behavior of the particular type of offender and may use his Fed. R. Evid. 702 opinion to conclude that the chats will be stored by this particular offender based on the investigator's own personal review of the evidence.

Investigators must also be aware of the most recent forms of computer storage devices in order to properly set forth a list of items to be seized during the search, as well as a summary of where the investigator expects to find the items. Child exploitation offenders tend to have extensive expertise in the area of computer usage, transmission, and storage. Recognizing that a pen or keychain can be a camera, that "flash drives" can be as small as an inch and still store thousands of images, and that computer cameras can be merely a pinprick above a screen, the law enforcement officer must make every effort to set forth a comprehensive, but also logically justifiable, list of items to be seized during the search.

3. Subpoenas to Third Parties

The types of information that can be obtained from a third-party provider include transactional information, account information, real-time chats, old e-mails that have been read already, and new e-mails that have not yet been opened. The investigator needs to know what he is looking for, because the level of privacy interest is different for each type of potential evidence. For example, there is little expectation of privacy in a defendant's account information. As such, serving a grand jury or administrative subpoena on a third-party service provider suffices to obtain basic account information such as the name of the subscriber, the address and the phone number linked to that account, and the associated screen names. Other types of information that can be obtained with a subpoena include the length and type of service and the manner in which the subscriber paid for the service. No notice to the subscriber is required to be given.

Federal agencies such as the FBI, in fact, have the ability to issue administrative subpoenas in child exploitation investigations to gather this type of information without the use of a grand jury. The benefit of such a subpoena is that, since the agency is not required to turn over the material to a prosecutor until the case is presented for prosecution, the operation can remain covert for a longer period of time, which provides the agency an opportunity to decide whether the material should be presented to the state for prosecution instead. With a grand jury subpoena, a court order is required before any materials can be provided to a state prosecuting authority.

In contrast to what can be obtained with a simple subpoena, unopened e-mails are much like an opened letter sitting in a mailbox. There *is* an expectation of privacy in its contents, and, as such, a search warrant will be required to open it.

The investigator can also employ a provision of the Patriot Act, 18 U.S.C. 2703(d), to enable him to gather this information. When collecting stored electronic communications, the investigator must determine where the particular communication sits along a continuum of privacy levels, one side being the least invasive (obtained with a subpoena) and the other end being the most invasive (a wiretap that records every keystroke of an offender's online communication).

At the "lower-privacy" end of the continuum are other options available to law enforcement: pen registers, trap and trace monitoring, and consensual recordings. The pen registers and trap and trace logs will not provide the investigator with content, but will provide him with the numbers that are placing the calls and the numbers that are receiving the calls. In the case of computer communications, this will be in the form of Internet protocol addresses. Consensual recordings will involve a cooperating individual who has agreed to have his side of the computer conversation recorded and, as such, is consensually agreeing to the recording of a normally private computer discussion. Search warrants (the often time-intensive holy grail for investigators) for an account can provide the investigator with stored e-mails, buddy lists, sites visited, newsgroups accessed, and chat rooms visited. All of these will be reflected on logs showing the times of each of the activities. Essentially, the warrant can gather the electronic footprint of every website an offender visited over a period of time, exactly when he visited there, and what he did while there.

The investigator's task here is to ensure that he obtains the information in a timely fashion, since huge volumes of information are regularly "dumped" by third-party providers. He must ensure that his probable cause does not get "stale," but rather reflects an *existing* link between recent activity and the likelihood that evidence of that activity will be retrieved from the third-party provider. Preservation orders are available to preserve the data if the law enforcement officer reaches out in a timely fashion. Staleness of the probable cause link can result in a warrant being rejected by a reviewing judge, or, even worse, the destruction of key evidence.

If this electronic evidence is not enough, and the agent can show that no other means of investigation will suffice to gather the information needed to prove the illegal activity, the investigator can seek a wiretap to gather real-time recordings of live conversations. The wiretap order must be approved by the Attorney General of the United States or his designee, and must be obtained following the strict requirements of 18 U.S.C. 2510 *et seq.* It will be "good" or "active" for a period of thirty days, and the agent will be required to provide activity or "status" reports every ten days. The agent will also be required to minimize any surreptitiously recorded private conversations that are either (1) privileged or (2) not pertaining to the subject illegal activity for which the authorization was sought. All of the tools described above have provisions for exigent circumstances, such as a likelihood of death and bodily harm, enabling the agent in the rare case to conduct searches without prior court authorization.

4. Identifying Key Categories of Evidence

In the early days of computer evidence seizures, a traditional search of a computer solely consisted of culling images from the subject computer's hard drive. As computer technology advanced, and more federal agencies began using computer analysis and recovery teams, the sophistication of the searches kept pace. Prosecutors now work side by side with computer analysts sharing their theories of the case, the knowledge obtained from the investigation, and potential charges that may be pressed.

As a result, law enforcement teams are now better able to identify items of evidentiary value, and can prune their searches to seek them out. Open communication between the computer analyst and the prosecution team also broadens the scope of the search; for example, rather than merely identifying child pornography, an analyst may be provided a list of potential victims sourced through interviews, chats, and materials obtained by subpoena. Word searches may result in recovering travel documents, background information regarding a victim or potential victim, and Internet browser logs showing mapping requests for the victim's residence or school. The computer analysis is also no longer deemed a one-time project, but rather one that must be addressed again as evidence develops, and as new leads develop. What may seem like an unimportant receipt for a piece of jewelry at the time of the initial agent review, for example, may turn out to be, after the victim is interviewed, the crucial gift that helped to lure and lower the defenses of the minor victim.

a. Online Sexual Exploitation

The investigative team will determine what charges to bring based on the evidence recovered. Rarely is possession of child pornography the only offense that can be charged after a thorough computer search, because Internet logs will also reflect when various images were (1) *received*, and (2) whether those images were *sent* to another offender. File-sharing software can reflect vast volumes of images of child pornography being traded among offenders, many of whom will be required to upload certain "acceptable" images before being given access to the collections of others in the file-sharing group. These file sharers will often catalog their images in such a way that the offender can shop for the exact type of image: for example, "four-year-old twins," "fellatio," or "thirteen-year-old and daddy."

Searching for *manufactured* images may, howover, require more time. Comparing images recovered from the residence of an offender that depict distinctive features of that residence (for example, blankets recovered from the bedroom) can reveal whether images were created within the offender's domicile. The search team should take photos of each room of the residence, and, as the computer search team reviews images, the team can parallel the background setting of photos to identify images that may have been created within the residence.

E-mail communications and chats can further support a finding of production of child pornography where offender(s) discuss events that support that manufacturing took place on a particular date and time. A sleepover party for a child documented on a computer calendar, coupled with an e-mail regarding the minors within the offender's home to another offender, and child images saved on that same day can establish the manufacture of images on that date.

Deleted images within the computer's slack or cache area can, as discussed in the defenses section (chapter 13), often be retrieved in spite of an offender's efforts to destroy the files. The timing of the deletion can often be ascertained, aiding the prosecutor in developing a theory of the defendant's intent. Deletion of images shortly after being approached by law enforcement can also lead to an obstruction of justice charge.[21]

Internet logs can also serve to negate an offender's claim that images were obtained by mistake or accident while collecting adult pornography. Investigations have shown instances of an offender's Internet log reflecting an hour-long e-mail communication with a potential victim, followed by an hour-long downloading session of child pornographic images, followed by a five-minute "research" session on the possession statute on a law school's website.[22]

The way in which an offender catalogs his contraband can also hold significant evidentiary value. Aside from the catalog itself, which mirrors the offender's interests and demonstrates how he personally views the images (for example, storing pornographic images of a victim in the same file as nonpornographic images), the amount of time spent downloading and cataloging the images (which can be determined by an analyst) reflects the intensity of the offender's interest (and, thus, can help establish intent). Ascertaining the number of hours spent downloading and cataloging can also speak to the dangerousness of an offender's actions by demonstrating his willingness to take on the risk of being detected while at work, home, or in the presence of others.

Encrypting his contraband also reflects the offender's knowledge of the criminality of his actions. Encryption poses a significant obstacle for the investigator. In spite of significant advancements in computer searching tools, if an offender uses a long enough encryption key, he may effectively prevent law enforcement's ability to access his contraband. In one such case, the defendant so effectively encrypted the massive amounts of data on his computer that the prosecutors' efforts to partner with both NASA and NSA to crack the code failed after a two-year effort.[23]

Aside from images, banking and financial tracking software can show purchases of equipment for manufacturing, gifts for travelers to use in the grooming process, and even evidence of the purchase of child pornography.[24] Electronic address books can provide access to both other offenders and other victims. Selected "friends" on Facebook and other social networking sites may lead to the same.

The bottom line is that, as technology develops, so must the investigator and prosecutor's level of sophistication and understanding; only by keeping up to date can search warrants be most effectively drafted and executed, can evidence be most efficiently reviewed, and the most appropriate charges be brought.

b. Exploitation

In spite of an offender's efforts to encrypt and hide his contraband, it remains a common trait of online molesters that they (1) seek to share their exploits with other offenders in an effort to both rationalize their behavior and bolster their ranks within the online molesting community, and that, as discussed above, they (2) eventually seek out actual "hands-on" victims to exploit (and, typically, to film during such exploitation).[25] As such, offenders often document their molestations either through video "snags," where their sexual exploitation is documented in a short video that can be shared with other offenders, or they perform their molestations live by broadcasting to their well-vetted group of known offenders.[26] This need to boast about their illegal sexual exploits has led to the demise and subsequent prosecution of more than one molester.[27] In the case of the offender whose encrypted contraband could not be cracked by the National Aeronautics and Space Administration (NASA) and the National Security Agency (NSA), it was a live broadcast of a molestation of his "grandson" David that was "snagged" by another offender (in violation of the rules of the molester group), which led to his conviction for production of child pornography. Five-year-old David's truthful interview describing the events could not be corroborated until the other offender's computer was seized and the video snag was retrieved.[28]

An expert in the field of videography and photography can also provide the investigation team with significant links to the locale of the molestation and the photo. This link can often lead to information regarding the dates and times of the molestation and the presence of other individuals.

Traditional sexual molestation investigative tools, moreover, can prove to be equally useful in the child molestation context: a rape kit employed by a professional medical care provider, a blood test and DNA test linking semen and other bodily fluids to the offender, and crime scene analysis collecting fiber and hair samples and taking photographs. Yet, in the child molestation context, this collection rarely occurs as a reactive process. In the child exploitation world, as discussed earlier, the offenders are master manipulators who prey on the weakest personalities in society, and, therefore, their crimes often remain undetected, sometimes for years. The investigator in this context is more like an archeologist digging for clues, and his personal Valley of the Kings is generally the world of electronic evidence.

c. Labor Trafficking

Although this book primarily examines child sexual exploitation, child *labor* exploitation is an equally important, and often interconnected, topic that we want to at least flag for the reader. The labor *and* sex trafficker's key tools are falsified documents. If the labor trafficker can create a false persona of a legal individual working for an entity that has allegedly checked her visa, driver's license, birth certificate, or other identifying documents, it will be very difficult for the prosecutor to press charges until he can prove that the provision of the documents was an intentional effort on the part of the labor trafficker to hide the age, identity, nationality, and visa status of the victim. False document cases, when viewed in isolation, fail to illustrate the significant impact that false identification documents have on the proliferation of labor trafficking. The insidiousness of the crime is magnified when one recognizes that the victim is often told that she is being aided by obtaining the false documentation that allows her to "work" within the community. Often these victims come from countries where public corruption is pervasive. As such, the victim may not recognize any potential avenue of escape, and follows the "company line" when confronted by law enforcement, due to her fear of being deported back to a place of high risk.

Labor investigations, like child trafficking investigations, also require financial analysis of the work being performed by the trafficker's victims. Only with a complete analysis of the cost of the labor can the reality of the harm be understood.

Careful and complete site searches are critical in the investigation of all human trafficking cases. Nothing is more effective in explaining the victim's constraints than viewing the scene where she was held. Often these sparse quarters will house only mattresses, and victims will be supplied with just a single change of clothes. In extreme instances, the rooms will be locked from the outside by the trafficker, but often, it is merely the lack of any basic clothing that allows the trafficker to keep hold of his victims. Preying on the understanding that these victims often do not speak the local language, have no money to go elsewhere, and have no basic food or clothing to even exit the premises and seek out work, the traffickers keep control over their victims, psychologically and physically narrowing their world and reinforcing their perceived need to rely on the trafficker to survive. Documenting the material items within a trafficking premises, taking photographs, and interviewing victims regarding their daily lifestyle brings the reality of the slavery to life for the court and the jury.

d. Sex Trafficking

Although confinement, false identification, and psychological control are factors common to both labor trafficking and sex trafficking, the trafficker's habit of displaying grooming behavior and manipulation often differentiate these two practices. Girls who have been trafficked for sexual purposes often describe an offender who treats his victim kindly and furnishes her with gifts, food, drugs, and attention. Due to the gifts and attention, the victims often believe that they want to go with the offender.[29] Providing drugs to girls who are trafficked is a common way for offenders to maintain control over their victims. This method has the added benefits for the trafficker of lowering the girl's inhibitions to extreme sexual deviance and numerous sexual acts, and provides incentives to the victim not to flee. Drug addiction, moreover, hampers the victim's ability to think independently and separate herself from the confinement by clouding her rational thoughts and blocking her problem-solving capabilities. For a graphic example, see the movie *Taken*.

Sex trafficking takes numerous forms, but almost all have one common thread: money. Sex trafficking is lucrative for the offender, and, as such, an investigation into the money remains a top priority of any investigation. One investigator always includes an IRS agent on her task force team, repeating the common understanding that the offenders are more concerned about losing their profits than about getting caught.[30]

Nor are sex traffickers necessarily particularly adept at hiding their profits. Some have been known to have their clients use credit cards to pay for sex acts; most, however, resort to a pure cash trade. Cash equates to money laundering because the offender who is reaping the profits of tens of thousands of dollars from the sexual victimization of minor girls must find a way to process that money through some seemingly legitimate entity or business. Tax charges, money laundering charges, and forfeiture charges are available. At a bare minimum, the statutes provide that the profits of the illegal trade can be seized.

A traditional sex crimes investigation must be conducted as a part of the child sex trafficking investigation, and, as such, all the victims—child and adult—must be physically examined for injuries and abuse. The pimp makes his money from selling the girl as often as possible to as many "clients" as possible. A thorough medical examination with a rape kit can reveal multiple DNA types within the girl, bruising, lacerations, burns, and unique injuries that come from the idiosyncratic and perverse desires of different customers. Such medical examination can significantly aid a prosecutor by corroborating a victim's testimony (for example, a rope burn on a victim's arm can support testimony that she was tied up by one of the men to whom she was sold).

5. Conducting Online Investigations and Undercover Work

Certain federal agencies, including the FBI, ICE, and the U.S. Postal Inspection Service, are trained in the sensitive area of undercover operations. A growing number of local authorities have also expanded their ability to train and support local police officers in their efforts to conduct undercover operations. Agents are trained to spot the types of messages that offenders post on Internet chat rooms, message boards, and on social networking websites, and are experienced at identifying the underlying meaning in a disguised invitation to engage in illegal sexual activity. Accessing the secretive world of the sexual offender remains one of the most promising ways to reveal intent and to disprove claims of "fantasy" or "mistake."

Offenders communicate with other offenders in chat rooms, through e-mails, text messages, twitter, and on the phone. Gaining access to private chat rooms by posing as a like-minded fellow traveler can provide open access to the offender's thoughts. A Craigslist ad for a "dating service," for example, may appear to be unremarkable to the untrained eye, whereas a trained agent may be able to spot the criminal intent through uniquely coded word choice and phraseology.

Entrapment is another pitfall awaiting the unwary. The trained agent will understand the ramifications of the Supreme Court's ruling in *Jacobson v. United States*,[31] will be certain to document the offender's predisposition to commit the crime, and will be careful not to offer the offender any improper inducements to engage in the illegal conduct. Generally, this is not a problem, as evidenced by the few cases where entrapment has actually been advanced as a successful defense.[32] Trained investigators learn quickly that commonplace statements and everyday images can have an entirely different meaning to the sexual offender.

Once, in an interview with convicted child molester Brian Urbanawiz, one of the authors asked him how he knew that a particular image was created by now-convicted child molester Charles Burt. The image was banal in that it did not depict nudity, but rather showed another child molester, Richard Fleming (convicted by the other coauthor), with his arm gently around a five-year-old boy victim. Urbanawiz excitedly described the photo's strong allure to him: the placement of the arm of the offender, the innocent look of the victim as he smilingly looked over his shoulder at the photographer, and the message of "pure innocence and beauty mixed with devilishness." As he held the photo for minutes, he gasped, "Do you know how much this is worth? At least $5,000." Trained agents learn to spot the characteristics of photos, chats, and postings that suggest something more than an average everyday message. The trick becomes how to obtain entry into their highly protected (largely online) world.

One successful way is to pose as a potential victim. Creating a persona of a thirteen-year-old girl, going to a website regarding Justin Beiber, and talking about his songs is an example. There is no need for the agent to find a private webpage at this introductory stage, because the offender is in his grooming stage and will be trolling the places where he can find his preferred age level and gender. An open chat will begin, which will generally turn into an opportunity for the offender to invite the minor to a separate, private chat room.

The groomer will attempt to elicit an e-mail address from the victim in order to continue his communication. The agent, therefore, must create an entirely false identity, including a residence, school, etc., because investigations have shown that while the offender is chatting to his new victim, he is also investigating where she lives, what grade she is in school, details about the school, and any information about the family that he can obtain. Indeed, the offender may well question the victim on details concerning the above in an attempt to ferret out law enforcement posing as a child. The agent, meanwhile, will be recording each keystroke via screen-capture software such as Camtasia in order to document the luring.

As so vividly brought to the American public's attention by Chris Hansen in his Dateline NBC undercover show *To Catch a Predator*, in a matter of days, in a traveler case, the offender may travel to meet his new victim. The diligent agent throughout this process has been careful to portray his child persona as someone who is not sexually active, is not permitted to see the adult during school hours (thus verifying the age of the victim), and will be sprinkling the record of his e-mails and chats with various facts that can later be used to corroborate the offender's criminal intent. The more details about the meeting the agent can obtain from the offender during this process, the stronger the likelihood of proving the defendant's unlawful objectives. If the offender tells the "minor" that he will bring condoms, champagne, and flowers, and he then arrives at the meeting place with those items in his car, the defense claim that this was all merely a fantasy will be rendered unpersuasive.

If the agent is required to actually get on a telephone and pose as a minor girl, moreover, there are a number of voice synthesizing tools that she can use. But generally, a higher-pitched voice of a female law enforcement officer is all that is needed. When agents are trained to use age-specific jargon and nervous laughter or giggles at the moments that sexual activity is being discussed, these consensual recordings can be quite effective and have duped many offenders in the past. It, in the end, will be up to the trier of fact to determine whether the defendant actually believed the young-sounding officer to be a child.

As for undercover operations in the area of distributing child pornography, agents generally must have the electronic "goods" to gain access to a file-sharing site. Once a particular site is located, the agent must be able to upload an image that will be acceptable to the file server. In the past, corrupted images of space shuttle photos have been used in undercover operations, allowing the agent to access the server and gather some images before the "bogus" image is rejected or questioned by those running the child pornography site or server.

The use of confidential informants—meaning an individual who provides information to law enforcement for leniency or a fee—is, not surprisingly, rare in child exploitation investigations. However, cooperating defendants remain an option as more cases are charged and defendants face increasingly significant sentences. Often these cooperators provide historical information that aid law enforcement in identifying victims or locations; but occasionally, a cooperating defendant can provide "real-time" information that will enable a law enforcement officer to assume his identity and stand in for him on the Internet. Being able to assume the identity of an offender can allow the investigator to gain the trust of other targets in closed communities or membership-based web communities. This access is invaluable in overcoming the barriers offenders set up to block such access.

The challenging aspect of such cooperation will be the extent of the deal the government chooses to offer such a cooperator. As will be discussed in chapter 12, victim issues should remain front and center in the prosecutor's analysis concerning whether to provide leniency to a potentially cooperating child exploitation offender. A balance must, after all, be struck between the rights of the victim to restitution, resolution, information, and redress and the prosecutor's need to remove another offender from society and protect any unidentified victims.

a. Some New Challenges Associated with Online Cases

Successful undercover operations create some unique issues. First, the proliferation of undercover operations in recent years has caused a virtual backlog of cases being federally prosecuted. By taking down a large file-sharing conspiracy, an agency might generate hundreds, if not thousands, of "leads" to other jurisdictions. As these leads are sent out, critical time is passing and the freshness of the probable cause may wane, causing the warrant to become stale and rejected by the reviewing judge. Agents are permitted to return to the source and once again engage in undercover activity to freshen the probable cause, but this is not always possible if the site has been taken down, the server is no longer operating, or the offenders have changed identities. This is one type of case that the above-described Attorney General's Advisory Committee attempts to avoid by providing quick and helpful advice to agents in the field about how to efficiently disseminate leads in order to protect victims and have successful prosecutions across numerous jurisdictions.

Due to the proliferation of federal undercover operations, federal authorities have recently seen offenders return to the traditional in-person file-sharing gatherings. Taking the illicit material off the networks and bringing it back to traditional one-on-one distribution creates obvious challenges for law enforcement. How does one pose as a man/boy lover in order to be invited to such an event? How does an agent record the event's activities? Although there are reported cases of agents who have infiltrated such groups as North American Man/Boy Love Association (NAMBLA) those cases are not the norm.

6. Documenting Predisposition and Grooming

Ken Lanning, formerly of the FBI's Behavioral Analysis Unit, in the 1990s began to describe grooming behavior when sexual grooming was just being identified as a critical step in Internet and electronic-based child exploitation cases.[33] Lanning described the previously identified distinction between a situational child molester—an individual who was regressed and sexually indiscriminate—and a preferential molester—a highly intelligent, manipulative individual motivated by his need to have sex with a particular type of victim.

Lanning's testimony in *United States v. Romero* described how Romero held numerous adolescent boys in his "grooming pipeline," each at a different stage of the grooming process.[34] One had already been successfully lured into the defendant's residence and was living with him, engaging in sexual activity with him, and aiding him in the viewing and storage of his massive child pornography collection; others, meanwhile, were being flattered and cajoled depending upon their own idiosyncratic interests and identified weaknesses. The problem for preferential molesters like Romero was not how to lure his victims, but, rather, how to "dump" a child once that boy aged to a point where he grew beyond Romero's preferential age, and, thus, his interest.

Indeed, when agents searched the Romero residence and the computers he used, they discovered a veritable treasure trove of luring items. One group of boys in his pipeline was interested in a Wiccan-type religion, and Romero fed them rituals and prayers, replete with candles, oils, and chants. One item used at his trial was the "altar box" containing his manufactured religious articles. Victim interviews revealed that one ritual performed around the altar box included the boys circling and touching each other's erect penises. Another of his victims was fascinated with Area 57 and UFOs. A search of Romero's home revealed hundreds of pages of downloaded articles on UFOs that Romero used to educate himself and feed his victim's interest.

The searched computers provided details of the grooming process and contained the identities of numerous victims in his pipeline. Voice recordings that Romero made of himself talking to unknown boys were saved on his computer. None of the boys were ever identified, but the recordings serve as a glimpse into Romero's grooming process, including how he changed his persona and even his voice as he tailored his message of seduction to the interests of each particular victim.

Romero's chameleon-like ability to juggle the ongoing seduction of numerous minors simultaneously easily negated any defense that he was unaware of what he was doing when he spoke to the boys. The large number of potential victims became most apparent when pages of scrap paper, which were located surrounding his computer, were presented to the jury. Each page was filled with e-mail addresses obtained during his daily and nightly jaunts on the Internet. Eerily, the victim whose kidnapping Romero was charged with was listed as just one of hundreds of e-mail addresses on the scrap papers strewn around the computer, evidence of the ease with which Romero was able to gain emotional—and physical—access to his victims.

7. Collecting Electronic Evidence

Gathering electronic evidence from child exploiters requires a team that has knowledge of all of the potential types of storage. Gone are the days of seizing a hard drive and sending it to the lab. Cell phones with cameras, cameras that shoot video, flash drives, jump drives, CD-ROMs, DVDS, and external hard drives must all be collected and reviewed. A trained computer analyst on the team will be able to make a mirror image of the drives and can preserve the state of the computer as it was upon entry. For example, in *Romero*, a fifteen-year-old boy received an e-mail from Romero while Romero was on a Greyhound bus—just moments before FBI agents boarded the bus and arrested him. Romero instructed the boy to get rid of what was bad for him (Romero) on the computer. When agents in Florida entered the residence, the boy was in the process of deleting hundreds of images of child pornography—all of which were recovered because a knowledgeable agent retrieved them *prior* to shutting down and removing the computer. The direction to the child to destroy the images provided additional evidence of Romero's malicious intent, and provided an additional basis for an obstruction of justice charge. A knowledgeable computer agent will also recognize that the defendant will have required certain operating software, cables, and plugs, and, to recreate those images, will seize those key items as well.

8. Conducting Forensic Analysis

The main attack on an electronic-based child exploitation case will be based on the computer analyst's results. Most analysts will use a standard software program that will allow them to identify images and cull them from the rest of the evidence. As mentioned earlier, however, the analyst who works side-by-side with the investigator and prosecutor will likely obtain a higher volume of material of an evidentiary nature. The way an offender labels his files, for example, opens a window into how valuable the offender believed his material was. Furthermore, analysts can obtain deleted files, pieces of files in the slack and cache areas of the hard drive, and files that have had their endings changed to hide their character and contents. All of these actions can serve as evidence of the defendant's intent and, relatedly, consciousness of guilt.

Preserving a mirror image of the computer is the primary task of the computer analyst. What occurs with that mirror image has been the subject of judicial scrutiny for several years. As noted above, some defense attorneys have requested that the computer (not merely the mirror image) be turned over to a defense expert in order to challenge the government's computer searching expert. The government has traditionally treated the computer hard drive as containing contraband and, as such, has argued that it should not be out of the government's hands without a court order—much like when a defense expert chooses to test the seized illegal drug.

Regional Crime Computer Labs now provide rooms where defense experts and defense attorneys may review the images within the confines of the lab, preventing any disclosure of the contraband. In all cases, it is both the court's and the government's duty to ensure that the contraband is treated in accordance with the strictures of 18 U.S.C. § 3509, ensuring that it is not shared, disseminated, or placed in the public record, because each time the child pornography is viewed, the victim depicted in that contraband is being revictimized.[35] More fully set forth in chapter 12, it remains the court's obligation to ensure that the illicit materials remain under seal and protection while the trial or appeal proceed.

9. Interviewing Suspects

As in all criminal cases, whether the suspect is in custody will govern the manner in which the agents interview him. Talented law enforcement agents recognize that the key to learning anything from a child exploitation defendant is understanding the type of offender that he is. A member of NAMBLA is approached differently than a situational molester. The situational offender can be interviewed in a traditional manner, but the NAMBLA member must be approached with the understanding that this offender does not believe he is offending (rather, he simply is being punished for violating an ill-conceived "social construct," namely, the criminalization of adult-child sexual relationships). As such, employing language that is not accusatory, that is not an attack on his actions, will allow the agent to gather more information about the preferential defendant and his actions. This is a slow process, but an offender who does not believe that he has engaged in illegal activity may provide a significant amount of information in an interview with law enforcement officers.

Taking breaks from the interview, providing food or drink during a longer interview, and generally keeping a respectful tone (in spite of the information that may be provided to the interviewer during the process) will result in a more comprehensive statement of the offender's involvement. This statement can then be used to show voluntariness and lack of coercion at trial or during a pretrial hearing. The calm—and perhaps even empathetic—atmosphere created by the agent also provides an opportunity for the investigator to clarify terminology used by the offender. An interview with a sexual offender can offer insights not only into the particular offender's crime, but, more broadly, into the unique world of sexual offenders. Understanding the idiosyncrasies of the interactions between offenders and their victims can train an investigator on how best to approach both in the future.

Finally, sexual offenders with a large collection of electronic evidence are generally quite proud of their collection, their techniques, and their personal expertise with computers. These are, in the main, savvy computer users who have the latest in electronic gadgetry and software. An interview would not be complete if it did not include a comprehensive discussion about the manner in which the offender stored his collection and shared it, his interactions with fellow travelers, and how he used electronic tools to maintain and secure all of the above. Seeking encryption codes, full names and locations of victims and other offenders who are identified only by nicknames or screen-names, and identification of all types of equipment that either manufactured or stored contraband are essential topics for a professional offender interview.

a. Gender Issues in Interviewing

One challenging complication that often occurs during the interview of child exploiters is the role of the female interviewer and the manner in which the male offender responds to her. In the authors' experience, most male offenders do not open up directly to female interviewers, often looking at them in a paternalistic and condescending way. This is especially true of offenders who identify themselves as man/boy lovers. This particular type of offender believes that the sexual relationship that he has with a boy is more pure, and, therefore, superior, to any heterosexual relationships because it involves a higher level of psychological, even spiritual, intimacy. As such, the man/boy lover looks upon the female interviewer as someone simply incapable of understanding or appreciating this relationship. A male interviewer who takes on the persona of someone who "gets it" and appreciates the offender's motivations, on the other hand, may be more successful than a female interviewer during the initial stages of the interview. Understanding the "moral philosophy" driving some of the offenders (or, at least, used by them to justify their conduct) is, therefore, key, because the angry Andy Sipowicz (*NYPD Blue*) "you are just scum" approach to interviewing may make the interviewer feel good, but will typically not produce the same level of cooperation and openness from the defendant.

This is not to say that female interviewers are unsuccessful. The interviews of Brian Urbanawiz were conducted over a three-day period in Michigan by a female local law enforcement officer and followed up with a two-day interview by the female author. Once Urbanawiz began telling his story, the female interviewers seemed harmless to him; he let down his defenses and gave one of the most comprehensive interviews of a man/boy sex offender ever recorded. Over days, Urbanawiz described his psychology, his motivations, and the reasons why offenders like him act the way that they do. He even spent hours identifying photos of victims. In the end, this offender did not feel threatened by the female interviewer and appeared to relish the opportunity to educate her. As a result, powerful testimony and historical knowledge was obtained for use in other investigations and in trial.

C. Medical and Psychological Evaluations of Suspects and Defendants

18 U.S.C. § 4241 provides for a mental examination of a defendant for a determination of whether the defendant is suffering from a mental disease or defect rendering him incompetent to understand the nature of the proceedings against him or to assist properly in his defense. This section of the code can be invoked by the defense attorney, the prosecutor, or the judge at any point during the proceedings based on the behavior of the defendant and his interaction with his counsel or the bench.

Although such an examination is more frequently performed in child exploitation cases than in others, the end result of a finding of incompetence is rare. Most criminal defendants may be deemed to have some sort of psychological disorder, even a mental defect, but rarely are they so impaired that they do not actually understand the nature of the proceedings. Even those offenders deemed incompetent at one stage of the proceedings may be treated over a period of time through hospitalization, mental health treatment, and medications, and may be found competent at a later stage in the proceedings, allowing for the defendant to proceed to trial. As such, psychological evaluations generally provide more insight into the issues governing detention in the pretrial stage and issues of likely recidivism in the sentencing stage.

As for the pretrial period, the court must make a determination regarding whether a defendant is a danger to the community or a flight risk in order to detain him pursuant to 18 U.S.C. § 3142. Often judges are faced with conflicting images of the man before them: the law-abiding pillar of the community vs. the insidious child predator. In seeking to determine dangerousness, the court may seek to have the defendant evaluated. If the defendant agrees to such an evaluation, the discussions with the treating doctor are turned over to both the government and the court, and the defense waives his right to privacy. When a defendant waives his right to privacy, he usually believes that, by presenting the evaluation to the court, he will show the court that he is not a danger to the community.

In many instances, this may be an uphill climb because there is a presumption of pre-trial incarceration applicable in offenses involving a minor brought under sections 1201, 1591, 2241, 2242, 2244(a)(1), 2245, 2251, 2251A, 2252(a)(1), 2252(a)(2), 2252(a)(3), 2252A(a)(1), 2252A(a)(2), 2252(a)(3), 2252A(a)(4), 2260, 2421, 2422, 2423, and 2425—the familiar presumption is that no condition, or combination of conditions, will reasonably assure the appearance of the defendant. Further, offenses under chapter 117 are defined as crimes of violence, which hold a presumption that the defendant is a danger to the community. Even if the defense were able to overcome these presumptions, the same code section requires that in any case involving a minor victim under the above-mentioned statutes, or a violation of a failure to register as a sex offender, any release order shall contain, at a minimum, a condition of electronic monitoring.

The psychological evaluation may, therefore, be used as a tool for the government to show dangerousness, potential recidivism, and lack of remorse or even awareness of the harm that he has allegedly inflicted. The same report will then be used by the defense to rebut dangerousness by showing that the offender has not been charged in the past, has a job and a family, and is willing to engage in mental health treatment while awaiting trial. In short, the judge will find herself grappling once again with the dichotomy of the individual standing before her.

Notes

1. Criminal Prosecutions Bureau (2008), www.statesattorney.org.
2. See, for example, *United States v. Burt*, 495 F.3d 733 (7th Cir. 2007) (investigation into Burt's manufacturing of child pornography led to the investigation of William Martin and twelve other offenders who shared molestation images with Burt in Milwaukee and other jurisdictions).

3. U.S. Attorney's Manual, 9-75.100, Multiple District Investigations and Prosecutions (2010).

4. 18 U.S.C. §§ 2510–2522.

5. See, for example, *United States v. Laine*, 270 F.3d 71 (5th Cir. 2001); *United States v. Nanda*, 178 F.3d 1287 (4th Cir. 1999).

6. Ibid.

7. *United States v. Manion*, 54 Fed. App'x 372 (4th Cir. 2002); *United States v. Cottle*, 355 Fed. App'x 18 (6th Cir. 2009).

8. *Georgia v. Randolph*, 547 U.S. 103 (2006).

9. Ibid.

10. Ibid.

11. *United States v. Sager*, 2008 WL 45358 (N.D. Ind. Jan. 2, 2008).

12. *United States v. Meek*, 366 F.3d 705 (9th Cir. 2004).

13. *United States v. Hoffa*, 385 U.S. 293 (1966).

14. See, for example, *United States v. Simons*, 206 F.3d 392 (4th Cir. 2000).

15. *United States v. Hall*, 142 F.3d 988 (7th Cir. 1998).

16. See, for example, *United States v. Barth*, 26 F. Supp. 2d 929 (W.D. Tex. 1998).

17. *United States v. Brunette*, 76 F. Supp. 2d 30 (D. Me. 1990), *aff'd* 256 F.3d 14 (1st Cir. 2001).

18. N.D. Ill. Computer Search Protocol.

19. *United States v. Falso*, 554 F.3d 110 (2nd Cir. 2008).

20. See, for example, *United States v. Hodson*, 543 F.3d 286 (6th Cir. 2008).

21. *United States v. Romero*, 189 F.3d 576 (7th Cir. 1999) (defendant instructed minor living in his home to delete images after law enforcement closed in on him on a Greyhound bus while transporting another victim to the residence).

22. *United States v. David Sanders*, No. 00-CR-675 (N.D. Ill.).

23. *Burt*, 495 F.3d at 733 (defendant sentenced to one hundred years in prison after testimony of minor victims and the retrieval of a video from another offender's computer in spite of prosecutor's inability to break encryption codes of computers seized from defendant's residence).

24. *United States v. Watzman*, 486 F.3d 1004 (7th Cir. 2007) (defendant sent money orders to Russia to purchase his personally selected child pornographic videos).

25. See, for example, *United States v. Urbanawiz*, No. 04-001853-FC (Mich. filed June 4, 2004) (during Urbanawiz's proffer, he described a process wherein offenders must gain access to other offenders' collections only after proving that each was worthy of viewing the other's cache, often by providing an image worthy of the offender's collection).

26. *United States v. Laney*, 189 F.3d 954 (9th Cir. 1999); *United States v. Tank*, 200 F.3d 627 (9th Cir. 2000); *United States v. Anderson*, 27 Fed. App'x. 931 (10th Cir. 2001).

27. *Burt*, 495 F.3d at 733; *Laney*, 189 F.3d at 954; *Tank*, 200 F.3d at 627; *Anderson*, 27 Fed. App'x. at 931; *United States v. Fleming*, No. 07-CR-00276 (N.D. Ill. filed May 3, 2007).

28. *Burt*, 495 F.3d at 733.

29. See, for example, Amy Fine Collins, *Sex Trafficking of Americans—the Girl Next Door*, VANITY FAIR (May 24, 2011).

30. Ibid.

31. 503 U.S. 540 (1992).

32. Courts have found that the affirmative defense of entrapment does not apply where the government invites the defendant to participate in a crime and does not employ any pressure tactics or other type of coercion to induce the defendant. See *United States v. Orr*, 622 F.3d 864 (7th Cir. 2010) (no entrapment where defendant, without provocation, initiated contact with undercover agent, his first inquiry to agent was about sexually abusing her children, and he bragged about molesting other children); *United States v. Fernando*, 2008 WL 4107241 (4th Cir. Sept. 5, 2008) (no entrapment jury instruction necessary when government agents merely offer an opportunity to commit a crime and the defendant promptly avails himself of the opportunity—in this case, chatting online about sexually explicit topics with an undercover agent posing as a fourteen-year-old girl that defendant attempted to meet in person); *United States v. Gamache*, 156 F.3d 1 (1st Cir. 1998) (no entrapment where sting operation merely provides opportunity to commit a crime); *United States v. Gifford*, 17 F.3d 462 (1st Cir. 1994) (no entrapment where defendant was mailed open-ended solicitations to purchase child pornography because the solicitations made no appeal to the sympathy of any obviously reluctant person and they required the defendant to prepay); *United States v. Gendron*, 18 F.3d 955 (1st Cir. 1994) (no entrapment where government mailed solicitations from sham companies that did not progress from innocent lure to frank offer, did not, with one exception, appeal to any motive other than the desire to see child pornography, did not claim to come from a lobbying organization, and did not ask defendant to commit crime as a matter of principle); *United States v. Byrd*, 31 F.3d 1329 (5th Cir. 1994) (no entrapment where defendant eagerly and promptly responded to undercover sting operation and defendant already possessed foreign sex education text containing pictures of children as well as a sexually explicit questionnaire for nine-year-old boys); *United States v. Harvey*, 991 F.2d 981 (2d Cir. 1993) (no entrapment where defendant promptly accepted government-sponsored invitation to buy child pornography because a jury could rationally infer that his prompt action demonstrated predisposition); *United States v. Osborne*, 935 F.2d 32 (4th Cir. 1991) (no entrapment where defendant responded to advertisement placed by postal inspector offering both adult pornography and child pornography with a letter indicating his interest in purchasing two videos containing child pornography); see also *United States v. Ross*, 2008 WL 4963045 (N.D. Cal. Nov. 19, 2008) (jury instruction for entrapment that lacked a specific instruction to consider the defendant's reluctance was not legally improper or misleading), and also *United States v. Poehlman*, 217 F.3d 692 (9th Cir. 2000) (distinguishing willingness from predisposition and finding entrapment where government engaged in protracted communication with defendant who, based on his earliest messages to the undercover agent, was not otherwise predisposed to commit the offense).

33. Kenneth V. Lanning, CHILD MOLESTERS: A BEHAVIORAL ANALYSIS, 4th ed. (Washington, DC: Office of Juvenile Justice and Delinquency Prevention and Department of Justice, 2001).

34. 469 F. 3rd 1139 (7th Cir. 2006).

35. See *Ferber*, 458 U.S. at 747.

10

The Syndicate and the Scholar

Examining the Anatomy of the Prosecution of University of Chicago Pediatrician Dr. H. Marc Watzman

---

THE SAD CASE OF thirty-seven-year-old Dr. H. Marc Watzman, the then–chief resident at the University of Chicago Medical School, specializing in pediatrics and anesthesiology, illustrates the difficulty in predicting those who are involved in the sexual exploitation of children, and the challenges facing prosecutors and agents tasked with investigating such cases. Moreover, this case provides a vivid demonstration of the global danger posed by organized crime groups running large-scale child pornography manufacturing and distribution networks.

By way of full disclosure, we prosecuted this case, and are, therefore, particularly familiar with the extraordinary facts that in a very tangible sense played out on the streets of Russia, Ecuador, and other countries, and that, in the end, led to Dr. Watzman's dramatic downfall. Walking through this case—from the beginning of the investigation to the sentencing—should give the reader a better understanding of (1) what investigators and prosecutors should look for when the investigation first starts; (2) how child pornography syndicates on a day-to-day basis generate millions of dollars in profits; (3) how evidence is most effectively collected; (4) what legal arguments the defense can make; and (5) what factors play a role in determining not only a defendant's ultimate guilt, but also the appropriate sentence.

A. The Investigation Begins

In February 2003, an international undercover operation revealed that a company called "Regpay," located in Minsk, Belarus, and operated by a Moscow,

Russia, based child pornography syndicate, owned and operated a global network of members-only Internet websites containing images of real children engaging in pornographic conduct with other children and with adults.[1] In the late summer of 2003, federal agents, operating in an undercover capacity, in fact obtained memberships to, and visited, the Russian syndicate's members-only websites.

The Regpay investigation was, in many ways, exactly the type of transnational investigation that the Attorney General's Advisory Committee on Child Exploitation Cases was designed to facilitate. The Regpay targets spanned multiple jurisdictions domestically and internationally. Having a concrete plan of how material would be shared among agents and prosecutors, how victims would be identified and protected, and how investigative efforts could be streamlined so as not to be duplicative or cumulative was critical to the successful prosecution of the individual child exploitation cases that were spawned from the initial take-down.

Turning back to the investigation, it revealed early on that the syndicate transferred funds from U.S.-based customers accessing Regpay's child pornography websites to an account maintained by a company known as "Connections," located in Fort Lauderdale, Florida. The Russian child pornography syndicate, in fact, through Regpay *alone,* received at least $2,500,000 worldwide from customers paying for membership to its various members-only child pornography websites.[2]

The federal agents who in July and August 2003 reviewed some of Regpay's sites discovered that Regpay placed numerous Internet advertisements offering membership to its websites. When a customer purchased Regpay's services, the billing page automatically appeared on the computer screen. This billing page sought the prospective customer's personal and financial information, including billing address and credit card information. The top of each billing page included a logo containing the word *Regpay,* and the name of the particular website that the client was seeking to purchase.

After completing the form, the customer was instructed to hit the "JOIN NOW!" button on the screen. Shortly after clicking on the "JOIN NOW!" button, Regpay sent the customer a message stating that Regpay "successfully" charged the customer's credit card. The message also provided the customer with a unique transaction number, log-in information, and password to log in to the members-only child pornography site(s) the customer had purchased.

Practice Tip: It is important to "isolate" the defendant's conduct in this way to ward off subsequent claims that some third person (perhaps a roommate, a friend visiting the defendant's house, or a neighbor "hacking into" the defendant's server) was the person who in fact accessed the pornographic websites. Because a password was required, and the customer (Dr. Watzman) was sent a unique transaction number and log-in information, it is much less likely that he will later be able to credibly claim that, in fact, it was someone else who (repeatedly) logged into the child pornography accounts.

The message also advised that a nondescript entry would appear on the customer's credit card statement as a beneficiary of this transaction.

B. Federal Agents Seize Regpay's Customer List

Federal agents, using subpoenas and search warrants in October 2003, seized Regpay's customer database. While the syndicate operated out of Russia, it demonstrated a rare oversight by housing one of its servers in the United States (specifically, in Houston, Texas; other servers were located in cities including Hong Kong, China, and Karlsruhe, Germany). The customer database contained Regpay's records for each customer who purchased access to one of Regpay's child pornography websites. This information included the purchaser's name, home address, e-mail address, credit card number, names of websites purchased, and date(s) of purchase. Illustrating the incredible profit-generating potential of child pornography, in Illinois alone there were some *three thousand* paying customers to just one of the syndicate's child pornography websites.

> **Practice Tip:** The regrettable reality is that the number of individuals engaged in child pornography dramatically outpaces law enforcement's ability to investigate and prosecute them. As a result, law enforcement tends to pursue those who have the most ready access to children, those with child exploitation in their backgrounds, and those whose conduct appears to be particularly aggravated. In this case, Dr. Watzman was one of a handful of targets law enforcement was able to fully investigate. Suffice it to say that limited law enforcement resources allowed thousands of other Illinois clients (and tens of thousands of clients located elsewhere) to escape Dr. Watzman's well-deserved fate.

C. "H. Marc Watzman," One of Regpay's Top-Paying Customers

Federal agents reviewing Regpay's customer databases soon discovered that Dr. Watzman was one of Regpay's many paying Illinois customers. The

TABLE 10.1
Payment Information

Customer Name	Customer Address	Website	Purchase Date
Dr. Watzman, aka chiefer4″doglover.com	858 W. Armitage, Chicago, IL 60614	www.darkfeeling.com	June 2, 2003
Dr. Watzman, aka chiefer4″doglover.com	858 W. Armitage, Chicago, IL 60614	www.dark-video.com	May 28, 2003
Dr. Watzman, aka chiefer4″doglover.com	858 W. Armitage, Chicago, IL 60614	www.onlinesharingcommunity.com	May 3, 2003
Dr. Watzman, aka chiefer4″doglover.com	858 W. Armitage, Chicago, IL 60614	www.video-2000.com/regpay	May 2, 2003
Dr. Watzman, aka chiefer4″doglover.com	858 W. Armitage, Chicago, IL 60614	www.lust-gallery.com	April 30, 2003
Dr. Watzman, aka chiefer4″doglover.com	858 W. Armitage, Chicago, IL 60614	www.darkfeeling.com	April 13, 2003
Dr. Watzman, aka chiefer4″doglover.com	858 W. Armitage, Chicago, IL 60614	www.wildnymphets.biz/trust	April 8, 2003
Dr. Watzman, aka chiefer4″doglover.com	858 W. Armitage, Chicago, IL 60614	www.lolitacastle.com/trust	March 21, 2003
Dr. Watzman, aka chiefer4″doglover.com	858 W. Armitage, Chicago, IL 60614	www.lust-gallery.com	March 13, 2003

purchasing information contained on Regpay's customer database for Dr. Watzman is listed in table 10.1.

> **Practice Tip:** Evidence that a defendant *paid* for the services can be key in establishing that the defendant had good reason to ensure that he *knew* what he was paying for. Put another way, it shows the defendant's commitment to obtaining the materials, and blunts later defense claims that the defendant inadvertently "happened upon" the pornographic materials while casually surfing the Internet.

Thereafter, federal agents with extensive background in child pornography investigations visited all of the above-listed websites to which Dr. Watzman had purchased memberships. The agents used their expertise in the area to preliminarily determine that these websites contained exclusively photographic and video images of what appeared to be real children engaged in pornographic activities with other children and adults. The agents, when visiting the websites, also captured the contents of these websites.

> **Practice Tip:** It is important that agents visiting such sites have a significant level of experience and expertise so that their findings and conclusions concerning, among other things, the estimated age of the victim and the fact that the victim is, indeed, a "real child," will withstand the scrutiny of federal judges later reviewing the sufficiency of the search warrant or criminal complaint that is, at least in part, premised on these critical findings. If a reviewing judge finds that the agent lacked the requisite background and training to reliably reach these conclusions, the entire case may be put in jeopardy.

D. Contents of "www.video-2000.com"

The evidence revealed that on May 2, 2003, Dr. Watzman joined the neutrally titled www.video-2000.com. Federal agents determined that potential customers of the website must go through a number of individual webpages prior to providing his or her name, address, credit card number, and so forth. Federal agents who reviewed these subsidiary pages found that these "access" pages contain a number of images of naked girls in their early teens in various sexually explicit poses.

> **Practice Tip:** Evidence of these types of content-specific notices is key because it demonstrates that the defendant knew full well what he was paying for—he was not paying for images of pornography; he was paying

for images of *child* pornography, which will assist the reviewing judge who is evaluating the sufficiency of the search warrant or complaint.

The text accompanying these images of child pornography stated, among other things, to "enjoy the pure beauty and charm of [the] young female body!"; boasted that the webpage contained "2,500 assorted pics of extreme uncensored content"; offered "video nymphette updates twice a week"; advertised the "LS Magazine," which contained images of girls "age 12 to 14 years old"; claimed to feature images of girls "from 11 to 17 y.o."; and stated that it offers "exclusive content." Customers, such as Dr. Watzman, who purchased membership to www.video-2000.com were, in short, made well aware that the website contained exclusively child pornography.

> **Practice Tip:** Whenever an ad uses the term *exclusive content*, it is implying that the people operating it, or their associates, have access to children and are, as a result of this access, able to manufacture child pornography that is "exclusive" to them and their websites or other avenues of distribution.

The access page one had to click through to reach the registration page for www.lust-gallery.com, moreover, stated that its sister-site www.darkfeeling.com is "famous for: leg spreads and close-ups, shots from behind and some peeing shots. . . . All models are 14 and younger and *have never shown at our sites before*"[3]; the website also informed the potential customer that it is "the place where Dark Feelings come true."

The initial access page preceding the registration page for www.darkfeeling.com, moreover, advertised a number of "our sites," including "Lo!Littles.com," which featured "exclusive content" of girls "under 14."

E. Credit Cards Dr. Watzman Used to
Open Child Pornography Accounts Sent to P.O. Box

On October 14, 2003, federal agents with this information in hand contacted MBNA and determined that Marc Watzman was, in fact, the account holder of the particular credit card number used to open the child pornography accounts. Agents, furthermore, discovered that the credit card statements were sent to Dr. Watzman's home address, where he lived alone. (Dr. Watzman was, indeed, a very good customer. He signed up for undergroundlolita studio.com; wildnymphets.biz; lolittles.com; lust-gallery.com; lolitacastle.com; darkfeeling.com; and lust-gallery.com. He also obtained access to syndicate-run websites with titles leaving little to the imagination, including "photololitabiz," "eternal virgins," "little-pussy-studio," "Young Pussy Video," "My Little Lolita," "brutalgames.com," "Barefoot Teen Girls," "Children in Cinema," "Brutal Porno," "Teenieworld," "Tinywomen Virginz," "Lolitasforever," "Teenshols," "Lolitafix," "PEDO Shop," "Very big child porno collections," "Immoral Underages," and "Defloration.")

> **Practice Tip:** From the perspective of the prosecution it is always helpful if the websites themselves have addresses indicating their content—in this case, the references to "wildnymphets" and "undergroundlolitastudio" make defense arguments of inadvertence less credible.

Subsequently, federal agents drove to Dr. Watzman's purported home address and determined that the location was an affiliate of the United Parcel Service that offers mail boxes for rent. Agents discovered that Dr. Watzman leased mail box #180. The paperwork Dr. Watzman filled out and signed when he initially rented the P.O. Box listed one of his earlier Chicago addresses as his home address.

Later that day, federal agents reviewed Dr. Watzman's Illinois insurance card, and his driver's license, both of which listed that prior address as his home address. The link between Dr. Watzman and payments for child pornography was, in short, becoming ever-stronger.

Later that day, federal agents also confirmed with MBNA Bank that Dr. Watzman was, in fact, the account holder of the credit card used for the online child pornography purchases; this was the credit card number used to sign up for www.dark-video.com; www.onlinesharingcommunity.com; www.video-2000.com; and www.darkfeeling.com, all of which contained exclusively child pornography images and videos.

F. The Early Mistake—Dr. Watzman Provided Home Address during First Purchase of Membership to "Lolita-gates.com"

On or about February 1, 2003, Dr. Watzman had signed up for membership with Regpay's "www.lolita-gates.com." Dr. Watzman at the time provided his Chicago home address as his billing address. In contrast, for all future purchases Dr. Watzman used his P.O. Box.

> **Practice Tip:** Such an "evolution" in a defendant's risk awareness is quite common and can help demonstrate that the defendant early on may have not been as conscious of the danger of law enforcement detection, but ultimately took various "new" precautions in order to remain undetected. In

this case, the search warrant affiant used this evidence to argue consciousness of guilt to the reviewing judge: "Dr. Watzman has used his P.O. Box
address to avoid detection by law enforcement."

G. Dr. Watzman's Background

A concurrent review of Dr. Watzman's driver's license and the paperwork he
filled out to obtain his P.O. Box conducted at the initiation of the investigation revealed that at the time he was a thirty-seven-year-old male. Documents
from the Illinois Department of Professional Regulation, moreover, indicated
that Dr. Watzman was a board-licensed physician and surgeon.

> **Practice Tip:** Developing the defendant's background, even during the
> preliminary stages of an investigation, is an important step toward provid-
> ing the reviewing judge (or the jury) with a sense of who this person is.
> Although not necessarily that telling in itself, it can be key for issues such
> as detention; and the reviewing judge will likely notice its absence from a
> search warrant or criminal complaint.

Indeed, in July 2003, Dr. Watzman had completed his residency at the University of Chicago Hospitals, specializing in anesthesiology. Dr. Watzman
was licensed on July 28, 1999, and his license was current at the time of the
investigation. Federal agents also determined that until October 8, 2003, Dr.
Watzman was employed by Edward Hospital in Naperville, Illinois, as a pe-
diatrician in the Critical Care Unit.

> **Practice Tip:** In a case such as this, a defendant's ready access to chil-
> dren raises serious concerns, and necessitates considerable follow-up
> investigation—after all, what law enforcement learns about an individual
> during their initial investigation is typically only the proverbial tip of the
> exploitation iceberg. The authors have prosecuted pedophile priests, dea-
> cons, nurses, Boy Scout leaders, and other individuals with regular (often
> unsupervised) contact with minor children; in each of those cases, the
> defendant had used his position for sexual gratification.

H. Border Search of Certain Items of Mail Sent to Dr. Watzman

The investigation was beginning to build up steam. On September 30, 2003,
federal agents, pursuant to their border-search authority, inspected a letter-
sized parcel sent from a fictitious P.O. Box in Sweden to Dr. Watzman's
P.O. Box in Chicago. The parcel contained a video titled "The Wild Life

Report, Volume 4." Agents viewed the video and found it to contain what appeared to be homemade voyeuristic scenes of nude people on a beach. Agents, the next day, inspected another parcel from Sweden, which contained the identical video.

Less than two weeks later, agents intercepted a parcel from Germany that was addressed to Dr. Watzman. The parcel was inspected and was found to contain encryption software commonly used to hide pictures within pictures, to hide text within pictures, and to encrypt computer files. The agents noted that, in their expert opinions, such software is commonly used by child pornographers to reduce the risk that they will be discovered when they receive and distribute child pornography.

> **Practice Tip:** Demonstrating a defendant's use of encryption software is another way of establishing that the defendant knew what he was doing was illegal, and that he was trying to hide his communications and files from law enforcement. Although some defendants may claim that this software was merely used to hide lawful adult pornography or other private items from husbands, wives, children, or roommates, standard computer and e-mail account passwords usually suffice for those purposes. The possession of such software may, alone, not demonstrate much, but when combined with other evidence of evasion it can be extremely probative.

I. The Investigation Narrows and Agents Conduct a "Trash Pull" at Dr. Watzman's Residence

On October 8, 2003, federal agents performed surveillance of Dr. Watzman's residence (in law enforcement parlance, the "subject premises"). Agents who had previously reviewed Dr. Watzman's Illinois driver's license picture and his photograph on the University of Chicago Medical School's website observed Dr. Watzman enter and leave the subject premises.

> **Practice Tip:** Visual surveillance helps corroborate that the defendant's identity was not somehow stolen and used by a third party to engage in the crime; this may not seem like a significant piece of evidence, but failure to be thorough and follow through on such routine investigatory steps can end up jeopardizing the investigation and threaten to leave the reviewing judge or jury with the impression that the investigators were "sloppy" in their approach.

Agents further observed Dr. Watzman take out his trash. Agents recovered Dr. Watzman's trash and found, among other things, a cover letter dated October 1, 2003, in Dr. Watzman's name and written to Edward Hospital; a

Walgreens prescription bottle for Valtrex (used to treat herpes) dated "7/7/03" in Dr. Watzman's name, and listing the subject premises and his home address; a Nationwide Advantage Mortgage refinancing solicitation addressed to "Marc Dr. Watzman" at the home address; and an envelope addressed to "Doctor Mark Dr. Watzman" at the home address and postmarked January 27, 2003.

> **Practice Tip:** "Trash pulls," an understandably undesirable task typically left to new agents, can be critical in securing physical evidence and establishing that a particular person resided (and, perhaps, resided alone) at a particular residence.

J. Public Information Search

Additional public information database searches conducted on October 14, 2003, confirmed that Dr. Watzman was the sole listed occupant at his residence. Specifically, a search conducted on LexisNexis revealed that the address was Dr. Watzman's most recent/current address.

> **Practice Tip:** Obtaining such basic information early during a subsequent defendant interview is critical because the questions seem to be neutral and nonthreatening, but ultimately help ward off subsequent claims that someone else had ready access to the defendant's computer. Agents and prosecutors must work in close cooperation throughout the process, and must cross-check that no investigatory step is overlooked.

K. Federal Agents Conduct Court-Authorized Search of the Garden Apartment at 1454 N. Wieland Street, Chicago, Illinois[4]

Based on a search warrant detailing the evidence and investigatory steps we have discussed, on October 24, 2003, the assigned U.S. Magistrate Judge issued a warrant to search the Garden Apartment at 1454 N. Wieland Street, Chicago, Illinois, for evidence relating to Dr. Watzman's receipt and possession of child pornography.

The next day, at approximately 10:15 a.m., federal agents, assisted by members of the Chicago Police Department, executed the search warrant on Dr. Watzman's residence. The agents found Dr. Watzman was alone; he voluntarily admitted to them that he had lived at this residence since 2001, and that he resided there alone. The agents, moreover, during their search did not find any indicia of occupancy by anyone other than Dr. Watzman.

L. Federal Agents Recover Dr. Watzman's Compaq Desktop Computer Containing Child Pornography

Agents near Dr. Watzman's bedroom recovered a Compaq desktop computer. This Compaq computer was plugged in and connected to a wireless Internet router. Thereafter, a federal agent with extensive experience in the forensic analysis of computers and the investigation of child pornography cases conducted a preliminary forensic examination of the computer.

The agent's preliminary forensic analysis revealed that the Compaq computer contained in excess of approximately 200,000 erased images. The agent was able to recover some of these erased images from folders and from unallocated space. These images featured, among other things, two nude boys and a girl aged approximately eight to twelve engaging in sexual activity. The agent, furthermore, recovered approximately dozens of nonerased images from the Compaq's hard drive that depicted nude girls who appeared to be eight to twelve years old engaging in sexually explicit conduct, as well as e-mails in Dr. Watzman's name.

M. Federal Agents Recover Dr. Watzman's Laptop Computer Containing Child Pornography

Agents also recovered a Sony Vaio laptop computer from the living room of the Watzman residence. (During surveillance conducted on or about October 7, 2003, federal agents had observed Dr. Watzman with what appeared to be this same computer at Edward Hospital in Naperville, Illinois.)

A preliminary forensic examination of this laptop revealed, among other items, a computer program called "Evidence Eliminator," used to erase, among other things, images that were received/stored on computers.

Practice Tip: As noted previously, the recovery of such sophisticated software used to eliminate, or hide, evidence of a person's online activity can be used to establish the defendant's sophistication, the absence of mistake, and consciousness of guilt, but can also be used to explain why certain e-mails, images, or videos obtained by the defendant are no longer recoverable from his computer.

In addition, the preliminary forensic examination revealed approximately three thousand to five thousand images stored in various directories. These images depicted real nude children, aged eight to ten, exposing their genitals and otherwise engaging in sexually explicit activity and poses.

Practice Tip: In all search warrant affidavits, criminal complaints, and other filings it is important to specify that the images were, or appeared to be, of "real" (as opposed to "virtual" or "computer-generated") children.

N. DVDs and Encrypted Materials Recovered from the Residence

Agents also recovered from Dr. Watzman's home multiple Digital Video Disks (DVDs) featuring nude girls ages eight to fourteen in various states of undress. Agents, furthermore, determined that Dr. Watzman was a paid member to adult "fetish" websites in the same manner in which he was a paid member to websites featuring child pornography.

Practice Tip: Establishing such "routine" use of computers and the Internet to access online materials, including non-illicit pornography, helps counter any claims of mistake or inadvertence.

Agents also recovered a number of DVDs stored near Dr. Watzman's desktop computer. Although a majority of these DVDs had "Music" written on them in marker, subsequent forensic examination revealed that they contained various encrypted files of child pornography images and movies that could only be viewed with the appropriate software and a secret password.

Practice Tip: Suffice it to say that such attempts to hide evidence of illegal activity can fatally undermine any defense case. Here, Dr. Watzman had good reason to keep the true nature of his expensive collection secret from, among others, his girlfriend.

O. Consent-Search of Dr. Watzman's Nissan Pathfinder

During that initial law enforcement contact, Dr. Watzman also consented orally and in writing to a search of his 2001 Nissan Pathfinder. The vehicle contained, among other items, a resume/curriculum vitae in the name "H. Marc Watzman, MD."

Agents during their search also recovered hidden in a side-panel of the vehicle's rear compartment a number of recent wire transfers to Guayaquil,

Ecuador. These transfers, which were in the thousands of dollars, were in Dr. Watzman's name, but did not list Dr. Watzman's accurate address.

P. Narcotics Recovered from Dr. Watzman's Residence and Vehicle

Agents during their search also recovered various narcotics from Dr. Watzman's vehicle (primarily in the side panel in the rear of the car's interior, where the wire transfers were recovered), and in his residence (primarily in the kitchen drawer). These narcotics included injectable Morphine; injectable Diprivan (which, according to a physician contacted by federal agents, is used to induce unconsciousness); Ketamine (used to induce unconsciousness); injectable Nimbex (used to induce temporary muscle paralysis); injectable Midazolam (used to sedate persons prior to surgical procedures), and a bottle of Viagra tablets. Inquiries through the DEA indicated that Dr. Watzman did not have prescriptions for these drugs, and no legitimate reason for his possession of these drugs was known.

Q. Dr. Watzman Charged

Dr. Watzman was first charged by way of a criminal complaint. Thereafter, the Grand Jury returned an indictment, and two subsequent superseding indictments, against Dr. Watzman. The second superseding indictment listed some of the aliases Dr. Watzman used to purchase his images of the sexual exploitation of children: "Marvin Barash," "Herb Watman," and "Chiefer4"doglover .com."[5] Dr. Watzman also employed aliases such as "VDbutthead," "Marcus Waltman," and "RMChief."

> **Practice Tip:** The use of such aliases is clearly relevant in a case such as this. Prosecutors should, therefore, in all but the most exceptional cases include all aliases used by a defendant in the course of committing the offense.

Specifically, the indictment in count one charged that on the date of the search, Dr. Watzman possessed materials containing no fewer than 1,000 images and no fewer than 200 digital video clips of child pornography that had been mailed, shipped, and transported in interstate and foreign commerce.

Counts two through ten, in turn, charged that Dr. Watzman on nine separate occasions knowingly received, and attempted to receive, digital computer video files containing child pornography that had been mailed, shipped, and transported in interstate and foreign commerce.

Finally, and most significantly, count eleven charged that Dr. Watzman transferred money from the United States to a place outside of the United States to promote the manufacture and distribution, and attempted manufacture and distribution, of child pornography.

> **Practice Tip:** Prosecutors should be flexible when matching the evidence to appropriate charges. Here, Dr. Watzman's conduct assisting the Russian child pornography syndicate by sending them tens of thousands of dollars to have "new" or "custom-made" child pornography arguably provides them with at least as much assistance as that provided by a driver or complicit banker. Put simply, Dr. Watzman and others like him bankrolled the syndicate's day-to-day exploitation of children, and the charges appropriately took this reality into consideration.

R. The Defense Fires Back

Unlike many defendants facing such an overwhelming amount of evidence of guilt, Dr. Watzman from the outset displayed a fighter's mentality. At first, Dr. Watzman characterized himself as the victim of an overreaching government. Later, Dr. Watzman claimed, among other things, that the computer images seized from his computer were "digitally morphed," and, thus, were not of real children being sexually exploited.

Dr. Watzman, as part of his more offensive strategy, also alleged that, because the government added the money laundering charge to the second superseding indictment, it had engaged in "truly nothing more than a blatant attempt to bludgeon a guilty plea from [Dr. Watzman] and penalize him for exercising his sixth amendment trial rights." Dr. Watzman claimed that the purported prosecutorial "vindictiveness" entitled him to discovery of the government's internal work-product, including its prosecution memorandum, to an evidentiary hearing, and to the dismissal of the second superseding indictment.

S. The District Court Rules

The district court, following a hearing, concluded that defendant's claims lacked merit, and that the presumption of prosecutorial good faith stood undisturbed because Dr. Watzman failed to establish that the government in any way retaliated against him for exercising his protected statutory or constitutional rights.[6] The district court pointed out that a prosecutor is completely within his bounds to seek additional charges after a defendant refuses to enter a plea agreement, and this legal and permissible act, by itself, will not be deemed prosecutorial vindictiveness.[7] Indeed, even in cases where a defendant exercises his constitutional right to go to trial after having agreed to plead guilty and the prosecutor presses superseding charges, courts have refused to find a presumption of vindictiveness on the part of the prosecution.[8] The district court, furthermore, confirmed that a defendant is not entitled to discovery on the issue of vindictiveness until he presents a colorable basis on which to conclude that the prosecutors acted with such animus.

T. Defendant Pleads Guilty on the Eve of Trial

The defense, despite this setback, continued its vigorous and aggressive posture in court, as well as in the media. Following a string of defeats on various motions *in limine*, however, Dr. Watzman may have begun to see the writing on the wall. On the day jury selection was to begin, he entered a conditional guilty plea (reserving the right to challenge the government's court-authorized search of his residence—a challenge subsequently resolved in favor of the government).

> **Practice Tip:** Filing appropriate motions *in limine* not only streamlines the case and provides some predictability in terms of what evidence will be ruled admissible for what reasons, but also may serve to resolve certain key evidentiary disputes that can impede pre-trial resolution of the case.

U. Aggravating Sentencing Factors

By the time of sentencing, Western Union had provided the government a list of Dr. Watzman's wire transfers (wires Dr. Watzman obtained using an expired address and aliases such as "Herb Watman," "Herbert Watman," and "Herbert M. Watman"). The government also learned that Dr. Watzman had sent some seventeen individual wire transfers to men in Russia and in Ecuador, all of whom were members of a transnational Russian pornography syndicate. Indeed, Dr. Watzman spent well over $100,000 on child pornography, thereby directly and materially helping the Russian child pornography syndicate continue its operations.

Dr. Watzman was not alone in funding this syndicate. The Russian syndicate had thousands of similar wire transfers from around the world, including the United States, England, Russia, and Spain.

Although Dr. Watzman pled guilty to the offense, he certainly was not cooperative. For example, throughout the investigation and up to his sentencing, he steadfastly refused to provide law enforcement with the passwords for his encrypted child pornography (much of which to this day remains undiscovered due to the sophistication of the software Dr. Watzman used).

Despite Dr. Watzman's lack of assistance, agents were still able to break the code on some of the folders contained in one of Dr. Watzman's "music" DVDs—those seven folders contained approximately thirty videos (each of which were up to sixty minutes long) showing various boys and girls between the ages of eight and twelve engaging in various sexual acts, including sexual intercourse with adults, other children, and so forth. Notably, the vast majority of the videos were produced by the same persons, featured the same background, and depicted Russian-speaking children coerced into engaging in these sexually explicit acts while syndicate cameramen recorded the crime in progress.

> **Practice Tip:** Just because a defendant pleads guilty does not mean that law enforcement's job is done. Prosecutors and agents, like the defense, must use the time between plea and sentencing to nail down any remaining loose ends, identify the likely key sentencing issues, and gather evidence targeted at resolving those remaining issues.

Agents, furthermore, were able to recover Dr. Watzman's coded e-mail exchange with a representative of the child pornography syndicate in Russia. Critical to the government's theory of aggravation, Dr. Watzman engaged in a number of e-mail chats with the Russian syndicate revealing his knowledge that the syndicate was *creating* the images he was paying for.

For example, the following e-mail correspondence between Dr. Watzman and "Pedo Shop" erased any doubt about the defendant's knowledge that real children were being sexually exploited as a direct result of the defendant's significant financial contributions to the Russian child pornography syndicate:

September 17, 2003	Pedoshop: "GOOD NEWS!!!!! . . . we have *made* this summer 24 vcd! The quality is better than previous vcd! *All was made using digital camera*! The films have gantastic quality. 1 vcd cost—$290. If you will order more than 5 vcds we will make you discounts!!"
September 20, 2003	Pedoshop: [Says received money order; provides password to download videos.]
September 20, 2003	Watzman: "OK. It is pretty good. Except #4 and #7 did not open and a few videos *I already had*. Make me a good discount offer for more and I will buy them."

September 20, 2003	Watzman: "*Is it all NEW material? Not the same as old movies?*"
September 21, 2003	Pedoshop: "Sure its *new material*!! please tell me how much vcd=s you have decided to order???"
September 21, 2003	[Watzman tells Pedoshop he will send four money transfers and complains that links for] "vcd 11, 14, 16, 13, 17, 29, 33, 35 no longer work. My files got corrupted so I have to download them again. I paid for them already." [Watzman previously ordered 24 VCDs for $170 each.]
September 21, 2003	Watzman: "OK. I will send as you say. It may take a few days to complete. I will start now. Maybe you start giving me some vcd links as I send you the transfer numbers."
September 23, 2004	Watzman: "I sent money. Total of $4,200 as you say for new 24 vcds and fixed old links. Please hurry. My time to download is short." [Watzman then provides money order routing numbers.]
September 27, 2003	Pedoshop: [Indicates they received Watzman's $3,000.] "Soon *we will have VERY BIG STUDIO and we can make films special for you*!!! You will tell what you want to see, what actions, which girls, etc. And *we will make films using your scenario. . . .* We will make you big discounts for this. . . . No money to grow, to give you more opportunities . . . another we want to make offices in USA, Germany, Australia, and some other countries and offer sex with lolitas . . . are you interested in it? . . . . As you see we are the ONLY ONE all over the Internet which shop doesn't cheat." [Goes on to request money. Emphasis added.]
October 2, 2003	Watzman: "*OK maybe I can send more money.* But first I have to see some new vcd's as you promised. I have been a good customer. I have already sent a lot of money."[9]
	[Defendant subsequently sends Pedoshop the requested money.]

Dr. Watzman, indeed, on at least one occasion provided Pedoshop with money above and beyond what he owed because Pedoshop said their Internet servers were expensive to run. According to the prosecution, in so doing, he knowingly provided material support for the syndicate's ongoing child exploitation "studios."

Watzman, in short, went beyond his role as a mere purchaser of goods, and became a financial supporter of this degrading operation. Moreover, he was fully aware that Pedoshop sexually exploited and sadistically abused real children. Not only did he not complain about this horrifying conduct, but he also encouraged it and fed the demand.

On October 27, 2003—a date coinciding with the "takedown" of the server—a representative of the syndicate e-mailed Dr. Watzman that he had "very bad news. . . . All peoples who received wires from our clients via Western Union . . . were arrest and put into jail! *Our studio* was closed."[10] This obviously confirmed what agents (and Dr. Watzman) already knew—namely, that the syndicate Dr. Watzman was helping fund was manufacturing child pornography.

V. The Sentencing of, and Parting Thoughts on, Dr. Watzman

The district court had access to all of the above evidence, and in late November 2005 sentenced Dr. Watzman to five years of incarceration (less time than the eight years of incarceration the government requested, but more than the sentence of probation urged by the defense based on claims that Dr. Watzman suffered from depression caused by a congenital heart defect).

The case of Dr. Watzman, in the end, tells a story sadly familiar to those of us who have spent careers in the field of criminal law. Indeed, one need not look far to see its several tragic dimensions. Most obviously, perhaps, is the identity of its direct victims; the little girls living half a world away who had their childhoods stolen and their lives ruined by members of a ruthless child pornography syndicate focused solely on raking in fortunes by feeding the perverse desires of their paying clients, largely well hidden by their sheer normalcy. On the other hand are the friends and family of this man, who in many senses could be a character in a Robert Louis Stevenson novella—the handsome, successful, highly educated doctor with a stellar future who, to the enduring shock and disbelief of those nearest him, secretly spent much of his disposable time—as well as income—funding a brutally exploitative Russian consortium willing to mercilessly sexually abuse children, and then memorialize this abuse for all time through "homemade" video clips and images. The devastation caused by the much-admired doctor's sinister side was tangible.

Practice Tip: In one particularly memorable case prosecuted by one of the authors, a pedophile priest not only allocuted at sentencing but also elected to assume the witness stand and allocute *under oath* in an effort to explain to the court what he had done, and why. This, as a matter of strategy, turned out to be a colossal blunder, as the defrocked priest spent two full days on cross-examination, ultimately agreeing with the prosecutor that he had lost count of the number of young boys he had victimized, and that he was not, and would never be, able to control his desires for sexual contact with minors. Exacerbating the situation, the defendant also minimized the full scope of his conduct, causing the judge to deny him a reduction in his sentence for acceptance of responsibility. The net result was the longest-ever sentence in the United States for possession of child pornography. The lesson from this series of errors is that defense counsel, particularly in such highly charged cases, must carefully consider how to proceed at sentencing (realizing that less, in this context, really can be more), and must spend considerable time with his or her client determining the best course of action.

As for defendants in Dr. Watzman's shoes, even they, in a sense, are pathetic figures driven by deep-seated sexual desires and fantasies that ultimately take over and, in the end, generally ruin their personal and professional lives. Whether the Internet and its associated explosion of readily available child pornography deserves a share of the blame is a topic for another book (or, perhaps more appropriately, for another few decades of research), but suffice it to say that never in human history has it been possible to so effortlessly explore and nourish secret sexual thoughts and desires.

Notes

1. All facts relayed here are contained in the well-publicized public record of the case.

2. This extremely conservative estimate is based on traceable purchases only.

3. Emphasis added.

4. A ful copy of the search warrant affidavit is available at www.dmholmeslaw .com/appiesboard/viewtopic.php?f=2&t=757 (last visited June 5, 2011).

5. The "Chiefer" alias represented Dr. Watzman's position as chief resident.

6. See generally *United States v. Bullis,* 77 F.3d 1553, 1158 (7th Cir. 1996) ("A prosecution is vindictive and a violation of due process if undertaken to punish a person because he has done what the law plainly allowed him to do"; quotations omitted); *United States v. Polland,* 994 F.2d 1262, 1266 (7th Cir. 1993) (same).

7. See generally *Bordenkircher v. Hayes,* 434 U.S. 357, 364–65 (1978).

8. See, for example, *United States v. Yarbough,* 55 F.3d 280, 282 (7th Cir. 1995) (defendant's withdrawal of guilty plea followed by superseding indictment with six new narcotics charges did not give rise to presumption of vindictiveness); *United States v.*

Bernal, 28 F.3d 630, 632 (7th Cir. 1994) (defendant's refusal to plead to state firearms charge followed by federal charges of felon in possession, which carried a much stiffer sentence, did not constitute vindictive prosecution); see also *United States v. Stanley,* 928 F.2d 575, 579 (2d Cir. 1991) (defendant's withdrawal of guilty plea followed by superseding indictment that added a firearm charge does not give rise to a presumption of vindictiveness); *United States v. Cooks,* 52 F.3d 101, 105–6 (5th Cir. 1995) (defendant's withdrawal of guilty plea followed by government seeking the career offender enhancement not vindictive).

    9. Emphasis added.

   10. Emphasis added.

11

The Challenge of
Transnational Investigations

A N ENDURING REALITY OF CRIMINAL JUSTICE is that, at least collectively, criminals are an extraordinarily adaptive and innovative lot, often leaving law
enforcement lagging woefully behind. Indeed, the criminal occupation itself is
all about having the first-move advantage, with law enforcement, in the main,
occupying a reactive posture. This is certainly true of domestic criminality,
but it is even more of a reality in the context of unlawful ventures crossing
U.S. borders.

In the context of child sexual exploitation, the inescapable contemporary
truth is that commercial and noncommercial exploiters alike satisfy a global
demand by selling and trading sexually explicit images of children, as well
as the children themselves, across national borders as if they were guns or
narcotics (the other top-dollar commodities headlining the global black market).[1] Put simply, the sexual exploitation of children, in whatever form, is now
big business; the fact that Crime, Inc., wants a piece of the lucrative action
should provoke little surprise.

Child exploitation, constantly spurred on by more readily available and
sophisticated modern communications technologies, is, indeed, a bona fide
transcontinental phenomenon, and law enforcement is finally recognizing it
as such. Today's investigators and prosecutors must, therefore, not only know
how to put together and present a domestic child exploitation case, but must
also be comfortable with the key weapons in the fight against transnational
child exploitation, including (1) letters rogatory; (2) Mutual Legal Assistance
Treaties (MLATs); and (3) extradition treaties.

Understanding the nuances involved in seeking the extradition of a wanted fugitive, and understanding the process of gaining the cooperation of a foreign nation in order to secure a critical witness interview and to collect certain evidence, are no longer rarely used, "exotic" skills. After all, no prosecutor or investigator wants to find himself drinking downstream from the (criminal) herd. To maximize the chances that the system's, and the victims', interests are properly vindicated, modern law enforcement personnel must, therefore, (1) understand the key challenges of transnational investigations; (2) have in mind a plan of attack for dealing with these challenges; and (3) be prepared to change that plan, as necessary, in order to overcome any potential stumbling blocks.

A. Today's Child Exploitation Prosecutor
Must Be a Public International Lawyer

The emotional, evidentiary, and technical challenges facing investigators and prosecutors handling purely domestic child exploitation cases are, as we have seen, formidable. And once these cases go transnational, the challenges multiply.

There can be little doubt that modern communications technology, and particularly the Internet, has been a net boon for child exploiters. With almost two billion people online,[2] and new members to the online community added by the tens of thousands each and every day, the world is in a very tangible sense becoming progressively smaller. And while this global interconnectedness and immediate access brings with it a host of public benefits, for those entrusted with the task of stemming the tide of child predators, cross-border cooperation in the digital age, as we shall see, also poses unique and complex challenges.

In the face of this ever-shrinking world, today's child exploitation prosecutors must also be public international lawyers. For instance, prosecutors must understand and be capable of effectively utilizing the various international legal instruments at their disposal to address the logistical, legal, and bureaucratic challenges posed by cases involving cross-border criminality. They must know how to secure foreign legal assistance to effectuate searches, arrests, and extraditions, and to otherwise collect foreign information and evidence in a manner rendering it admissible in a U.S. courtroom.[3]

In the pages that follow, we will sketch out the archetypal categories of challenges facing U.S. and foreign law enforcement once the crime being investigated has "gone global."

B. Understanding the True Scope of the Challenge

Federal prosecutors and investigators who for the first time are confronted with a case requiring assistance from a foreign jurisdiction are often taken aback by how difficult—not to mention frustrating—securing timely and meaningful foreign assistance can be. But prior to discussing how to overcome the particular challenges posed by transnational investigations, we must first gain a better understanding of what the most common challenges actually are; for only such an understanding permits effective planning.

1. No Longer Just London Calling: Exploiters Use Advances in Communications and Computer Technology to Live Local while Operating Global

The worst-kept secret in the world of child exploitation is that the proliferation of the Internet, cell phones, and other modern communications technologies has dramatically diminished the deterrent role that national boundaries play in warding off child exploiters.[4] Twenty years ago, smuggling photographs or videos of child pornography across national borders, sending these images through the mails, or smuggling children for sexual purposes was a high-risk activity, typically engaged in by extremely insular groups of like-minded child predators. Advances in computer and communications technology have drastically expanded the ability of those involved in the sexual exploitation of children to feel they are part of a larger and legitimized pedophile "community."[5] In addition, the advances also permit exploiters, regardless of geographic location, to coordinate their illicit activities, and to use online banking, e-mail accounts, f-servers, and the like to buy and sell (and re-sell) their "product" almost instantaneously, and with astonishingly limited risk of government detection.[6]

Contemporary exploiters, put simply, rely heavily on the Internet to (1) produce, obtain, and distribute child sexual exploitation content, (2) advertise their illicit wares, (3) "groom" and otherwise recruit innocent children, and (4) gather and launder their ill-gotten gains.[7] The ever-evolving Internet and related telecommunications, e-banking, and e-commerce capabilities are, therefore, but recent examples of how criminals adapt to change and successfully pursue the latest opportunities for amassing greater profits.

The global presence of the Internet, moreover, also permits individual and organized criminals to carry out their business *remotely*. Whether in Frankfurt or Freetown, the Internet and its various applications function the same. Communications, moreover, are not only immediate, but are, with even the slightest effort, rendered largely secure and anonymous.[8] Such reduced transaction costs—not to mention transaction risks—have transformed child exploitation, once a rarely charged offense, into a true multibillion-dollar global industry.[9] Indeed, in the time it takes to read this paragraph, hundreds of exploiters will have used their online accounts to receive and send thousands of images of previously created child pornography; while others will have digitally captured themselves, or their associates, sexually exploiting children, and will be in the process of downloading these images onto hard drives or anonymous servers for purposes of trade or financial gain.

And, as noted above, where money is to be made, organized crime is rarely far behind. Indeed, various organizations, including the International Organization for Migration, report that organized crime groups, including the Italian, Russian, and Balkan Mafias, South American cartels, Chinese and Vietnamese Triads, and the Japanese Yakuza have used the Internet to forge highly profitable transnational alliances to more efficiently and safely facilitate their human trafficking and related child exploitation activities.[10]

By way of example, consider the case of the "Blue Orchid," a "club" operated out of Moscow. The men running this club manufactured and distributed videos showing boys aged eight years and older being physically and sexually abused, and offered a child pornography series titled "Russian Flowers."[11] Another commercial ring, managed by Russian and Indonesian webmasters, was run by associates out of Fort Worth, Texas.[12] "Landslide Industries, Inc.," on the other hand, counted 250,000 subscribers worldwide (30,000 of them in the United States) who paid $29.95 a month for access to sites named "Child Rape," "Cyber Lolita," and "Children Forced to Porn."[13] Notably, these sites had a strictly commercial goal. Clubs such as "Wonderland" and "Our Place," on the other hand, were part of the virtual community of pedophiles, which seeks to constantly satisfy its need for new and more images of children engaged in sexual activity.

The plight of child trafficking victims aptly underscores the true magnitude of the problem. Although reliable statistics are notoriously difficult to come by, there is little debate that traffickers each year use their carefully coordinated channels to traffic internationally hundreds of thousands of young women and children for the purpose of selling them into a life of sexual exploitation.[14] The U.S. State Department and UNICEF estimate that each year more than two million children fall victim to commercial sexual exploitation.[15] The number of offenders is also uncertain because few are held accountable. And the groups responsible for these mass crimes clearly rely on the Internet and other modern communications technologies to coordinate transportation, to obtain fraudulent identity documents, to set up local safe houses, and to divide up and transfer the proceeds of their crimes.

But organized criminals are not the only ones taking advantage of modern communication technologies to help their crimes "go global." Even "independent" child traffickers and sexual exploiters benefit from the economies of scale and streamlined logistics that the technological revolution has made possible—frequently formally or informally affiliating with larger organized criminal collectives and groups.[16] For example, exploiters who were once regionally isolated can now expand their operations by collaborating through the Internet and by cell phone with organized criminal groups and other like-minded individuals. In the process, these exploiters forge criminal connections throughout the world. A good example of this symbiotic relationship can be seen in Macedonian and Russian human traffickers who force or dupe children and young girls to travel to the Balkans, where Albanian organized crime groups "break them in" at their brothels prior to routing them on to various European syndicates. This sad cycle, which continues virtually uninterrupted every day, is only possible as a result of the cooperation between and among organized crime groups.

2. Diminished Risks of Transnational Detection through Some Basic Tech Savvy

Complicating matters for law enforcement conducting transnational investigations is that only the rare (and, frankly, sloppy) foreign exploiter will employ communications technologies that are directly traceable back to him. Instead, the vast majority of today's child pornographers and human traffickers take great care to anonymize their communications and to encrypt their computer files. Even if law enforcement were to one day gain access to these criminals' computers, hard drives, or servers, they will usually be unable to actually open the files contained therein. Moreover, although the targets of the investigation of course know the usernames and passwords that would enable decryption, they, for obvious reasons, typically refuse to reveal them to law enforcement.

So is there a work-around solution for law enforcement? Although mechanisms such as gaining access to encrypted data by, say, remotely installing "key-logging" programs[17] onto subject computers to capture usernames and passwords are no longer the stuff of crime novels, their transnational use is hardly commonplace, and, for the reasons discussed below, often raise serious legal and diplomatic concerns. Such means of obtaining password information from overseas targets, moreover, require substantial technical sophistication (not to mention, in most countries at least, warrants).

Today's communications technology, in short, makes it easier than ever before to generate vast sums of money from transnational child exploitation.

But, more than that, our shrinking world also drastically—and effectively—extends the exploiters' "reach," that is, their ability to threaten, coerce, and control victims and witnesses, as well as their families and friends. Time and again, one-time witnesses are located through social networking sites and similar online means of tracking people down, and are, once contacted, "persuaded" to cease their cooperation. And if the direct approach fails, it does not take more than a few threatening e-mails or phone calls to friends or family to make even the most committed cooperator, and particularly one living in a jurisdiction with weak police and law enforcement, think twice about whether taking the risk is worth it. In short, while silence once was traditionally obtained through an in-person visit after the exploiters used phone books or friends and family to locate the (usually domestic) witness, today's virtual world permits criminals to obstruct justice anonymously, and from thousands of miles away, through the simple click of a mouse or a call using an untraceable cell phone.

Compounding these challenges, today's exploiters routinely rely on technology to operate out of fragile, weak states where they are, effectively, shielded from the long arm of the law. And while they may coordinate their criminal activities, produce their child pornography and do their online banking from places like Russia, Ecuador, or Thailand, they sell their "product" to citizens living in developed states who offer them the most lucrative opportunities, such as the United States. Consequently, exploiters' profits are now larger, as is their effective immunity from prosecution; this, from a criminal's perspective, is nothing short of a dream combination. Thus, while the fabled Italian crime syndicates of *Godfather* fame once employed accountants to ensure that the "technical" parts of their organizations ran smoothly, today's child exploitation syndicates employ IT and hacking experts to do their bidding, to develop and implement bespoke software programs, and to maintain and update the tech infrastructure driving their criminal empires.

In summary, then, today's virtual world promises transnational exploiters increased profits and decreased chances of law enforcement detection:

- *Anonymizing Software.* Exploiters and their networks develop and/or purchase increasingly sophisticated software in order to shield their anonymity, to expand their online storage capacities, and to encrypt their files, rendering them safe from potential digital forensic examination by police.
- *Trust-Based Systems.* Exploiters, particularly noncommercial ones, rely on "hidden channels" to secure their communications. Requiring private access that is granted only to those who have been "selected," based on

their perceived reliability and the trust-enhancing purchasing and/or sharing of sexually explicit materials over time.

- *Vulnerable Child Victims Found Abroad.* Exploiters continue to travel to developing countries where children are offered up by their families or other facilitators for the purpose of sexual exploitation and/or the production of sexually explicit material. Within minutes, the materials can be anonymously distributed to thousands of paying customers world-wide via the Internet.

- *Using the Internet to "Recruit."* Exploiters use online "grooming" and other recruiting techniques to persuade and coerce vulnerable children from around the world to produce pornographic materials, or to make themselves available for such production.

- *Finding a Secure Perch from Which to Set Up Shop.* Most child exploitation syndicates create their pictures and films and do their banking in overseas locations such as Russia, South America, and the Balkan states. The rule of law is less developed in these areas, and the chances of their detection, arrest, and conviction is accordingly minimized.

These are just some of the ways that today's modern communications technologies benefit the exploiters' supply chains and bottom lines, while concurrently according them a greater sense of security than ever before.

3. Who to Charge from One Thousand Miles Away: The Long and Bumpy Transnational Road to Identifying Criminal Targets

In the domestic context, identifying the targets/suspects/subjects of a particular child exploitation investigation is usually accomplished by traditional investigative techniques, such as residential and/or computer searches, witness interviews, grand jury subpoenas, video surveillance, and the collection of other circumstantial evidence of the person's guilt.

One of the most fruitful sources of evidence in the child sexual exploitation arena, in fact, is the seizure of the actual computers or external hard drives believed to be involved in the creation, possession, receipt, or distribution of child pornography—the computers the sexual exploiter used to communicate with the producer/supplier of the pornographic materials or which he used to "chat" with the child victim.[18]

Once the computer, whether through a court-ordered search warrant or a consent-search, is in hand, a careful forensic examination of the computer's files will, in the typical case, virtually seal a suspect's fate. If, for example, the seized computer in fact contains child pornography or e-mails believed to be evidence that the computer's user sexually abused children, evidence that the computer was (1) purchased by the suspect, and/or (2) contains exclusively the subject's e-mails, bills, online banking information, and other subject-specific data is the kind of rock-solid evidence even the most skilled defense attorney will have a hard time explaining away.[19] Likewise, DNA samples and fingerprints obtained from the computer's keyboard or CDs containing contraband images can answer the question of whether a particular suspect ever used (or at least handled) the computer.[20]

But such examinations, of course, presuppose physical access to a suspect's computer. And physical access requires, as a prefatory step, law enforcement to have substantially narrowed the field of potential suspects (typically to one). But that initial step of identifying the suspect—or, at least, of drastically cutting down the universe of potential suspects—on the other end of a chain of electronic communications becomes infinitely more difficult once these communications traverse national borders. Moreover, proving with certainty who the sender of pornographic images was, or who used the Internet to handle a criminal organization's logistics and fund transfers, is exceptionally tricky without physical access to the computer suspected of being used to draft and transmit the communications.

Even today's most basic online technologies permit computer users to disguise their identities, to create fictitious identities, or to use someone else's true identity.[21] "Re-mailing" services, for instance, permit users to strip outgoing e-mail messages of any potential identifying information.

But re-mailing is, in fact, one of the more sophisticated means of hiding one's true online identity. At least equally straightforward and familiar means of creating anonymity include:

- Using false names to purchase free or prepaid Internet access from a service provider or e-mail service.[22]
- Accessing public computers used by many, such as at Internet kiosks, cyber cafés, libraries, and schools.[23]
- Using overlay network/onion routing, proxy servers, or circumventors to hide the user's IP address and obscure the path the user's data took.[24]
- Using "ping servers" to hide one's identity while getting information out quickly.

Although privacy groups may well disagree, those who study computer crime trends have seen time and again that the e-mail and privacy systems offering the most sophisticated encryption and "anonymizer" services find their most loyal following within the online pedophile and organized crime communities. But, regardless of how one views the global availability of modern communications technology and modern means of hiding one's identity, there can be little debate that the proliferation of these technologies will, if anything, only accelerate, particularly in developing economies.[25] For U.S. law enforcement to have a significant domestic impact on the supply and demand dynamics of both commercial and non-commercial child exploitation, it must develop effective systems for tracking and identifying those who use modern communications technology outside the United States to engage in criminal conduct within the United States.

C. Key Methods of Obtaining Foreign Judicial Assistance

As tempting as it may be at times, a U.S. prosecutor or investigator risks his career by proactively contacting foreign authorities or witnesses, whether by telephone, e-mail, postcard, or other means, absent prior notice and authorization. An e-mail or postcard sent to a suspected criminal confederate living overseas will likely be considered a violation of the sovereignty of the nation into which the e-mail or card is sent. Moreover, as we shall see, even once such official clearance and authorization is in hand, actually receiving the foreign assistance almost inevitably involves significant delays. Prosecutors and investigators seeking such help from abroad must, therefore, as soon as possible initiate the process through the appropriate avenues.

1. The Promises and Pitfalls of the World's #1 Judicial Assistance Tool: Mutual Legal Assistance Treaties (MLATs)

Assume that U.S. law enforcement has been able to identify the name and location of an individual who is running a child pornography production syndicate in, say, Ukraine. More specifically, U.S. investigators have chat logs and IP addresses showing that Individual X over the course of a year provided a U.S.-based customer with thousands of dollars of custom-made child pornography.

Having this information is, of course, a great start. But the above-described issues of national sovereignty prevent U.S. law enforcement from simply flying to Ukraine to conduct a search of Individual X's residence and computers, to question and arrest Individual X, or to bring him back to the United States to stand trial for his alleged crimes. Stated most plainly, the default is that U.S. prosecutors and investigators are prohibited from conducting *any* part of their investigation in a foreign country without *first* obtaining that country's cooperation.

a. What MLATs Can Achieve

Larger-scale international criminal investigations, as a result, are virtually im-possible without resorting to the cooperation provisions contained in coun-try-specific MLATs (or, in the case of countries such as China, Taiwan, and Hong Kong, Mutual Legal Assistance *Agreements* [MLAAs]). Some MLATs even contain provisions on the release of bank records and other financial information from abroad (and these provisions in many cases even trump any restrictive domestic bank secrecy laws).[26] Because MLATs are so ubiquitous, most federal prosecutors who have occupied their positions for more than a few years will likely have functioned as "commissioners" for other countries seeking legal assistance in the United States pursuant to an MLAT (such com-missioners are, as discussed in chapter 6, in essence "deputized" to carry out the seeking country's wishes within the United States). Most federal prosecu-tors may have also relied on the MLAT procedure to gain the cooperation of their counterparts in other countries.

As their names suggest, MLATs provide for bilateral, mutual assistance in the gathering of legal evidence for use by the "requesting" state (that is, the state asking for the assistance) in its criminal investigations and proceedings. In general terms, then, MLATs are used to request foreign law enforcement assistance, such as the following:

- taking the testimony and statement of persons;
- providing documents, records, and evidence;
- serving documents;
- executing requests for searches and seizures;
- transferring persons in custody for testimonial purposes;
- locating persons;
- initiating proceedings upon request; and
- freezing and confiscating proceeds and instrumentalities of crime.

b. The United States as the Requested State: U.S. Cooperation and Accommodation Fosters Foreign Reciprocity

Although some MLATs contain provisions limiting their applicability (such as sections specifying that those requests having the potential of interfering with ongoing investigations in the "requested" country need not be acted on), a chief benefit of using an MLAT is that, unlike the below-described extradi-tion treaties, MLATs typically do not contain "dual criminality" (also known as "double criminality") requirements (more on this *infra*). Thus, if a U.S. prosecutor needs to interview a child sexual exploitation victim in Thailand, the prosecutor can ask the Thai authorities for assistance pursuant to the

TABLE 11.1
**Compilation of Bilateral Mutual Legal Assistance Treaties
to which the United States Is a Party**

Country	Date Ratified	Effective Date
Anguilla	July 3, 1986	November 9, 1990
Antigua & Barbuda	April 18, 1996	July 1, 1999
Argentina	December 4, 1990	February 9, 1993
Australia	April 30, 1997	September 30, 1999
Austria	February 23, 1995	August 1, 1998
Bahamas	June 12, 1987; August 18, 1987	July 18, 1990
Barbados	February 28, 1996	March 3, 2000
Belgium	January 28, 1988	January 1, 2000
Belize	September 19, 2000	July 2, 2003
Brazil	October 14, 1997	February 21, 2001
British Virgin Islands	July 3, 1986	November 9, 1990
Bulgaria	September 19, 2007	
Canada	March 18, 1985	January 24, 1990
Cayman Islands	July 3, 1986	November 9, 1990
China	June 19, 2000	March 8, 2001
Colombia	August 20, 1980	
Cyprus	December 20, 1999	September 18, 2002
Czech Republic	February 4, 1998	May 7, 2000
Czech Republic	May 16, 2006	
Dominica	October 10, 1996	May 25, 2000
Egypt	May 3, 1998	November 29, 2001
Estonia	April 2, 1998	October 20, 2000
European Union	June 25, 2003	
Europol	December 6, 2001	December 7, 2001
Europol Supplement	December 20, 2002	December 21, 2002
France	December 10, 1998	December 1, 2001
Greece	May 26, 1999	November 20, 2001
Grenada	May 30, 1996	September 14, 1999
Hong Kong	April 15, 1997	January 21, 2000
Hungary	December 1, 1994	March 18, 1997
India	October 17, 2001	October 3, 2005
Ireland	January 18, 2001	
Israel	January 26, 1998	May 25, 1999
Italy	November 9, 1982	November 13, 1985
Jamaica	July 7, 1989	July 25, 1995
Japan	August 5, 2003	July 21, 2006
Korea, Republic of (South Korea)	November 23, 1993	May 23, 1997
Latvia	June 13, 1997	September 17, 1999
Liechtenstein	July 8, 2002	August 1, 2003
Lithuania	January 16, 1998	August 26, 1999
Luxembourg	March 13, 1997	February 1, 2001

(*continued*)

TABLE 11.1
(Continued)

Country	Date Ratified	Effective Date
Malaysia	July 28, 2006	
Mexico	December 9, 1987	May 3, 1991
Montserrat	July 3, 1986	April 26, 1991
Morocco	October 7, 1983	June 23, 1993
Netherlands	June 12, 1981	September 15, 1983
Nigeria	September 13, 1989	January 14, 2003
Panama	April 11, 1991	September 6, 1995
Philippines	November 13, 1994	November 23, 1996
Poland	July 9, 1996	September 17, 1999
Romania	May 26, 1999	October 17, 2001
Romania Protocol	September 10, 2007	
Russian Federation	June 17, 1999	January 31, 2002
South Africa	September 16, 1999	June 25, 2001
Spain	November 20, 1990	June 10, 1993
St. Kitts & Nevis	September 18, 1997	February 25, 2000
St. Lucia	April 18, 1996	February 2, 2000
St. Vincent & the Grenadines	January 8, 1998	September 8, 1999
Sweden	December 17, 2001	
Switzerland	May 25, 1973	January 23, 1977
Thailand	March 19, 1986	June 10, 1993
Trinidad & Tobago	March 4, 1996	November 29, 1999
Turkey	June 7, 1979	January 1, 1981
Turks & Caicos	July 3, 1986	November 9, 1990
Ukraine	July 22, 1998	February 27, 2001
United Kingdom	January 6, 1994	December 2, 1996
Uruguay	May 6, 1991	April 15, 1994
Venezuela	October 12, 1997	
Venezuela—Cooperation/ Money Laundering	November 5, 1990	January 1, 1991
Venezuela—Mutual Assistance/ Financial Institutions	March 17, 1995	March 17, 1995

U.S.-Thai MLAT,[27] regardless of whether the prosecutor has charged anyone, or, if he has charged someone, with what that person was charged.

Moreover, in contrast with the below-described extradition process, which requires that all requests be made through formal diplomatic channels, MLAT requests are handled between law enforcement "central authorities" (typically, the respective Attorney General, Ministry of Justice, Ministry of the Interior, or his designee).

In the United States, the Office of International Affairs (OIA) in Washington, DC, functions as the designee of the Attorney General. Incoming and outgoing requests for law enforcement assistance are, therefore, in the first instance handled by OIA. As a consequence, prosecutors "in the field" (that is, not living in Washington, DC) typically only come in contact with their foreign counterparts *after* OIA has processed the request (and even then, direct law enforcement to law enforcement contact remains the exception rather than the rule; the OIA attorneys generally function as the intermediaries).

Particularly in the area of high-tech crime, however, obtaining evidence through the use of formal MLATs between nations can, as practitioners can attest, prove to be exceedingly slow and ineffective. The central difficulty is the required level of legal formality, resulting in sluggish and cumbersome official requests (and actions thereon). Moreover, foreign law enforcement counterparts often lack the training necessary to conduct, say, sophisticated forensic searches of subject computers (in such cases, it is preferable to have them simply ship the entire seized hard drive to the United States).

And delays are, of course, always annoying when a prosecution team is in the midst of a ramped-up investigation. Particularly in child exploitation cases, it is vital that searches and document requests be executed as quickly as possible in order to preserve evidence, secure witness statements, remove child victims from danger, and/or question or arrest suspects. Having to wait for weeks or longer for the official diplomatic channels to process and approve a request not only can be extremely frustrating, but often also guarantees that the action, once approved, will serve little value.

Although economics perhaps shouldn't matter in the hunt for the world's transnational child predators, the "money plays no part" argument is most often brought to the fore by well-funded law enforcement agencies not engaged in a daily struggle to find funds sufficient to cover their most basic needs. The costs associated with mutual legal assistance, after all, are almost always borne by the party *providing* that assistance (that is, by the "requested" country).

This financial arrangement can create significant hardships for poorer countries, such as Thailand, which on a daily basis are served with multiple requests for assistance from wealthier countries, while rarely seeking such foreign assistance for themselves. The result of this virtual one-way foreign assistance street is that these poorer countries are, in a very real sense, subsidizing the legal processes of much wealthier nations.

That said, the United States in particular also finds itself inundated with requests from around the globe for information concerning online sites and hosts such as Facebook, Hotmail, Google, and Yahoo!. The FBI, which typically in the first instance handles such requests, is required to process and route these requests to the subject company's corporate offices, and countless federal prosecutors are tasked with shepherding the foreign requests through the U.S. legal process. This process causes significant administrative costs to, and places man-power burdens on, the Department of Justice. These economic realities at some point will likely have to be reevaluated as we transition into an increasingly interactive and integrated global law enforcement community.

The legal and diplomatic hurdles and corresponding delays associated with MLATs (particularly when issued to countries already over-taxed and unable to properly accommodate the mounting requests) often dissuade U.S. prosecutors from requesting assistance pursuant to them. Often months will pass without the requested country taking any action on the MLAT, and even once action is taken, it is not always the top-flight, professional assistance the U.S. prosecutor may have expected. Particularly in the context of requesting electronic evidence, there is a constant concern that, as the hours and days pass, the evidence is being destroyed, altered, or transferred. Careful planning and considerable patience are, therefore, still important tools in the prosecutor's arsenal.

2. "Letters Rogatory"

In many cases, the United States and the particular foreign nation in whose jurisdiction assistance is needed will not have negotiated and entered into a formal MLAT. In such cases, U.S. prosecutors can request that a U.S. District Judge issue traditional "letters rogatory" (also known as "letters of request"), which is a particularly nondescriptive term referring to a judicial request that a foreign tribunal provide certain documents or assistance. Put another way, a letter rogatory is a request from a U.S. judge to the judiciary of a foreign country for the performance of an act that, if done without the sanction of the foreign court, would constitute a violation of that country's sovereignty. (For a very useful "fill-in-the-blank" sample letter rogatory, see appendix 4.)

a. Advancing Reciprocity by Assisting with "Incoming" Letters Rogatory

Prior to discussing how U.S. prosecutors and investigators can use letters rogatory to seek foreign assistance, a few words are in order concerning how U.S. responses to *foreign* requests for assistance help pave the way for future reciprocity (and, perhaps, even future MLATs).

Ever since the mid-nineteenth century, Congress has authorized non-U.S. parties to request legal assistance from the federal courts in the collection of evidence for use in a foreign proceeding. More specifically, the statute now codified at 28 U.S.C. § 1782 permits federal courts to provide such assistance.[28] Section 1782, in its current form, states:

> The district court of the district in which a person resides or is found may order him to give his testimony or statement or to produce a document or other thing for use in a proceeding in a foreign or international tribunal, including criminal investigations conducted before formal accusation. The order may be made pursuant to a letter rogatory issued, or request made, by a foreign or international tribunal or upon the application of any interested person and may direct that the testimony or statement be given, or the document or other thing be produced, before a person appointed by the court. By virtue of his appointment, the person appointed has power to administer any necessary oath and take the testimony or statement. The order may prescribe the practice and procedure, which may be in whole or part the practice and procedure of the foreign country or the international tribunal, for taking the testimony or statement or producing the document or other thing. To the extent that the order does not prescribe otherwise, the testimony or statement shall be taken, and the document or other thing produced, in accordance with the Federal Rules of Civil Procedure.
>
> A person may not be compelled to give his testimony or statement or to produce a document or other thing in violation of any legally applicable privilege.[29]

To invoke § 1782 and obtain federal-court assistance, the requesting entity presents a written request in the form of a letter rogatory (which, if presented by an "interested person" rather than a requesting *entity*, is known as a "letter of request") to the applicable federal district court.[30] Today, both foreign tribunals and private parties, including corporations and natural persons, can make requests for use in both civil lawsuits and criminal prosecutions,[31] and can ask that a federal prosecutor be designated a commissioner who acts on that party's request.

Answering the question of why U.S. prosecutors and investigators should care about U.S. assistance provided to foreign authorities, consider that one of the important congressional purposes in broadening the scope of federal-court assistance was to *encourage reciprocity* by other nations.[32] By providing broad assistance to foreign nations and tribunals via § 1782, the U.S. encourages foreign nations and tribunals to do the same.

The courts, moreover, have stressed that U.S. District Courts still retain the discretion to deny a request.[33] "Congress gave the federal district courts broad discretion to determine whether, and to what extent, to honor a request for assistance under 28 U.S.C. § 1782."[34] The courts have described a wide range of potentially applicable factors they consider when making such a discretionary determination.[35] Most significantly, the U.S. Supreme Court has held that those factors include whether "the person from whom discovery is sought is a participant in the foreign proceeding"; "the nature of the foreign tribunal, the character of the proceedings underway abroad, and the receptivity of the foreign government or the court or agency abroad to U.S. federal court judicial assistance"; whether the request "conceals an attempt to circumvent foreign proof-gathering restrictions or other policies of a foreign country or the United States"; and whether the request is "unduly intrusive or burdensome."[36]

b. Using "Outgoing" Letters Rogatory to Secure Judicial Assistance Abroad

As the nomenclature implies, while MLATs are *legally binding treaties*, under the letters rogatory approach requested countries or tribunals make available whatever assistance they are willing to provide as a matter of comity. There is, simply, no guarantee that the requested country or tribunal will act on a letter, or, if it acts, how it will act.

Law enforcement, moreover, must proceed on the assumption that the letters rogatory process will take at least a year. While this delay may be cut short by transmitting a copy of the request through Interpol or some other more direct route, even in urgent cases such requests take over a month to execute.

Here is what the U.S. Attorney's Manual advises in terms of letters rogatory *procedure*:

A. Content: The form of a letter rogatory depends on the country to which it is addressed and the assistance sought. Some countries have statutory guidelines for granting assistance. Assistant United States Attorneys should seek specific guidance from the Office of International Affairs (OIA) before drafting a letter rogatory. . . .

   Letters rogatory generally include: (1) background (who is investigating whom and for what charge); (2) the facts (enough information about the case for the foreign judge to conclude that a crime has been committed and to see the relevance of the evidence that is being sought); (3) assistance requested (be specific but include an elastic clause to allow subsequent expansion of the request without filing an additional letter rogatory); (4) the text of the statutes alleged to have been violated; and (5) a promise of reciprocity.

   Letters rogatory must be signed by a judge and, normally, authenticated by (1) an apostille, (2) an exemplification certificate, (3) a chain certificate of authentication, or (4) as directed by OIA. If the requested state has ratified the Hague Convention Abolishing the Requirement of Legalization of Foreign Public Documents, it is preferable to use an apostille. The chain certification is a cumbersome process involving authentication by the Department of Justice, the Department of State, and the embassy of the foreign country to which the letter rogatory is directed. Consult OIA to ascertain which method to use because authentication requirements change frequently.

B. Procedure: First, obtain a model from OIA and check with OIA to ascertain the requirements of the particular country.

Second, prepare a draft . . . and send it to OIA for clearance.

Third, secure a judge's signature. Submit the cleared final to the district court in two originals under cover of an application for issuance of letters rogatory and a memorandum in support, models of which have been obtained from OIA. One signed original letter rogatory remains with the court.

Fourth, authenticate as directed by OIA. Unless OIA has instructed you differently, affix an apostille or other authentication to the signed duplicate original and send it and two copies to OIA.

Fifth, make arrangements for translation . . . of the letter rogatory (not the application or supporting memorandum) and send the duplicate original with translation to OIA, which will transmit it to the Department of State, the American Embassy in the country concerned, or directly to the appropriate ministry or authority in the country concerned. If OIA transmits the letter rogatory with translation via the diplomatic channel, the Embassy will send it to the Foreign Ministry under cover of a diplomatic note, the Foreign Ministry will usually refer it to the Ministry of Justice, and the Ministry of Justice will usually forward it to the proper judicial authority where it will be executed. Normally, the evidence, once obtained, is returned through the same channel by which the request was transmitted. In some cases, the request is sent to an attorney in the foreign jurisdiction who is retained to present the request, obtain the evidence, and deliver it to the United States.[37]

In terms of drafting style and content, the U.S. Attorney's Manual advises the following:

A. Style: A request for judicial assistance is necessarily directed to a judicial system that is different from our own. Even common law countries do not always have the same legal concepts and philosophies found in our legal system (although, confusingly, they may use some of the same terms). Civil law systems differ even more markedly. In drafting a request for assistance, it is therefore imperative to describe simply and clearly the facts of the case and the nature of the assistance requested. Do not use the kind of language that they would include in an indictment or application for search warrant.

Most applications will be translated. Avoid the use of technical legal terms (e.g., ITAR, ITSP, RICO or even probable cause) that are impossible to translate. A clear, narrative style eases the job of the translator and the judicial authority that receives the request. OIA reviews draft requests to ensure conformity with these requirements.

B. Grand Jury Information: Sufficient facts should be included in the request to show that a crime has been committed and that the information sought is relevant to the investigation or prosecution. If the request will not make sense without incorporating information obtained through the grand jury and protected by secrecy requirements, the Assistant United States Attorney (AUSA) should obtain an order authorizing disclosure under Fed. R. Crim. P. 6(e). (Because letters rogatory are signed by the court, an order authorizing disclosure is superfluous. However, the AUSA should draw the court's attention to the grand jury material in the application.)[38]

3. Extraditions—the Promised Land of Delays and "Red Tape"

From an investigative perspective, identifying the subject of the investigation, determining what charges the evidence supports, and filing these charges completes the bulk of the heavy lifting. In the context of international investigations, however, extradition is a considerable additional hurdle that must be cleared.

In those cases in which defendants either reside in or are visiting other jurisdictions, formal requests for a particular defendant's (1) arrest and (2) extradition are the standard mechanisms for returning the defendant to stand trial in the United States. And while extraditions and legal assistance both typically are achieved through formally negotiated international treaties, there are some notable differences. For one, extradition proceedings can be extraordinarily time-consuming and legally complex, requiring familiarity with the process's legal nuances, the ability to put on a "mini-trial" in the requested country to demonstrate sufficient proof (usually judged by a preponderance standard of proof) of the defendant's guilt, and a willing requested nation.

In terms of the big picture, then, extradition requires (1) a legal mechanism (usually a bilateral treaty) between the two countries, as well as (2) a finding that the alleged conduct is "an extraditable offense." Although determining whether a country has a formal extradition treaty with the United States is a relatively straightforward undertaking, answering the question of whether the offense for which the defendant is indicted in the United States is, in fact, "extraditable" can be far more complex (and, therefore, is something the astute federal prosecutor must think about prior to indictment; when multiple charges are on the table in a case where the defendant is known to be outside the United States, some advance homework can ease the post-indictment burden and help make the extradition a more straightforward process).

a. Modern Extradition Treaty Trends: From "Dual Criminality" to the "Rule of Specialty"

Early U.S. extradition treaties contained straightforward, comprehensive lists of all extraditable offenses. Today's treaties, in contrast, tend to replace such lists with a simple requirement of "dual criminality." Dual criminality safeguards both the interests of states in which the crimes occur, and those of foreign nationals traveling abroad. Because jurisdiction is based principally on territoriality, states generally set the legal norms within their own borders. Usually these norms exhaustively describe the legal duties of persons, including foreign nationals. The dual criminality requirement appreciates that retaining legal assistance in a foreign state can be problematic when the subject offense is not one recognized as something illegal by that state.

Thus, instead of a schedule of extraditable crimes, modern treaties require (1) that the offense be considered an imprisonable crime under the laws of the requested country, had those acts taken place within the jurisdiction of that country, as well as (2) some negotiated minimum term of imprisonment signaling the offense's severity.[39] That said, a minority number of treaties contain a hybrid combination of explicitly enumerated extraditable offenses, as well as a requirement of dual criminality.

The most clear-cut benefit of the dual criminality approach is its flexibility. Dual criminality permits the criminal law in both treaty countries to develop, while concurrently obviating the need to renegotiate and amend the treaty whenever a new offense is on the books. However, certain conduct that qualifies as a child exploitation offense in the United States is not similarly illegal in other jurisdictions. For example, if a destination country has not criminalized the prostitution of children, or has set the age of sexual consent particularly low, home countries are hampered in their efforts to prosecute their nationals and permanent residents who sexually abuse children abroad.

Predictably, such a foreign "safe harbor," whether created due to legislative shortcomings or ineffective enforcement, particularly in the context of sex crimes, encourages "criminal preference" among offenders who seek out states with reduced child protections. Absent extraterritoriality provisions discussed in chapter 11, perpetrators can offend U.S. laws and then return home with impunity. For example, by some estimates, among the roughly five million tourists who visit Thailand annually, over half are believed to be sex tourists, 10 percent of whom reportedly engage in sex with minors.[40] A strong argument can be made that international legal norms relating to child exploitation, such as those enshrined in the United Nations Convention on the Rights of the Child, create an affirmative international duty upon states to protect the defenseless; a failure to prosecute because of dual criminality restrictions implies an abdication of these duties and a prioritization of those within the state's borders.

Although the requested jurisdiction may invoke the dual criminality doctrine to prevent extradition when it does not have the same child exploitation *laws* as the United States, the same alleged *acts* may constitute some other criminal violation under the foreign law (such as, say, battery, or child neglect in the case of child prostitution). In Kosovo, for example, being a "John" who purchases the services of a prostitute is not illegal; however, aiding and abetting prostitution is—and it is difficult to argue that the customer who gives a pimp, young woman, or child money in order to have her engage in prostitution is not, thereby, also aiding and abetting the conduct.

In such cases, thus, the U.S. prosecutor must be prepared to argue that, for the purposes of extradition, the dual criminality requirement is satisfied because it should not matter that the parties to the treaty place the crime in a different *category* of offense or describe the offense using different terminology. What matters is that the *conduct* is criminal in both countries. Reference to the U.N.'s Model Treaty on Extradition[41] may provide some support for the U.S. prosecutor's request, in that it provides that:

> The treaty provision should require differences in the names of offenses, as well as different categorizations, to be disregarded in determining double criminality. The introduction of such explanatory clauses to reinforce a generic double criminality standard explicitly minimizes the significance of the particular legislative language used to penalize certain conduct and encourages a more pragmatic focus on whether the underlying factual conduct is punishable by both contracting States, even if under differently named statutory categories. Many difficulties that arise because of the need to make highly technical distinctions between different crimes (for example theft, fraud, embezzlement; malversation and breach of trust; degrees of homicide; financial misconduct by public officials; or various forms of participation in organized criminal activities) are thereby avoided. In extradition treaties between civil and common law States, what otherwise could be difficult double criminality issues could be preempted by specific provisions on how common law offenses such as attempt and conspiracy relate to the civil law concepts of criminal association.[42]

In terms of additional considerations relating to the extradition process, most of today's treaties are explicit as to what their requirements are and what documents the requesting state must provide, such as (1) the charging documents, (2) a description of the applicable evidentiary standard(s), (3) copies of arrest warrants, and (4) identifying documents such as copies of passports. Some treaties, moreover, also include explicit *limitations*; some countries, for example, will refuse to extradite their nationals, or will not extradite if the sought person is facing the death penalty, has already been prosecuted for the same offense, or is wanted in connection with "political offenses."[43]

The "rule of specialty," moreover, prevents the requesting country from prosecuting an extradited defendant for any prior offenses for which the formal extradition was not sought; this, in effect, prevents the requesting nation from trying a "bait and switch," seeking formal extradition only for Crime A, but then prosecuting that individual for Crime B.[44] To determine whether the rule was violated, courts consider whether the surrendering country would view the charged crimes as interconnected with the crimes for which he was extradited. For example, the rule may be violated if a defendant was extradited for a child pornography possession offense, but, once in the United States, was additionally charged with manufacturing and distributing child pornography.[45] Of course, the rule of specialty can be waived by the requested state.

Prosecutors must, therefore, be on the lookout for defendants who consent to being extradited on the least aggravated charges, for in those receiving jurisdictions where defendants have standing this strategy can act as a bar to prosecution for the more aggravated offense. In jurisdictions where the extraditing country has standing to waive a violation of the rule of specialty, moreover, such a defense strategy can impose heavy burdens on the requesting government to obtain a waiver from the extraditing country.[46]

Finally, most modern extradition treaties to which the United States is a signatory provide that extradition must be granted *regardless* of where the act(s) constituting the offense were committed.[47]

Rounding out this part of our discussion, when an urgent pre-extradition arrest is sought, the requesting state, pursuant to most standard treaties, can also seek a "provisional arrest warrant." Other standard treaty provisions include mechanisms for the sought person to waive formal extradition proceedings, the provision of legal representation, and grounds for deferred surrender of the sought person.[48]

b. Extradition Logistics

We now turn from extradition treaty content to the equally important extradition logistics. The process, as noted above, is certainly far from informal. Extradition requests, including urgent ones, must be accompanied by the requisite paperwork and diplomatic notes, and must be routed through formal diplomatic channels. The process is in stages:

1. If a U.S. prosecutor is seeking the arrest and extradition of a defendant, he must, as with MLATs, first contact OIA.
2. OIA prosecutors handle different regions of the world, and are assigned to assist on matters depending on their regional expertise and current caseload. The assigned OIA attorney functions as an intermediary between the U.S. and foreign prosecutor, and helps the U.S. prosecutor determine what documentation the applicable treaty requires.
3. Assuming the prosecutor and OIA attorney have gathered the needed paperwork, OIA then sends it on to the U.S. Department of State.

4. The State Department, in turn, sends the package (which by now has been translated into the requested state's language) on to the appropriate U.S. embassy.
5. The embassy then transmits the package to the requested government.
6. Once the extradition (or provisional arrest) package is in the hands of the requested government, the requested government will usually convene some form of preliminary extradition hearing to determine whether the requesting state has complied with the applicable treaty provisions.
7. Assuming the extradition request passes muster, the defendant has been arrested, and the court has ordered the defendant's extradition, the U.S. Marshal's Service typically handles escorting the person back to the United States.

The U.S. prosecutor is expected to, on an ongoing basis, provide any paperwork, evidence, or other documentation their foreign counterparts need in order to satisfy the requested country's court that the court is dealing with (1) the right person (that is, the person who's extradition is sought is in fact the person who stands before the court), and that (2) the United States has satisfied its applicable burden of proof (typically, probable cause or lower)[49] to support the claim that the defendant committed the offense on which the extradition is based.

c. Alternative Extradition Approaches

Sometimes either logistical or legal considerations make formal extradition impractical. In those cases, OIA can provide useful guidance as to alternative approaches worth considering. For example, OIA, through the State Department, can ask another country to expel or deport a U.S. citizen by using a U.S. arrest warrant to cancel the person's U.S. Passport. In such a case, OIA asks the State Department to send a cable to the Embassy in the country in which the defendant is located. The cable will typically inform the embassy and local national law enforcement of the identity of the defendant (providing identifying information and the like), and will point out that the defendant is a fugitive residing in the country without valid travel documents. The cable will, of course, also request that the country use its immigration laws to deport the defendant back to the United States.

Not surprisingly, the success of this approach in large part depends on the willingness of the requested country to use its local laws to assist in executing the deportation request. To this end, and as practitioners know well, providing the requested country with detailed information on the offense and/or the defendant's criminal background (particularly when either or both are aggravated) can help motivate a perhaps otherwise sluggish bureaucracy to spring into action to remove the undesirable person from their midst.

Federal law enforcement may, of course, also attempt to "lure" a target or defendant to the United States using trick or subterfuge.[50] The problem with this technique is that it will often raise the ire of officials in the country in which the individual is residing. In the typical case, the lure will require e-mails or letters to be sent, or calls to be made, to that country without having first obtained the country's permission via an MLAT request or letter rogatory. The aggrieved jurisdiction's claim will be that, even though such contacts are fairly minimal, they violate the country's sovereignty (and may even violate their domestic laws). Once again, setting aside exceptional circumstances, prior authorization for any such lure should be obtained directly from OIA.

4. Whose Case Is This Anyway? Confronting Jurisdictional Challenges

Transnational child exploitation cases, by their very nature, frequently serve up extremely complicated jurisdictional issues. After all, if the offense takes place in multiple countries, the defendant(s) are typically eligible of being charged in multiple jurisdictions. In recent years, and particularly in the wake of the enactment of the Comprehensive Crime Control Act of 1984 (P.L. 98-473) and the Omnibus Diplomatic Security and Antiterrorism Act of 1986 (P.L. 99-399), U.S. statutes have begun to include targeted extraterritorial provisions for misconduct engaged in outside the United States, but which causes harm in, or is intended to cause harm in, the United States.

The "Protect Act," for example, which targets both U.S. citizens and residents in the United States, makes it a crime for any person to travel abroad with the purpose of engaging in child sex tourism.[51] Under the act, the government can establish the offender's guilt by proving one of the following: (1) that the accused traveled with the intent to engage in sexual conduct with a minor, (2) actually engaged in sexual conduct with a minor overseas, or (3) otherwise attempted to violate the law. The act, furthermore, permits prosecution based solely on evidence of *intent* to travel abroad for the purpose of engaging in sexual conduct with a minor.[52] Not requiring evidence that any actual sexual misconduct took place, to some extent, has the added benefit of eliminating the difficult task of cross-border evidence collection.

But sometimes the foreign authorities will be quite eager to handle the case themselves. The foreign jurisdiction in which the defendant finds himself may persuasively argue that the "requesting" jurisdiction should permit local law enforcement to pursue the matter because this approach permits both sides to bypass the above-described issues relating to extradition or evidence-gathering, and/or because the foreign jurisdiction has strong public policy grounds for wanting to bring the defendant to justice where he was found.[53]

5. Searching For, and Seizing, Evidence in a Foreign Country

Speaking broadly, there are two means of retrieving evidence stored on computers and hard drives. First, law enforcement can conduct a physical search of the premises where the computer is located (and, thereafter, a forensic exam of the actual computer). Second, and less common, law enforcement can monitor, in real time, interceptions of data transmitted from or to the computer.

As we already know, the Internet and computers have vastly expanded child exploiters' collective capacities to transport, store, and distribute images of sexual exploitation; to share information; and to smooth out logistical problems relating to the movement of images or persons, receipt and transfer of payment, establishment and operation of safe houses and production facilities, and so forth. Seizing overseas computer evidence through MLATs or, if that is not available, letters rogatory is, therefore, a critical component in most transnational child exploitation investigations.

Obtaining computer-based evidence, however, also poses serious *technical* and *logistical* challenges to global law enforcement. The challenges include:

- Obtaining permission to conduct searches remotely (that is, through the Internet).
- Having local law enforcement make reliable copies of hard drives or storage devices ("mirror-imaging" them) without corrupting the evidence (or, alternatively, obtaining permission for U.S. law enforcement to retrieve this evidence).
- Gaining access to encrypted or password-protected files.
- Properly retaining the seized evidence and establishing a solid chain of custody.

Careful and close coordination between law enforcement agencies is, as we have already seen, the most fundamental prerequisite to successful transnational operations. For example, foreign arrests and/or search warrants frequently need to be simultaneously executed in multiple jurisdictions in order to minimize the chances that the targets either flee or have an opportunity to destroy evidence or otherwise interfere with the investigation.[54] The coordination of these activities in a manner that does not corrupt the evidence or raise doubts about the professionalism of the witness or defendant interview is difficult to achieve in the best of circumstances; once national borders are traversed, such coordination concerns only multiply.

D. Additional Practical Solutions For
Today's Complex Transnational Challenges

Conducting an investigation across national borders is, as we have seen, a potential minefield of practical and legal problems threatening to result in mounting delays, increased costs, and significant uncertainty concerning whether the sought assistance will be accomplished in the hoped-for manner. In addition to the challenges discussed above, additional day-to-day practical problems facing U.S. prosecutors and investigators include:

- Securing timely, reliable, and professional document translation and interpreters.
- Dealing with foreign counterparts who do not prioritize the foreign cases—or child exploitation cases—in the same way the referring law enforcement officers do.
- Scheduling conference calls when law enforcement personnel live in different time zones.
- Legal, linguistic, and cultural barriers and differences between officers working, formally or informally, across borders.

In the face of these significant obstacles, governments have devised a variety of approaches to minimize the additional burden already inherent in transnational—and, often, transcultural—investigations. At the heart of all successful solutions, however, is a basic realization that the global law enforcement community must continue to strive to harmonize laws and procedures, facilitate the seamless transfer of information, and build up the professional capacity of U.S. and foreign investigators and prosecutors.

- *Improved Law Enforcement Intelligence Sharing and Communication*: As we have seen, today's exploiters of children are extremely facile when it comes to adopting the latest tools of the criminal trade. E-mail, the Internet, cell phones, web-based servers, and online banking are as much of the contemporary criminal's arsenal as forged identity documents, public telephones, and nominee bank accounts once were. It is, therefore, incumbent on modern law enforcement not only to keep up with the latest technological advances, but to also strive to stay one step ahead of the criminal class. By understanding the capacities of foreign counterparts, and harmonizing information-sharing technologies, evidence, and tips, law enforcement in different countries can use both formal and informal channels to identify, pursue, and bring to justice those involved in commercial and noncommercial child exploitation.

Consider, by way of example, chapter 10's discussion of University of Chicago pediatrics resident Dr. Marc Watzman.[55] In that case, Russian law enforcement seized a server operated by a Russian child pornography syndicate with thousands of U.S. clients and sophisticated billing, banking, and money laundering operations in Ecuador and elsewhere. Although some of the syndicate members, shortly after the first wave of arrests, were able to use the Internet to tip off their paying "customers," the Russian authorities quickly shared the names, credit card numbers, and other identifying information they obtained from the server with their law enforcement counterparts in the United States and elsewhere.

The upshot of the Russian investigation was that federal and local law enforcement in the United States within a matter of days received the names and addresses of over three thousand customers who paid top dollar for "original" and "custom-made" pornography produced by the syndicate. Although law enforcement, unfortunately, was not able to bring cases against most of these customers who, through their purchases, supported the syndicate's ongoing criminal activities, they were able to identify the largest financial backers of the syndicate and those who had the most likely access to actual children in the United States. As a result, within a twenty-four-hour period officers and agents obtained search warrants and initiated "knock and talks" with hundreds of suspects, sending a virtual shockwave through this particular "community" of exploiters. Dr. Watzman's criminal conduct was exposed, and he, on the eve of trial, pled guilty to using the Internet to order tens of thousands of dollars' worth of child pornography.

- *Increased Law Enforcement Sensitivity to Reality That Seemingly "Local" Conduct Can Be a Tip-Off to the Presence of Transnational Crime:* It is often too easy for the law enforcement community to overlook clear "red flags," and to treat instances of exploitive criminality occurring on their streets as just that—little more than local matters. In response to what can be an overly myopic view of child exploitation, the U.S. law enforcement community has collectively worked to sensitize its members and to raise awareness that criminal conduct observed locally may well be part and parcel of more involved transnational crime.

Thus, when well-trained officers interview minor women whom they believe to be engaged in prostitution, they are now looking for evidence of false documentation; evidence of foreign nationality; the absence of meaningful local contacts, parents, and other family who live overseas in "source" countries such as Moldova or Ukraine; the absence of any traceable home that is either paid for or controlled by the young woman; and the presence of similarly situated girls. Following up on such "red flags," today's investigators understand that they may well be dealing with a trafficking victim when they are unable to get straight answers to some key questions, such as:

- Do you live with your employer?
- Can you leave your job if you want?
- Can you come and go as you please?
- Have you been hurt or threatened if you tried to leave?
- Has your family been threatened in connection with your job?
- Where do you sleep and eat?
- Are you in debt to your employer?
- How did you arrive at this destination?
- Do you have your passport/ID/immigration paperwork? If not, who has it?

Answers to such red-flag questions may prompt logical follow-ups in order to determine whether the minor or young adult was brought to the United States by human traffickers for the purposes of organized prostitution. By becoming aware of these connections, by gaining a better sense of what appropriate steps to take once such red flags come to law enforcement's attention, and by collaborating with their regional, national, and international peers, today's prosecutors and investigators are able to more effectively identify and build cases that go beyond the national jurisdiction.

- *Recruiting IT Experts*: Law enforcement must become more adept at confronting the reality that the exploiters are increasingly tech-savvy and are using modern communications technologies to expand their unlawful reach. Law enforcement, in response, must more heavily recruit IT professionals possessing the specialized training and skills needed to effectively initiate an online pursuit. Such professionals can, once the suspect is identified, conduct forensic examinations of the suspect computer system, external hard drives, and so forth. One of the enduring problems is that law enforcement agencies can rarely compete with the private sector for the top talent. Cooperative relationships with private-sector consultants may, at times, be the only viable alternative. Nevertheless, law enforcement agencies not only must conduct in-house training to get the officers, agents, and prosecutors familiar with the basics of online investigation and forensic examination, but also must begin to more aggressively cultivate "home-grown" IT talent. In this, the FBI has made extremely positive strides; the FBI has put together dedicated groups of agents who are specifically trained to pursue such cases, who receive ongoing IT training, and who are able to develop focused subject-matter expertise.[56]

- *Continued Support for, and Enforcement of, Multinational Treaties and Conventions*: We have already discussed the basic purpose and operation of MLATs, letters rogatory, and other international treaties, conventions, and assistance in its various forms. But to gain a more fulsome understanding of why bilateral and multilateral judicial assistance treaties and similar initiatives are, generally speaking, in the interest of U.S. law enforcement agencies pursuing foreign child exploitation cases, a brief discussion of the history of such instruments is in order.

By the mid to late 1970s, the U.S. had negotiated several thousand treaties with foreign countries on a myriad of topics affecting legal relationships, including extradition treaties with most other countries. Nevertheless, negotiating MLATs was not of primary concern.

Indeed, the first such treaty was the 1977 MLAT with Switzerland. This agreement, as it turned out, initiated a virtual flood of similar agreements between the United States and virtually every country with (1) functioning law enforcement capabilities and (2) democratic governments.

The United States, concurrently, also became a party to other mutual legal obligations, including key conventions issued by the U.N. and the Organization of American States (OAS; see appendix 5). These agreements, however, were put in place primarily to deal with those cases in which *no* bilateral agreements exist.

Responding to the growing realization that transnational threats demand a transnational law enforcement response, from 1993 to 2000 the Clinton Administration developed various unilateral, multilateral, and bilateral law enforcement initiatives to build capacity and spread pro-U.S. goodwill within and among "friendly" nations. The creation of integrated databases to share law enforcement information among U.S. law enforcement agencies, and the development in 1966 of a national global anticrime strategy reflected a healthy understanding of the pressing need to work together to fight transnational crime.

The U.S. Department of State, the Treasury Department, and the U.S. Department of Justice, indeed, increasingly collaborated to devise memoranda of understanding (MOU) calibrated to coordinate the handling and sharing of law enforcement information in foreign jurisdictions, while harmonizing (and deconflicting) the efforts of liaison offices throughout the world. As a result, teams of law enforcement officers began to work together in a task force approach within embassies and U.S. missions worldwide.

The 1990s also witnessed the United States sign on to various substantive multilateral initiatives, primarily through the 1995 Lyon Group of the G8, which developed new arrangements to combat, among others, organized crime, trafficking in women, cyber crime, and corruption.

In 2003, moreover, the United States and the European Union signed very important legal assistance and extradition treaties.[57] These treaties had the added benefit of putting the European Union in the position of bilateral partner, capable of negotiating on behalf of all of its member states (something the United States had previously bridled against). The United States, for its part, secured the European Union's consent to set up joint investigative teams and share information concerning the bank accounts of criminal suspects, something E.U. law had previously prohibited. The net result of these developments was, in short, a win-win, reflecting a hard-fought harmonization of trans-Atlantic interests and approaches.

To build on this gaining momentum, the United States, with its dominant global market power and infrastructure, must continue to develop approaches and standards that other countries will, more or less willingly, adopt. And, as the old saying about global acquiescence to U.S. approaches and initiatives goes, "Where Goliath walks, others will follow."

• *Expanding Informal Channels*: Although formal MLATs, letters rogatory, and conventions may be the "public face" of the world's cooperative law enforcement community, a comparable amount of exchange of information occurs through tried-and-tested informal investigator-to-investigator and prosecutor-to-prosecutor contacts. (Indeed, these personal cooperative relationships can be so informal and "off the grid" that agencies frequently only learn of them by accident.)

The FBI and other U.S. law enforcement agencies, recognizing how hard it is to receive law enforcement cooperation "remotely" (and primarily through formal channels), have embarked on aggressive efforts to set up shop in many, if not most, foreign countries. U.S. law enforcement, for example, commenced a very deliberate goodwill strategy focused on building counterpart relationships in countries such as Russia, Estonia, Ukraine, Poland, the Czech Republic, Serbia, Egypt, Pakistan, Israel, Kazakhstan, India, and Argentina.

The purpose of such bricks-and-mortar outreach is to forge indispensable cop-to-cop relationships through which U.S. law enforcement is able to cultivate ties to other sources of information in the host countries. Echoing this understanding, then–FBI director Louis Freeh described the FBI's Legal Attaché ("Legat") program as "the single most significant factor in the Bureau's ability to detect, deter, and investigate international crimes in which the United States or our citizens are victims."[58]

Valuable relationships are also forged daily through joint trainings and the ongoing placement of liaison officers drawn from all branches of the U.S. law enforcement community; the FBI, DEA, ATF, ICE, Secret Service, and Coast Guard now all post their officers and agents overseas. Conversely, the United States also encourages other countries to send their officers to the United States to get training and share information. In an effort to build capacity and foster reliable partner relationships in other countries, the United States has established international law enforcement academies in Southeast Asia, Europe, Africa, and Latin America for joint training involving U.S. and foreign law enforcement officials. The United States has also established subject-area-specific working groups with selected partner countries, such as China, Russia, Ukraine, and Italy. The United States must also continue to seek to enter into MLATs with transition countries, such as Russia and Kosovo, which present the greatest global crime threat.

While old-guard institutions such as Interpol[59] and the World Customs Organization[60] continue to struggle to keep up with contemporary law enforcement developments, new organizations such as the Southeast European Cooperative Initiative (SECI)[61] housed in Bucharest make increasing strides to develop integrated law enforcement capacities that address the burgeoning crime problem facing countries like those in the newly independent Balkans.

In its first year of operation, for example, SECI (a self-described "mini-Interpol") handled thousands of requests for information relating to transborder crimes, and, since then, has facilitated the establishment of specialized task forces to combat, among other offenses, trafficking in persons and organized prostitution rings.

On balance, then, the trend in transnational cooperation is very positive, no doubt driven in large part by the realization that no country is able to unilaterally protect itself against criminal elements within and outside its borders. Law enforcement officers around the globe are collaborating to stop the creation and dissemination of child pornography, the sexual abuse of children through forced prostitution, and the trafficking of children for purposes of sexual exploitation. Politicians, in turn, understand that their reelection hopes are tied to the public's perception that they have delivered a reasonable degree of security to their constituents. Thus, while policies and ideologies may wax and wane, the long-run balance is clearly tilting toward cooperation, and away from unilateralism and isolationism.

E. Parting Thoughts

When a prosecutor or investigator realizes that his investigation requires assistance in a foreign country, the first thing he should do is to determine what mechanisms he has at his disposal. In terms of steps, he must:

1. Identify the country from which the assistance is needed;
2. Determine whether the United States has an MLAT with that country that applies to the kind of case he is dealing with, as well as to the kind of evidence being sought; and
3. If no MLAT exists, consider the letters rogatory procedure (and survey all potentially applicable international conventions and treaties that may provide some persuasive authority).

Although great progress toward stemming the tide of child exploitation has been made during the past decades, cooperation among national and local law enforcement agencies continues to be more *ad hoc* than systematic, internal information-sharing leaves much to be desired; information systems are frequently incompatible, and transnational trust and respect have yet to completely replace skepticism and derisiveness. The principal limitations of transnational cooperation, in short, are frequently not only ideological, but also pragmatic. Armed with a realistic understanding of the promises and pitfalls of transnational investigation, prosecutors and investigators will be best positioned to decide on the most promising investigative path.

Key Sources for Guidance:

- U.S. Department of State Guidance on Preparing Letters Rogatory: http://travel.state.gov/law/judicial/judicial_683.html#countryspecific
- U.S. Attorneys Manual Section on Letters Rogatory: www.justice.gov/usao/eousa/foia_reading_room/usam/title9/crm00275.htm
- U.S. Department of State Country-Specific Judicial Assistance Information: http://travel.state.gov/law/judicial/judicial_2510.html
- U.S. Department of Justice's Office of Overseas Prosecutorial Development, Assistance, and Training Program Homepage: www.justice.gov/criminal/opdat/about/
- U.S. Department of Justice's Office of International Affairs Homepage: www.justice.gov/criminal/about/oia.html
- U.S. Department of Justice's Office of International Affairs Contact Info: www.justice.gov/criminal/about/contact.html
- Interpol: www.interpol.int/

- USDOJ Office of Justice Program's National Institute of Justice's International Center: www.nij.gov/international/
- USDOJ Office of the Legal Advisor U.S. Treaty and Other International Agreements List: www.state.gov/www/global/legal_affairs/tifindex.html

Notes

1. See generally *United States v. Sullivan*, 451 F.3d 884, 891 (D.C. Cir. 2006) (comparing the market for child pornography with the market for drugs, and concluding that, "in contrast to wheat or marijuana, the supply of electronic images of child pornography has a viral character: every time one user downloads an image, he simultaneously produces a duplicate version of that image. Transfers of wheat or marijuana merely subdivide an existing cache; transfers of digital pornography, on the other hand, multiply the existing supply of the commodity, so that even if the initial possessor's holdings are destroyed, subsequent possessors may further propagate the images. This means that each new possessor increases the available supply of pornographic images. This multiplying effect highlights the importance of eliminating a possessor's stash in the first instance, before it can be disseminated into the marketplace").

2. See generally Shadid M. Shahidullah, *Federal Laws and Judicial Trends in the Prosecution of Cyber Crime Cases in the United States: First and Fourth Amendment Issues*, 45 CRIM. L. BULL. ART. 2 (2009) ("More than 1.3 billion people world-wide are now connected to the global cyber space—the Internet and the World Wide Web. It is estimated that by 2015, another one billion of the world's population will be connected to cyber space. The Internet use is currently growing at a rate of 72.2% in North America, 56.4% in Oceania and Australia, and 46.8% in Europe. The rest of the world, however, is more aggressive in catching up. Between 2000–2008, Internet usage has grown 923.7% in the Middle East, 903.9% in Africa, 603.4% in Latin America and the Caribbean, and 348.1% in Africa. During the same period, Internet usage has grown 125.2% in North America and 256.1% in Europe. The discovery and expansion of the Internet and the World Wide Web have brought significant advances in communications among different groups, cultures, and civilizations. Cyber space has enlarged the boundaries of human knowledge, science, technology, and productivity. It has taken societies and civilizations to a new threshold of power and possibilities for transformations. But it has also brought new crimes and criminality, and an entirely new domain of criminal law and statutes").

3. As a general matter, evidence obtained overseas relating to a criminal defendant who is a nonresident alien will be admissible unless the manner in which the evidence was obtained does not "shock the conscience" of the U.S. court. See generally *Stonehill v. United States*, 405 F.2d 738 (9th Cir. 1968) (ruling that "(1) all evidence is admissible unless there is an exclusionary rule; (2) even the Fourth Amendment does not by itself provide for the exclusion of evidence unlawfully obtained; (3) the Supreme Court, in order to force United States officers to abide by the Fourth Amendment,

created the exclusionary rule; and (4) there is nothing our courts can do that will require foreign officers to abide by our Constitution").

4. See Shahidullah, supra note 2.

5. See generally James E. Baker and Melanie Krebs-Pilotti, *Internet Pandemic? The Not-So-Secret and Expanding World of Child Pornography*, 53 FED. LAW. 50, 50 (2006) ("Child pornography is not a tragic sideshow to the Internet age; it is endemic to the Internet").

6. See generally Federal Bureau of Investigation, INNOCENT IMAGES: ONLINE CHILD PORNOGRAPHY/CHILD SEXUAL EXPLOITATION INVESTIGATIONS, available at www.fbi.gov/stats-services/publications/innocent-images-1 ("Today, computer telecommunications have become one of the most prevalent techniques used by pedophiles to share illegal photographic images of minors and to lure children into illicit sexual relationships. The Internet has dramatically increased the access of the preferential sex offenders to the population they seek to victimize and provides them greater access to a community of people who validate their sexual preferences") (last visited June 15, 2011).

7. See *United States v. Young*, 613 F.3d 735, 739 n. 3 (8th Cir. 2010) (noting that *grooming* is a term that refers to "a way that subjects, adult subjects [converse] with persons on the Internet that are under the age of 18. For example . . . the subject might talk about things that the . . . person under age 18 would be interested in such as what they like to do with their friends, where they like to eat, what they like to do for fun. . . . The purpose of the grooming is to build a trusting relationship between the two parties").

8. See generally Jay M. Zitter, *Propriety of Civil or Criminal Forfeiture of Computer Hardware or Software*, 39 A.L.R.5th 87 (2011) ("The computer has become an indispensable tool in the world of business. However, like any other advance in technology, computer equipment and software can not only be used to benefit mankind, but can also be used to the detriment of society, such as advancing criminal designs. For example, computers can be used for disseminating obscenity through Internet and other systems, for criminals communicating with henchmen, for hacking into personal and business records, or for the more prosaic tasks of keeping records of illicit drug or gambling transactions").

9. See generally Maureen Walterbach, comment, *International Illicit Convergence: The Growing Problem of Transnational Organized Crime Groups' Involvement in Intellectual Property Rights Violations*, 34 FLA. ST. U. L. REV. 591, 599 (2007) ("Facilitating transnational operations is easier with the Internet and other instantaneous communication methods. Exchange of ideas can be sent thousands of miles in seconds with various online communication methods. Organized crime groups use the Internet for communications as well as for their criminal targets that can be exploited for considerable gain at low risk") (citations and quotations omitted); see also James R. March, *Masha's Law: A Federal Civil Remedy for Child Pornography Victims*, 61 SYRACUSE L. REV. 459, 469–70 (2011) (discussing Congressional findings in support of the Child Abuse Victims' Rights Act of 1986).

10. See generally James R. Richards, TRANSNATIONAL CRIMINAL ORGANIZATIONS, CYBERCRIME, AND MONEY LAUNDERING, at 3 (1999); Claire Sterling, CRIME WITHOUT FRONTIERS: THE WORLDWIDE EXPANSION OF ORGANISED CRIME AND THE PAX MAFIOSA (1994);

Carol Hallett, *The International Black Market: Coping with Drugs, Thugs, and Fissile Materials*, in Global Organized Crime: The New Empire of Evil, at 74, 76 (Linnea P. Raine and Frank J. Ciluffo, eds., 1994).

11. See Press Release, U.S. Customs Service, *Russian Police Take Down Global Child Pornography Web Site* (Mar. 26, 2001), available at www.customs/gov/hot-new/pressre1/2001 (last visited June 15, 2011).

12. See Naftali Bendavid, *Huge Child Porn Web Site Broken Up*, Chi. Tribune, Aug. 9, 2001, at 9.

13. See Christopher Marquis, *U.S. Says It Broke Ring That Peddled Child Pornography*, N.Y. Times, Aug. 9, 2001, at A1.

14. See generally Viviana Waisman, *Human Trafficking: State Obligations to Protect Victims' Rights*, 33 Hastings Int'l & Comp. L. Rev. 385, 391 (2010) ("Data collection [is] extremely difficult. In fact, the range of estimates varies to such an extent that higher estimates are as much as ten times that of lower estimates. Despite the fact that estimates vary by several million persons, the International Labor Organization, in a comprehensive report, calculates that approximately 2.4 million persons are trafficked each year; 43% for commercial sexual exploitation, of which 98% are women and girls. An estimated 500,000 women are trafficked annually to Western Europe") (citations omitted).

15. See 2010 TIP Report, supra chapter 1, note 1; see also 2008 TIP Report, supra chapter 1, note 1.

16. See Florida State University Center for the Advancement of Human Rights, Florida Responds to Human Trafficking, at 10 (2003) (noting that "advanced electronic forms of communication and Internet advertisements facilitate this oppressive and exploitive industry").

17. See generally Neal Hartzog, *The "Magic Lantern" Revealed: A Report of the FBI's New "Key Logging" Trojan and Analysis of Its Possible Treatment in a Dynamic Legal Landscape*, 20 J. Marshall J. Computer & Info. L. 287, 289 (2002).

18. See generally Ty E. Howard, *Don't Cache Out Your Case: Prosecuting Child Pornography Possession Laws Based on Images Located in Temporary Internet Files*, 19 Berkeley Tech. L.J. 1227 (2004).

19. See, for example, *United States v. Dobbs*, 629 F.3d 1199, 1213 (10th Cir. 2011) ("The existence of copies of the images in the cache of his computer was, like fingerprints left at the scene of a crime, merely evidence of his actual criminal activity").

20. See, for example, *United States v. Acosta*, 619 F.3d 956, 960 (8th Cir. 2010) ("Acosta's fingerprints were found on child pornography CD labels and on related materials. Handwriting analysis also revealed that Acosta's handwriting appeared on various child pornography materials").

21. See generally Citizens Media Law Project, How to Maintain Your Anonymity Online, www.citmedialaw.org/legal-guide/how-maintain-your-anonymity-online (guidance on maintaining online anonymity and keeping your identity hidden from, among others, law enforcement and the courts) (last visited on May 27, 2011).

22. See, for example, *United States v. Allen*, 625 F.3d 830 (5th Cir. 2010) (defendant used false name to open e-mail account). Note, however, that when a user signs up for a free e-mail account, the server used to access the site logs the user's IP address. If

that IP address can be traced to the user's home or work computer, and if the e-mail (or blog-hosting) provider is subpoenaed, the user's true identity could be revealed.

23. By using an Internet café, library, or university computer lab, the user is able to set up an e-mail account with far fewer risks that his or her IP address can be traced and identity revealed.

24. See, for example, *United States v. Vosburgh*, 602 F.3d 512, 527 n.14 (3rd Cir. 2010) ("The trial evidence showed that proxy servers can be used to mask IP addresses, and that knowledgeable users can 'spoof' the IP addresses of others").

25. See generally Shahidullah, supra note 2 ("The Internet use is currently growing at a rate of 72.2% in North America, 56.4% in Oceania and Australia, and 46.8% in Europe. The rest of the world, however, is more aggressive in catching up. Between 2000–2008, Internet usage has grown 923.7% in the Middle East, 903.9% in Africa, 603.4% in Latin America and the Caribbean, and 348.1% in Africa. During the same period, Internet usage has grown 125.2% in North America and 256.1% in Europe").

26. However, if this approach does not work, a more straightforward method of gaining access to such potentially incriminating documents can be to simply serve a grand jury subpoena on the U.S. branch of an overseas bank with which the suspected human trafficker, for example, maintains bank accounts tied to his criminal endeavors. Such subpoenas are referred to as "extraterritorial subpoenas," "Bank of Nova Scotia subpoenas," or "BNA" subpoenas. The latter two names come from the key U.S. case in which the Eleventh Circuit Court of Appeals ruled that the U.S. government may compel a foreign bank doing business in the United States to comply with a U.S. grand jury subpoena seeking records from an overseas branch, and permitting U.S. courts to hold noncompliant banks in contempt for failing to do so. That said, and in light of foreign nations' repeated assertion that this extraterritorial approach infringes on their national sovereignty and domestic laws, U.S. courts in most cases in which the compliance is challenged will employ a "vital U.S. interests" test intended to limit forced compliance to only the most important cases. Because of the potential diplomatic friction caused by such BNA subpoenas, and in light of the proliferation of MLATs, OIA concurrence is required before an assistant U.S. attorney (AUSA) issues such a subpoena. AUSAs may also seek to enforce "consent directives," by which a U.S. court orders a person subject to its jurisdiction to consent to the foreign bank's disclosure of its records (such consent has been found nonviolative of the Constitution because the directives are not "testimonial" and are only signed to accomplish compliance with a valid grand jury subpoena).

27. See appendix 3 for the U.S.-Thai MLAT, which is fairly standard and should provide readers with a more tangible sense of what these MLATs actually look like in the real world.

28. See *Intel Corp. v. Advanced Micro Devices, Inc.*, 542 U.S. 241, 247–49 (2004) (discussing Section 1782's history).

29. 28 U.S.C. § 1782(a).

30. See generally *In re Comm'r's Subpoenas*, 325 F.3d 1287, 1290 (11th Cir. 2003); abrogation in other part recognized by *In re Clerici*, 481 F.3d 1324, 1333 n.12 (11th Cir. 2007).

31. See, for example, *Intel*, 542 U.S. at 246 (request by private corporation for use in underlying civil lawsuit); *In re Letter of Request from Crown Prosecution Serv. of United Kingdom*, 870 F.2d 686, 687 (D.C. Cir. 1989) (request by foreign government for use in underlying criminal investigation).

32. See, for example, *United Kingdom*, 870 F.2d at 690 ("The expectation or hope was that by making assistance generously available through the good offices of United States officials and courts, our country would set an example foreign courts and authorities could follow when asked to render aid to United States courts, authorities, and litigators"); *John Deere Ltd. v. Sperry Corp.*, 754 F.2d 132, 135 (3d Cir. 1985) ("'It is hoped that the initiative taken by the United States in improving its procedures will invite foreign countries similarly to adjust their procedures'" [quoting the Senate Report for the 1964 amendment]).

33. See, for example, *Intel*, 542 U.S. at 264 ("As earlier emphasized, a district court is not required to grant a § 1782(a) discovery application simply because it has the authority to do so") (citation omitted).

34. *Four Pillars Enters. Co. v. Avery Dennison Corp.*, 308 F.3d 1075, 1078 (9th Cir. 2002); accord *In re Clerici*, 481 F.3d at 1331; *Edelman v. Taittinger (In re Edelman)*, 295 F.3d 171, 181 (2d Cir. 2002); *Al Fayed v. United States*, 210 F.3d 421, 424 (4th Cir. 2000).

35. See, for example, *In re Request for Assistance from Ministry of Legal Affairs of Trinidad & Tobago*, 848 F.2d 1151, 1156 (11th Cir. 1988) (holding that the district court should deny the request if the district court "suspects that the request is a 'fishing expedition' or a vehicle for harassment"), abrogated in other part by *Intel*, 542 U.S. at 259.

36. *Intel*, 542 U.S. at 264–65.

37. U.S. Attorney's Manual, 9-275, Letters Rogatory (2010).

38. Ibid. at 281.

39. See generally *United States v. Saccoccia*, 18 F.3d 795, 800 n.6 (9th Cir. 1994) (holding that "an accused may be extradited only if the alleged criminal conduct is considered criminal under the laws of both the surrendering and requesting nations"); Jonathan O. Hafen, *International Extradition: Issues Arising under the Dual Criminality Requirement*, 1992 B.Y.U. L. Rev. 191 (1992).

40. See Vickie F. Li, *Child Sex Tourism to Thailand: The Role of the United States as a Consumer Country*, 4 Pac. Rim L. & Pol'y J. 505, 516 (1995); see also Lucy Ward, *Cook Cracks Down on Child Sex Tourism; Britain Leads Crusade against Paedophiles: International Co-operation to Target Prostitution Trade*, Guardian, Apr. 1, 1999, at 3 (reporting 250,000 Western child-sex tourists visiting Asia yearly); Aaron Sachs, *The Last Commodity, Child Prostitution in the Developing World*, World Watch, Jul./Aug. 1994, at 26, 28 (discussing explosive growth of the sex tourism industry).

41. U.N. Office on Drugs and Crime, Revised Manuals on the Model Treaty on Extradition and on the Model Treaty on Mutual Assistance in Criminal Matters (2002), available at www.unodc.org/pdf/model_treaty_extradition_revised_manual.pdf.

42. Ibid. at para. 21.

43. On the political offense exception, see generally *Kroeger v. The Swiss Federal Prosecutor's Office*, 72 Int'l L. Rep. 606 (Swiss Fed. Trib. 1966) ("The [purported political] offense must have been committed in the course of a struggle for power in the State and must also be in appropriate proportion to the object pursued, in other words suitable to the attainment of that object. The extinction of human life, one of the most reprehensible crimes, can only appear excusable if it constitutes a last resort in the pursuit of a political objective. On the facts . . . such a situation does not come into question. The accused was acting at a time when the nationalist socialist regime stood at the pinnacle of its power. He acted against helpless women, children and sick persons who could not possibly have threatened German dominion"). However, article VII of the Genocide Convention explicitly states that "genocide and the other acts enumerated in article III *shall not* be considered as political crimes for the purpose of extradition" (emphasis added). Such clauses rejecting the political offense exemption are extremely rare in international treaties (see the 1973 International Convention on the Suppression and Punishment of the Crime of Apartheid, the 1998 International Convention for the Suppression of Terrorist Bombings, and the 2000 International Convention for the Suppression of the Financing of Terrorism); see also *Quinn v. Robinson*, 783 F.2d 776, 792–93 (9th Cir. 1986) ("The political offense exception is premised on a number of justifications. First, its historical development suggests that it is grounded on the belief that individuals have a right to resort to political activism to foster political change. This justification is consistent with the modern consensus that political crimes have greater legitimacy than common crimes. Second, the exception reflects a concern that individuals—particularly unsuccessful rebels—should not be returned to countries where they may be subjected to unfair trials and punishments because of their political opinions. Third, the exception comports with the notion that governments—and certainly their non-political branches—should not intervene in the internal political struggles of other nations").

44. This rule was first recognized under U.S. law in *United States v. Rauscher*, 119 U.S. 407 (1886).

45. The First Circuit in one case found no violation where the defendant was extradited for conspiracy to murder and was charged with attempted murder because the facts underlying the offenses were interconnected. See *United States v. Tse*, 135 F.3d 200, 205–6 (1st Cir. 1998).

46. See, for example, *United States v. Najohn*, 785 F.2d 1420 (9th Cir. 1986).

47. *Cf.* Charles Doyle, Extraterritorial Application of American Criminal Law (Congressional Research Service 2010) ("Crime is ordinarily proscribed, tried, and punished according to the laws of the place where it occurs. American criminal law applies beyond the geographical confines of the United States, however, under certain limited circumstances. State prosecution for overseas misconduct is limited almost exclusively to multi-jurisdictional crimes, that is, crimes where some elements of the offense are committed within the state and others are committed beyond its boundaries. A surprising number of federal criminal statutes have extraterritorial application, but prosecutions have been few. This may be because when extraterritorial criminal

jurisdiction does exist, practical and legal complications, and sometimes diplomatic considerations, may counsel against its exercise").

48. On the issue of deferred surrender, consider the following relatively standard proviso in the U.S.-Korean Extradition Treaty:

1. If the extradition request is granted in the case of a person who is being proceeded against or is serving a sentence in the Requested State for an offense other than that for which extradition is requested, the Requested State may temporarily surrender the person sought to the Requesting State for the purpose of prosecution. The person so surrendered shall be kept in custody in the Requesting State and shall be returned to the Requested State after the conclusion of the proceedings against that person, in accordance with conditions to be determined by mutual agreement of the Contracting States.
2. The Requested State may postpone the extradition proceedings against a person who is serving a sentence in that State for an offense other than that for which extradition is requested or who is being prosecuted in that State. The postponement may continue until the prosecution of the person sought has been concluded or until such person has served any sentence imposed.

Extradition Treaty between the Government of the United States of America and the Government of the Republic of Korea, U.S.-Korea, June 9, 1998, art. 12, available at www.state.gov/documents/organization/112483.pdf (last visited June 5, 2011).

49. See *Hand 'Em Over: Britain's Tough Extradition Laws Face a Shake-Up*, THE ECONOMIST, Sept. 23, 2010 (noting that the burden of proof for extraditions from the United States—namely, probable cause—is higher than that for extraditions out of Britain), available at www.economist.com/node/17103867?story_id=17103867 (last visited July 6, 2011).

50. For example, in 2000, unknown persons believed to be in Kazakhstan attempted to extort Michael Bloomberg, founder and owner of Bloomberg L.P. The subjects demanded via the Internet that Bloomberg pay them money in exchange for information on how they had managed to infiltrate Bloomberg L.P.'s computer system. FBI undercover agents, with the assistance of Mr. Bloomberg, engaged in e-mail communications with the subjects while they were in Kazakhstan—a country without an extradition treaty with the United States—and convinced them to travel to London for a meeting. On August 10, 2000, they were identified as the authors of the communications to Bloomberg and arrested for extradition to the United States by the London Metropolitan Police and New Scotland Yard. See Nick Fielding, *Hackers Caught in Bloomberg E-Sting*, SUNDAY TIMES (London), Aug. 20, 2000, at 10.

51. Note, for example, that Section 506 of the PROTECT Act, amending 18 U.S.C. § 2251 (making it illegal to travel abroad with the intent of taking illicit pictures of children), is titled "Extraterritorial Production of Child Pornography for Distribution in the U.S." Congress, thus, clearly intended for the law to apply outside the boundaries of the United States. The amendment itself, in fact, makes Congress's intent even more apparent: "Any person who . . . employs, uses, persuades, induces, entices or coerces any minor to engage in, or who has a minor assist any other person to engage in, any sexually explicit conduct outside of the United States, its territories or possessions, for the purpose of producing any visual depiction of such conduct,

shall be punished"; see also Ellen S. Podgor, *New Dimension to the Prosecution of White Collar Crime: Enforcing Extraterritorial Social Harms*, 37 McGEORGE L. REV 83, 94–95 (2006) ("In recent years, extraterritorial prosecutions have increased, and it is likely that globalization factors into this expansion. Increased travel, commerce, and accessibility to communicate with other countries have the unfortunate side effect of increased extraterritorial criminal activities. Prosecuting crimes with an international dimension presents new challenges for federal prosecutors. The initial question in all of these cases is whether there is appropriate jurisdiction to proceed with the criminal action. At the heart of this question is whether the statute at issue encompasses activities occurring outside the United States"); see also *United States v. Knox*, 776 F. Supp. 174 (MD Pa. 1991) (holding that there can be no extraterritorial application of child pornography statute where the defendant was not prosecuted for producing pornography in a foreign country, but for receiving it).

52. See ibid.

53. To round out this discussion, note also the opposite problem of "jurisdictional passivity," which occurs when cases that could be brought in a number of countries, are eventually not prosecuted at all because nobody takes the initiative.

54. For example, in one online child pornography sting the U.S. Customs Service coordinated the execution of thirty warrants for twelve different suspects in ten countries. In another case, the New York Attorney General's office seized a news server as part of "Operation Sabbatical," an anti-child-pornography sweep that resulted in thirteen arrests in twelve states and three foreign countries. The Attorney General argued that the operator of the server (Dreamscapes) knew or should have known that child pornography was on its servers, and failed to remove it.

55. See *Watzman*, 486 F.3d at 1004.

56. The FBI's Computer Analysis and Response Team (CART) and Regional Computer Forensic Laboratory (RCFL) programs are good examples of this forward thinking. See Douglas A. Schmitknecht, *Building FBI Computer Forensics Capacity: One Lab at a Time*, 1 DIGITAL INVESTIGATION 177 (2004), available at www.rcfl.gov/downloads/documents/DigitalInvestigator.pdf.

57. See Select Committee on the European Union, EU/U.S. AGREEMENT ON EXTRADITION AND MUTUAL LEGAL ASSISTANCE, 2002–2003, H.L. 153, available at www.statewatch.org/news/2003/jul/useuhol.pdf (last visited on June 7, 2011).

58. *FBI International Training: Hearing before the Subcomm. on Foreign Operations*, 105th Cong. (1997) (statement by Louis J. Freeh, director, Federal Bureau of Investigation), available at www.fas.org/irp/congress/1997_hr/s970320f.htm (last visited June 15, 2011).

59. Interpol homepage, www.interpol.int/ (last visited May 27, 2011).

60. World Customs Organization homepage, www.wcoomd.org/home.htm (last visited May 27, 2011).

61. Southeast European Cooperative Initiative: Regional Center for Combating Trans-border Crime, www.secicenter.org/ (last visited May 27, 2011).

12

Victim Witness Protection
in Child Exploitation Cases

AₗₜₕₒᵤGH LAW ENFORCEMENT OFFICERS and social service providers receive specialized training in the handling of child sexual exploitation victims, most will candidly concede that their desire to investigate the cases, prosecute the offenders, and serve the victims did not fully develop until they met their first actual child victim of sexual exploitation. Although one can address the issues academically and antiseptically describe the medical or psychological injuries, nothing quite prepares the responder for his first interview of a victim. Most responders will say that it is, in fact, the victims that keep them working in such a uniquely psychologically and emotionally draining field. The perseverance of victims in the face of denigration, lack of hope, physical harm, and insidious manipulation serves as a beacon for those entrusted with the important job of both aiding the victim and serving justice. In recent years, Congress and the Department of Justice (DOJ) have made significant steps toward appropriately recognizing these challenges and ensuring the rights of individuals who in the past were all too often left voiceless.

A. The Crime Victims' Rights Act of 2004—
Giving a Voice to the Formerly Voiceless

As part of the Justice for All Act, federal crime victims' rights were expanded significantly in 2004 with the enactment of the Crime Victims' Rights Act (CVRA). One significant provision under the act accords victims a recognized role in court proceedings—whereby victims are, accordingly, notified of those proceedings. The notification process is initiated by the specific U.S. attorney's office handling the case, and is carried out by the designated victim/witness coordinator.

Once a case is indicted, the CVRA requires the prosecutor's office to provide the victim with notice of court hearings and other "critical stages" throughout the process. The victim coordinator is also required to inform the victim that she has a right to her own legal representation as the case winds its way through the justice system. The CVRA takes into account certain cases where the victim numbers may be significant, and, for such cases, mandates that the trial court develop and implement a reasonable plan for notifying all the victims of upcoming court proceedings.

Enforcement of the CVRA comes in two forms: (1) through the government acting on behalf of the victims, and (2) through the victim herself. In the former scenario, the government can file a motion with the court signaling adherence to the CVRA, and in the latter, the victim can file an administrative complaint seeking that the representative of the DOJ comply with the act. If an administrative complaint is filed, the DOJ is required to investigate the matter; if it is later determined that the DOJ employee willfully disregarded the rights of the victim, the Department is required to sanction that employee.[1] The Attorney General's Manual requires that the main federal law enforcement agencies (FBI, DEA, ATF, Inspector General's Office, U.S. Marshal Service), federal prosecutors, Department of Corrections, and Parole Officers are designated as "responsible officials," thereby requiring them each to have a dedicated victim coordinator to monitor and oversee the particular agency's compliance with the CVRA.

The CVRA covers the entire span of the criminal case, and, as such, the victim is to be notified as early as the defendant's initial appearance before the court. The victim, moreover, is given an opportunity to be "reasonably heard" on the question of whether bond is to be set or denied. The CVRA does not describe the precise manner in which victims are to be heard, nor does it specify the weight the court is required to give the victim's statement. Presumably, a court may take into equal account a written or oral statement. The act, moreover, does not mandate that the victim's statement be given more or less weight than any other statement, but rather, simply provides that the victim be given the *opportunity* to provide the court with information concerning the court's detention decision.

The various hearings at which a victim has a right to be heard include: the arraignment, any joint representation hearing, and any waiver of indictment. Consistent with its counterpart, the Federal Child Victim Protection Statute,

Section 3509 (further described below), a victim is also to be heard at any hearing where time will be excluded under the Speedy Trial Act, because it is presumed that the victim is entitled to proceedings free from unusual delay. Under both acts, the prosecution team must be cognizant of the impact of unusual delays in cases involving minor victims. A reasonable delay, for example, in a fraud trial against an adult offender requiring review of voluminous documents, could extend over a period of two years; this may not be reasonable for a thirteen-year-old victim attempting to put her molestation behind her by seeking treatment and moving into her high school years. The psychological impact delays can have on child victims is, put simply, severe. In fact, the act requires that a victim have a reasonable right to confer with the government attorney in a case as it progresses, and be invited to provide her input regarding delays, plea agreements, and any other agreements that the government may make with a criminal defendant.

Once the trial begins, moreover, the CVRA requires the court to "make every effort to permit the fullest attendance possible by the victim and shall consider reasonable alternatives to the exclusion of the victim from the criminal proceeding."[2] This varies from the generally accepted procedure in most federal courts where witnesses are not permitted to appear in court to hear the testimony of other witnesses in order to preserve the integrity of the testimony and prevent witnesses from tailoring their testimony in response to other testimony presented at trial. The court has discretion to take into account unique circumstances, but the CVRA suggests that the court at least notify the victim of the reasons why she would be excluded from any portion of the trial. While the trial is occurring, the court is also required to ensure that there is a separate waiting area for the victim and her guardian or attendant so she is not brought into contact with or in view of her exploiter.[3]

If the trial concludes in a conviction, the most significant role for the victim will be during sentencing. Under the post-*Booker* sentencing regime, courts have greater leeway in taking into account all types of information in making a determination as to what a "reasonable" sentence should be. Generally, defense attorneys have taken advantage of this change in the law by presenting comprehensive overviews of their client's life, disadvantages, and other mitigating circumstances. Although the materials presented in open court may be shared with the victim, at least one court has held that a victim does not have a right of access to the federal probation officer's confidential report.[4] This report is provided to the court and the parties—it forms the basis for the court's sentencing hearing, and the parties are permitted to file objections to the report's contents or conclusions.

The act, nevertheless, ensures that the victim's voice will be heard at sentencing. The CVRA is not limited to felonies, but extends to *all* persons harmed "as a result of the commission of a federal offense."[5] It is, therefore, appropriate under the act for victims of an exploiter's relevant conduct to be heard and/or to present victim impact statements to the court.[6]

Finally, at sentencing, the CVRA mandates full and timely restitution to victims. To determine whether a victim of child sexual exploitation is entitled to restitution, a court need not view the circumstances under a proximate cause analysis, since there is a "clear and indisputable right to restitution, under the statute which mandates restitution for sexual exploitation of children, without the requirement of causation."[7] For most federal offenses, and in all federal crimes of violence, the CVRA also requires courts to impose the full amount of restitution *without* regard to the defendant's economic circumstances.[8] The restitution award can be added as a condition of probation, so that when the offender is released, he will be required to make monthly payments toward the restitution award for the victim. Failure to do so can result in the revocation of supervised release.

But victims' rights extend even beyond the sentencing hearing. A victim, by way of example, is entitled to notice if (1) the defendant is going to be released from prison or (2) the defendant has violated his terms of supervised release and is scheduled for a revocation hearing. A victim is also entitled to know if her exploiter has (3) escaped from prison, (4) been released from a prison to a work camp, or (5) died. In the case of an offender who is released to a jurisdiction other than the one within which he was convicted, the victim is also entitled to (6) have her victim impact statement forwarded to the probation officer monitoring the convicted exploiter during his probationary period. These rights, therefore, are not only extensive but also provide victims with much-needed practical assistance, notice, and an opportunity for input.

B. The More Focused Federal Child Victim Protection Statute—18 U.S.C. § 3509

The Federal Child Victim Protection Statute, Section 3509, gives federal prosecutors a toolkit to protect child witnesses and abuse victims from the sharpest elbows of the criminal justice system. Its child-friendly alternative procedures include testimony by closed-circuit television and adult attendants to provide emotional support. Critically, it also ensures that, where relevant, child pornography is not disseminated during the criminal discovery process, requiring that the pornography in question stay in the government's custody (while providing reasonable access to the defendant).

1. Background and Specific Provisions

Section 3509's protections are, as we shall see, as extensive as they are targeted.

a. Maryland v. Craig and the Victims of Child Abuse Act

In 1990, the Supreme Court in *Maryland v. Craig* approved a state procedure that allowed a six-year-old victim of sexual abuse to testify via one-way closed-circuit television (CCTV).[9] That procedure required the trial judge to find that the child would suffer "serious emotional distress" if she testified in the presence of the defendant. Over a bristly dissent by Justices Scalia, Brennan, Marshall, and Stevens, the Court found that the CCTV procedure did not violate the defendant's right "to be confronted with the witnesses against him," guaranteed by the Confrontation Clause of the Sixth Amendment. Though the CCTV testimony undoubtedly sacrificed the subtlety of face-to-face confrontation, the Court found that it preserved the other hallmarks of confrontation, including cross-examination and the jury's evaluation of credibility. Most importantly, the Court relied on a string of its previous decisions that recognized protecting child victims as valid public policy, including *Globe Newspaper v. Superior Court*, which favored protecting the child victim over the media's and public's right to attend criminal trials.[10] Citing two dozen state statutes containing some variant of Maryland's CCTV procedure, *Craig* reasonably concluded that "a State's interest in the physical and psychological well-being of child abuse victims may be sufficiently important to outweigh, at least in some cases, a defendant's right to face his or her accusers in Court."[11]

Spurred by *Craig*, Congress passed the Victims of Child Abuse Act, codified at 18 U.S.C. § 3509, as part of the Comprehensive Crime Control Act of 1990.[12] Congress explicitly recognized that the federal law had fallen behind the state law listed in *Craig*, noting that Section 3509 was "the culmination of close to a decade of detailed study and analysis, and reflects a broad consensus among child, victim, and legal advocacy organizations."[13] More bluntly, Congress wanted to protect the child victim from the "potential second assault" of testifying under the glare of his or her abuser.[14] The chairman of the Senate Judiciary Committee (and the bill's chief sponsor), then-Senator Joe Biden, hoped that Section 3509 would make the criminal justice system "more gentle" on child abuse victims.[15]

b. Section 3509's Robust Protections for Children

Section 3509 applies to those under the age of eighteen who are victims of a crime of (1) physical abuse, (2) sexual abuse, or (3) other exploitation.[16]

It also applies to children who (4) witnessed a crime, even if that crime did not involve abuse or exploitation.

i. The Use of CCTV

The most important (and most litigated) protection offered by Section 3509 is testimony by the above-described two-way CCTV, requested by the government or the child through his or her attorney or guardian.[17] Section 3509(b) narrowly defines the court's discretion to allow CCTV testimony.

The court, prior to permitting CCTV testimony, must find that the child is unable to testify in open court in front of the defendant for one of four specific reasons: (1) the child cannot testify because he or she is afraid; (2) an expert has determined that there is a "substantial likelihood" that the child would suffer emotional trauma by testifying; (3) the child suffers from a "mental or other infirmity"; or (4) the defendant or defense counsel's conduct caused the child to be unable to continue testifying. To properly justify CCTV, the court must put its findings on the record. Section 3509(b)(1)(C) also permits the judge to question the child outside the courtroom with counsel and guardians present to determine if one of the four criteria has been met.

Once the judge approves CCTV testimony, Section 3509 provides very specific procedures that balance the child's needs with the defendant's rights. The statute only allows the following people into the room when the child testifies: trial counsel, the child's attorney or guardian, a judicial officer appointed by the court, the CCTV technician, and anyone else the court deems necessary for the "welfare and well-being of the child," including an adult to provide emotional support. As a result, a defendant acting as his or her own attorney cannot enter the testimony room. To preserve the defendant's right to confrontation, the statute requires that the child have a monitor where he or she can see the defendant, who is also being filmed. The defendant, in turn, must have a method to communicate privately and contemporaneously with his or her attorney in the testimony room.

Section 3509(b)(2) provides a similar procedure, effectively a mini-trial, to create admissible video deposition testimony in instances where the child may not be available to testify at trial.[18] Under this provision, the prosecutor or the child's representative may ask the court to take the child's videotape deposition. Once that request is made, Section 3509 requires the court to make a preliminary finding to determine whether, at the time of trial, the child "is likely to be unable" to testify in open court before the defendant, jury, judge, and the general public for the same four reasons identified above. There is one caveat, as previously described: the expert testimony must establish a substantial likelihood that the child will suffer emotional trauma from testifying *in open court*, not just from testifying in general. Once the court determines that the child likely cannot testify in open court, the judge must order the child's deposition to be taken by videotape.

The statute allows the same people to be present at the deposition as in the testimony room under CCTV subsection (b), but with one notable exception. The defendant may be present at the deposition *if* the court's preliminary finding is based on something besides the child's inability to testify in the defendant's presence. In the event that the court found that the child cannot testify before the defendant, the statute requires the same CCTV setup as discussed above. Defense counsel may then cross-examine the child, and the statute requires that the judge preside over the deposition and rule on objections as if it were any other trial testimony.

Finally, if the court finds, at the time of trial, that the child is unable to testify for one of the four reasons, the court may admit the deposition testimony into evidence, supported by specific findings on the record. The statute also provides for additional video depositions if the trial turns up new evidence not known at the time of the original video deposition.

ii. Limitations on Competency Findings for Child Victims

Section 3509 also makes it more difficult for defendants to challenge the competence of children as witnesses. First, children are presumed competent under the statute.[19] Any challenge to a child's competence must be supported by evidence, and the court may only order a competency examination if the court determines, on the record, "that compelling reasons exist."[20] The statute is also clear that the child's age, by itself, is not a compelling reason for any competency examination. Second, psychological and psychiatric examinations are only permitted if there is a "compelling need."[21] If there are compelling reasons to question a child witness's competence, only the judge, the parties' counsel, a court reporter, and anyone necessary for the child's well-being may be present during the examination.

The statute directs the judge to examine the child, using questions submitted beforehand by counsel. The lawyers may examine the child only after the judge determines that it will not cause the child to suffer emotional trauma. The questions cannot pertain to the issues of the trial but, instead, must focus narrowly on the child's ability to understand simple questions.

iii. Confidentiality of Child Victims

Additionally, subsections (d) and (e) of Section 3509 offer strong confidentiality protections for child witnesses. They obligate all parties involved in the criminal case—including prosecutors, law enforcement agencies, court employees, defense counsel, the defendant, and the jurors—to keep in a secure place all documents disclosing the child's name or other information about the child. These provisions require any such documents to be filed under seal with the court. The statute also gives the court wide latitude to enter protective orders if there is "a significant possibility" that the disclosure in question "would be detrimental to the child" (which, as a practical matter, will be true in most cases). It also allows the judge to close the courtroom in two circumstances: (1) when the judge finds that testifying in open court would cause "substantial psychological harm" to the child or affect his or her ability to communicate, and (2) when a witness's testimony will disclose information about the child.

iv. Minimizing the Length of Proceedings and Staying Civil Matters

Section 3509 has two provisions to ensure that the child's time in court is minimized. The first allows the prosecutor or the child's guardian to ask the court to find that the case is of special public importance. Following such a finding, the court can expedite the trial to "minimize the length of time the child must endure the stress of involvement with the criminal process."[22] The statute also requires the court to justify, in writing, any continuance granted when a child is involved, whether or not the trial has been expedited.

The second provision, presumably to avoid the child having to testify in multiple proceedings at one time and to prevent inconsistent statements from being generated, stays any civil action for injury to the child until after the defendant's trial.[23]

v. Guardians and Adult Attendants for Child Victims

Section 3509 also provides two categories of adults to help guide the child through the criminal justice system. Subsection (h) allows the court to appoint, and pay for, a guardian *ad litem* "to protect the best interests of the child."[24] Though the statute does not require such a guardian to have any formal qualifications, it suggests that the guardian be familiar with the judicial process, social services, and child abuse issues. The guardian has broad rights under Section 3509 to attend all proceedings and to have access to all reports, evaluations, and records, and confers the responsibility to "marshal and coordinate" social services for the child. The guardian is also responsible for completing the child's victim impact statement under subsection (f).

Child witnesses are also entitled to "adult attendants" for emotional support during hearings and the trial.[25] Attendants are allowed to stay in close physical contact with the child while he or she is testifying, and the statute expressly allows the child to sit on the attendant's lap. In a similar vein, the statute also permits the child to use dolls, puppets, or other aids to help his or her testimony.[26]

vi. Multidisciplinary Approach Encouraged

Finally, the statute requires, whenever possible, the use of "multidisciplinary child abuse teams," composed of health and social workers, law enforcement, and legal assistance personnel.[27] Prosecutors must consult with such teams "as appropriate," and the team must provide services to the child consistent with their professional backgrounds, including expert testimony and training for court personnel.

2. Section 3509(m)—Limiting Defendants' Access to Child Pornography during the Pretrial Discovery Process

In 2006, Congress passed the Adam Walsh Child Protection Safety Act, named for the murdered son of *America's Most Wanted* host John Walsh. Though most notable for creating a federal sex offender registry, it also added subsection (m) to Section 3509, which modifies Federal Rule of Criminal Procedure 16. Rule 16, stated broadly, requires prosecutors to turn over all evidence the government anticipates using at trial. Subsection (m) modifies that rule by requiring, in all criminal proceedings, that child pornography stay in the government's or the court's possession.[28] The subsection, moreover, requires the court to deny any request to reproduce child pornography as part of discovery, but obligates the government to give the defendant "reasonable access"—defined as "ample opportunity for inspection, viewing, and examination at a Government facility" by the defendant and his or her attorneys and experts.

3. Constitutionality, Current Interpretation, and Use of § 3509

Though Section 3509, at the time of this publication, has not been considered by the Supreme Court, its provisions have (with one limited exception) survived all constitutional attacks at the appellate level. One circuit court's analysis was straightforward: it found that Section 3509's two-way CCTV setup passes muster under the Confrontation Clause because the Supreme Court approved a one-way setup in *Craig*.[29] Another circuit technically found unconstitutional the provision of Section 3509 allowing a child to testify via CCTV because of the child's "fear" of the defendant.[30] That court interpreted *Craig* to require, under the Confrontation Clause, that a witness could testify via CCTV only after the district court found the child was scared of the *defendant specifically,* and not of the courtroom in general. If the fear of the courtroom was the problem, the court reasoned, the child could testify somewhere else with the defendant present, keeping the defendant's traditional confrontation rights intact. In other words, the district court must find that fear of the defendant is the dominant reason the child does not want to testify. Other courts have similarly interpreted that provision of Section 3509, some simply interpreting the statute to align with *Craig*'s holding.[31] The only circuit court to consider the facial constitutionality of subsection (m) (the provision limiting pretrial discovery) found it to be constitutional because defendants have no constitutional right to pretrial discovery, and because Congress has a rational basis to seek to reduce the amount of child pornography in circulation.[32]

District courts often hold evidentiary hearings with expert testimony to determine if a child may testify by CCTV under Section 3509.[33] One circuit court found that testimony from a psychiatrist, psychologist, or other children's mental health specialist—but not necessarily a social worker—is required to demonstrate that the child is unable to testify in open court. Appellate courts generally allow the factual findings required by Section 3509 to stand, evaluating the district courts' determinations under the deferential "clearly erroneous" standard.[34] The exception is when the district court does not bolster its decisions with specific findings, as required by the statute.[35]

Specific guidance from the circuit courts as to how to set up the CCTV system is limited. Only one appellate court has evaluated in great detail what satisfies Section 3509's CCTV requirements.[36] That court found that the monitor showing the defendant must be pointed out to the child and be "readily visible" from where the child is sitting, but does not have to be in the child's direct field of vision.[37] With respect to Section 3509's requirement that the defendant have access to "contemporaneous communication," it is clear that it means instantaneous communication between the defendant and his or her attorney, not just the ability to talk to counsel during breaks.[38]

C. Other Federal Regulations That Provide Victim Protections

Supplementing the above-discussed evidentiary rules and victim protection acts, there are a number of discrete federal regulations that can be used to aid victims. One such regulation is 42 U.S.C. § 14011, which provides a mechanism for obtaining an HIV test from a defendant. In the case of a sexual molestation, this regulation provides at least some degree of comfort to a victim concerning the ongoing need for long-term HIV testing.

Specific victim services are set forth in the same title under Section 10607, which is the U.S. Attorney General's Guidelines regarding victim services. According to these guidelines, a victim must be informed of the following services:

(a) His or her rights as enumerated in 18 U.S.C. § 3771(a). (18 U.S.C. § 3771(c)(1))

(b) His or her entitlement, on request, to the services listed in 42 U.S.C. § 10607(c). (42 U.S.C. § 10607(b)(2))

(c) The name, title, business address, and telephone number of the responsible official to whom such a request for services should be addressed. (42 U.S.C. § 10607(b)(3))

(d) The place where the victim may receive emergency medical or social services. (42 U.S.C. § 10607(c)(1)(A))

(e) The availability of any restitution or other relief (including crime victim compensation programs) to which the victim may be entitled under this or any other applicable law, and the manner in which such relief may be obtained. (42 U.S.C. § 10607(c)(1)(B))

(f) Public and private programs that are available to provide counseling, treatment, and other support to the victim. (42 U.S.C. § 10607(c)(1)(C))

(g) The right to make a statement about the pretrial release of the defendant in any case of interstate domestic violence.

(h) The availability of payment for testing and counseling in cases of sexual assaults. The responsible official of the investigative agency is required to inform victims of the Attorney General's obligation to provide for the cost of up to two anonymous and confidential tests of the victim for sexually transmitted diseases during the 12 months following the assault, as well as the cost of a counseling session by a medically trained professional regarding the accuracy of such tests and the risk of transmission of sexually transmitted diseases to the victim as a result of the assault. (42 U.S.C. § 10607(c)(7)) That same individual is to advise the victim of a sexual assault that poses a "risk of transmission" of the AIDS virus of the circumstances under which the court may order that a defendant be tested for this condition. The official should explain that such an order is only available after the defendant has been charged. (42 U.S.C. § 14011)

(i) The availability of services for victims of domestic violence, sexual assault, or stalking. Responsible officials are required to take appropriate steps to inform victims of domestic violence, sexual assault, or stalking of assistance that may be available to them under programs that have received grants from the Attorney General, such as legal assistance services funded by grants under 42 U.S.C. § 379 6gg-6, housing assistance for child victims of domestic violence, sexual assault, or stalking funded by grants under 42 U.S.C. § 13975, and other similar services.

(j) The option of being included in a Victim Notification Service (VNS). Victims are to be notified of their opportunity to receive notification of case developments through VNS as well as their right to decline to be included in the VNS database.

(k) Available protections from intimidation and harassment. Whenever appropriate, victims are to be informed of legal protections and remedies (including protective orders) that are available to prevent intimidation and harassment.

(2) Referral. The responsible official is also required to assist the victim in contacting the person or office responsible for providing the services and relief described in paragraph A.3. (42 U.S.C. § 10607(c)(1)(D)) When charges are filed, the responsibility for making referrals is transferred to the responsible official in the prosecutor's office.

(3) Notice during the investigation. During the investigation of a crime, a responsible official is required to provide the victim with the earliest possible notice concerning both:

(a) The status of the investigation of the crime, to the extent that it is appropriate and will not interfere with the investigation. (42 U.S.C. § 10607(c)(3)(A))

(b) The arrest of a suspected offender. (42 U.S.C. § 10607(c)(3)(B))

b. Protection From Harassment/Intimidation. The responsible official is required to arrange for a victim to receive reasonable protection from a suspected offender and persons acting in concert with or at the behest of the suspected offender. (42 U.S.C. § 10607(c)(2)) These arrangements may vary from aiding a victim in changing her telephone number to placing the victim in extreme circumstances in the Federal Witness Security Program.

c. Return of Property Held as Evidence. The responsible official is required to ensure that any property of a victim that is being held for evidentiary purposes is maintained in good condition and returned to the victim as soon as it is no longer needed for evidentiary purposes. (42 U.S.C. § 10607(c)(6)) Contraband, however, is not to be returned to victims.

d. Notification to Victims' and Witnesses' Employers and Creditors. Upon request by a victim or witness, the responsible official is required to assist in notifying:

(1) The employer of the victim or witness if cooperation in the investigation of the crime causes his or her absence from work; and

(2) The creditors of the victim or witness, when appropriate, if the crime or cooperation in its investigation affects his or her ability to make timely payments.

e. Payment for Forensic Sexual Assault Examinations. The responsible official or the head of another department or agency that conducts an investigation into a sexual assault is required to pay the cost of a physical examination of the victim and the costs of materials used to obtain evidence. The department or agency conducting the sexual assault investigation is to be responsible for the cost of the examination unless payment is provided by other means. (42 U.S.C. § 10607(c)(7))

f. Logistical Information. Victims and witnesses are to be provided information or assistance with respect to transportation, parking, childcare, translator services, and other investigation-related services.

g. Programs for Department Employees Who Are Victims of Crime. Responsible officials are required to ensure that Department employees have access to an Employee Assistance Program as well as generally available victim assistance programs. Responsible officials are to assist employees in accessing appropriate victim services.

D. Special Considerations When
Interviewing Victims of Sexual Exploitation

Interviewing a victim and preparing her for the court process is the most challenging of all aspects of a child exploitation prosecution. Although the trial attorney is cognizant of the legal attacks that may be made on his victim/ witness, he is also aware that the most significant attack will always be on the victim's credibility. Often, the victim's words will be the most damaging piece of evidence against the defendant.

Relying on a victim advocacy center to assist during the initial interview provides the forward-thinking prosecutor and agent with some assurance that the initial questions will be asked by a trained interviewer, and that the interview will be conducted in a victim-friendly environment. Usually, the advocacy center will have the ability to videotape the interview so that the victim does not provide unnecessarily duplicative statements that can later be used to impeach her credibility through minor inconsistencies. More importantly, the ability to videotape the interview is key because each interview revictimizes the minor to the extent that she is repeating and reliving the traumatic experience.

Establishing a rapport with the victim is, of course, essential. The interview process will depend significantly on the age of the victim and on whether the victim is represented by counsel, a guardian, or a parent. Rapport may be established first with the caregiver, and can be promoted by providing a preview of the next steps in the criminal justice process, by using layman terms to explain what is happening, and by appropriately managing expectations. If a victim and her family are told up front that it may be months before the next court hearing, and possibly years before a trial, they are better able to plan the rehabilitation process. After all, taking a child out of school for purposes of trial and away from her support system, including her mental health caregiver, can be very disruptive, especially if the child is already suffering from some other mental or emotional challenges (which, as discussed earlier, is a common characteristic of victims targeted by exploiters).

The first part of any victim interview should cover general background information in order to set the victim at ease. Only the prosecutor, the advocate, and the law enforcement officer should be present. A careful explanation of how this approach will protect the child in the courtroom needs to be given to the worried parent who will be separated from the minor. The interviews should also be relatively short, and every effort should be made to take breaks to accommodate emotional drain. The interviewer must define each term used by the victim in order to understand exactly what happened. The interviewer can never be judgmental. In fact, the authors discovered early in their interviews of child victims that the mildest of comments, such as "I'm sorry he did that," enabled the minor to continue on without fear of negative moral or social judgment. Explaining the entire court process, including cross-examination and what types of questions will be asked, is critical if the victim is of the appropriate age. To the extent possible, the interviewer should allow the victim to control the direction of the interview and the interviewer should take cues from the victim and turn to other areas when the victim is upset.

One of Charles Burt's victims (as previously discussed) was only seven years old when he testified in federal court against Burt. One of the authors was prosecuting that case and brought "David" to the courtroom the night before the trial, sat him in the witness stand, and showed him where each person would be. The following day during trial, David bravely told the jury about how Burt sexually molested him behind a locked door, and then broadcast the abuse live to his friends on the Internet. On cross-examination, the defense attorney challenged whether the prosecutor had fed David the story, and whether he was just "doing what the prosecutor said." David replied that he was. A momentarily shocked prosecution team listened as David continued, informing the defense attorney that he was doing exactly what the prosecutor said. She had told him that the courtroom is a very special place and only the truth can be spoken there. He continued to explain that the prosecutor told him that when someone asks him a question, no matter who it is, he must just tell the truth—and so yes, he was doing exactly what the prosecutor told him to do. Sometimes, the simple and most direct statements work most efficiently when preparing a minor for the witness stand.

Much progress has been made during the past decade. Today, each U.S. Attorney's office has a victim coordinator tasked with handling victim notification, travel, and services coordination. Yet one of the prevailing themes the authors note is that victims too often continue to be left in the dark concerning the consequences of agreeing to testify. This is a regrettable oversight. If a prosecution team treats the victim and her family with respect, and provides them with a realistic understanding of the criminal justice process and what they will be facing, that team not only will have satisfied its legal obligations, but will have also paved over a myriad of potential pitfalls.

Notes

1. 18 U.S.C. 3771(d)(3)): "The district court shall take up and decide any motion asserting a victim's right forthwith. If the district court denies the relief sought, the movant may petition the court of appeals for a writ of mandamus." The attorney general must take and "investigate complaints relating to the provision or violation of the rights of a crime victim" and provide for disciplinary sanctions for department employees who "willfully or wantonly fail" to protect those rights. 18 U.S.C. 3771(f)(2).

2. Section 3771(b).

3. 42 U.S.C. § 10607(c)(4).

4. *In re Brock*, 262 Fed. appx. 510 (4th Cir. 2008).

5. Section 3771(e).

6. See, for example, *United States v. Spiwak*, 377 Fed. appx. 319 (4th Cir. 2010); *United States v. Clark*, 335 Fed. appx. 181 (3d Cir. 2009).

7. See *In re Amy Unknown*, 636 F.3d 190 (5th Cir. 2011).

8. 18 U.S.C. § 3663A.

9. See *Md. v. Craig*, 497 U.S. 836 (1990).

10. See *Globe Newspaper Co. v. Sup. Ct.*, 457 U.S. 596 (1982).

11. *Md. v. Craig*, 497 U.S. 836 (1990).

12. Pub. L. No. 101-681 (1990).

13. H.R. Rep. No. 101-681(I) at 6572 (1990).

14. H.R. Rep. No. 101-681(I) at 6572 (1990).

15. 101 Cong. Rec. S17600 (Oct. 27, 1990) (statement of Sen. Biden).

16. 18 U.S.C. § 3509(a)(2).

17. 18 U.S.C. § 3509(b)(1).

18. 18 U.S.C. § 3509(b)(2).

19. 18 U.S.C. § 3509(c).

20. 18 U.S.C. § 3509(f)(4).

21. 18 U.S.C. § 3509(f)(9).

22. 18 U.S.C. § 3509(j).

23. 18 U.S.C. § 3509(k).

24. 18 U.S.C. § 3509(h).

25. 18 U.S.C. § 3509(i).

26. 18 U.S.C. § 3509(l).

27. 18 U.S.C. § 3509(g).

28. 18 U.S.C. § 3509(m).

29. See *United States v. Etimani*, 328 F.3d 493, 499 (9th Cir. 2003).

30. See *United States v. Bordeaux*, 400 F.3d 548, 552–53 (8th Cir. 2005), citing *United States v. Turning Bear*, 357 F.3d 730, 737 (8th Cir. 2004).

31. See *United States v. Moses*, 137 F.3d 894, 898 (6th Cir. 1998) (collecting cases finding a general fear of the courtroom is insufficient to support CCTV testimony); *United States v. Garcia*, 7 F.3d 885, 888 (9th Cir. 1993) (interpreting 18 U.S.C. § 3509 to require fear of the defendant under *Craig*).

32. See *United States v. Schrake*, 515 F.3d 743, 745–46 (7th Cir. 2008).

33. See, for example, *Etimani*, 328 F.3d at 497 (9th Cir. 2003); *United States v. Fee*, No. 09-15343, 2011 U.S. App. LEXIS 8854, at 2–3 (11th Cir. Apr. 2011).

34. See *United States v. Moses*, 137 F.3d 894, 898 (6th Cir. 1998).

35. See *United States v. Thunder*, 438 F.3d 866, 868 (8th Cir. 2006) (faulting the trial court for failing to make any finding supporting closing a courtroom under 18 U.S.C. § 3509(e)).

36. See *Etimani*, 328 F.3d at 497.

37. See ibid. at 495.

38. See *United States v. Miguel*, 111 F.3d 666, 670 (9th Cir. 1997).

13

The Difficult Defense

Surveying the Most Common Issues When Representing Individuals Accused of Child Exploitation

AN ATTORNEY CHARGED WITH DEFENDING any kind of child exploitation case will often face an uphill battle. Setting aside the personal and emotional issues that can make it difficult for even the most hard-boiled defense counsel to get fully invested in defending alleged exploiters, counsel will typically find that winning a child exploitation trial is almost as difficult as persuading the government to drop the charges or offer the defendant a generous plea. For one, given the nature of the investigations, the government usually has a mountain of evidence with which to buttress its charges. Fair or not, the fact is that individuals accused of child exploitation in the main can expect little sympathy or empathy from prosecutors or judges, let alone from members of the public empanelled to sit on a jury.[1]

A. Defendants' Chances of Acquittal at Trial Are Staggeringly Low

By way of illustration, consider the child pornography statistics in figure 13.1. Providing additional context for this graph, in 2009 the federal government indicted 2,074 individuals—of those, only 3 were acquitted.[2] Of course, many indictments in 2009 were not disposed of in 2009, and those who pled or went to trial that year were not likely indicted in 2009. That said, the rough proportions remain stable. The bottom line is that the chances of acquittal following trial are exceptionally low (indeed, only roughly .001 percent of those indicted will be acquitted—even the authors, after crunching the numbers, were surprised at this astonishing outcome).

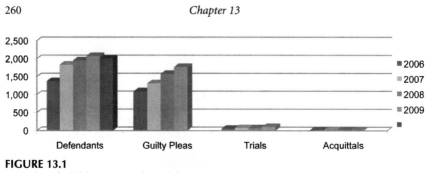

FIGURE 13.1
Statistics of Child Pornography Trial Outcomes

B. Acquittal Is Perhaps Overly Ambitious. . . . Seek Out Case Defects as Negotiating Points

Despite these very significant obstacles facing most counsel defending an accused child exploiter, there are a variety of issues that routinely come up in these cases which may provide potential full or partial defenses, grounds for challenging the admissibility of certain evidence, a basis for challenging the sufficiency of an indictment, and so forth. While these potential weaknesses in the government's case may not promise an acquittal, they can be a valuable means of persuading a prosecutor to cut a more favorable deal, or to dismiss certain charges. Indeed, negotiating an appropriate non-trial disposition of the case that is fair to the defendant should, in most cases, be the focus from the start (though not a focus the government should be aware of—defense counsel, though privately expecting to plead, should act to the outside world as if he or she is preparing for trial, or at least putting the government's case under a meticulous pre-trial microscope).

Although surveying the complete range of issues defense counsel may face in the different categories of child exploitation cases is beyond the scope of this book, our goal over the next pages is to sketch out some of the more familiar and, at times, promising defense arguments that can be raised prior to, or during, trial. As no prosecution case is perfect, identifying the flaws is the job of the zealous advocate. Defense counsel should not get greedy, and should consider how to use every possible defect. Any defect, no matter how small, may help persuade the government to drop charges or treat the defendant more leniently.

On the other hand, we will also identify arguments that, despite their popularity in federal defense circles, are, stated bluntly, nonstarters. This exercise is intended to benefit not only defense counsels but also prosecutors, investigators, and victim advocates who are investigating suspected child exploitation cases and want to ensure that they do not commit errors that could jeopardize the entire case.

C. The Overarching Problem: Jurors and
Judges Despise Child Exploitation Defendants

Child exploitation is as easy to despise as it can be to prosecute. After all, there is near-universal agreement that there are few offenses more reprehensible than crimes against children. As a complicating factor for the defense, many jurors have either themselves been victimized, or have close friends or family members who have. They are, therefore, often acutely familiar with the damage such exploitation can cause, and will be particularly unsympathetic to those who they believe knowingly elevated their personal sexual gratification over the interests of defenseless minors. Moreover, even for those who have not had direct contact with victims, the media, and in particular shows like *To Catch a Predator*, hardly portray exploiters in a sympathetic light.

How to traverse the emotional minefields these cases present will largely be dependent on the type of defendant involved. Meaning, if the client is able to credibly deny any involvement with the alleged conduct, defense counsel will be able to occupy the rare, sought-after moral high ground. In these cases defense counsel, whether at trial or during negotiations with the government, can condemn this type of offensive and destructive conduct/material, and concentrate his defense on pointing to evidence that distances the defendant from the charged conduct.

A harder row to hoe is in store for defense counsel faced with a manufacturing or distribution case in which the evidence of the defendant's involvement is difficult to deny. In such a case, the jury, prosecutor, and judge will likely be outraged by the subject matter.

Given that defense counsel is already starting behind the eight ball, assuming the defendant takes the case to trial, the *voir dire* will be particularly critical, in that it (1) presents an opportunity to weed out those jurors most unable to keep their emotional reactions in check and most disinclined to give the defendant a fair trial, and (2) provides a forum in which defense counsel can begin (very delicately!) to at least partially desensitize jurors' sensibilities to what is in store for them. And, as to the latter, the only realistic goal defense counsel should have at that point is to detach the jury's revulsion from the defendant, and to direct as much of it as possible toward the conduct (however, a word of caution: taking the "it's just kiddie porn—what's the big deal?" approach during plea negotiations or at trial, something that in fact happens surprisingly often, will in all cases be a sure loser).[3]

It is, indeed, during the process of trying to segregate out these deep-seated emotions that a defense counsel's skill and commitment to his client must come through. Tone and sensitivity are the keys to success. It is only the rare client who will testify and single-handedly persuade the jury that the government got it all wrong.

Jurors will also, from the outset of the trial, look at child exploitation defense counsel—particularly after the prosecution opening—and ask themselves some variant of "how can anyone defend this animal . . . and why in the world should anyone give him the benefit of any doubt?" Indeed, the same will happen, though perhaps in somewhat more muted form, when defense counsel first walks through the assigned prosecutor's office door to explain why it is his client is either not guilty or deserving of more lenient treatment (in this context, it undoubtedly helps if the defense counsel and the prosecutor have had prior, positive interactions; like it or not, the slick "hired gun" with the "I will beat the government in all cases" advertising[4] is less likely to receive the prosecutor's trust and benefit of the doubt).

Jurors', prosecutors', and judges' biases and prejudices are largely indelible, and, if left unidentified and unaddressed, can remain latent and lethal. Confronting this very tough question head on, without offending the jury, prosecutor, or judge, is the true art of skilled defense counsel.

One of the few approaches that seems to work for defense counsel in the trial context is to lay all the cards on the table. Following this path, counsel candidly concedes at the outset that:

1. Counsel had the same initial reaction to the case when it came through the door (a tricky argument to make during trial as a matter of the evidentiary rules—so perhaps best deployed during *voir dire*); and
2. Struggling to balance fairness for the accused against the natural inclination to condemn anyone in any way associated with such conduct is an understandably difficult task for anyone in the courtroom.

Once the groundwork has been laid—both during the *voir dire* and, again (and as permitted by the court), during opening—counsel can transition to the argument that, once viewed fairly and objectively, the government's case is fatally flawed.

Confronting the jurors', prosecutors', and the courts' deep-seated feelings, asking that they recognize them, and very subtly suggesting that they, like all trial participants, must separate their feelings from their consideration of the government's case is easier said than done (and, at trial at least, is all too frequently attempted through the blithe and workmanlike "the Constitution is important, patriotism requires fealty to it, so let's all please assume my client innocent" manner that will never win the jurors' hearts and minds). Again, this area is a tough uphill battle for even the most experienced and talented defense attorney. Once overcome, however, persuading judges to treat the defendant fairly, prosecutors to recognize either the defects in their case or mitigating circumstances relating to the accused's upbringing or conduct in the case, and jurors to give the defendant a fair shake all become more manageable.

D. Child Exploitation Takes Many Forms,
But Online Pornography Is the Clear Standout

We now move from tone and approach to substance. By way of a quick recap, under federal criminal law, the sexual exploitation of children encompasses:

1. The sale of children for purposes of sexual exploitation[5];
2. Interstate and international transportation of adults and children for purposes of prostitution or for any other illegal sexual activity[6];
3. Kidnapping (including of minors)[7]; and
4. The production, distribution, dissemination, importation, export, offering, selling, or possession of child pornography.[8]

Of these, offenses relating to the last category of offenses—namely, crimes relating to child pornography—are those with which practitioners and judges are most familiar because they are prosecuted most frequently.

Although the statutes relating to the distribution of child pornography require the government to prove that "defendant had knowledge, or a reason to know, that such visual depiction will be transported or transmitted" in interstate commerce, there is no requirement that a defendant have knowledge, or even reason to believe that a child subject has yet to turn eighteen years of age. The statute, thus, facially imposes strict liability on producers of visual depictions of children engaging in sexually explicit conduct.

Note also that there is no requirement that expert testimony be presented in child pornography cases to establish the age of children in the pictures. Under rule 701, a lay witness may give an opinion that is rationally based on his or her perceptions, including an assessment of a child's age, if the opinion is helpful to a clear understanding of the witness's testimony or to the determination of a fact in issue.

Moreover, pursuant to 18 U.S.C. § 2, an individual who aids, abets, counsels, commands, induces, or procures the commission of a federal crime, including those relating to child exploitation, is punishable as a principal—that is, the same as the person who committed the crime.

1. Section 2252A's Broad Proscriptions

Although child sexual exploitation cases can cover a wide variety of individual conduct, far and away the most common category of charges filed in federal court relating to child pornography are child pornography charges related to the Internet.

Moving from the general to the specific, 18 U.S.C. § 2252A provides, in relevant part:

(a) Any person who—

    (1) knowingly mails, or transports or ships using any means or facility of interstate or foreign commerce or in or affecting interstate or foreign commerce by any means, including by computer, any child pornography;

    (2) knowingly receives or distributes—

        (A) any child pornography that has been mailed, or using any means or facility of interstate or foreign commerce shipped or transported in or affecting interstate or foreign commerce by any means, including by computer; or

        (B) any material that contains child pornography that has been mailed, or using any means or facility of interstate or foreign commerce shipped or transported in or affecting interstate or foreign commerce by any means, including by computer;

    (3) knowingly—

        (A) reproduces any child pornography for distribution through the mails, or using any means or facility of interstate or foreign commerce or in or affecting interstate or foreign commerce by any means, including by computer; or

        (B) advertises, promotes, presents, distributes, or solicits through the mails, or using any means or facility of interstate or foreign commerce or in or affecting interstate or foreign commerce by any means, including by computer, any material or purported material in a manner that reflects the belief, or that is intended to cause another to believe, that the material or purported material is, or contains—

            (i) an obscene visual depiction of a minor engaging in sexually explicit conduct; or

            (ii) a visual depiction of an actual minor engaging in sexually explicit conduct. . . .

    (6) knowingly distributes, offers, sends, or provides to a minor any visual depiction, including any photograph, film, video, picture, or computer generated image or picture, whether made or produced by electronic, mechanical, or other means, where such visual depiction is, or appears to be, of a minor engaging in sexually explicit conduct . . . for purposes of inducing or persuading a minor to participate in any activity that is illegal; or

    (7) knowingly produces with intent to distribute, or distributes, by any means, including a computer, in or affecting interstate or foreign commerce, child pornography that is an adapted or modified depiction of an identifiable minor [shall be punished].

Although Section 2252A is drafted in the rather cumbersome fashion of most federal criminal statutes, its proscriptions are clearly delineated (and, from the defense perspective, pretty much all-encompassing).

2. Section 2252A's Two Affirmative Defenses

A (very slight) glimmer of hope is offered by way of two affirmative defenses.

a. First Affirmative Defense—"Virtual" Child Pornography

Section 2252A(c) provides an "affirmative defense," provided the defendant can convince the jury of the following:

(1) (A) the alleged child pornography was produced using an actual person or persons engaging in sexually explicit conduct; and
      (B) each such person was an adult at the time the material was produced; or
(2) the alleged child pornography was not produced using any actual minor or minors.

Although the government has the burden of proving beyond a reasonable doubt that the defendant committed the crime of possessing child pornography, the defense is permitted to raise this affirmative defense, which, if established, defeats the government's case (note, however, that defendants, no less than fourteen days prior to the trial, must notify the government of their intention to challenge the government's proof that a child was used[9]). The reason the defendant carries the burden of establishing this affirmative defense is that it does not negate an element of the offense (which would be an unconstitutional shifting of the burden of proof to the defendant), but, rather, mitigates culpability once guilt is proven—in other words, it does not negate one of possession's elements.

Tracking the turbulent history of this affirmative defense begins when it became part of the statute in 1996. Congress at that time passed the Child Pornography Prevention Act,[10] which for the first time outlawed virtual child pornography—pornography involving a computer simulation of a child rather than an actual child: an image "that . . . appears to be . . . of a minor engaging in sexually explicit conduct."[11] This "appears to be" language could have been thought to reach a case in which an adult who looked like a child was used in the production of pornography, rather than an actual child. But that was not Congress's intent; its concern was with computer simulations. The Senate committee report explained the purpose of the affirmative defense as follows:

> [The bill] . . . does not, and is not intended to, apply to a depiction produced using adults engaging in sexually explicit conduct, even where a depicted individual may appear to be a minor. Accordingly, the bill includes . . . an affirmative defense provision for material produced using adults. Under that provision, it is an affirmative defense to a charge under section 2252A that the material in question was produced using an actual person or persons engaging in sexually explicit conduct, each of whom was an adult at the time the material was produced, provided the defendant did not intentionally pander the material as being child pornography.[12]

The history makes clear that the purpose of the affirmative defense was to exculpate pornography made with adult rather than child models.

Within a few years, however, the defense was overtaken by the Supreme Court's decision in *Ashcroft v. Free Speech Coalition*, holding that the production of (1) nonobscene pornography (2) in which no child was involved cannot constitutionally be prohibited, because there is no sexual abuse in such a case.[13] The Court ruled that only the presence of that abuse justifies the suppression of pornography not crossing the line to obscenity. According to the Court, therefore, the government is required to prove that an *actual child* was used, unless the pornography is considered obscenity (a small subset of pornography, and prosecuted extremely rarely).[14]

For obvious reasons, the *Ashcroft* holding buoyed defense counsel, seeing this as an opportunity to argue that the government is unable to prove that the images or videos actually depicted real children (videos, however, being almost impossible to convincingly make "virtual," due to continuing technical limitations when it comes to moving images). Reality soon doused their hopes.

For one, the courts quickly explained that (1) defendant bears the burden to prove the affirmative defense because the defense does not negate an element of the crime, and (2) the government is not required to take the step of introducing evidence that images of children are of actual children, rather than "virtual" children.[15] In the typical trial, however, the government may, nevertheless, present testimony that the children have been identified by law enforcement, or will call forensic analysts to the stand to testify that the images depict actual children (perhaps a reflection of the rarity of child exploitation trials—and the corresponding motivation for prosecutors and agents not to cut any corners when it comes to proving their case or disproving any defenses).[16]

It is, therefore, only the rare case in which a defendant will seek to demonstrate that the images on which he was charged did not portray real children.

b. Second Affirmative Defense: Extremely "Small Scale" Possession

Section 2252A(d) sets forth the second affirmative defense:

> It shall be an affirmative defense to a charge of violating subsection (a)(5) that the defendant—
>
> (1) possessed less than three images of child pornography; and
> (2) promptly and in good faith, and without retaining or allowing any person, other than a law enforcement agency, to access any image or copy thereof—
>   (A) took reasonable steps to destroy each such image; or
>   (B) reported the matter to a law enforcement agency and afforded that agency access to each such image.

This affirmative defense has some intuitive public policy appeal—after all, given the realities of today's online world discussed below, it certainly is possible to completely[17] inadvertently find one or two images that appear to be child pornography in one's inbox or cache, and to "promptly" erase them "in good faith" (in other words, you can't simply, as a matter of daily routine, download child pornography in twos and just erase them later in the day). That said, in our experience cases involving simple *possession* of only one or two images will never be prosecuted. After all, in a world in which our government, due to resource constraints, each year takes a pass on thousands of targets each possessing thousands of images or more, the idea of formally indicting a case involving one or two images seems farfetched.

3. A Brief Summary of Constitutional Challenges That, Despite Being Nonstarters, Continue to Be Popular with Defense Counsel

There is a small group of evergreen challenges with which experienced prosecutors will be very familiar. Even though courts will typically dispose of these challenges in less time than it takes to print out the motion, they continue to be part of many child exploitation defense attorneys' stock pretrial filings. For the reasons discussed below, counsel should pick her battles, and should, therefore, think twice before filing motions that the court will likely deem meritless (if not frivolous).

a. Void for Vagueness

In order to be void for vagueness, a statute must contain enough indeterminacy that it fails to provide a person of ordinary intelligence notice of what is prohibited or is "so standardless that it authorizes or encourages seriously discriminatory enforcement." The child pornography statutes, whatever one may say about their public policy grounding, are not vague.[18]

b. Invasion of Privacy

Attempts to extend the right to possess obscene material in the privacy of one's home[19] to the possession of child pornography have consistently failed.[20]

c. Free Speech Violations and "Morphed" Images

The Supreme Court has long recognized the government's compelling—and, indeed, rather obvious—interest in protecting minors from becoming victims of child pornography because of the physiological, reputational, and emotional harm imposed on them.[21] The possession and distribution of child pornography has been found to be "intrinsically related" to the sexual abuse of children,[22] and it is now settled law that child pornography is not protected expressive speech under the First Amendment.[23]

Indeed, even the act of using children's faces to create what appear to be minors engaging in sexually explicit conduct using morphed images of adult bodies—not to distribute, but merely to personally possess—has been declared outside of the scope of the First Amendment.[24]

In *United States v. Hotaling*, for example, the defendant admitted that he created and possessed sexually explicit images of six minor females that he had digitally altered by a process known as "morphing." Specifically, the defendant had cut the heads of minor females from their original, nonpornographic photographs and superimposed them over the heads of images of nude and partially nude adult females engaged in "sexually explicit conduct," as defined by 18 U.S.C. § 2256(2). The defendant's claim, however, was that 18 U.S.C. § 2256(8)(C) was overbroad and unconstitutionally vague. According to the defendant, no actual minor was harmed or exploited by the creation of the photographs, which, in his mind, existed solely to "record his mental fantasies," and thus were protected expressive speech under the First Amendment.[25]

The Court of Appeals note that the necessary underlying inquiry is whether an image of child pornography implicates the interests of an actual minor.[26] "Although morphed images may fall within the definition of virtual child pornography, they implicate the interests of real children and are in that sense closer to the images in *Ferber*."[27] Applying this analysis to defendant's case, the court ruled that the interests of actual minors are implicated when their faces are used in creating morphed images that make it appear that they are performing sexually explicit acts. The court held that, even though the bodies in the images belonged to adult females, they had been digitally altered such that the only recognizable persons were the minors. Compounding the situation, defendant added the actual names of the minors to many of the photographs, making it easier to identify them and bolstering the connection between the actual minor and the sexually explicit conduct:

> Unlike the computer generated images in *Free Speech Coalition*, where no actual person's image and reputation were implicated, here we have six identifiable minor females who were at risk of reputational harm and suffered the psychological harm of knowing that their images were exploited and prepared for distribution by a trusted adult.[28]

Moreover, although some attorneys seek to invoke the First Amendment and "community standards" to defend child pornography cases, cases such as *New York v. Ferber*[29] render this line of argumentation pointless—child pornography is unprotected by the First Amendment even when it is not obscene; put another way, child pornography need not meet the *Miller* test to be illegal. The rationale announced by the court is that such materials are "intrinsically related to the sexual abuse of children. . . . Indeed, there is no serious contention that the legislature was unjustified in believing that it is difficult, if not impossible, to halt the exploitation of children by pursuing only those who produce the photographs and movies."[30]

d. Overbreadth

The overbreadth doctrine "prohibits the Government from banning unprotected speech if a substantial amount of protected speech is prohibited or chilled in the process."[31] The Supreme Court describes facial invalidation for overbreadth as "strong medicine" that "has been employed by the Court sparingly and only as a last resort."[32] The Court, moreover, has "vigorously enforced the requirement that a statute's overbreadth be substantial, not only in an absolute sense, but also relative to the statute's plainly legitimate sweep," before it may be invalidated.[33] The defendant bears the burden as challenger to prove substantial overbreadth.[34] Setting aside the *Ashcroft* case, courts have ruled that the child pornography statutes do not criminalize speech that is neither child pornography nor obscenity, and, therefore, are not overbroad.[35]

e. Lack of Commerce Nexus[36]

As every first-year law student knows, the Commerce Clause has given Congress the constitutional authority to criminalize various types of conduct at the federal level.[37] Provided that the criminal statutory scheme regulates economic activity that Congress could rationally determine to have a substantial effect on interstate commerce, the statute will be deemed constitutional under the Commerce Clause. Thus, to the extent that Congress rationally concludes that a certain type of criminal activity is one of the conduits of a national or international pipeline of illegal activity, it may justifiably step in and regulate that activity pursuant to its commerce power, even though the activity is wholly intrastate.[38]

Employing this logic, courts routinely reaffirm that Congress properly exercised its powers under the Commerce Clause in enacting, for example, statutes prohibiting the possession of child pornography.[39]

In terms of practical considerations, counsel should think twice prior to raising the above arguments. Unless the particular facts of the case dictate otherwise, there is a significant chance that raising facially meritless arguments reduces the advocate's credibility in the court's eyes, and unnecessarily diverts attention and resources from the advocate's stronger factual or legal claims.

4. Some Promising Legal Challenges to Consider

Although the above-described constitutional challenges may provide only the slimmest reed of hope, below we discuss some fact-based challenges that, on occasion, can prove fruitful.

a. Were the Images Simply "Child Erotica"?

Although we now know that Section 2252A criminalizes all forms of production, ownership, and trade in child pornography, it leaves untouched the trade in visual depictions of children that are *not sexually explicit*, but are "sexually arousing to a given individual" (generally referred to as "child erotica").[40]

Agents and prosecutors, perhaps in part because of their dislike of actually viewing the images, will often provide the defense, court, or probation officer with an estimate of the number of images of child pornography, only to discover on closer inspection that many of the images are in fact not of child pornography, but, rather, are child erotica. Although the mischaracterization of some images may not matter in a case involving tens of thousands of images of undeniable child pornography, as the numbers get smaller (or, rather, small enough to matter for purposes of the sentencing calculations), the importance of carefully reviewing each image becomes greater.

In *United States v. King*, for example, the Ninth Circuit agreed with the defense's argument that, during the sentencing phase, the preponderance of the evidence did not support a finding that defendant's offense involved possession of "300 or more images" of child pornography:

There was inadequate information in the record from which the district court could conclude that the case agent had the qualifications to evaluate and define which images constituted child pornography as opposed to child erotica or adult pornography.

The district court's error was not harmless because it is not clear that the district court would have imposed the same sentence had it properly found facts supporting the sentencing enhancement. Accordingly, we vacate King's sentence and remand for resentencing for factual findings consistent with this opinion.[41]

Defense counsel must, therefore, never simply take the agent or prosecutor's word for it when it comes to whether a client received, distributed, possessed, or produced images of child pornography, and how many such images the client is or should be responsible for. Instead, counsel should make time to review the allegedly criminal images and derive an independent estimate.

After all, the sentencing guidelines are in large part driven by the number of pornographic images the defendant is found to have received, distributed, possessed, or produced. Section 2G2.2 provides:

- 10–149 images = two-level enhancement
- 150–299 images = three-level enhancement
- 300–600 images = four-level enhancement
- 600+ images = five-level enhancement

For example, in *United States v. Burke,* the District Court found that a four-level enhancement in the total offense level was appropriate because the defendant possessed more than three hundred images of child pornography, but less than six hundred images.[42] More specifically, the District Court made a factual finding that the defendant possessed exactly 314 images (a conclusion very difficult to overturn on appeal, given the clear error review for factual findings[43]). Burke's attorney had not challenged the number of images at sentencing (and perhaps for good reason), but this is the type of case where counsel's ability to argue that fifteen or more of the images did not qualify would have translated into a substantially reduced sentence. And in Burke's case, that would have dropped the category 1 defendant (no criminal history) from a level 24 (fifty-one to sixty-three months' imprisonment) to a level 20 (thirty-three to forty-one months' imprisonment).

b. Are the Images Actually Child Pornography?

Picking up on the theme in the preceding section on child erotica, "sexually explicit conduct," in the context of child pornography, includes the "lascivious exhibition of the genitals or pubic area of any person."[44] The question of whether materials depict "lascivious exhibition of the genitals or pubic area," an element of the crime, is for the finder of fact.[45] Note that nudity alone does not qualify; instead, there must be (1) an "exhibition" of the genital or pubic area, and (2) this exhibition must be "lascivious."[46]

A picture, moreover, is "lascivious" only if it is sexual in nature,[47] meaning, "a depiction which displays or brings forth to view in order to attract notice to the genitals and pubic area of children, in order to excite lustfulness or sexual simulation in the viewer."[48] As with "child erotica," then, it is up to the defense counsel to fulfill his or her professional obligation to perform due diligence by inspecting the actual images with which his client allegedly was involved.

c. Were the Images "Knowingly Possessed" by the Defendant?

Per our prior analysis, today's typical child pornography case will involve pornography obtained or distributed through the Internet, and maintained on computers. Among the many unique challenges facing lawyers defending such Internet pornography cases is the relatively amorphous nature of "possession" of an image or video on a computer. Most laws criminalizing possession, including possession of narcotics, firearms, and pornographic magazines and photos, after all, target the *physical* possession of *tangible* objects. Arguing to a court or jury that a defendant was involved in this concrete form of commonsense possession is generally a fairly straightforward undertaking.

A more serious challenge arises, however, when the allegation is that the defendant "possessed" a stream of binary digits lying latent and innocuous somewhere on the hard drive of the defendant's computer until they are interpreted and rendered by software in another location in the same computer. Indeed, the very nature and ephemeral quality of computer technology raises a number of discrete questions that defense counsel must (1) understand, and (2) be able to incorporate into the defense. Some basic questions that must be answered include:

- What role, if any, did the particular software package used to access the data play?
- Today's software engineers, in the interest of increasing processor speed, constantly develop new programs that, among other things, create, save, move, and delete working files without the user's input (and, potentially, without the user's knowledge). How does this impact a user's knowing possession?
- If others were granted access to a computer, and, through the subject computer, were able to exercise dominion and control over pornographic material residing on that computer, do they have possession over the material rendering them potentially legally culpable? Does the analy-

sis alter if such users, with or without the computer owner's knowledge, access the computer (or hack into the system) to save or store images of child pornography?

- Is there legal exposure for similar users who are not aware that they could view the pornographic images, or who simply "happened upon" them?
- Assume a user receives a data file from a friend, only later to discover that it contains child pornography. Does that user have criminal exposure? What if he only suspects that the data file *might* contain child pornography (which, in fact, it does), but never opens or deletes it?
- What if the user deletes a data file containing child pornography, but the file still remains latent in the computer's cache (more on this below)? Does this qualify as "knowing" possession?

E. Expertise Needed: Some Thoughts on the Forensic Analysis of Computers and Data

Whether to retain a computer forensics expert is a decision that, as discussed below, depends largely on the procedural posture of the case and on the nature of the evidence in the government's possession. Defense counsel, in any event, must be (or become) educated on the basics of forensic analysis in order to identify potential problems with the government's case, and to know whether and when adding a forensics expert is appropriate and adds the most value. What is more, the attorney's ability to explain to the judge, jury, or prosecutor in a plain and nontechnical manner computer technology nuances with which they may not be familiar can be critical to a defendant's fortunes.

By way of example, it may be important that the jury understand how much of what they see on their work and personal computer screens is the result of unseen activities going on "behind the screen," the result of software engineers' collective efforts to make life easier for us as users. The goal is to convey to the jury that not everything the agent who conducted the forensic exam discussed with the jury is information necessarily known by the person sitting in front of the screen (that is, known to the defendant). The fact that certain undeniably incriminating information was found on the user's computer does not, therefore, in and of itself necessarily establish that its presence is proof that the defendant *knowingly* engaged in criminal conduct.

1. What Is the "Cache," and Why Is It So Dangerous?

Perhaps the most accessible example of how little the public knows about what is "going on" inside their computers is the ubiquitous web cache. At its most basic level, the cache is the computer component that stores data for future use. Many of our searches, most frequently conducted through web browsers such as Google, produce identical results ("data sets"). Rather than having to go find the same data over and over again by repeating time-consuming searches, software developers store recently found data in the cache.[49]

If requested data is already contained in the cache (a "cache hit"), it can simply be pulled up by "reading" the cache. If the sought-after data is not in the cache (a "cache miss"), the data has to be recomputed or "fetched" from its original storage location, which is, relatively speaking, a more time-consuming process. For users of Microsoft's Internet Explorer, for example, the cache storage area is located deep within the Windows system folder under the "Temporary Internet Files" heading.

Although the data obtained through web browser searches will land in a user's cache, so will the information the user simply sees when he points his browser to a particular web location. A typical website, after all, can contain hundreds of individual images. Thus, when a user, say, visits the "www.usdoj. gov" website, the user opens up a data connection to that webpage and, in effect, instructs the computer to download *each and every* data file that exists on that page.

The very act of visiting a website, therefore, results in the downloading of the website's content to the user's computer. And these downloads occur without the user's permission, without any conduct such as keeping a particular file using the "save as" function, and, in most cases, even without the user's knowledge. This computer reality comes as news to most jurors.

Viewed from the perspective of a child pornography case, a user may be surfing a lawful pornography site, click a seemingly innocuous banner, and suddenly see a pop-up window displaying images of a child engaging in sexually explicit conduct. Without knowledge or intent, this user has now "downloaded" child pornography onto his computer (that is, into his cache).[50] Of course, if this happens hundreds, thousands, or hundreds of thousands of times, the "inadvertence" argument loses significant bite, but, as illustrated by the above discussion of the different enhancements for possessing certain numbers of images, for a situation where the number of images is smaller, it may be important for the defense to point out that not all of the images on the client's computer were in fact "knowingly" downloaded. Consider the ruling in *United States v. Pruitt*:

> Inadvertent receipt of child pornography is not a violation of the statute. We stress that Section 2252A(a)(2) criminalizes only "knowing" receipt. This element of scienter carries critical importance in the Internet context given spam and the prevalence and sophistication of some computer viruses and hackers that can prey upon innocent computer users.
>
> Under the statute, courts will address "knowing . . . recei[pt]" mainly as issues of fact, not of law; and the specter of spam, viruses, and hackers must not pre-

gas. But the owner has a roadside sign letting all passersby know that, if they choose, they can stop and fill their cars for themselves, paying at the pump by credit card.[61]

c. P2P Pitfalls

But P2P can also be the source of false allegations. For example, files can be shared inadvertently. Illustrating this point, the federal government in 2009 installed P2P software, and inadvertently shared various sensitive Secret Service documents and IRS tax returns.[62] Indeed, because the actual content of the materials being shared is not known to the software, it is entirely possible for a person to, say, download what he thinks is the latest episode of "The Office," only to find that the downloaded clip is in fact child pornography.

The U.S. General Accounting Office, seeking to determine the ease of access to child pornography over P2P networks and juvenile P2P users' risk of inadvertent exposure to pornography, including child pornography, conducted its own study.[63] The study not only showed that the P2P networks are overflowing with child pornography, but it also revealed that *inadvertent* downloading of child pornography is a very real danger.

> Juvenile users of peer-to-peer networks are at significant risk of inadvertent exposure to pornography, including child pornography. Searches on innocuous keywords likely to be used by juveniles (such as names of cartoon characters or celebrities) produced a high proportion of pornographic images: in our searches, the retrieved images included adult pornography (34 percent), cartoon pornography (14 percent), child erotica (7 percent), and child pornography (1 percent).[64]

Of course, these findings apply equally to adults who are looking for lawful materials, only to find they have inadvertently downloaded child pornography.

Another potentially fertile argument for defense counsel is that P2P software has so automated the file-sharing process that downloads can occur without any human intervention. The default setting on the Gnutella file-sharing network, for example, is for documents downloaded from the network to continue to be shared on the network. Users must affirmatively disable this default in order to have files downloaded off the network remain private.

Because law enforcement tracks the IP addresses of users who download known files containing child pornography, any such inadvertent download can lead to serious troubles. But, again, if the defendant has hundreds of downloaded, categorized videos, the "someone put this on my computer" defense is a sure loser. The defense lawyer sorting through the facts of his or her case must at all times keep this technological context in mind. When the client claims no knowledge of how a file got on their computer, it is counsel's responsibility to determine how those images *could* have gotten there. A thorough understanding of the technologies that can lead to the acquisition of illegal materials on a personal computer is therefore a must for defense counsel.

Ideally, a computer forensics expert will be able to provide counsel with sufficient information to persuade, as appropriate, the government not to indict or not to seek an enhanced sentence, or, if the case proceeds to trial, to explain to the jury why the presence of small amounts of child pornography on the defendant's computer is not evidence that the defendant engaged in criminal conduct.

4. Listservs

Users can also subscribe to automatic mailing list services called "listservs" (an abbreviation of "list server') and "mail exploders." These e-mail lists facilitate communications about particular subjects of interest to different groups.

For example, someone interested in birds can subscribe to a listserv that focuses on that subject. The subscriber can submit or "post" messages to the listserv by sending them to the listserv's e-mail address, such as birder@listserve .com. The message is then automatically (or through a human moderator overseeing the listserv) sent to everyone who subscribes to that particular listserv.

The function of listservs is to keep subscribers updated on developments or events in that particular subject area—and, not surprisingly, there are hundreds of listservs that are dedicated to child pornography. Just as with any other e-mail, a recipient of such a message can reply to the message, but here the reply will be distributed to everyone on the mailing list. The obvious risk (and defense) is that images were not intentionally "ordered" or "downloaded," but, rather, came to the user via an unsolicited listserv post.

5. News Groups

Distributed message databases, such as USENET newsgroups, provide a service similar to listservs. User-sponsored newsgroups are organized by topics, subtopics, and sub-subtopics. An example is "alt.binaries.pictures .birders." A newsgroup with this title is an alternate newsgroup, thus the "alt" in the name.

Newsgroups deal in binary files (usually graphic images), and the group in our example focuses on pictures of birds. There may even be a subtopic under birds that focuses on jays, for example (alt.binaries.pictures.birds.jays).

Many newsgroups, on the other hand, are dedicated to child pornography. Most, moreover, are not moderated. When a message is posted to a newsgroup, it generally is forwarded automatically to all USENET servers. Each such server temporarily stores all the messages for all the newsgroups, some for differing periods of time and others based on space limitations. While they are temporarily stored on the servers, users can access them using software that is usually provided by their ISPs.

Relevant here, child pornography investigations often turn up logs of newsgroup messages, and agents assume (often incorrectly) that the user viewed all of the messages (often images) listed in such logs. In reality, however, it is very possible that only the "headers" downloaded onto the user's computer; simply finding the header on a log is not proof that the user actually viewed or downloaded the file(s).

6. Instant Messaging

Particularly in the case of "hands-on" child sexual abuse, the in-person meeting will often be preceded by lengthy instant-messaging sessions. Defense counsel should understand that instant-messaging programs automatically save chat logs on the user's computer unless the user manually locates the folder and deletes it.

Most "IM logs" appear in one of two places: the user's "My Documents" folder (on Windows OS), or within the user's folder located in the "Program Files" on the C drive. There now are commercially available software programs designed specifically to delete these chat logs. The chat logs, of course, can be helpful, but also may end up being the nail in a defendant's coffin; even if defense counsel has not thought about this possible source of evidence, the government probably has.

F. The Questionable Viability of the "Legitimate Use Defense"

United States v. Lamb allowed defendants to present what might be thought of as a First Amendment–grounded "legitimate-use defense" to charges of transporting or possessing child pornography.[65] *Lamb* involved a prison psychiatrist who claimed that the possession of child pornography image files on his computer hard drive was necessary for his research. The trial court in *Lamb* ruled the defendant should be allowed to present an "unconstitutional-as-applied defense" to the jury. The trial court, citing *Ferber*, also articulated how academic research on the topic of child pornography is closely related to wise and informed legislation in that area. The Court of Appeals, however, rejected this reasoning. Indeed, other courts have similarly declined the opportunity to rule that the First Amendment protects such research or "news gathering" activities, holding that such conduct violates valid criminal laws, which, in this case, are the laws against possession of child pornography.[66]

G. Search Warrants

Most child exploitation cases will involve the execution of search warrants relating to the defendant's computers, external hard drives, PDAs, or residence. In fact, search warrants relating to just about any crime will include a general authorization to search "computers, hard drives, and other computer-related media." Because the literature on search warrants is extensive, the analysis highly fact-dependent, and the law constantly shifting, we will not cover the topic in depth.

That said, one of the most critical search-related issues to bear in mind is that, under well-established search and seizure law principles, if agents find contraband in a location where they are authorized to be, that contraband may be seized as well.[67] There are, of course, exceptions, but as a general rule, if agents are authorized to search for image files on a computer, they will usually be authorized to seize child pornography files they locate on the computer.

Search Warrant Checklist:

- Did the target have a reasonable expectation of privacy in the area searched?
- Is the affidavit facially invalid?
- Is there a lack of probable cause?
- Is the information in the affidavit reasonably detailed?
- Is there a nexus between the purported offense and the location to be searched?
- Does the warrant contain a particularized description of (1) the place to be searched, and (2) the items to be seized?
- Did the warrant specifically authorize a search for "image files"?
- Did the agent make unwarranted assumptions "based on his training and experience" when, in fact, he had little of both?[68]
- Are there any potential exceptions to the warrant requirement, such as search incident to arrest; exigent circumstances; plain-view search; direct-[69] or third-party-consent search; car search; *Terry* stop; lack of state action; or search by probation officer?
- Is the affidavit based on stale information?

- Has a confidential informant's background and/or other evidence of lack of veracity or motivation to lie been appropriately disclosed?
- Does the affidavit reveal the basis of the confidential informant's knowledge/information?
- Does the affidavit contain any potentially deliberate falsehoods, or evidence of a reckless disregard for the truth?
- Is there a potential good-faith exception for the search?
- Did the "neutral magistrate" have jurisdiction to issue the warrant? (Consult a map of the particular district.)
- Was the warrant executed within the time provided by the issuing court?
- Did the officer give appropriate notice (was this a "no knock" or a "knock and announce" warrant)?
- Did the agents read or show the warrant to the target and/or leave a copy of the inventory (items seized)?
- Did the warrant explicitly contemplate that file names might be selected to disguise their content (thereby authorizing that individual files be opened irrespective of their names)?
- Did any part of the agent's search exceed the scope of the warrant?[70]

The results of searches typically seal the defendant's fate. Defense counsel must, therefore, in all cases scour each warrant, as well as the agent documentation relating to the actual search, for potential inconsistencies and mistakes pointing to deeper issues that could potentially justify suppression of the seized evidence.

H. Mistake of Age Defense in Production Cases

To date the Supreme Court has not directly addressed whether the First Amendment requires a reasonable mistake of age defense to crimes of child pornography production. However, in *United States v. X-Citement Video*, the Court held that the federal child pornography statute requires prosecutors to show that distributors and retailers of child pornography had knowledge that material they sold contained sexually explicit images of minors.[71] As of this writing, the Courts of Appeals of the Fourth, Eighth, and Ninth Circuits have addressed the issue, and only the Ninth Circuit has concluded that the First Amendment requires a reasonable mistake of age defense. The other courts, in contrast, have adopted a strict-liability standard. Thus, given the circuit split, defense counsel should consider requesting a jury instruction on the mistake of age defense (if only to preserve the issue on appeal).

I. Preparation Should Accompany Negotiation

Most child exploitation cases are, as noted above, resolved through a plea deal—and this is for good reason, given that the evidence of defendant's guilt is typically overwhelming and pleading can result in some very tangible sentencing benefits.

In more "marginal" cases, however, defense counsel should make clear to the prosecutor that, unless a favorable resolution is reached, trial is on the horizon. This is not necessarily a "bluff," but prosecutors can sense when defense counsel simply lays down because he is not fully engaged with the case.

Performing a complete forensic work-up after discovery demands is certainly one way to signal to the government that counsel is prepared to take the case to trial if a mutually acceptable outcome is not in the cards.

Conversely, counsel should not be shy about explaining to the prosecutor the weaknesses counsel has identified and/or why this particular defendant deserves more lenient treatment (up to, and including, dismissal of charges). Today's prosecutors are more computer literate than in years prior, so explaining how an individual could inadvertently have a few images of child pornography[72] on his computer, for example, will not necessarily require a forensic expert to resonate with the prosecutor.

J. Thoughts on Defending Child Trafficking Cases

The most serious trafficking charge involving children is found under 18 U.S.C. § 1591, which proscribes "sex trafficking of children by force, fraud, or coercion":

(a) Whoever knowingly—
  (1) Recruits, entices, harbors, transports, provides, obtains, or maintains by any means a person; or
  (2) benefits, financially or by receiving anything of value, from participation in a venture which has engaged in an act described in violation of paragraph (1), knowing, or in reckless disregard of the fact, that means of force, threats of force, fraud, coercion described in subsection (e) (2), or any combination of such means will be used to cause the person to engage in a commercial sex act, or that the person has not attained the age of 18 years and will be caused to engage in a commercial sex act, shall be punished as provided in subsection (b). . . .
  (c) In a prosecution under subsection (a)(1) in which the defendant had a reasonable opportunity to observe the person so recruited, enticed, harbored, transported, provided, obtained or maintained,

the Government need not prove that the defendant knew that the person had not attained the age of 18 years. . . .

(e) In this section:

(1) The term "abuse or threatened abuse of law or legal process" means the use or threatened use of a law or legal process, whether administrative, civil, or criminal, in any manner or for any purpose for which the law was not designed, in order to exert pressure on another person to cause that person to take some action or refrain from taking some action.

(2) The term "coercion" means—

(A) threats of serious harm to or physical restraint against any person;

(B) any scheme, plan, or pattern intended to cause a person to believe that failure to perform an act would result in serious harm to or physical restraint against any person; or

(C) the abuse or threatened abuse of law or the legal process.

(3) The term "commercial sex act" means any sex act, on account of which anything of value is given to or received by any person.

(4) The term "serious harm" means any harm, whether physical or nonphysical, including psychological, financial, or reputational harm, that is sufficiently serious, under all the surrounding circumstances, to compel a reasonable person of the same background and in the same circumstances to perform or to continue performing commercial sexual activity in order to avoid incurring that harm.

(5) The term "venture" means any group of two or more individuals associated in fact, whether or not a legal entity.

1. The Defendant's Difficult Argument

The crime of child trafficking is one with which most judges and jurors will be unfamiliar.[73] Though it is often in the news, actual prosecutions are extremely rare. From the government's perspective, the job is to show jurors that such child slavery is actually occurring on U.S. soil. From the defense perspective, the (often quite strained) argument will be some variant of the claim that the defendant-trafficker is, in fact, helping the children's parents by giving them a better life in the United States (an argument that gets harder to make if there is evidence that the defendant was actually involved in, or had knowledge of, the child(ren) being forced to work in brothels or the like). Of course, depending on the allegations and the facts, the defense argument could also be that the government simply "got the wrong guy."

2. "Human Trafficking Experts"

Because this is a relatively "exotic" crime, both the government and the defense may be tempted to consult with a human trafficking expert, or to call such an expert to the witness stand to explain human traffickers and their business.

a. Limiting the Government Expert

The defense should consider requesting a *Daubert* hearing[74] to challenge the purported expert's background, anticipated testimony subject-matter expertise, or credentials.[75] Also, defense counsel should remember that, while expert testimony may be used to "assist the trier of fact to understand the evidence or to determine a fact in issue,"[76] the expert witness may not usurp the jury's function to weigh evidence and make credibility determinations.[77]

In *United States v. Farrell*, for example, the government's purported human trafficking expert testified as to "red flags" in employer-employee relationships indicative of coercion and the presence of a "climate of fear." The expert went on to testify that the employees in the case were working under such a climate of fear that the witnesses were credible, and that the evidence of guilt was "incredible." The Eighth Circuit Court of Appeal ruled that, under these circumstances, "the expert's testimony was not simply a factual conclusion but rather an attempt to express an opinion as to the guilt of [defendants] and a manner of stating that the forthcoming worker witnesses were telling the truth."[78]

Defense counsel must, accordingly, be prepared to challenge the government's trafficking expert on certain potentially critical issues:

- the expert's subject-matter expertise in child trafficking;
- any specialized practical experience or consultation with credible studies or reference materials;
- the "climate of fear" created by traffickers;
- the psychological dynamics and effect of human trafficking on victims;
- whether the instant evidence is consistent with common practices and behavior patterns in human trafficking cases;
- what impacts cultural differences, hierarchy, deference, and class stratification may have; and
- the power of nonviolent psychological coercion.

b. Considerations When Dealing with Defense Human Trafficking Experts

On the other hand, the defense may also wish to consult with, or call, its own expert. Steps the defense counsel can take include the following:

- limit communications to phone or in-person conversations, rather than potentially discoverable documents or e-mails;
- explain to the expert the level and type of expertise you really need;
- clarify the precise scope of work that will be required (reports, trial testimony, etc.);
- make sure the expert has full access to all the documentation or other information he needs;
- discuss the precise legal posture of the case; and
- determine whether the expert should meet with or interview the client.

K. Summary "To-Do" List in Child Exploitation Case[79]

As we discussed, the potential issues defense counsel may have to confront in representing a child exploitation defendant could fill many books. We, therefore, have truly only skimmed the surface. But the point of the exercise is to at least sensitize the reader to some of the most common issues that come up in real-world child pornography cases. In terms of a summary, the following steps should be taken by competent and zealous defense counsel:

- Interview client to gauge his level of computer sophistication.
- Ask client about possible ways images could have come into his possession.
- Request all reports or documentation used by government as basis for any search.
- Determine what version of what software the government used during its forensic exam.
- Find out whether the target computers' components had been used before their installation into the defendant's system. Did the defendant purchase a used hard drive or computer from a friend or computer shop or bring either in for repair (opening the possibility of contamination of the hard drive)?
- Determine where the files were found (in the cache? in unallocated space?).

- Did an untrained investigator view the original files on the system (as opposed to on a mirror image of the hard drive), not realizing that by doing so he changed the system data logs that may establish identity and intent? Did such alterations leave room for reasonable doubt or justify suppression of the evidence or dismissal of the case?
- Review public databases for information on forensic software bugs and their impact.
- Review search warrants for specificity.
- Determine how the copies or mirror images were made. If the copies were made by connecting the target computer with a law enforcement computer that had previously been used for investigating child pornography cases, the investigator may not have ensured that inadvertent file transfer was foreclosed.
- Demand that the government provide full access to the mirror image of the seized computer hard drive.
- Review *all* reports, documents, images, and other relevant evidence (and do not be afraid to ask what different fields or notations mean).
- Consider whether hiring a computer forensic expert will add value to the negotiations/trial.
- Determine whether instant messaging was involved and review any chat logs.
- If the case proceeds to trial, inoculate the jurors to the graphic information involved in the case and segregate that evidence from the defendant in the minds of the jurors.

Notes

1. See generally Sharon Nelson, et al., In Defense of the Defense: The Use of Computer Forensics in Child Pornography Cases, at 1 (2009) ("Pity the poor child pornography defendant? Maybe. These days, even battle-hardened, cynical types like the authors have some sympathy for these defendants and even more for the attorneys who represent them. It is not a level playing field for these defendants and they are regularly denied due process of law"), available at www.senseient.com/articles/pdf/In_Defense_of_the_Defense.pdf.

2. In 2009, the number of cases not resulting in a plea or acquittal (that is, being dismissed, having defendants who fled or committed suicide, etc.) was roughly 300.

3. The converse of the flippant defense counsel is the prosecutor or agent who refers to "kiddie porn." Though, on its face, the term may not seem offensive, to those with more than cursory involvement with child pornography cases this term is particularly reviled since it minimizes the seriousness of the conduct. Even so, however,

it is surprising how many in law enforcement who should know better still employ the term.

4. Defense counsel, in fact, should be cognizant of what they put on the web, say during conferences, and distribute as marketing materials. These days, legal professionals will almost inevitably Google attorneys they do not already personally know in order to get a flavor of their backgrounds. One particular defense counsel presents a perfect illustration of what not to do. He has a website claiming (falsely, as it turns out) to never have lost a case, says government prosecutors and agents are always corrupt, claims to never have his clients plead guilty, and promises to "bring it to the government" at trial. Setting aside the ethical concerns raised when an attorney elevates his ego above his professional responsibility by not negotiating cases (which, as discussed above, is not always in a defendant's interests), the tone will virtually assure defense counsel (and his/her unfortunate clients) that the government will go out of its way to ensure that no stone is left unturned when it comes to proving the defendant's guilt. In an ideal world, perhaps, attorneys would work like automatons and not be swayed by emotion; in the real world, however, defense counsel must carefully guard his reputation for being a "straight shooter," lest the client's interests suffer.

5. See 18 U.S.C. § 1591 (passed as part of the Trafficking Victims Protection Act of 2000; prohibits recruiting, enticing, harboring, transporting, providing, obtaining, or maintaining a child knowing that the child "will be caused to engage in a commercial sex act").

6. See 18 U.S.C. §§ 2421–2423.

7. See 18 U.SC. § 1201.

8. See 18 U.S.C. §§ 2251–2252A.

9. See 18 U.S.C. § 2252(c).

10. Pub. L. No. 104-208, § 121, 110 Stat. 3009–26 (1996).

11. 18 U.S.C. § 2256(8)(B) (1996).

12. S. Rep. No. 358 (1996).

13. 535 U.S. 234, 250–51 (2002).

14. See, for example, *United States v. Kain*, 589 F.3d 945, 950 (8th Cir. 2009) (holding that evidence was sufficient to support finding that the images found on defendant's computer depicted real minors, as required to support a conviction for knowing possession of child pornography. Evidence included twenty-seven images found on the computer, testimony of the detective who conducted the forensic examination of a copy of the computer's hard drive claiming it contained images of prepubescent, female minors based on their physical features, and testimony of another law enforcement agent that the girl depicted in one image was about nine years old when he interviewed her some years after the photograph was taken, and defendant's admission that he owned the computer and had used it to download forty to fifty images of child pornography to the file folder); see also *United States v. Schales*, 546 F.3d 965, 971–72 (9th Cir. 2008); 18 U.S.C. § 1466A.

15. See generally *United States v. Deaton*, 328 F.3d 454, 455 (8th Cir. 2003); see also *United States v. Salcido*, 506 F.3d 729, 734 (9th Cir. 2007) (*per curiam*) (collecting

cases) ("There seems to be general agreement among the circuits that pornographic images themselves are sufficient to prove the depiction of actual minors"); *United States v. Hall,* 312 F.3d 1250, 1260 (11th Cir. 2002) (holding that no reasonable jury could have found that the images were virtual children created by computer technology, as opposed to actual children); *United States v. Richardson,* 304 F.3d 1061, 1064 (11th Cir. 2002) (same); *United States v. Nolan,* 818 F.2d 1015, 1020 (1st Cir. 1987) (stating that uncorroborated speculation that some undefined technology exists to produce pornographic pictures without the use of real children is not sufficient basis for rejecting a lower court's determination to admit evidence).

16. Several appellate courts have assumed the testimony of experienced forensic or medical professionals, establishing the authenticity of alleged child pornography, constitutes appropriate expert testimony. See *United States v. Bynum,* 604 F.3d 161, 167 (4th Cir. 2010) (collecting cases).

17. *Williams,* 553 U.S. at 304, 306.

18. See, for example, *United States v. Fogarty,* 663 F.2d 928, 930 (9th Cir. 1981); see also *United States v. Hockings,* 129 F.3d 1069, 1072 (9th Cir. 1997).

19. *Stanley v. Georgia,* 394 U.S. 557 (1969).

20. See, for example, *United States v. Miller,* 776 F.2d 978, 980 (11th Cir. 1985); *United States v. Marchant,* 803 F.2d 174, 177 (5th Cir. 1986); *United States v. Anderson,* 803 F.2d 903, 904 (7th Cir. 1986).

21. See *Free Speech Coal.,* 535 U.S. at 249.

22. *Ferber,* 458 U.S. at 758–59 and n. 10.

23. Ibid. at 758–60.

24. See *Hotaling,* 634 F.3d at 729–30.

25. Ibid. at 727.

26. Ibid., citing *Williams,* 553 U.S. at 289 ("The child-protection rationale for speech restriction does not apply to materials produced without children"); *Free Speech Coal.,* 535 U.S. at 258 (holding that "virtual" child pornography, which did not use images of actual minors, was protected expressive speech under the First Amendment because it did not harm any real children through its production and continued existence).

27. *Free Speech Coal.,* 535 U.S. at 242; see also *Bach,* 400 F.3d 622, 630–32 ("The government responds that morphed images such as the one in count 6 involve real children with consequential mental harm. It asserts that a morphed image may victimize several children at once because it may contain an underlying picture of real children being abused and exploited, as well as the face of an identifiable child whose own mental health and reputation may suffer. . . . Unlike the virtual pornography or the pornography using youthful looking adults which could be prosecuted under subsections (B) and (D) [of § 2256(8)], as discussed in *Free Speech Coalition,* this image created an identifiable child victim of sexual exploitation. . . . Although there may well be instances in which the application of § 2256(8)(C) violates the First Amendment, this is not such a case. The interests of real children are implicated in the image received by [defendant] showing a boy with the identifiable face of AC in a lascivious pose. This image involves the type of harm which can constitutionally be prosecuted under *Free Speech Coalition* and *Ferber*").

28. *Hotaling,* 634 F.3d at 730.

29. 458 U.S. at 764.

30. Ibid. at 759–60.

31. See generally *Free Speech Coal.,* 535 U.S. at 255; *Williams,* 553 U.S. at 292; *Weaver v. Bonner,* 309 F.3d 1312, 1318 (11th Cir. 2002).

32. *Broadrick v. Oklahoma,* 413 U.S. 601, 613 (1973).

33. *Williams,* 553 U.S. at 292.

34. *Virginia v. Hicks,* 539 U.S. 113, 122 (2003).

35. See generally *Ferber,* 458 U.S. at 773; *United States v. Dean,* 635 F.3d 1200, 1204–5 (11th Cir. 2011).

36. See, for example, *United States v. Robinson,* 137 F.3d 652 (1st Cir. 1998); see also *United States v. Bausch,* 140 F.3d 739 (8th Cir. 1998).

37. See generally *United States v. Hook,* 195 F.3d 299 (7th Cir. 1999).

38. See generally *United States v. Rodia,* 194 F.3d 465 (3d Cir. 1999).

39. See, for example, *United States v. Kimler,* 335 F.3d 1132, 1139 (10th Cir. 2003); see also *United States v. Smith,* 459 F.3d 1276, 1284–86 (11th Cir. 2006) (upholding the application of section 2251(a) to a defendant who produced intrastate pornographic photographs, but used materials that had traveled in interstate commerce); *United States v. Maxwell,* 446 F.3d 1210, 1218 (11th Cir. 2006) (ruling that "it is within Congress's authority to regulate all intrastate possession of child pornography, not just that which has traveled in interstate commerce or has been produced using materials that have traveled in interstate commerce").

40. See generally *Martin,* 426 F.3d at 78–79.

41. *United States v. King,* 378 Fed. Appx. 748, 751 (9th Cir. 2010) (unpublished) (citations omitted).

42. *United States v. Burke,* 252 Fed. appx. 49 (6th Cir. 2007) (unpublished).

43. See generally *United States v. Hazelwood,* 398 F.3d 792, 795 (6th Cir. 2005).

44. *United States v. Horn,* 187 F.3d 781, 789 (8th Cir. 1999), quoting 18 U.S.C. § 2256 (2)(E).

45. See *United States v. Rayl,* 270 F.3d 709, 714 (8th Cir. 2001).

46. See *Horn,* 187 F.3d at 789; see also *United States v. Kemmerling,* 285 F.3d 644, 645–46 (8th Cir. 2002) ("We have held that more than mere nudity is required before an image can qualify as 'lascivious' within the meaning of the statute").

47. See *Kemmerling,* 285 F.3d at 646.

48. See *United States v. Larkin,* 629 F.3d 177, 182 (3rd Cir. 2010).

49. See generally *Kain,* 589 F.3d at 948n3, citing MICROSOFT COMPUTER DICTIONARY 81 (5th ed. 2002) (defining *computer cache* as a "special memory subsystem in which frequently used data values are duplicated for quick access").

50. See *United States v. Kuchinski,* 469 F.3d 853, 861–63 (9th Cir. 2006) (finding no evidence the defendant was a sophisticated computer user, that he tried to get access to the cache files, or that he knew of the cache's existence, the court ruled that "where a defendant lacks knowledge about the cache files, and concomitantly lacks access to and control over those files, it is not proper to charge him with possession and control of the child pornography images located in those files." The court concluded that charging someone with possession and control over cache files without "some other

indication of dominion and control over the images . . . turns abysmal ignorance into knowledge and a less than valetudinarian grasp into dominion and control"); see also *United States v. Stulock*, 308 F.3d 922, 925 (8th Cir. 2002) (summarizing a district court's unchallenged observation that "one cannot be guilty of possession for simply having viewed an image on a web site, thereby causing the image to be automatically stored in the browser's cache").

51. *United States v. Pruitt*, 638 F.3d 763 (11th Cir. 2011), citing *Child Pornography, the Internet, and the Challenge of Updating Statutory Terms*, 122 HARV. L. REV. 2206, 2211–14 (2009) (describing ways a person could unintentionally receive child pornography); see also *United States v. Romm*, 455 F.3d 990, 998 (9th Cir. 2006) (finding that the "[defendant] exercised dominion and control over the images in his cache by enlarging them on his screen, and saving them there for five minutes before deleting them" sufficient for "receiv[ing]" under Section 2252A).

52. Common examples are "Encase" by Guidance Software and "Forensic Toolkit" by AccessData.

53. High Technology Crime Investigation Association, www.htcia.org (last visited May 30, 2011).

54. International Association for Computer Information Systems, www.iacis.org (last visited October 3, 2011).

55. See generally *United States v. Flyer*, 633 F.3d 911, 918 (9th Cir. 2011) ("Unallocated space is space on a hard-drive that contains deleted data, usually emptied from the operating system's trash or recycle bin folder, that cannot be seen or accessed by the user without the use of forensic software. Such space is available to be written over to store new information. Even if retrieved, all that can be known about a file in unallocated space (in addition to its contents) is that it once existed on the computer's hard-drive").

56. See IPOQUE, INTERNET STUDY (2007), available at www.ipoque.com/ (last visited June 15, 2011).

57. *Children's Exposure to Pornography on Peer-to-Peer Networks: Hearing before the H. Comm. on Oversight and Gov't Reform* (2003), available at http://oversight.house.gov/documents/20040817153704-85383.pdf.

58. 492 F.3d 867 (7th Cir. 2007).

59. Ibid. at 870.

60. Ibid. at 876.

61. Ibid., quoting *United States v. Shaffer*, 472 F.3d 1219, 1223–24 (10th Cir. 2007).

62. See Declan McCullagh, *Congress: File Sharing Leaks Sensitive Government Data*, July 29, 2009, available at CBSNews.com.

63. See GAO, PEER-TO-PEER NETWORKS PROVIDE READY ACCESS TO CHILD PORNOGRAPHY (2003), available at www.gao.gov/new.items/d03351.pdf.

64. Ibid.

65. *United States v. Lamb*, 945 F. Supp. 441, 449 (N.D.N.Y.1996); see also *United States v. Bryant*, No. CR 92-35R (W.D. Wash. May 13, 1992) (unpublished order) (holder of a doctoral degree in psychology who had previously researched child prostitution for his master's thesis claimed that the child pornography he possessed was

"for additional research on the subject of child prostitution," and was permitted to present legitimate-purpose defense).

66. *United States v. Matthews*, 209 F.3d 338 (4th Cir. 2000).

67. See generally *Horton v. California*, 496 U.S. 128, 142 (1990) ("In this case the items seized from petitioner's home were discovered during a lawful search authorized by a valid warrant. When they were discovered, it was immediately apparent to the officer that they constituted incriminating evidence. He had probable cause, not only to obtain a warrant to search for the stolen property, but also to believe that the weapons and handguns had been used in the crime he was investigating. The search was authorized by the warrant; the seizure was authorized by the 'plain-view' doctrine"); see also *United States v. Williams*, 592 F.3d 511, 521 (4th Cir. 2010) (ruling that seizure of images portraying child pornography was justified by the plain view exception to the warrant requirement, even if the discovery of the images was not inadvertent; images were found on DVD, officers had warrant to search defendant's computers and digital media for evidence relating to crimes of making threats and computer harassment. Warrant impliedly authorized officers to open each file and view its contents, at least cursorily, to determine whether the file fell within the scope of the warrant's authorization, and contraband nature of pornographic images was immediately apparent); *United States v. Mann*, 592 F.3d 779, 784 (7th Cir. 2010) (search was lawful where investigator conducted search within scope of warrant and did not knowingly expand the scope of the search to discover child pornography).

68. For example, a claim of child molestation does not provide probable cause to search for evidence of child pornography. See generally *Hodson*, 543 F.3d at 292 ("It is beyond dispute that the warrant was defective for lack of probable cause—Detective Pickrell established probable cause for one crime (child molestation) but designed and requested a search for evidence of an entirely different crime (child pornography). Consequently, the warrant did not authorize the search and, barring some other consideration, the evidence obtained during that search must be excluded from trial"); *United States v. Falso*, 544 F.3d 110, 124 (2d Cir. 2008) ("Although Falso's crime allegedly involved the sexual abuse of a minor, it did not relate to child pornography. That the law criminalizes both child pornography and the sexual abuse (or endangerment) of children cannot be enough") (citation omitted).

69. Determining voluntary consent is a particularly tricky and fact-intensive part of the law. Considerations include whether the target was told he could refuse the search, whether he was told what was being sought, whether a large number of police were in close proximity, had their guns drawn, or otherwise created an intimidating environment, whether there was any trickery, the length of time between the first contact and the giving of consent, tone of voice of the agents, whether *Miranda* warnings were given, and the age, background, national origin, and education of the target.

70. See, for example, *United States v. Carey*, 172 F.3d 1268, 1272–73 (10th Cir. 1999) (ruling that seizure of images of child pornography, beyond the first, from defendant's computer hard drive was not authorized by the warrant. Since the images were in closed files, they were not in plain view, but, instead were seized pursuant to a general, warrantless search. The warrant permitted only the search of

the computer files for "names, telephone numbers, ledgers, receipts, addresses, and other documentary evidence pertaining to the sale and distribution of controlled substances"; instead, it was the contents of the files and not the files themselves that were seized, and it was evident from the police officer's testimony that each time he opened a "JPG" file after the first, he expected to find child pornography and not material related to drugs).

71. 513 U.S. 64 (1994).

72. Note that 18 U.S.C. § 2252(c) provides an affirmative defense in the following situation:

The defendant—

(1) possessed less than three matters containing any visual depiction proscribed by that paragraph; and
(2) promptly and in good faith, and without retaining or allowing any person, other than a law enforcement agency, to access any visual depiction or copy thereof—
   (A) took reasonable steps to destroy each such visual depiction; or
   (B) reported the matter to a law enforcement agency and afforded that agency access to each such visual depiction.

73. Indeed, as of this writing, the U.S. Courts of Appeal have dealt with child trafficking convictions less than a dozen or so times.

74. *Daubert v. Merrell Dow Pharm., Inc.*, 509 U.S. 579 (1993) (holding that, faced with proffer of expert scientific testimony, trial judge must determine at the outset whether the expert is proposing to testify to (1) scientific knowledge that (2) will assist trier of fact to understand or determine a fact in issue; preliminary assessment must be made of whether reasoning or methodology underlying testimony is scientifically valid and of whether that reasoning or methodology properly can be applied to facts in issue).

75. See, for example, *Shaffer*, 472 F.3d at 1225 ("Exclusion of defendant's computer expert's proffered testimony, that based upon the file structure of defendant's computer hard drive defendant was on a pornography fishing expedition with no particular calculation toward any particular type of material, other than generally sexually explicit material, was warranted, in prosecution for distribution and possession of child pornography; the proposed testimony went to defendant's state of mind or whether he knowingly committed the charged offenses, and expert witnesses were prohibited from testifying regarding such ultimate issues").

76. Fed. R. Evid. 702.

77. See *United States v. Azure*, 801 F.2d 336, 339–40 (8th Cir. 1986).

78. *United States v. Farrell*, 563 F.3d 364, 377–78 (8th Cir. 2009).

79. These suggestions are, of course, in addition to other more "routine" criminal defense actions.

14

Overview of Selected Trial Issues

W HAT FOLLOWS IS A VERY BASIC DISCUSSION of the trial process, as well as a summary of some key practical pointers and tips. Although this summary will likely be too introductory for the seasoned trial attorney, we include it so that others less familiar with what happens during a trial might gain a better understanding of some of the issues facing investigators and attorneys charged with presenting these difficult cases to judges and juries. And although this chapter is predominantly drafted from the perspective of the prosecutor, many of the issues covered apply equally to defense counsel (with some of the technical issues specific to child exploitations cases discussed above in chapter 12).

A. Developing the Theory of the Case

Developing a working theory is essential to organizing the volume of evidence obtained in a child exploitation prosecution. A working theory helps the investigative team explain various types of evidence, and similarly aids the defense team in disproving the case. Again, knowing the type of offender and understanding how that offender operates will help in putting the case together and proving or disproving intent. For example, in the *Romero* case described in chapter 9, one theory used by the prosecution team at trial was that Romero was a chameleon who changed his colors to fit his victims—all for one goal: to lure the boys to his home where his true colors would be revealed. The theory was supported by the evidence that during the luring phase of Romero's contact with each victim he never revealed his sexual intentions. Only after the victim was safely under his control would he begin the desensitization process of showing the boy child pornography and preparing him to accept the sexual act. The various phone calls, e-mail solicitations, stories, physical items, and letters could be presented to the jury to show that Romero manipulated each of his victims by adjusting his persona. The defense chose to flip that theory and sought to show that Romero was engaged in all types of fantastical communications with children, but had no intent to lure and molest a child.

A theory of the case also always aids the trial attorney when he is faced with evidentiary objections. Being able to tell the judge that a particular piece of evidence is relevant based on the theory increases the likelihood that an objection will be overruled. For example, a defense attorney might easily challenge the admission of the "altar box" in the Romero case by stating to the court that the altar box is not relevant to the kidnapping charge or the possession of child pornography charge. The defense might state that the altar box should not be presented to the jury because it is overly prejudicial in that it is just being used to enflame the passions of the jury and the government has not charged any of the activity associated with the box. In response, the prosecutor would use the theory of the case to make the box relevant by stating that the government's case is built around the premise that Romero portrayed himself differently to different boys, manipulated those boys by luring them into his net through the use of items that they desired, and that the box shows his intent to deceive, manipulate, and lure. The prosecutor also argued that it further revealed that Romero's luring worked on boys, since witness testimony from those boys would reveal that they had taken his story, hook, line, and sinker by engaging in his fabricated altar ritual. By using the theory of the case, the box takes on more relevance and has a higher likelihood of being admitted.

B. Identifying and Developing Critical Facts

If two people were to meet for a cup of coffee and discuss something important that had happened to one of them the night before, the other would ask many commonsense and reactive questions in an effort to understand and assess the situation. Take, for example, two friends discussing how one of them had an unfortunate and upsetting experience in the morning: she had come out of her apartment that morning and found her car vandalized by someone who wrote some derogatory remark on it. The listener wants to comprehend the situation and might ask: Why would someone do that to you? Is anyone upset with you? Where were you when this happened? When did you first discover it? Did someone else also see it? Has this happened before? All of these seemingly banal questions offer opportunities to explore potentially relevant facts. Often lawyers tend to avoid the most obvious and relevant facts of a case while they seek to prove the elements of a crime. These commonsense questions offer insights into important legal issues: intent of the offender, relationship between the offender and the victim, defendant's opportunity to commit the crime, and the timing of the crime. Unique facts offer highly relevant insights into identity. Why was that particular remark written? Is that a remark that links the victim to the offender in some unique way? If during the investigation of the case the lawyer was intrigued by a particular fact or circumstance, chances are high that the same fact or circumstance will be intriguing and beneficial to a juror hearing the case.

Addressing these unique facts involves assessing whether each fact is one that can be defined as a situational or tangible issue, such as the placement of the car on the street in front of the apartment; or a psychological and state of mind issue, such as the use of the derogatory term by a neighbor two days prior to the incident. Psychological issues respond to the juror's question: Why? Why did the neighbor react angrily on that day? Why didn't the victim call the police when she found the car vandalized? Failure to answer a "why" question in the theory of the case or through witness testimony can result in a frustrated and doubtful jury. Therefore, the big-picture commonsense questions asked by a layperson can be a helpful tool in identifying a critical issue in the case.

Using the *Romero* case as an example again, one common question that a juror would naturally have is why the boy left his home and agreed to go with Romero. Remember, the theory of the Romero case was that the boy was inveigled and deceived. The victim believed that he was joining a caring and loving caregiver who would provide him with gifts and a life of luxury. The boy was thirteen. Why would a boy that age think that leaving his family to live in Florida with a stranger was a realistic option? Answering this question is critical to the successful prosecution of this case. First, it identifies the reality that consent remains a complete defense to a charge of kidnapping. Second, there is no bright line test for the age of consent; instead, all circumstances that would impact consent must be taken into account. By considering these questions early in the pretrial preparation period, it became apparent that the government would be required to call experts to testify about the boy's weakened psychological state—namely, his diagnosed depression and attention deficit hyperactivity disorder, and his inability to control his impulses and understand future consequences of his actions. The government would need to present all of the circumstances of the grooming process and the boy's inability to understand that he was being lured in order to prevail on this theory. It would be essential to contrast the manipulative and intentional conduct of the exploiter with the psychologically weak and malleable personality of the victim.

C. Preparing a Preliminary Trial Checklist

The preliminary trial list enables the trial attorney to have contact with all law enforcement officers, witnesses, experts, and other contacts that may have information regarding the case. This initial contact list may eventually morph into a witness list, but having quick access to those who have information regarding the case is essential. The checklist will serve as a deadline list for getting items to the lab for evaluation, getting information to experts for their reports, getting key motions filed pursuant to the court's scheduling order, and keeping track of any conflicts that law enforcement and witnesses may have preventing the trial attorneys access to them. All of the criminal histories of the witnesses and any other legal documents that may apply to an evidentiary dispute regarding that history must be obtained at an early stage. Key items on the trial checklist include preparing transcripts of tape recordings; preparing electronic duplicates of evidence for the defense; determining in what manner the images, transcripts, and e-mails will be displayed, and obtaining the necessary equipment; and preparing the evidence to be used according to the equipment's specifications. This list will evolve and expand over time; yet a running list will keep the trial preparation moving efficiently and appropriately.

D. Creating a Trial Notebook

A common and simple method for staying organized during trial is to keep a comprehensive "trial notebook" containing the most important information about the case, including everything from the contacts list and indictment to the attorney's preliminary thoughts on how to argue certain issues that may arise at trial. Putting together such a trial notebook enables the trial attorney to properly separate, outline, and arrange all aspects of the case. The attorney will come to rely on this notebook, as it contains, in an organized and easily accessible fashion, all the pertinent information used by the attorney. The notebook should also contain the attorney's legal research, pretrial motions, evidence to be presented, draft outlines for opening statement, direct examination of each witness, cross-examination of opposing witnesses, and a draft closing argument. Each section should be separately divided within the trial notebook. The pretrial motions section should contain the actual motions the attorney has argued, or will argue. Similarly, the legal research section should contain relevant statutes as well as legal memoranda on anticipated issues in the trial. In the exhibit list, documentary evidence should be arranged chronologically in the order in which it is expected to be introduced at trial. This will allow quick access when documents are needed. A document that cannot be found during trial is the same as no document at all. The use of notebook software with search capabilities also facilitates quick access to needed documents, exhibits, and research.

E. Jury Issues

Selecting the jury in a child exploitation case, or related human trafficking case, can be even more challenging than the reading of tea leaves that normally goes into the jury selection process. Take, for example, a typical drug distribution trial: during *voir dire*, the prosecutor can explore a particular juror's ideas about law enforcement, about the use of drugs, about legalization of drugs, and about whether drug use has impacted a prospective juror or his family in a significant way. Drug use is discussed in grammar schools, there are national television and radio ads regarding drug use, and mainstream media has incorporated drug dealers and drug dealing into television series and movies for years. In contrast, child abuse and child sexual exploitation has been traditionally viewed as a taboo topic that is inappropriate to discuss in most circles. Many victims of sexual abuse never share their victimization with even their most intimate friends. There is also an archaic understanding of child sexual abuse, as discussed in chapter 2.

Stated plainly, it is highly unlikely that counsel will get direct and open discussion regarding the issues with jury members. It is critical, therefore, that counsel work with the judge to encourage the jurors to be candid in a safe setting—a sidebar conversation with the lawyers and the judge. Although this conversation will be on the record, it will not be in open court. As such, the parties have a greater likelihood that the potential jurors will be candid and honest.

Each attorney will have his own theory about who is a good juror for a child exploitation case—and the authors will not attempt to second-guess the skills of any seasoned attorney. In the authors' experience, however, from the prosecutor's perspective, the best jurors for a child exploitation case are jurors who have children or work with children, so that there is a clear and unmistakable knowledge of just how young, naïve, and malleable children can be. If a juror has not interacted with minors in the past, he may be less likely to understand the power differential between the mature adult and the easily manipulated child. Jurors with stable backgrounds evidencing a strong work history, ties with the community, and friendships are, moreover, generally jurors who will be more inclined to view the defendant's conduct as a crime, as opposed to some type of psychological perversion or, worse, an "accident" for which the child is largely at fault. Interestingly, in spite of the layperson's belief that race and gender play critical roles in jury composition, the authors find that, in the exploitation context, race and gender have far less impact during the selection process than the individual juror's stability, education, and interaction with children.

F. Opening Statement

For a juror who has never been in a federal court, or has never been exposed to a trial, the courtroom setting can be quite intimidating. From the moment jurors enter the building, they are sent the message that this place is different and less accessible. They pass through a security review, are exposed to jargon they are likely unfamiliar with, and are restricted in their ability to talk with others about what they are experiencing as jurors. Add to this discomfort the complexity and perversion of learning about a child sexual offense, something completely foreign to the average layperson, and you have a combination of circumstances not conducive to learning. This, as we explored in chapter 12, is the challenge of the federal exploitation trial lawyer.

In the opening statement, the trial attorney must set the tone for what she will present throughout the course of the trial. In doing so, she must use plain and direct diction and avoid euphemisms. Each term she uses must be clearly defined. This is the opening of an educator—one who wants to enlighten his jury about the crime because this is not a topic that comes instinctively to a juror. From the prosecutor's perspective, the best way to do so is through the eyes of the victim (for the defense perspective, consult chapter 13). By telling her story in a direct and conversational manner, the trial attorney can begin to educate the jury. Using a theme to sort through all the facts will enable the jury to understand the relevance of the evidence more clearly.

For example, the trial attorney in a sexual trafficking case may use the theme of "control," and start by informing the jury that this case involves control in many ways: control over a girl's freedom, control over her income, control over her emotions, control over her body, and control over her daily needs, all for one purpose—to put money in the trafficker's pocket. This foundational theme sets the tone for key facts that the trial attorney must sort out for the jury: the trafficker's confinement in a squalid hotel room, the profit from the victim's molestation, and the psychological and physical denigration inflicted upon the victim.

The opening statement must of course also address the elements of the crime and the burden of proof. Each fact should be set forth as fulfilling an element of the crime, and should telegraph to the jury what the trial lawyer believes the evidence will show.

The attorney should also always operate with a theory of the case. The theory is different from the theme. It explains why individuals acted the way they did, and how it was that certain facts played out the way they did. The opening is not a time for argument or hyperbole. Rather, the trial lawyer should keep a calm and professional tone to lessen any concerns that the case is being brought on the basis of raw emotion or to "get even" with the defendant. By methodically examining the facts that will be presented, the trial attorney encourages the jury to do the same. The trial attorney needs the jury to look at the facts boldly, and not to shy away from the difficult, uncomfortable, or painful ones. By doing so himself, the professionally detached prosecutor sets the tone for how the jury should go about its work.

This is not to say that the opening statement will be cold or bland. Telling the story of molestation through the eyes of the victim is bound to be painful and, frankly, shocking. The key here is to present that story by personalizing it and not arguing it. There will be plenty of time during closing arguments to argue, assess the credibility of the witnesses, and test the theory of the defense. This, in contrast, is the time to set the stage for the coming days.

The prosecutor should start with an introduction that grabs the attention of the jury and suits his theme. He should introduce the parties to the jury and explain their roles. Then it is time to tell the story. The facts should be presented with attention to the scenes and should paint visual pictures that make those scenes come to life for the jurors. Once the story has been told, the attorney should discuss the elements of the crime and embrace the burden on him to prove those elements. Then each fact is pulled out of its normal chronological sequence and is placed within the category of the element of the crime that particular fact proves. In the end, the prosecutor must directly ask the jury for the relief that he seeks; for example, "and I will return and ask you to return a verdict of guilty of human trafficking."

In the opening, it is also appropriate—and, in fact, generally sound trial strategy—to address certain weaknesses that the attorney believes may hamper his case. If, for example, the alleged victim of human trafficking is psychologically damaged and her memory is poor regarding certain events, the attorney might address the victim's poor recall of facts and can put it into context of his theme—due to the trafficker's control over her, she does not know the details of how certain aspects of the trafficking operation took place because the exploiter kept her, both literally and figuratively, in the dark. He might also prep the jury for an expert witness who will testify on the impact that extended periods of confinement can have on an individual's ability to recall details. These potential weaknesses will have been identified far in advance of trial during the pretrial investigation phase. The trial attorney should not try to brush these weaknesses under the carpet; rather, he should embrace and address them.

G. Direct Examination of Witnesses

Direct examination gives the party presenting the witness an opportunity to have that witness tell a particular part of the story and "fill in the blanks" for the jury.

1. Purpose of Direct: Telling the Story from the Victim's Perspective

Having a victim tell her story is the primary purpose of the direct examination, which is why the examiner steers clear of leading questions. Leading questions suggest the answer to the question. Direct questions, in contrast, merely set forth the who, what, when, where, why, and how of what happened. If nonleading questions are asked, the focus will remain on the victim, where it should always be during a direct. The victim will use her own words, her own phraseology, and gestures and emotions to bring to life the story she is telling. Leading questions, in contrast, demand an almost robotic response that depersonalizes the story and separates the human emotional reactions from the witness.

2. Structuring the Direct

A common way to order a direct examination is to tell the story chronologically. In a trafficking case or a luring case, this makes particular sense because there will be a beginning moment when the victim meets her exploiter and an end moment when she has been victimized (or when law enforcement's intervention prevented victimization and/or uncovered the defendant's illicit conduct). Telling a story chronologically also helps the jury to understand the grooming or luring process so that by the time the victim describes her first molestation, the jury has an understanding of how it was that she was in that place at that time. Throughout the direct, the examiner must slow the witness down and continue to render alive those small snapshots of the locations and actions being described. "He kept us in a room" is a very different description than "he kept us in a small hotel room where there were no beds, only mattresses on the floor, no bathroom, no windows, and he locked the door each night." The difference between the former answer and the latter is in the preparation. It will take hours of witness preparation to help get a victim ready to tell her story in the appropriate level of detail (without, of course, "coaching" the witness).

Many evidentiary objections can be avoided if questions are crafted appropriately in advance. For example, a question that asks, "What did the officer tell you?" will appropriately call for a hearsay objection. Phrased differently, the examiner might ask, "What did you do as a result of what the officer told you?"

3. Conducting Direct

The focus of the jury's attention should, as noted above, remain on the victim witness throughout the direct examination. Therefore, the examiner should stand away from the witness stand, requiring the jury to keep its focus on the storyteller and not the examiner. If the examiner is standing too close to the witness, the examiner may draw the attention of the jurors to him rather than to the victim. The examiner should allow the victim to use the words that the jurors would use in describing what happened. Victims rarely use anatomical terms in describing their molestation. During the pretrial preparation stage, the examiner can determine what each term means so that when the examination occurs in the courtroom, the words will come naturally to the witness and may be followed by a clarifying question by the examiner.

a. Dealing with a Particularly Young Witness

Special attention must be paid to the child victim. The obligations of the court and all those involved in the judicial proceeding are set forth in chapter 11. For one, recognizing the shorter attention span and the need to take breaks for bathroom, snacks, and rest are critical to an effective trial preparation. Taking a child to the courtroom where she will testify is also a helpful step in preparing her for testifying. The more familiar she is with the setting, the less likely it is that she will freeze on the stand due to fear of the unknown. As the provisions of 18 U.S.C. § 3509 set forth, she may have an attendant with her throughout her testimony, and she should be provided private access to the courtroom that keeps her out of the exploiter's gaze. Assessing whether she is able to confront her exploiter will depend in significant part on her own treating doctor and his assessment of her progress.

Moreover, the risks of having a case upset for failure to protect the confrontation rights of the defendant are documented by regular reversals.[1] It requires testimony from a professional, usually a psychologist or a social worker, to set forth the reasons why testifying in the presence of the defendant will be harmful to the child. Only then can a judge safely implement a screening mechanism such as CCTV.

Younger children will also be difficult to prepare for cross-examination. By explaining that other individuals in the courtroom may ask the minor questions, the child will be less intimidated by those questions. Bringing the minor to the courtroom can also help in determining whether any special seating needs to be arranged so the jury can see the minor. Witness stands, after all, are designed for adults, and in some courtrooms a child can become dwarfed by the stand. Also, if an attendant is going to be present during the testimony, the logistics of where that attendant will sit and how she will have access to the minor must be worked out well in advance.

The minor witness must also practice identifying key pieces of evidence such as pointing to the offender in a photo, identifying his voice on a phone call, and identifying a location from a photograph. All of this is done over a period of short visits to ensure that the minor is not overly taxed, and in a manner that does not suggest that the minor was inappropriately coached or cajoled into providing false or misleading evidence. In all, the basic elements of preparation of the minor for testimony will be similar to that of any other witness—the more the witness is aware of what will happen, the better prepared she will be in the courtroom.

b. The Expert Witness

Expert witnesses can be critical to the successful prosecution of a child exploitation case. Experts who explain a child's psychological condition that made her more susceptible to the defendant's manipulations can help clarify unique child behavior.[2] Psychiatrists and medical doctors may be critical to explaining the extent of injuries inflicted on a child. But the type of expert that can turn a jury's lack of understanding to one of enlightenment are those who explain the behavior of child molesters themselves. Numerous courts have approved this type of expert because the expert is an individual who has knowledge about a topic outside that of the ordinary layperson, that knowledge is relevant, and that knowledge, if imparted to the jury, would likely aid the jury in making its decision.[3]

Early notice of experts is required by the rules of evidence so an opposing party can determine whether they want to challenge the expert under *Daubert v. Merrell Dow Pharmaceuticals.*[4] The court may be required to have a *Daubert* hearing in advance of trial to determine if the expert's testimony would be helpful to the fact finder, whether it is accepted within its field, and whether the scope of the testimony is relevant to the case. Pretrial hearings are given after one side opposes the other's expert and challenges its admission at trial. This challenge comes after the moving party provides the opposition the expert's report of opinion and a proffer of what the expert's testimony will cover. In the end, the court will determine whether the expert's opinion can be admitted.

If the court allows an expert to testify, the expert is permitted to give an opinion based on his training and expertise. Interestingly, although an expert can be effectively crossed for lack of education, the expert's level of academic education may not be as critical as the expert's "opportunity and ability" to observe real-world phenomena that permit the expert to provide his conclusions and findings. For example, a rape victim advocate who has no formal medical training may be able to testify about the hundreds of rape victims that she has met at the hospital and describe their demeanor based upon that personal knowledge if at trial there is an issue about whether the victim reacted emotionally upon her arrival at the hospital.

c. Cooperating Witness

The jury will be informed that the cooperating witness's testimony should be treated with "caution and great care" *if* that witness received some benefit from the government in exchange for his cooperation. Usually, that benefit comes in the form of a reduction in his sentence pursuant to a plea agreement with the government. In presenting a cooperating witness to the jury, the examiner must not hide the agreement, but, rather, should embrace it. The prosecutor must place the agreement in front of the jury with an explanation that this type of inside information can only be provided by those within the inner circle of the defendant, and, as such, they have criminal backgrounds or perverse interests like the defendant. Cooperating witnesses can be powerful tools in a prosecution because they can offer a perspective of this type of criminal activity that is simply beyond the common understanding of the layperson.

Serious consideration must always be given to the decision of whether to offer a cooperating defendant a reduced sentence in exchange for testimony. The victim of a crime is entitled to weigh in on this decision and may have a significant impact on the decision. Factors such as whether the case can be prosecuted without the cooperation of the criminal, whether it is in the best interest of the victim to have the criminal cooperator testify, and the broader societal interest of prosecuting a child exploiter all factor into this equation. Often these decisions can be fraught with challenges. For example, is the victim of the cooperating defendant entitled to have their exploiter prosecuted without a benefit from the government? In the end, the executive branch will have the ultimate say as to whether a cooperating defendant should receive a reduced sentence, but that decision should be based on a balancing of interests and made with a keen eye on the rights of the victim.

4. Introducing Exhibits

The presentation of child pornography and other disturbing pieces of evidence demands attention to various competing interests. The job of the prosecutor is to present the evidence that will prove the elements of the crime he has charged. This can be photographs, videos, chats, e-mails, voicemails, medical tests, medical photos, and crime scene photos. It is the obligation of the prosecutor to ensure that the evidence is presented, but he also must bear in mind that the evidence will be displayed in an open courtroom. As such, careful placement of close up viewing screens seen only by the jury can help ensure that the child pornography is being shown solely for the narrow purpose of the government meeting its burden of proof, and that it is not inadvertently being displayed to the public in what would be deemed victimization by the viewer. Use of computer programs to show chats and how they are entered in real time make the chat evidence come to life, and scrolling software that can depict the transcript of a phone call while it is being played make it more understandable to the jury.

Warning the jurors in advance, as early as during *voir dire*, that they will be required to view the evidence is imperative. Warning them prior to the viewing that they will now be presented with what the government asserts is child pornography is also essential because the viewing can be disturbing. The prosecutor can seek to time the first presentation before a break in the trial so that jurors can overcome the visceral reaction to the evidence and to also help ease the transition into the fact finder's obligatory role.

Effective presentation of computer evidence also includes showing the Internet logs chronicling the defendant's progression, from downloading child pornography to chatting with a minor on the Internet. Demonstrating the vast number of hours that a defendant spent collecting his images can also be powerful evidence of how important that collection is to him, and of the absence of "mistake" or "inadvertence." Displaying images in the way that they were stored on the defendant's computer can also have non-obvious evidentiary value. Some offenders will have a file folder with a victim's name on it, and the file will include both sexual photos and nonsexual photos. The juxtaposition of the boy on a bike next to the boy in a sex act shows that the defendant only viewed the child in one way—as a sexual tool.

H. Cross-examination

1. Confrontation and Other Special Issues

A defendant has a Sixth Amendment right to confront his accusers (see chapter 12 for a detailed discussion on this topic), and neither the trial attorney nor the court should take this fundamental right lightly.

2. Cross-examining with a Prior Inconsistent Statement

Witness credibility remains the key to success in almost all criminal cases, and it plays a critical part in the trials of accused sexual exploiters. As mentioned previously, the prosecutor will have worked hard to minimize the number of times that a victim was interviewed in order to reduce the defense attorney's opportunities to impeach the victim by using minor inconsistencies. Even minor inconsistencies, in the hands of a skilled cross-examiner, can diminish credibility. If the defense attorney is successful in breaking down the credibility of the victim, some cases will fall apart completely.

Similarly, if the defendant spoke to law enforcement at any point, and that statement was recorded by an agent in any format, the government attorney will now have an opportunity to challenge the defendant if he testifies and says anything inconsistent with that prior statement. This tool of impeachment can serve to break down the credibility of the defendant, potentially resulting in a conviction.

3. Cross-examining Expert Witnesses

Experts can be crossed in a different way. First, the expert's qualifications can be challenged. If she is merely an academic, she can be challenged about her lack of hands-on experience. If she is a practitioner, she can be challenged about her lack of academic credentials. In the world of expert testimony cross, the expert is deemed to have knowledge of the major texts and treatises in her area of expertise. Therefore, she can be challenged with hypothetical situations that the opposing party will use to show that she is unqualified. Essentially, anything that the expert has written or said on the subject is fair game during a cross-examination of the expert. Preparing the expert for cross-examination is, therefore, even more important than preparing her direct examination because her opinion is only good as long as it holds up.

I. Closing Arguments

Closing arguments are finally the time for passion and argument. The evidence is in, the testimony is complete, and it is now time to argue the reasonable inferences that can be made from the evidence. The prosecutor is permitted to comment about the demeanor of the witnesses on the stand, on their answers, and on the manner in which they testified. Most importantly, the closing argument is the time for the prosecutor to summarize the evidence that shows guilt. Use of the jury instructions is generally permitted in most federal jurisdictions, but if the exact instruction is not permitted, the statutes and their elements must be used in order to show how the evidence presented supports a finding of guilt beyond a reasonable doubt on each charge. The trial lawyer can now circle back to his opening and use the same theme and theory to demonstrate to the jury that he has done exactly what he set out to do. He should use the evidence demonstratively during the closing and boldly address the issues that he calmly described before.

Defense closing arguments, in contrast, will focus on the impeachment of the witnesses in an attempt to have the jury not credit that testimony. The defense attorney will challenge the victim's story by pointing to inconsistencies or to her demeanor in answering the prosecutor's questions. In short, the defense's goal is solely to show that the government has failed to meet its burden.

At the conclusion of closing arguments, the prosecutor will always have the rebuttal argument—an exclusive opportunity of the prosecution because the government bears the burden of proof. The rebuttal is the prosecution's opportunity to respond to any attacks on his witnesses made by the defense. This is the time that the victim's testimony is, once again, corroborated, and the weaknesses the defense attorney identified are explained as irrelevant or unimportant to the jury's decision. Chronological structure is less critical in the rebuttal, since the purpose is solely to rehabilitate those areas of attack that need to be rehabilitated. In conclusion, the prosecutor will always ask the jury to do exactly what the government asserts the evidence has proven, namely, that the defendant is guilty and that they must, therefore, return a conviction.

Notes

1. See, for example, *Bordeaux*, 400 F.3d at 548.

2. See, for example, *Romero*, 189 F.3d at 576 (7th Cir.).

3. See, for example, *United States v. Hayward*, 359 F.3d 631 (3rd Cir. 2004) (testimony of Ken Lanning of the Behavioral Sciences Unit of the FBI regarding profiles of types of offenders).

4. 509 U.S. 579 (1993).

15

Sentencing Considerations in Sexual Exploitation Cases

Does Anything Work?

IF YOU WERE TO ASK A FEDERAL JUDGE what the most difficult part of her job is, one might expect the answer, "sentencing." If you were to ask what the most difficult type of sentencing is, the majority would most likely answer, "sex offenders." Sentencing a sex offender creates unique challenges for all parties involved and for the judge, in significant part, because it is at this point that the question must be asked, "What should we do with this offender?" Answering this question, of course, opens up a whole host of subsidiary inquiries: for example, was the offense triggered by mental illness, childhood abuse, obsessive compulsive disorder, or just plain evil intent?

In balancing the well-known sentencing factors set forth in 18 U.S.C. § 3553, the court, after all, must take into account (1) the impact of the crime on the victim, (2) the impact that the offender's sentence will have on others who may offend similarly, and (3) the unique characteristics of the offender. At no point during the criminal case are the issues as crystallized as they are at sentencing, and at no point are more factors and sources of evidence at play. Graphic images, victim statements, relevant conduct, family history, mental health, physical health, and passionate arguments on both sides make the sentencing process even more challenging.

A. Recidivism Rates and the Challenge of Rehabilitating Sex Offenders

The U.S. Supreme Court has noted "grave concerns over the high rate of recidivism among convicted sex offenders and their dangerousness as a class," and found that "the risk of recidivism posed by sex offenders is frightening and high."[1] Further, the Court has found that "when convicted sex offenders reenter society, they are much *more likely than any other type of offender* to be rearrested for a new rape or sexual assault."[2]

As broadly touched on in chapter 2, any analysis of recidivism rates among sexual offenders, whether based upon re-arrests or re-convictions, must take into account the vast underreporting of sexual assaults by victims—estimates indeed indicate that fewer than 16 percent of such victims ever report the offense.[3] And of those offenses reported, even fewer lead to prosecution and eventual conviction.[4] As a result, many sexual offenders are able to commit large numbers of offenses before ever being caught—as many as an average of 533 sex offenses over a twelve-year period before the first detection.[5] Similarly, one study of child molesters revealed that each of the offenders studied "reported having hundreds of previously unknown sexual contacts with children."[6]

On the whole, an average period of ten to sixteen years elapses between the time of a sex offender's first offense and his first arrest.[7] And there is no reason to believe that this scale of vast underreporting does not significantly impact analysis of recidivism rates as well; indeed, one study of "unofficial data" of subsequent sexual offenses after a conviction increased the researchers' recidivism measures by a staggering 170 percent.[8]

Thus, any study reporting recidivism rates on the basis of previous or subsequent "convictions" must be taken with a sizeable grain of salt. Moreover, even among those studies that have been done on re-offenses among sex offenders, "there is a great deal of variation in the offender populations studied, the size of the sample, the definition of recidivism, the length of the follow-up period, and in the use of control or comparison groups."[9]

Nevertheless, in examining the aggregate results of such studies, a number of significant realities must be taken into account.

1. Recidivism Rates Increase over Time

Researchers have found relatively low recidivism rates in the immediate years following the reentry of adult sex offenders into the community.[10] (Interestingly, recidivism rates among offenders who are on probation, without having served a significant period of incarceration, appear to be similar to those among individuals who have been released from prison.)[11] Recidivism rates spike, however, as researchers track offenders over longer periods of time.[12] Thus, "all current professional research potentially underestimates the accurate base rate for sex offender recidivism because the studies end too soon"— that is, before the offender commits his first post-conviction offense.[13] This is "in contrast to general criminal patterns, where the propensity to commit crimes decreases with increased age."[14]

2. Official Statistics Fatally Skew Results

Because victim-reporting and arrest rates for sexual offenders are so low, and there is no way to determine the accuracy even of self-reported re-offense rates, there is no way for researchers to determine whether any individual in their samples is a nonrecidivist or simply an unknown recidivist.[15]

3. Recidivism Rates Reflect Substantial Variation Depending on Offender Type

Overall, even setting aside that the statistics drastically underreport actual rate of reoffending, literature reviews reveal that exhibitionists have the highest reported recidivism rates of all sex offenders (between 41 and 71 percent), and that child molesters who offend against boys have substantially higher recidivism rates than those who offend against girls (between 13 and 40 percent for the former, and between 10 and 29 percent for the latter).[16] With respect to child pornography offenders, a 2005 study revealed that 17 percent of a sample of convicted child pornography offenders committed another offense within an average of about two and a half years after release into the community.[17]

Among these re-offenders, those who had been convicted of a sexual offense involving contact with a victim (only about one-quarter of the total sample) were the most likely to re-offend following a child pornography conviction.[18] However, only one of the 201 offenders who had only ever been convicted of a child pornography offense subsequently was convicted for committing a contact sexual offense, "contradict[ing] the assumption that all child pornography offenders are at very high risk to commit contact sexual offenses involving children."[19] But, again, these studies are, in a sense, flawed from inception because they rely on formal convictions (which, as we have seen, only reflect the proverbial tip of the sex-offender iceberg).

As for recidivism among the general category of "extrafamilial child molesters," a study analyzing the reoffending rates of offenders who had once been incarcerated produced a "52% failure rate for sexual re-offending" within the twenty-five-year period following release from incarceration.[20] Even this high rate is artificially low, however, as the researchers counted only those offenders who were (1) charged with a new offense, and only those offenses that (2) involved actual contact with a victim.[21] As these findings "are in keeping with the other research involving shorter-term measures of extra-familial child molester reconviction rates,"[22] it is fair to describe a recidivism rate of more than 50 percent as a very conservative estimation—indeed, a lower boundary—of re-offenses among convicted child molesters.[23]

B. The Prime Sentencing Challenge:
Understanding the Crime, the Offender, and the Victim

To fully understand the crime of which the defendant was convicted, the sentencing judge must first understand the offender, the victim, and the relationship between the two.

1. Surveying Key Factors Used to Gauge Recidivism Risk

As a general matter, sexual offense recidivism is associated with at least two broad factors: (a) deviant sexual interests and (b) antisocial orientation/lifestyle instability.[24] More specifically, researchers have consistently found that certain specified risk factors are key in predicting an offender's likely recidivism. These risk factors have, in fact, been used to create various actuarial risk prediction scales, with varying levels of reliability and acceptance in the criminal justice and psychological communities.[25]

Of these various risk factors, the ones considered highly indicative of the offender's risk of re-offending are the offender's

- sexual criminal history;
- diversity of the types of sexual offenses committed; and
- age.[26]

Also among the most frequently cited risk factors are

- the age of the victim;
- the offender's lack of education;
- unemployment; and
- presence of a history of alcohol or drug use.[27]

For example, a study of sex-offense probationers in Georgia revealed that "those who are married are less likely than those who are unmarried to commit a technical violation, commit a new crime, or fail probation"; similarly, probationers with full-time employment are less likely to violate probation or to re-offend.[28]

Other, less permanent characteristics also play a role in determining an offender's recidivism risk, including the following:

- the offender's willingness to accept responsibility for past criminal actions;
- the emotional state of the offender; and
- the offender's willingness to seek and cooperate with treatment programs.[29]

Additionally, certain characteristics of a particular offense may reveal the offender's risk of committing further sex offenses, such as the number, age, and sex of the victims, and whether force was used or injury to the victims resulted.[30] Interestingly, however, the study of Georgia sex-offense probationers revealed that, of the offense-specific variables, "only the presence of alcohol or drugs in the offense is related to probation outcomes," with those whose offenses involved substances being more likely to violate probation.[31]

On the subject of risk-reduction psychological and other treatment programs, the efficacy of a particular form of treatment is obviously affected by many offender- and community-specific variables. Indeed, meta-analysis of a myriad of studies provides only mixed reviews of the efficacy of treatment programs for sexual offenses.[32] And at worst, several studies have found that the groups of offenders who received treatment had "either similar or significantly higher sexual-offense reoffense rates than the untreated or refused groups."[33] Other studies, however, have found a positive relationship between treatment in a cognitive-behavior and offense-specific program and reduced risk of recidivism.[34]

2. Sentencing Considerations Dictated by the Federal Sentencing Guidelines

It is evident, therefore, that criminal sentencing of convicted sexual offenders poses difficult problems in light of the fluctuating recidivism research discussed above. In cases involving federal convictions, sentencing judges, after all, must consider not only the formal Sentencing Guidelines, but must also take into account the defendant's individual characteristics under 18 U.S.C. § 3553(a). Put simply, the sentencing of a convicted sex offender presents a complex puzzle, with easy answers in short supply.

a. Courts: "Proceed with Caution When Sentencing Child Pornography Defendants"

With respect to the federal Sentencing Guidelines, the Second Circuit Court of Appeals noted that the child pornography guidelines in particular are "fundamentally different from most and . . . unless applied with great care, can lead to unreasonable sentences."[35] This is largely a result of congressional action; Congress several times has directed the Sentencing Commission to modify the child pornography guidelines in order to provide for enhanced penalties for child pornography offenders.[36] As a result of these changes, the sentencing guidelines currently "concentrate . . . all offenders at or near the statutory maximum," and in fact often counter-intuitively mandate higher sentences for those involved with child pornography than for those who "actually engage . . . in sexual conduct with a minor."[37]

b. Considering a Defendant's "Propensity to Re-offend"

Of course, although a judge must abide by any applicable statutory mandatory minimum or maximum sentence set forth in the U.S. Code, the federal Sentencing Guidelines no longer bind federal sentencing judges. The guidelines only must be consulted and taken into account at sentencing.[38] In terms of the process, after determining the appropriate sentencing range under the guidelines, judges must next consider the defendant's individual characteristics, including his likelihood of committing subsequent crimes. Thus, in the landmark case of *United States v. Cossey*, the Second Circuit held that consideration of "a defendant's propensity to re-offend" is properly considered by a sentencing judge pursuant to 18 U.S.C. § 3553(a), particularly where evidence of such a propensity is demonstrated by psychiatrists' evaluations or other expert testimony.[39]

On the other hand, a sentencing judge's mistaken belief in a genetic basis for the proclivity to commit sexual offenses was held not to be a legitimate basis for sentencing under § 3553(a).[40] The court did find, however, that the sentencing judge's determination that Cossey would re-offend could have been properly reached on the basis that, according to the prosecution, Cossey had already re-offended at least once. The appellate court, therefore, remanded the case for resentencing and a determination of whether the alleged, but uncharged, recidivist conduct had been substantiated by a preponderance of the evidence.[41]

In another case, the Court of Appeals ruled it substantively unreasonable for a sentencing judge to assume that a defendant convicted of distribution of child pornography was "likely to actually sexually assault a child."[42] In the specific case at issue, this conclusion was buttressed by medical testimony; a therapist who examined the defendant had testified that the defendant was unlikely to act in an assertive, predatory manner.[43]

Sentencing judges may also consider, as suggested above, the fact that the crime for which a sexual offender is first convicted likely does not represent the defendant's true first offense, and that many offenders, indeed, arrive for their first sentencing with a long history of uncharged offenses behind them. For example, in *United States v. Phillips*, the Second Circuit held that a sentencing judge was permitted to take into account uncharged conduct that occurred when the offender was a minor, and described a long pattern of sexual conduct with children that had occurred stretching back into the offender's early teenage years.[44] Similarly, in *United States v. McCaffrey*,[45] a case prosecuted by one of the authors, the sentencing judge found that the defendant, a former priest, had throughout his life used his position with the Catholic Church to engage in the serial molestation of minors. The Seventh Circuit Court of Appeals found that the district court acted properly in determining that these prior uncharged criminal acts, for which the statute of limitations had long run out, could significantly enhance the defendant's sentence (yielding what was then the longest-ever sentence for an individual convicted of child pornography offenses).[46]

Sentencing judges are also permitted to consider a defendant's patterns of sexual offending, including both charged and uncharged incidents, in determining an appropriate sentence for a current offense. Thus, in *United States v. Angle*, the Seventh Circuit upheld an above-guidelines sentence for an offender who exhibited an extensive pattern of sexual offending characterized by (1) the abuse of a position of trust, (2) a history of producing child pornography, and (3) a failure to show remorse or seek counseling after two previous convictions for the sexual abuse of children.[47]

Finally, the unique nature of sex offenses, when considered in tandem with the high likelihood of eventual recidivism among offenders, gives sentencing judges significant leeway to impose ancillary restrictions on a defendant when these restrictions are designed to combat sexual re-offending (even where the conviction for which the defendant is currently being sentenced is not sexual in nature). Accordingly, the Fifth Circuit has found it permissible for a sentencing judge, who "must consider the defendant's history and characteristics," to consider a defendant's prior sex-offense conviction when imposing a sentence for a nonsexual offense.[48]

3. The Civil Commitment Problem

In the 1990s, states passed a variety of laws intended to "grapple with the problem of managing repeat sexual offenders," particularly those deemed "unamenable to existing mental illness treatment modalities," thus requiring long-term treatment outside of the prison or traditional mental institution context.[49] Civil commitment laws were generally passed with the promise of rehabilitation as the primary goal, but, in practice, those committed indefinitely as sexually violent predators were and are rarely discharged.

It therefore appears that incapacitation is, in fact, the primary mechanism through which civil commitment laws prevent recidivism.[50]

Scholars have argued that, as a matter of public policy, "civil commitment is not cost effective."[51] Civil commitment skeptics buttress their position by pointing to an eight-state housing and treatment average of $91,000 per year per offender and the additional burden of legal expenses and continual psychological re-examinations.[52]

In 1997, the Supreme Court addressed the constitutionality of Kansas's Sexually Violent Predator Act, which permitted the indefinite post-incarceration civil commitment of individuals who were deemed "likely to engage in 'predatory acts of sexual violence'" as the result of "a 'mental abnormality' or a 'personality disorder.'"[53] By way of brief background, Leroy Hendricks, the first offender to be committed under the act, challenged it on a variety of constitutional grounds. The Kansas Supreme Court, in turn, invalidated the act on the grounds that its requirement of a "mental abnormality" did not meet a substantive due-process requirement—namely, of allowing civil commitment only upon a finding of "mental illness."[54]

In *Kansas v. Hendricks*, the U.S. Supreme Court reversed, holding that the act satisfied substantive due process because it established adequate evidentiary and procedural safeguards, requiring a finding of both (1) future dangerousness and (2) a link between that prediction and some definite mental abnormality.[55] The Court further explained that its precedents did not require a diagnosis of some recognized mental illness as a predicate for civil commitment, but only required a mental state that, when combined with a prediction of future offenses, sufficed to distinguish the offender "from other dangerous persons who are perhaps more properly dealt with exclusively through criminal proceedings."[56] The Court additionally held that the act did not violate either the Double Jeopardy or *Ex Post Facto* Clauses, because it "does not establish criminal proceedings and . . . involuntary confinement pursuant to the Act is not punitive."[57] For obvious reasons, this ruling was hailed as a major victory by those who support long-term civil confinement for exploiters.

Subsequently, however, the Court reconsidered the constitutionality of Kansas's civil commitment act in *Kansas v. Crane*. The Kansas Supreme Court had interpreted *Hendricks* as requiring a finding that a defendant cannot control his dangerous behavior.[58] In *Crane*, the U.S. Supreme Court held that, although *Hendricks* did not require a demonstration that a defendant was completely or totally unable to control his behavior before civil commitment would be allowable under substantive due process doctrines, it did require "proof of serious difficulty in controlling behavior."[59] The Court hedged the exact parameters of this requirement, however, by explaining that "the States retain considerable leeway in defining the mental abnormalities and personality disorders that make an individual eligible for commitment."[60]

In sum, therefore, sexual predator commitment laws in the various states[61] require clinicians to determine, uncabined by bright-line rules from the courts, which offenders among a state's incarcerated population of sex offenders are so likely to re-offend as to merit involuntary civil commitment after the completion of their criminal sentences.[62] That said, research has indicated that it may be difficult for mental health professionals to accurately make "predictions of dangerousness," as required by *Hendricks* and its progeny.[63] Moreover, because, as we have discovered, the known base rate for recidivism among all sexual offenders is much greater than the percentage of offenders who are referred for possible civil commitment, "there is a very significant under-prediction of sexual predation when it comes to the commitment of sexual offenders within the sexual predator laws as they are currently implemented."[64]

C. The Role of the Victim in Sentencing Sexual Offenders

Earlier, we discussed how and why childhood sexual abuse has serious and lifelong effects on the victims of sexual crimes. Victims, for example, may experience a wide array of symptoms ranging from posttraumatic stress disorder to depression, neurotic mental illness, aggression, and suicidal behavior.[65] They, moreover, often experience difficulty in school and in the workplace, and are frequently characterized by abnormal expression of sexual behaviors, both as children and as adults.[66] Sexually abused girls, for example, are more likely to become runaways and, ultimately, more likely to be arrested as adults both for drug offenses and for violent crimes.[67] There is, indeed, a strong association between sexual victimization in childhood and subsequent drug abuse.[68] The question, therefore, becomes to what extent should the havoc wreaked upon the victims of sexual offenders factor into the calculation of what punishment is appropriate for the offenders.

In *Kennedy v. Louisiana*,[69] the Supreme Court held that the imposition of the death penalty for the offense of raping a child under twelve years of age violates the Eighth Amendment's prohibition of cruel and unusual punishment. The Court acknowledged that sexual offenses against children result in "prolonged physical and mental suffering" and can result in "years of long anguish that must be endured by the victim of child rape."[70] Nevertheless, the Court found that "imposing the death penalty for child rape would not further retributive purposes," and indeed, that "enlisting the child victim to assist it over the course of years in asking for capital punishment forces a moral choice on that child" and can prolong and worsen the emotional and psychological damage brought on by the offense itself.[71] The Court noted that the National Association of Social Workers reported that the problem of underreporting of sexual offenses was pervasive and serious, and reasoned, therefore, that "when the punishment is death, both the victim and the victim's family members may be more likely to shield the perpetrator from discovery, thus increasing underreporting."[72]

D. Understanding the Rationalizations Used by Offenders

As pointed out in chapter 2, certain types of sexual offenders are very adept at rationalizing their criminal behavior—to themselves, as well as to others— through a variety of psychological justifications. The "man/boy lover," for example, may affiliate with supporters of his sexual behavior through organizations such as the North American Man/Boy Love Association (NAMBLA). NAMBLA newsletters sent to its members include information about the age of consent in various states and countries, thereby allowing offenders to rationalize that the age of consent is arbitrary and shifting among the states and, as such, cannot be relied upon as a solid basis for determining one's criminal liability. Once part of such a "community," the offender begins to believe that his conduct is, in fact, not wrong—rather, it is society that has the "problem."

Other offenders may serve as leaders within their community, often situating themselves in positions of authority within either their churches or social structures. Coaching youth sports, supervising scouting events, and mentoring children, these offenders will send a mixed message to the sentencing court because there will always be those families whose interaction with the offender was positive. Without a criminal history, and with a sufficiently strong community network supporting him at sentencing, the judge must sort through the divergent purported personalities presented to her at sentencing. As described earlier, offenders often target minors who are less aware of their surroundings either through learning disabilities, familial fractures, mental deficits, or from being in some emotionally unstable period in their lives. This behavior can, at the time of sentencing, be presented as reflecting the genuine efforts of an individual seeking to mentor and care for the minor.

One of the more challenging justifications for a court is the Obsessive-Compulsive Disorder mitigation theory. The Diagnostic and Statistical Manual of Mental Disorders characterizes Obsessive-Compulsive Disorder as recurrent obsessions or compulsions that are severe enough to be time consuming (more than one hour per day) and cause marked distress. At some point, the person suffering from the disorder recognizes that the compulsions are excessive or unreasonable. The defense may use this disorder in mitigation to show the court that the offender was not voluntarily possessing significant amounts of pornography, but was instead "forced" to revisit the child pornography sites due to this compulsion. Defense attorneys who have attempted to use OCD as an affirmative defense have failed.[73] At sentencing, however, presenting the court with a documented finding by a psychiatrist that the offender actually suffers from the affliction can be used to minimize the massive amounts of child pornography that some offenders accumulate.

Offenders who justify or minimize their criminal activity, however, run the risk of a finding by the court of lack of remorse and little hope of rehabilitation. As any sentencing court may note, the first step toward rehabilitating an offender in any crime is for that offender to admit his wrong, express remorse for that wrong, and then show the court what efforts he has made to right that wrong. Justifications for convicted behavior may simply backfire for that reason alone.

E. Evaluating the Impact of Sex Offender Registration and Community Notification Efforts

Since 1994, a myriad of federal laws and amendments have mandated the creation of state sex offender registries and community notification schemes. In 2006, for example, the federal government enacted the Adam Walsh Child Protection and Safety Act, which consolidated and strengthened existing federal sex-offense laws.[74]

On the state level, many states' registration and notification laws rest on legislative findings regarding the social science evidence indicating high recidivism rates among convicted sexual offenders.[75] Among these states, laws impose either (1) compulsory schemes—in which all offenders convicted of certain sexual offenses must register and provide notification—or (2) discretionary schemes—in which varying combinations of judicial officers, executive agencies or prosecutorial authorities, and expert panels make specific determinations about an individual offender's level of threat to the community and likelihood of recidivism.[76] The courts have generally found such statutes to be constitutional in the face of Eighth Amendment, *ex post facto*, and double jeopardy claims.[77] Here, however, we limit ourselves to a brief examination of the literature concerning the efficacy of such laws, in the sense that they provide for the appropriate post-adjudication, post-incarceration handling of sex offenders.

Advocates, for their part, argue that sex offender registration and notification requirements decrease recidivism through several inter-related mechanisms, including increased monitoring by law enforcement authorities. The claimed benefit of such amplified monitoring is that it increases the risk of being caught. Moreover, registration and notification initiates "target hardening"—potential victims, once made aware of the offender's background and geographic proximity, change their behavior and make it harder for the offender to find a new victim.[78] Thus, some offenders report that registration and notification requirements kept them from recidivating, and others indicate that notification requirements "reduced their access to potential victims."[79] The public appears to consider the availability of information about sex offenders in their neighborhoods and communities quite valuable; one study, for example, indicates that "homes within close proximity of a registered offender sell for about $5,500 less than comparable homes."[80]

On the downside, widespread public awareness can cause registered sex offenders to suffer from significant adverse community attention. Consequently, they are much more likely to be fired from their jobs or evicted from their homes. Such negative externalities "may lower the offender's outside opportunities (in terms of jobs and social life) and thus lower the opportunity cost of choosing crime over more legal lifestyles."[81]

One study, in fact, revealed that more than 90 percent of the offenders surveyed "reported suffering disruptive effects, including ostracism, harassment or threats, loss of employment, expulsion from a residence, or the breakup of personal relationships."[82] Scholars have noted that the various harmful psychological consequences of such social ostracism, including "feeling alone, isolated, ashamed, embarrassed, or fearful, may threaten a sex offender's reintegration and recovery and may even trigger some sex offenders to relapse."[83] Noting these and similar stressors, several studies have found that recidivism rates among registered offenders may be higher, rather than lower, than would otherwise be expected.[84]

F. Facing the Sentencing Judge's Dilemma

As discussed before, since *United States v. Booker*,[85] the federal Sentencing Guidelines no longer mandatorily bind the federal sentencing judge's determination of a reasonable sentence. *Booker* and its progeny, instead, have created a sentencing regimen under which judges are required to (1) take into account the federal sentencing guidelines, and then (2) turn to the specific sentencing factors set forth in 18 U.S.C. § 3553. Section 3553, specifically, provides that the following (nonexhaustive) list of factors should be considered in imposing a sentence:

(1) the nature and circumstances of the offense and the history and characteristics of the defendant;

(2) the need for the sentence imposed—
    (A) to reflect the seriousness of the offense, to promote respect for the law, and to provide just punishment for the offense;
    (B) to afford adequate deterrence to criminal conduct;
    (C) to protect the public from further crimes of the defendant; and
    (D) to provide the defendant with needed educational or vocational training, medical care, or other correctional treatment in the most effective manner;
(3) the kinds of sentences available;
(4) the kinds of sentence and the sentencing range established for—
    (A) the applicable category of offense committed by the applicable category of defendant as set forth in the guidelines. . . .
(5) any pertinent policy statement—
issued by the Sentencing Commission . . . ;
(6) the need to avoid unwarranted sentence disparities among defendants with similar records who have been found guilty of similar conduct; and
(7) the need to provide restitution to any victims of the offense.

Because the sentencing court must still take into account the Sentencing Guidelines, a large body of law interpreting those guidelines remains pertinent and available to the sentencing judge. The guidelines provide for a number of enhancements potentially applicable to cases involving child sexual exploitation, depending, of course, on the specific circumstances of the case before the court. A defendant is also entitled to a sentencing reduction for acceptance of responsibility if he pleads guilty, remains cooperative, and is fully accepting of his criminal liability.

1. Acceptance of Responsibility

Generally, when a defendant pleads guilty within the federal system, he is entitled to an acceptance of responsibility reduction.[86] The guidelines require that the defendant truthfully accept responsibility for his actions; this has been interpreted as meaning someone who admits to his criminal involvement and does not minimize his criminal conduct.[87] As such, acceptance of responsibility remains another complex area in sentencing those involved in child sexual exploitation.

Considering whether a defendant has accepted responsibility, courts may still take into account whether he has engaged in violations during his supervised release, whether he has abided by all conditions while on bond, and whether he has committed any other criminal acts not covered in the indictment.[88] As described above, if the offender remains committed to somehow justifying his actions, he may easily fail to appear remorseful before the sentencing court. That said, at least one federal circuit has reversed a district court judge's refusal to award a defendant with an acceptance of responsibility reduction after the defendant stated that he believed the minors consented to the sexual conduct. That court commented that ruling in any other way would punish a defendant for acknowledging his disorder and for seeking the rehabilitation that he required.[89]

2. Criminal History Category and Career Offender

The guidelines and the statutes have provisions for career offenders who have engaged in two or more crimes of violent or sexual criminal activity. In making a determination as to whether certain crimes have been deemed crimes of violence, thereby supporting the career offender enhancement, courts have looked to whether the crimes create a serious risk of physical injury to the child. Courts have also noted the commercial nature of the offense, which commonly places minors at an additional risk of violence or illness from sexual disease. [90]

Often a judge will be faced with an argument that the defendant's criminal history is understated, and that the court should consider a higher criminal history category based on other uncharged criminal conduct.[91] As mentioned above, since many offenders have no criminal history and have not been detected by the police in the past, this can be a successful argument at sentencing if the prosecution team uncovers allegations of past conduct that have not been charged.

In *United States v. Bodenheimer*,[92] for example, the defendant had received one criminal history point for a misdemeanor conviction for disorderly conduct. When the prosecutor located the retired law enforcement officer who gave the defendant the ticket, the officer recalled vividly the details of the arrest. He had responded to a concerned call from a parent who had observed the defendant sitting in a car near her daughter's bus stop. When the officer arrived, he observed the defendant masturbating in his car. When the officer escorted the defendant to his home, he discovered enlarged photos of the girl papering the defendant's bedroom wall—photos he had taken at the bus stop. When asked why he gave a disorderly conduct misdemeanor ticket, the officer responded that he had no idea what else to call the conduct. The information was provided at the sentencing to support an upward departure for underrepresentation of Bodenheimer's lack of criminal history.

3. Concurrent and Consecutive State and Federal Sentences

Another unique complication for a federal sentencing judge is that a federal charge may be duplicative or overlap with a state charge. In manufacturing cases, for example, the actual sexual molestation of the minor will be charged by the local authorities, whereas the manufacturing of child pornography charge will be brought by the federal prosecutor. In those cases, the court will need to address the substantive similarities or differences between the two cases and determine whether the sentence imposed federally should be consecutive to or concurrent with the state sentence.[93]

4. Sentencing Enhancements

The guidelines provide for a number of enhancements that increase the advisory guidelines range for the defendant. Such enhancements include distribution of images of child pornography.[94] This distribution can come in the form of displaying an image to an undercover agent via a webcam,[95] using peer-to-peer file sharing,[96] and even leaving child pornography in a closet where a minor was bound to discover it and view it.[97]

Another enhancement that can increase the offender's sentence is the type of child pornography that the exploiter possesses. If the offender's collection contained images of children under the age of twelve, a two-level enhancement is required.[98] If the images are sadistic or violent in nature, another enhancement may be applied.[99] The court can also take into account the number of images when determining sentence. If the child was a particularly vulnerable victim or suffered extreme psychological injury, a higher sentence is warranted under the guidelines.[100] If a defendant poses as another individual and misrepresents himself to a minor as part of his crime, an additional enhancement applies.[101] Also, if the defendant obstructed justice in the investigation of the crime or during any part of the official proceedings, the defendant's sentence can be enhanced and he can lose his acceptance of responsibility reduction.[102]

After all of these preliminary considerations are addressed, the court will have an advisory guidelines range. At that point, the court must craft a sentence in keeping with the requirements of Section 3553. The court must also impose a sentence that comports with any applicable statutory minimum or maximum sentence. The PROTECT Act, for example, provides for a number of statutory minimum sentences for various crimes and mandatory increased minimum sentences for repeat offenders.

On appeal, the court's sentence will be upheld if it is deemed reasonable under all of the facts and circumstances. The burden of showing unreasonableness will be on the party appealing the sentence, and sentences that fall within the guidelines range are presumptively reasonable.[103] However, the court remains responsible for creating an adequate record of its reasons for seeking a sentence either within the guidelines range or one that departs from it.[104] If a court focuses on one aspect of the sentencing factors, but fails to take into account the other purposes of the sentencing factors, the sentence will not be deemed reasonable.[105] Reasonableness will depend significantly on the judge's record made during the sentencing hearing. In the end, it will be the thoughtful judge who takes into account the advisory guidelines factors, applies them to the unique traits of the defendant and circumstances of the case, and documents conclusions with evidence in the record who will have a sentence affirmed on appeal.

Notes

1. *Smith v. Doe*, 538 U.S. 84, 103 (2003) (quotation marks omitted).

2. *McKune v. Lile*, 536 U.S. 24, 33 (2002) (emphasis added).

3. Stephen Brake and Greig Veeder, RE-OFFENSE RATES OF ADULT SEX OFFENDERS, at 1 (unpublished literature review) (2007), available at www.stephenbrakeassociates.com/Reoffense_Rates_for_Website.pdf (last visited June 5, 2011).

4. Dennis M. Doren, *Recidivism Base Rates, Predictions of Sex Offender Recidivism, and the "Sexual Predator" Commitment Laws*, 16 BEHAV. SCI. LAW 97, 99 (1998) ("Only 15 of 315 rapes reported to the Seattle, Washington police in 1974 resulted in conviction").

5. Brake and Veeder, supra note 3, at 1.

6. Ibid. at 2.

7. Ibid.

8. Doren, supra note 4, at 99.

9. John R. Hepburn and Marie L. Griffin, AN ANALYSIS OF RISK FACTORS CONTRIBUTING TO THE RECIDIVISM OF SEX OFFENDERS ON PROBATION, at 2, unpublished report submitted to the Maricopa County Adult Probation Dep't and the Nat'l Institute of Justice (Oct. 2002).

10. Brake and Veeder, supra note 3, at 3.

11. Hepburn and Griffin, supra note 9, at 8–9; see also ibid. at 65 ("Those who enter probation directly from the court are no more or less likely to commit a technical violation, commit a new crime or fail probation than those who enter probation following a period of confinement").

12. Brake and Veeder, supra note 3, at 3 (noting that only 24 percent of groups of offenders tracked for less than five years had recidivism rates of 20 percent or greater, but that all groups of offenders tracked for fifteen years or more had recidivism rates greater than 20 percent, and most groups of offenders tracked for nineteen years or more had greater than 35 percent recidivism rates).

13. Doren, supra note 4, at 100.

14. Lin Song and Roxanne Lieb, Community Protection Research Project, Washington State Institute for Public Policy, ADULT SEX OFFENDER RECIDIVISM: A REVIEW OF STUDIES, at 7 (1994).

15. Doren, supra note 4, at 100.

16. Song and Lieb, supra note 14, at 5.

17. Michael C. Seto and Angela W. Elke, *The Criminal Histories and Later Offending of Child Pornography Offenders*, 17 SEXUAL ABUSE 201, 208 (2005).

18. Ibid.

19. Ibid.

20. Doren, supra note 4, at 101. In comparison to the population studied here, whose offenses had involved non-family members, "incest offenders quite consistently show lower recidivism rates." Ibid. at 102; see also Hepburn and Griffin, supra note 9, at 4 (summarizing one study that showed a recidivism rate of 15.1 percent within an average of 7.8 years among extrafamilial offenders, but a rate of only 6.4 percent within an average of 6.5 percent among intrafamilial offenders).

21. Doren, supra note 4, at 101.

22. Ibid. at 104.

23. See ibid. at 105 ("It is concluded that extrafamilial child molester sexual recidivism should be thought of as having a conservative approximation of about 52 percent").

24. R. Karl Hanson and Kelly E. Morton-Bourgon, *The Characteristics of Persistent Sexual Offenders: A Meta-Analysis of Recidivism Studies*, 73 J. CONSULTING & CLINICAL PSYCH. 1154, 1154 (2005).

25. Hepburn and Griffin, supra note 9, at 5–6. For more on the predictive accuracy of these various scales, see R. Karl Hanson and Kelly E. Morton-Bourgon, *The Accuracy of Recidivism Risk Assessments for Sexual Offenders: A Meta-Analysis of 118 Prediction Studies*, 21 PSYCH. ASSESSMENT 1 (2009).

26. Mario Scalora and Calvin Garbin, *A Multivariate Analysis of Sex Offender Recidivism*, 47 INT'L J. OFFENDER THERAPY & COMPARATIVE CRIMINOLOGY 309, 310 (2003).

27. Hepburn and Griffin, supra note 9, at 4–5 (compiling numerous studies).

28. Ibid. at 63.

29. Ibid. at 6.

30. Ibid. at 5 (compiling numerous studies).

31. Ibid. at 65–66.

32. Scalora and Garbin, supra note 26, at 311.

33. Ibid.

34. Ibid. at 318–19.

35. *United States v. Dorvee*, 616 F.3d 174, 184 (2d Cir. 2010).

36. Ibid. at 184–85; see also *United States v. Hanson*, 561 F. Supp. 2d 1004, 1009 (E.D. Wis. 2008) ("The guideline has been steadily increased despite evidence and recommendations by the Commission to the contrary. Congress has repeatedly amended it directly, ostensibly to target mass producers of child pornography and/or repeat abusers of children, a class of offenders that make up less than 5% of those affected by the changes").

37. *Dorvee*, 616 F.3d at 187.

38. See ibid. at 187–88, citing *United States v. Booker*, 543 U.S. 220 (2005).

39. 632 F.3d 82, 87–88 (2d Cir. 2011).

40. Ibid. at 88.

41. Ibid. at 89.

42. *Dorvee*, 616 F.3d at 183.

43. Ibid.

44. 431 F.3d 86, 91–92 (2d Cir. 2005).

45. 437 F.3d 684 (7th Cir. 2006).

46. Ibid.

47. 598 F.2d 352 (7th Cir. 2010).

48. *United States v. Weatherton,* 567 F.3d 149, 153 (5th Cir. 2009).

49. *Kansas v. Hendricks,* 521 U.S. 346, 351 (1997), quoting Kan. Stat. Ann. § 59-29a03 (Supp. 1996).

50. See also Hollida Wakefield, *The Vilification of Sex Offenders: Do Laws Targeting Sex Offenders Increase Recidivism and Sexual Violence?,* 1 J. SEXUAL OFFENDER CIV. COMMITMENT: SCI. & L. 141, 146 (2006).

51. Ibid.

52. Ibid.

53. 521 U.S. at 350, quoting Kan. Stat. Ann. § 59-29a01 *et seq.*

54. Ibid.

55. Ibid. at 358.

56. Ibid. at 359.

57. Ibid. at 368.

58. *Crane,* 534 U.S. 407 (2002).

59. Ibid. at 412–13.

60. Ibid. at 413.

61. The federal government also has a statute authorizing the detention of mentally ill and sexually dangerous federal prisoners beyond their dates of release from incarceration. See 18 U.S.C. § 4248. The statute allows a district court to order the civil commitment of an individual who is currently "in the custody of the [Federal] Bureau of Prisons," if that individual (1) has previously "engaged or attempted to engage in sexually violent conduct or child molestation," (2) currently "suffers from a serious mental illness, abnormality, or disorder," and (3) "as a result of" that mental illness, abnormality, or disorder, is "sexually dangerous to others," in that "he would have serious difficulty in refraining from sexually violent conduct or child molestation if released." Ibid. at §§ 4247(a)(5)–(6). The constitutionality of this statute was upheld by the Supreme Court in *United States v. Comstock,* 130 S.Ct. 1949 (2010), as a proper exercise of Congress's authority under the Necessary and Proper Clause.

62. Doren, supra note 4, at 108.

63. Ibid. at 97.

64. Ibid. at 110.

65. Kathleen Kendall-Tackett, et al., *Impact of Sexual Abuse on Children: A Review and Synthesis of Recent Empirical Studies,* 113 PSYCH. BULL. 164, 167 (1993).

66. Ibid. at 167–68.

67. Jane Siegel and Linda Williams, *The Relationship between Child Sexual Abuse and Female Delinquency and Crime: A Prospective Study,* 40 J. RES. CRIME & DELINQUENCY 71, 85 (2003).

68. Ibid. at 86.

69. 554 U.S. 407 (2008).

70. *Kennedy,* 554 U.S. at 435; see also *Ferber* 458 U.S. at 758n9 (1982) ("It has been found that sexually exploited children are unable to develop healthy affectionate relationships in later life, have sexual dysfunctions, and have a tendency to become sexual

abusers as adults"), citing Ulrich C. Schoettle, *Child Exploitation: A Study of Child Pornography*, 19 J. AM. ACAD. CHILD PSYCHIATRY 289, 296 (1980).

71. *Kennedy*, 554 U.S. at 442–43.

72. Ibid. at 445.

73. See *United States v. Black*, 116 F.3d 198 (7th Cir. 1997); *United States v. Polizzi*, 545 F. Supp. 2d 270 (E.D.N.Y. 2008).

74. Pub. L. No. 109-248, 120 Stat. 587 (2006).

75. See Wayne A. Logan, *A Study in "Actuarial Justice": Sex Offender Classification Practice and Procedure*, 3 BUFF. CRIM. L. REV. 593, 593n4 (2000) (collecting statutes and quoting legislative findings).

76. See generally ibid. at 602–19.

77. See ibid. at 596n11 (collecting cases).

78. Amanda Y. Agan, University of Chicago Department of Economics, SEX OFFENDER REGISTRIES: FEAR WITHOUT FUNCTION?, at 9–10 (Dec. 2008) (unpublished).

79. Jill S. Levenson and Leo P. Cotter, *The Effect of Megan's Law on Sex Offender Reintegration*, 21 J. CONTEMP. CRIM. JUST. 49, 56–57 (2005).

80. Agan, supra note 78, at 3, citing Leigh Linden and J. Rockoff, *There Goes the Neighborhood? Estimates from the Impact of Crime Risk on Property Values from Megan's Laws*, NBER WORKING PAPER 12253 (2006).

81. Ibid. at 9–10.

82. Levenson and Cotter, supra note 79, at 52, citing R. G. Zevitz, et al., *Sex Offender Community Notification: Managing High Risk Criminals or Exacting Further Vengeance?*, 18 BEHAV. SCI. & L. 375 (2000).

83. Ibid. at 62 (collecting various studies).

84. See Agan, supra note 78, at 10–11; see also Wakefield, supra note 50, at 145–46 (discussing "the vicious circle of persistent offending" that develops when an offender is prevented from reintegrating into normal society).

85. 543 U.S. at 220.

86. USSG Section 3E.1.

87. Ibid. Application notes.

88. See *United States. v. Winston*, 118 Fed. app'x. 980 (7th Cir. 2004) (unpublished).

89. See *United States v. Kise*, 369 F.3d 766 (4th Cir. 2004).

90. See, for example, *United States v. Williams*, 529 F.3d 1 (1st Cir. 2008), cert. denied, 129 S.Ct. 1580 (2009); *United States v. Patterson*, 576 F.3d 431 (7th Cir. 2009), cert. denied, 130 S.Ct. 1284 (2010).

91. See, for example, *Phillips*, 431 F.3d at 86 (court may take into account sexually exploitative conduct that occurred while defendant was a juvenile); *McCaffrey* 437 F.3d at 684 (no double counting if increase defendant's sentence on the basis of understated criminal history and for having engaged in pattern of exploitation).

92. 96 CR 717 (N.D. Ill.).

93. See, for example, *United States v. Bidwell*, 393 F.3d 1206 (11th Cir. 2004). The defendant in *Bidwell* had received thirty years' imprisonment from a Georgia state court for sexually abusing his daughter. For producing and transporting child pornography, the federal court imposed a fifteen-year sentence consecutive to the state

sentence due to substantive differences between the state and federal crimes, and the appellate court affirmed the sentence.

94. See, for example, *United States v. Maneri,* 353 F.3d 165 (2d Cir. 2003).

95. See, for example, *United States v. Hecht,* 470 F.3d 177 (4th Cir. 2006).

96. See, for example, *United States v. Carani,* 492 F.3d 867 (7th Cir. 2007), cert. denied, 128 S. Ct. 932 (2008).

97. *United States v. Clawson,* 392 F.3d 324 (8th Cir. 2004).

98. *United States v. Young,* 613 F.3d 735 (8th Cir. 2010).

99. See, for example, *United States v. Duane,* 533 F.3d 441 (6th Cir. 2008).

100. *United States v. Bentley,* 492 F. Supp. 2d 1050 (N.D. Iowa 2007), aff'd, 561 F.3d 803 (8th Cir. 2009), cert. denied, 130 S.Ct. 175 (2009); *United States v. DeCarlo,* 434 F.3d 447 (6th Cir. 2006); *United States v. Scott,* 529 F.3d 1290 (10th Cir. 2008) (vulnerable victim appropriate for teenage victim who was petite and frail, and unusually naïve for her age).

101. See, for example, *Young,* 633 F.3d at 735.

102. See, for example, ibid.

103. *United States v. Rodgers,* 2010 WL 1857366 (3d Cir. May 11, 2010).

104. *United States v. Kuchler,* 2008 WL 3318995 (3d Cir. Aug. 12, 2008).

105. *United States v. Morace,* 594 F.3d 340 (4th Cir. 2010), cert. denied, 131 S.Ct. 307 (2010); *United States v. Goldberg,* 491 F.3d 688 (7th Cir. 2007).

Conclusion

THE SEXUAL EXPLOITATION OF OUR CHILDREN, wherever it occurs, has earned a place among a discrete category of crimes universally recognized as striking at the very heart of civilized society. Providing meaningful protection to those who are the most innocent, as well as the least capable of defending themselves, is, after all, a duty recognized by all democratic nations. And while recent years have witnessed local and national governments and law enforcement agencies around the globe dramatically stepping up their collective efforts to stem child sexual exploitation in its many forms—from the production and dissemination of child pornography to the commercial trafficking of children—ever-developing communications and computer technologies have made these efforts more demanding, and more pressing, than ever before. Stated plainly, the epidemic of contemporary child sexual exploitation demands fresh thinking on the part of law enforcement, governments, and the citizenry. We, therefore, hope that this book has offered small-bore solutions for a large-scale need by providing a strong dose of technical and strategic advice and "best practices" for legal and nonlegal practitioners grappling daily with these complex challenges. Perhaps more than that, however, our objective is to also initiate a more nuanced and comprehensive transnational dialogue concerning the significance of this ever-rising threat, as well as what we, as a society, must do to effectively attack the root causes of child sexual exploitation. Only by recognizing, and in a practical manner responding to, the interconnected social, moral, political, and legal issues driving this particularly pernicious form of abuse can we hope to protect the defenseless and bring the perpetrators to justice.

Appendix 1

Convention on the Rights of the Child (1989) Preamble

The States Parties to the present Convention,

Considering that, in accordance with the principles proclaimed in the Charter of the United Nations, recognition of the inherent dignity and of the equal and inalienable rights of all members of the human family is the foundation of freedom, justice and peace in the world,

Bearing in mind that the peoples of the United Nations have, in the Charter, reaffirmed their faith in fundamental human rights and in the dignity and worth of the human person, and have determined to promote social progress and better standards of life in larger freedom,

Recognizing that the United Nations has, in the Universal Declaration of Human Rights and in the International Covenants on Human Rights, proclaimed and agreed that everyone is entitled to all the rights and freedoms set forth therein, without distinction of any kind, such as race, colour, sex, language, religion, political or other opinion, national or social origin, property, birth or other status,

Recalling that, in the Universal Declaration of Human Rights, the United Nations has proclaimed that childhood is entitled to special care and assistance, Convinced that the family, as the fundamental group of society and the natural environment for the growth and well-being of all its members and particularly children, should be afforded the necessary protection and assistance so that it can fully assume its responsibilities within the community,

Recognizing that the child, for the full and harmonious development of his or her personality, should grow up in a family environment, in an atmosphere of happiness, love and understanding,

Considering that the child should be fully prepared to live an individual life in society, and brought up in the spirit of the ideals proclaimed in the Charter of the United Nations, and in particular in the spirit of peace, dignity, tolerance, freedom, equality and solidarity,

Bearing in mind that the need to extend particular care to the child has been stated in the Geneva Declaration of the Rights of the Child of 1924 and in the Declaration of the Rights of the Child adopted by the United Nations on 20 November 1959 and recognized in the Universal Declaration of

Human Rights, in the International Covenant on Civil and Political Rights (in particular in articles 23 and 24), in the International Covenant on Economic, Social and Cultural Rights (in particular in article ten) and in the statutes and relevant instruments of specialized agencies and international organizations concerned with the welfare of children,

Bearing in mind that, as indicated in the Declaration of the Rights of the Child, "the child, by reason of his physical and mental immaturity, needs special safeguards and care, including appropriate legal protection, before as well as after birth,"

Recalling the provisions of the Declaration on Social and Legal Principles relating to the Protection and Welfare of Children, with Special Reference to Foster Placement and Adoption Nationally and Internationally; the United Nations Standard Minimum Rules for the Administration of Juvenile Justice ("The Beijing Rules"); and the Declaration on the Protection of Women and Children in Emergency and Armed Conflict,

Recognizing that, in all countries in the world, there are children living in exceptionally difficult conditions, and that such children need special consideration,

Taking due account of the importance of the traditions and cultural values of each people for the protection and harmonious development of the child,

Recognizing the importance of international cooperation for improving the living conditions of children in every country, in particular in the developing countries,

Have agreed as follows:

Part I: Substantive Provisions

Article 1

For the purposes of the present Convention, a child means every human being below the age of 18 years unless, under the law applicable to the child, majority is attained earlier.

Article 2

1. States Parties shall respect and ensure the rights set forth in the present Convention to each child within their jurisdiction without discrimination of any kind, irrespective of the child's or his or her parent's or legal guardian's race, colour, sex, language, religion, political or other opinion, national, ethnic or social origin, property, disability, birth or other status.
2. States Parties shall take all appropriate measures to ensure that the child is protected against all forms of discrimination or punishment on the basis of the status, activities, expressed opinions, or beliefs of the child's parents, legal guardians, or family members.

Article 3

1. In all actions concerning children, whether undertaken by public or private social welfare institutions, courts of law, administrative authorities or legislative bodies, the best interests of the child shall be a primary consideration.
2. States Parties undertake to ensure the child such protection and care as is necessary for his or her well-being, taking into account the rights and duties of his or her parents, legal guardians, or other individuals legally responsible for him or her, and, to this end, shall take all appropriate legislative and administrative measures.
3. States Parties shall ensure that the institutions, services and facilities responsible for the care or protection of children shall conform with the

standards established by competent authorities, particularly in the areas of safety, health, in the number and suitability of their staff, as well as competent supervision.

Article 4

States Parties shall undertake all appropriate legislative, administrative, and other measures for the implementation of the rights recognized in the present Convention. With regard to economic, social and cultural rights, States Parties shall undertake such measures to the maximum extent of their available resources and, where needed, within the framework of international cooperation.

Article 5

States Parties shall respect the responsibilities, rights and duties of parents or, where applicable, the members of the extended family or community as provided for by local custom, legal guardians or other persons legally responsible for the child, to provide, in a manner consistent with the evolving capacities of the child, appropriate direction and guidance in the exercise by the child of the rights recognized in the present Convention.

Article 6

1. States Parties recognize that every child has the inherent right to life.
2. States Parties shall ensure to the maximum extent possible the survival and development of the child.

Article 7

1. The child shall be registered immediately after birth and shall have the right from birth to a name, the right to acquire a nationality and, as far as possible, the right to know and be cared for by his or her parents.
2. States Parties shall ensure the implementation of these rights in accordance with their national law and their obligations under the relevant international instruments in this field, in particular where the child would otherwise be stateless.

Article 8

1. States Parties undertake to respect the right of the child to preserve his or her identity, including nationality, name and family relations as recognized by law without unlawful interference.

2. Where a child is illegally deprived of some or all of the elements of his or her identity, States Parties shall provide appropriate assistance and protection, with a view to speedily reestablishing his or her identity.

Article 9

1. States Parties shall ensure that a child shall not be separated from his or her parents against their will, except when competent authorities subject to judicial review determine, in accordance with applicable law and procedures, that such separation is necessary for the best interests of the child. Such determination may be necessary in a particular case such as one involving abuse or neglect of the child by the parents, or one where the parents are living separately and a decision must be made as to the child's place of residence.
2. In any proceedings pursuant to paragraph 1 of the present article, all interested parties shall be given an opportunity to participate in the proceedings and make their views known.
3. States Parties shall respect the right of the child who is separated from one or both parents to maintain personal relations and direct contact with both parents on a regular basis, except if it is contrary to the child's best interests.
4. Where such separation results from any action initiated by a State Party, such as the detention, imprisonment, exile, deportation or death (including death arising from any cause while the person is in the custody of the State) of one or both parents or of the child, that State Party shall, upon request, provide the parents, the child or, if appropriate, another member of the family with the essential information concerning the whereabouts of the absent member(s) of the family unless the provision of the information would be detrimental to the well-being of the child. States Parties shall further ensure that the submission of such a request shall of itself entail no adverse consequences for the person(s) concerned.

Article 10

1. In accordance with the obligation of States Parties under article 9, paragraph 1, applications by a child or his or her parents to enter or leave a State Party for the purpose of family reunification shall be dealt with by States Parties in a positive, humane and expeditious manner. States Parties shall further ensure that the submission of such a request shall entail no adverse consequences for the applicants and for the members of their family.

2. A child whose parents reside in different States shall have the right to maintain on a regular basis, save in exceptional circumstances, personal relations and direct contacts with both parents. Towards that end and in accordance with the obligation of States Parties under article 9, paragraph 1, States Parties shall respect the right of the child and his or her parents to leave any country, including their own, and to enter their own country. The right to leave any country shall be subject only to such restrictions as are prescribed by law and which are necessary to protect the national security, public order (ordre public), public health or morals or the rights and freedoms of others and are consistent with the other rights recognized in the present Convention.

Article 11

1. States Parties shall take measures to combat the illicit transfer and non-return of children abroad.
2. To this end, States Parties shall promote the conclusion of bilateral or multilateral agreements or accession to existing agreements.

Article 12

1. States Parties shall assure to the child who is capable of forming his or her own views the right to express those views freely in all matters affecting the child, the views of the child being given due weight in accordance with the age and maturity of the child.
2. For this purpose, the child shall in particular be provided the opportunity to be heard in any judicial and administrative proceedings affecting the child, either directly, or through a representative or an appropriate body, in a manner consistent with the procedural rules of national law.

Article 13

1. The child shall have the right to freedom of expression; this right shall include freedom to seek, receive and impart information and ideas of all kinds, regardless of frontiers, either orally, in writing or in print, in the form of art, or through any other media of the child's choice.
2. The exercise of this right may be subject to certain restrictions, but these shall only be such as are provided by law and are necessary:
   (a) For respect of the rights or reputations of others; or
   (b) For the protection of national security or of public order (ordre public), or of public health or morals.

Article 14

1. States Parties shall respect the right of the child to freedom of thought, conscience and religion.
2. States Parties shall respect the rights and duties of the parents and, when applicable, legal guardians, to provide direction to the child in the exercise of his or her right in a manner consistent with the evolving capacities of the child.
3. Freedom to manifest one's religion or beliefs may be subject only to such limitations as are prescribed by law and are necessary to protect public safety, order, health or morals, or the fundamental rights and freedoms of others.

Article 15

1. States Parties recognize the rights of the child to freedom of association and to freedom of peaceful assembly.
2. No restrictions may be placed on the exercise of these rights other than those imposed in conformity with the law and which are necessary in a democratic society in the interests of national security or public safety, public order (ordre public), the protection of public health or morals or the protection of the rights and freedoms of others.

Article 16

1. No child shall be subjected to arbitrary or unlawful interference with his or her privacy, family, home or correspondence, nor to unlawful attacks on his or her honour and reputation.
2. The child has the right to the protection of the law against such interference or attacks.

Article 17

States Parties recognize the important function performed by the mass media and shall ensure that the child has access to information and material from a diversity of national and international sources, especially those aimed at the promotion of his or her social, spiritual and moral well-being and physical and mental health. To this end, States Parties shall:

   (a) Encourage the mass media to disseminate information and material of social and cultural benefit to the child and in accordance with the spirit of article 29;

(b) Encourage international cooperation in the production, exchange and dissemination of such information and material from a diversity of cultural, national and international sources;

(c) Encourage the production and dissemination of children's books;

(d) Encourage the mass media to have particular regard to the linguistic needs of the child who belongs to a minority group or who is indigenous;

(e) Encourage the development of appropriate guidelines for the protection of the child from information and material injurious to his or her well-being, bearing in mind the provisions of articles 13 and 18.

Article 18

1. States Parties shall use their best efforts to ensure recognition of the principle that both parents have common responsibilities for the upbringing and development of the child. Parents or, as the case may be, legal guardians, have the primary responsibility for the upbringing and development of the child. The best interests of the child will be their basic concern.

2. For the purpose of guaranteeing and promoting the rights set forth in the present Convention, States Parties shall render appropriate assistance to parents and legal guardians in the performance of their child-rearing responsibilities and shall ensure the development of institutions, facilities and services for the care of children.

3. States Parties shall take all appropriate measures to ensure that children of working parents have the right to benefit from child-care services and facilities for which they are eligible.

Article 19

1. States Parties shall take all appropriate legislative, administrative, social and educational measures to protect the child from all forms of physical or mental violence, injury or abuse, neglect or negligent treatment, maltreatment or exploitation, including sexual abuse, while in the care of parent(s), legal guardian(s) or any other person who has the care of the child.

2. Such protective measures should, as appropriate, include effective procedures for the establishment of social programmes to provide necessary support for the child and for those who have the care of the child, as well as for other forms of prevention and for identification, reporting, referral, investigation, treatment and follow-up of instances of child

maltreatment described heretofore, and, as appropriate, for judicial involvement.

Article 20

1. A child temporarily or permanently deprived of his or her family environment, or in whose own best interests cannot be allowed to remain in that environment, shall be entitled to special protection and assistance provided by the State.
2. States Parties shall in accordance with their national laws ensure alternative care for such a child.
3. Such care could include, inter alia, foster placement, Kafala of Islamic law, adoption, or if necessary placement in suitable institutions for the care of children. When considering solutions, due regard shall be paid to the desirability of continuity in a child's upbringing and to the child's ethnic, religious, cultural and linguistic background.

Article 21

States Parties that recognize and/or permit the system of adoption shall ensure that the best interests of the child shall be the paramount consideration and they shall:

(a) Ensure that the adoption of a child is authorized only by competent authorities who determine, in accordance with applicable law and procedures and on the basis of all pertinent and reliable information, that the adoption is permissible in view of the child's status concerning parents, relatives and legal guardians and that, if required, the persons concerned have given their informed consent to the adoption on the basis of such counseling as may be necessary;

(b) Recognize that intercountry adoption may be considered as an alternative means of the child's care, if the child cannot be placed in a foster or an adoptive family or cannot in any suitable manner be cared for in the child's country of origin;

(c) Ensure that the child concerned by intercountry adoption enjoys safeguards and standards equivalent to those existing in the case of national adoption;

(d) Take all appropriate measures to ensure that, in intercountry adoption, the placement does not result in improper financial gain for those involved in it;

(e) Promote, where appropriate, the objectives of the present article by concluding bilateral or multilateral arrangements or agreements, and endeavor, within this framework, to ensure that the placement of the child in another country is carried out by competent authorities or organs.

Article 22

1. States Parties shall take appropriate measures to ensure that a child who is seeking refugee status or who is considered a refugee in accordance with applicable international or domestic law and procedures shall, whether unaccompanied or accompanied by his or her parents or by any other person, receive appropriate protection and humanitarian assistance in the enjoyment of applicable rights set forth in the present Convention and in other international human rights or humanitarian instruments to which the said States are Parties.

2. For this purpose, States Parties shall provide, as they consider appropriate, cooperation in any efforts by the United Nations and other competent intergovernmental organizations or nongovernmental organizations co-operating with the United Nations to protect and assist such a child and to trace the parents or other members of the family of any refugee child in order to obtain information necessary for reunification with his or her family. In cases where no parents or other members of the family can be found, the child shall be accorded the same protection as any other child permanently or temporarily deprived of his or her family environment for any reason, as set forth in the present Convention.

Article 23

1. States Parties recognize that a mentally or physically disabled child should enjoy a full and decent life, in conditions which ensure dignity, promote self-reliance, and facilitate the child's active participation in the community.

2. States Parties recognize the right of the disabled child to special care and shall encourage and ensure the extension, subject to available resources, to the eligible child and those responsible for his or her care, of assistance for which application is made and which is appropriate to the condition and to the circumstances of the parents or others caring for the child.

3. Recognizing the special needs of a disabled child, assistance extended in accordance with paragraph 2 of the present article shall be provided free

of charge, whenever possible, taking into account the financial resources of the parents or others caring for the child, and shall be designed to ensure that the disabled child has effective access to and receives education, training, health care services, rehabilitation services, preparation for employment and recreation opportunities in a manner conducive to the child's achieving the fullest possible social integration and individual development, including his or her cultural and spiritual development.

4. States Parties shall promote, in the spirit of international cooperation, the exchange of appropriate information in the field of preventive health care and of medical and psychological treatment of disabled children, including dissemination of and access to information concerning methods of rehabilitation, education and vocational services, with the aim of enabling States Parties to improve their capabilities and skills and to widen their experience in these areas. In this regard, particular account shall be taken of the needs of developing countries.

Article 24

1. States Parties recognize the right of the child to the enjoyment of the highest attainable standard of health and to facilities for the treatment of illness and rehabilitation of health. States Parties shall strive to ensure that no child is deprived of his or her right of access to such health care services.

2. States Parties shall pursue full implementation of this right and, in particular, shall take appropriate measures:

    (a) To diminish infant and child mortality;

    (b) To ensure the provision of necessary medical assistance and health care to all children with emphasis on the development of primary health care;

    (c) To combat disease and malnutrition including within the framework of primary health care, through inter alia the application of readily available technology and through the provision of adequate nutritious foods and clean drinking water, taking into consideration the dangers and risks of environmental pollution;

    (d) To ensure appropriate pre-natal and post-natal health care for mothers;

    (e) To ensure that all segments of society, in particular parents and children, are informed, have access to education and are supported in the use of basic knowledge of child health and nutrition, the advantages of breast-feeding, hygiene and environmental sanitation and the prevention of accidents;

(f) To develop preventive health care, guidance for parents and family planning education and services.

3. States Parties shall take all effective and appropriate measures with a view to abolishing traditional practises prejudicial to the health of children.

4. States Parties undertake to promote and encourage international cooperation with a view to achieving progressively the full realization of the right recognized in the present article. In this regard, particular account shall be taken of the needs of developing countries.

Article 25

States Parties recognize the right of a child who has been placed by the competent authorities for the purposes of care, protection or treatment of his or her physical or mental health, to a periodic review of the treatment provided to the child and all other circumstances relevant to his or her placement.

Article 26

1. States Parties shall recognize for every child the right to benefit from social security, including social insurance, and shall take the necessary measures to achieve the full realization of this right in accordance with their national law.

2. The benefits should, where appropriate, be granted, taking into account the resources and the circumstances of the child and persons having responsibility for the maintenance of the child, as well as any other consideration relevant to an application for benefits made by or on behalf of the child.

Article 27

1. States Parties recognize the right of every child to a standard of living adequate for the child's physical, mental, spiritual, moral and social development.

2. The parent(s) or others responsible for the child have the primary responsibility to secure, within their abilities and financial capacities, the conditions of living necessary for the child's development.

3. States Parties, in accordance with national conditions and within their means, shall take appropriate measures to assist parents and others re-

sponsible for the child to implement this right and shall in case of need provide material assistance and support programmes, particularly with regard to nutrition, clothing and housing.

4. States Parties shall take all appropriate measures to secure the recovery of maintenance for the child from the parents or other persons having financial responsibility for the child, both within the State Party and from abroad. In particular, where the person having financial responsibility for the child lives in a State different from that of the child, States Parties shall promote the accession to international agreements or the conclusion of such agreements, as well as the making of other appropriate arrangements.

Article 28

1. States Parties recognize the right of the child to education, and with a view to achieving this right progressively and on the basis of equal opportunity, they shall, in particular:
   (a) Make primary education compulsory and available free to all;
   (b) Encourage the development of different forms of secondary education, including general and vocational education, make them available and accessible to every child, and take appropriate measures such as the introduction of free education and offering financial assistance in case of need;
   (c) Make higher education accessible to all on the basis of capacity by every appropriate means;
   (d) Make educational and vocational information and guidance available and accessible to all children;
   (e) Take measures to encourage regular attendance at schools and the reduction of dropout rates.

2. States Parties shall take all appropriate measures to ensure that school discipline is administered in a manner consistent with the child's human dignity and in conformity with the present Convention.

3. States Parties shall promote and encourage international cooperation in matters relating to education, in particular with a view to contributing to the elimination of ignorance and illiteracy throughout the world and facilitating access to scientific and technical knowledge and modern teaching methods. In this regard, particular account shall be taken of the needs of developing countries.

Article 29

1. States Parties agree that the education of the child shall be directed to:
    (a) The development of the child's personality, talents and mental and physical abilities to their fullest potential;
    (b) The development of respect for human rights and fundamental freedoms, and for the principles enshrined in the Charter of the United Nations;
    (c) The development of respect for the child's parents, his or her own cultural identity, language and values, for the national values of the country in which the child is living, the country from which he or she may originate, and for civilizations different from his or her own;
    (d) The preparation of the child for responsible life in a free society, in the spirit of understanding, peace, tolerance, equality of sexes, and friendship among all peoples, ethnic, national and religious groups and persons of indigenous origin;
    (e) The development of respect for the natural environment.
2. No part of the present article or article 28 shall be construed so as to interfere with the liberty of individuals and bodies to establish and direct educational institutions, subject always to the observance of the principles set forth in paragraph 1 of the present article and to the requirements that the education given in such institutions shall conform to such minimum standards as may be laid down by the State.

Article 30

In those States in which ethnic, religious or linguistic minorities or persons of indigenous origin exist, a child belonging to such a minority or who is indigenous shall not be denied the right, in community with other members of his or her group, to enjoy his or her own culture, to profess and practise his or her own religion, or to use his or her own language.

Article 31

1. States Parties recognize the right of the child to rest and leisure, to engage in play and recreational activities appropriate to the age of the child and to participate freely in cultural life and the arts.
2. States Parties shall respect and promote the right of the child to participate fully in cultural and artistic life and shall encourage the provision

of appropriate and equal opportunities for cultural, artistic, recreational and leisure activity.

Article 32

1. States Parties recognize the right of the child to be protected from economic exploitation and from performing any work that is likely to be hazardous or to interfere with the child's education, or to be harmful to the child's health or physical, mental, spiritual, moral or social development.
2. States Parties shall take legislative, administrative, social and educational measures to ensure the implementation of the present article. To this end, and having regard to the relevant provisions of other international instruments, States Parties shall in particular:
    (a) Provide for a minimum age or minimum ages for admissions to employment;
    (b) Provide for appropriate regulation of the hours and conditions of employment;
    (c) Provide for appropriate penalties or other sanctions to ensure the effective enforcement of the present article.

Article 33

States Parties shall take all appropriate measures, including legislative, administrative, social and educational measures, to protect children from the illicit use of narcotic drugs and psychotropic substances as defined in the relevant international treaties, and to prevent the use of children in the illicit production and trafficking of such substances.

Article 34

States Parties undertake to protect the child from all forms of sexual exploitation and sexual abuse. For these purposes, States Parties shall in particular take all appropriate national, bilateral and multilateral measures to prevent:

(a) The inducement or coercion of a child to engage in any unlawful sexual activity;
(b) The exploitative use of children in prostitution or other unlawful sexual practises;
(c) The exploitative use of children in pornographic performances and materials.

Article 35

States Parties shall take all appropriate national, bilateral and multilateral measures to prevent the abduction of, the sale of or traffic in children for any purpose or in any form.

Article 36

States Parties shall protect the child against all other forms of exploitation prejudicial to any aspects of the child's welfare.

Article 37

States Parties shall ensure that:

(a) No child shall be subjected to torture or other cruel, inhuman or degrading treatment or punishment. Neither capital punishment nor life imprisonment without possibility of release shall be imposed for offences committed by persons below 18 years of age;

(b) No child shall be deprived of his or her liberty unlawfully or arbitrarily. The arrest, detention or imprisonment of a child shall be in conformity with the law and shall be used only as a measure of last resort and for the shortest appropriate period of time;

(c) Every child deprived of liberty shall be treated with humanity and respect for the inherent dignity of the human person, and in a manner which takes into account the needs of persons of his or her age. In particular every child deprived of liberty shall be separated from adults unless it is considered in the child's best interest not to do so and shall have the right to maintain contact with his or her family through correspondence and visits, save in exceptional circumstances;

(d) Every child deprived of his or her liberty shall have the right to prompt access to legal and other appropriate assistance, as well as the right to challenge the legality of the deprivation of his or her liberty before a court or other competent, independent and impartial authority, and to a prompt decision on any such action.

Article 38

1. States Parties undertake to respect and to ensure respect for rules of international humanitarian law applicable to them in armed conflicts which are relevant to the child.

2. States Parties shall take all feasible measures to ensure that persons who have not attained the age of 15 years do not take a direct part in hostilities.
3. States Parties shall refrain from recruiting any person who has not attained the age of 15 years into their armed forces. In recruiting among those persons who have attained the age of 15 years but who have not attained the age of 18 years, States Parties shall endeavour to give priority to those who are oldest.
4. In accordance with their obligations under international humanitarian law to protect the civilian population in armed conflicts, States Parties shall take all feasible measures to ensure protection and care of children who are affected by an armed conflict.

Article 39

States Parties shall take all appropriate measures to promote physical and psychological recovery and social reintegration of a child victim of: any form of neglect, exploitation, or abuse; torture or any other form of cruel, inhuman or degrading treatment or punishment; or armed conflicts.

Such recovery and reintegration shall take place in an environment which fosters the health, self-respect and dignity of the child.

Article 40

1. States Parties recognize the right of every child alleged as, accused of, or recognized as having infringed the penal law to be treated in a manner consistent with the promotion of the child's sense of dignity and worth, which reinforces the child's respect for the human rights and fundamental freedoms of others and which takes into account the child's age and the desirability of promoting the child's reintegration and the child's assuming a constructive role in society.
2. To this end, and having regard to the relevant provisions of international instruments, States Parties shall, in particular, ensure that:
    (a) No child shall be alleged as, be accused of, or recognized as having infringed the penal law by reason of acts or omissions that were not prohibited by national or international law at the time they were committed;
    (b) Every child alleged as or accused of having infringed the penal law has at least the following guarantees:
        (i)   To be presumed innocent until proven guilty according to law;

     (ii)   To be informed promptly and directly of the charges against him or her, and, if appropriate, through his or her parents or legal guardians, and to have legal or other appropriate assistance in the preparation and presentation of his or her defence;

     (iii) To have the matter determined without delay by a competent, independent and impartial authority or judicial body in a fair hearing according to law, in the presence of legal or other appropriate assistance and, unless it is considered not to be in the best interest of the child, in particular, taking into account his or her age or situation, his or her parents or legal guardians;

     (iv) Not to be compelled to give testimony or to confess guilt; to examine or have examined adverse witnesses and to obtain the participation and examination of witnesses on his or her behalf under conditions of equality;

     (v)   If considered to have infringed the penal law, to have this decision and any measures imposed in consequence thereof reviewed by a higher competent, independent and impartial authority or judicial body according to law;

     (vi) To have the free assistance of an interpreter if the child cannot understand or speak the language used;

     (vii) To have his or her privacy fully respected at all stages of the proceedings.

3. States Parties shall seek to promote the establishment of laws, procedures, authorities and institutions specifically applicable to children alleged as, accused of, or recognized as having infringed the penal law, and, in particular:

   (a) the establishment of a minimum age below which children shall be presumed not to have the capacity to infringe the penal law;

   (b) whenever appropriate and desirable, measures for dealing with such children without resorting to judicial proceedings, providing that human rights and legal safeguards are fully respected.

4. A variety of dispositions, such as care, guidance and supervision orders; counselling; probation; foster care; education and vocational training programmes and other alternatives to institutional care shall be available to ensure that children are dealt with in a manner appropriate to their well-being and proportionate both to their circumstances and the offence.

Article 41

Nothing in the present Convention shall affect any provisions which are more conducive to the realization of the rights of the child and which may be contained in:

(a) The law of a State Party; or
(b) International law in force for that State.

Part II: Implementation and Monitoring

Article 42

States Parties undertake to make the principles and provisions of the Convention widely known, by appropriate and active means, to adults and children alike.

Article 43

1. For the purpose of examining the progress made by States Parties in achieving the realization of the obligations undertaken in the present Convention, there shall be established a Committee on the Rights of the Child, which shall carry out the functions hereinafter provided.
2. The Committee shall consist of 10 experts of high moral standing and recognized competence in the field covered by this Convention. The members of the Committee shall be elected by States Parties from among their nationals and shall serve in their personal capacity, consideration being given to equitable geographical distribution, as well as to the principal legal systems.
3. The members of the Committee shall be elected by secret ballot from a list of persons nominated by States Parties. Each State Party may nominate one person from among its own nationals.
4. The initial election to the Committee shall be held no later than six months after the date of the entry into force of the present Convention and thereafter every second year. At least four months before the date of each election, the Secretary-General of the United Nations shall address a letter to States Parties inviting them to submit their nominations within two months.

   The Secretary-General shall subsequently prepare a list in alphabetical order of all persons thus nominated, indicating States Parties which have nominated them, and shall submit it to the States Parties to the present Convention.

5. The elections shall be held at meetings of States Parties convened by the Secretary-General at United Nations Headquarters. At those meetings, for which two thirds of States Parties shall constitute a quorum, the persons elected to the Committee shall be those who obtain the largest number of votes and an absolute majority of the votes of the representatives of States Parties present and voting.

6. The members of the Committee shall be elected for a term of four years. They shall be eligible for re-election if renominated. The term of five of the members elected at the first election shall expire at the end of two years; immediately after the first election, the names of these five members shall be chosen by lot by the Chairman of the meeting.

7. If a member of the Committee dies or resigns or declares that for any other cause he or she can no longer perform the duties of the Committee, the State Party which nominated the member shall appoint another expert from among its nationals to serve for the remainder of the term, subject to the approval of the Committee.

8. The Committee shall establish its own rules of procedure.

9. The Committee shall elect its officers for a period of two years.

10. The meetings of the Committee shall normally be held at United Nations Headquarters or at any other convenient place as determined by the Committee. The Committee shall normally meet annually. The duration of the meetings of the Committee shall be determined, and reviewed, if necessary, by a meeting of the States Parties to the present Convention, subject to the approval of the General Assembly.

11. The Secretary-General of the United Nations shall provide the necessary staff and facilities for the effective performance of the functions of the Committee under the present Convention.

12. With the approval of the General Assembly, the members of the Committee established under the present Convention shall receive emoluments from the United Nations resources on such terms and conditions as the Assembly may decide.

Article 44

1. States Parties undertake to submit to the Committee, through the Secretary-General of the United Nations, reports on the measures they have adopted which give effect to the rights recognized herein and on the progress made on the enjoyment of those rights:

(a) Within two years of the entry into force of the Convention for the State Party concerned,

(b) Thereafter every five years.

2. Reports made under the present article shall indicate factors and difficulties, if any, affecting the degree of fulfillment of the obligations under the present Convention. Reports shall also contain sufficient information to provide the Committee with a comprehensive understanding of the implementation of the Convention in the country concerned.

3. A State Party which has submitted a comprehensive initial report to the Committee need not in its subsequent reports submitted in accordance with paragraph 1(b) of the present article repeat basic information previously provided.

4. The Committee may request from States Parties further information relevant to the implementation of the Convention.

5. The Committee shall submit to the General Assembly, through the Economic and Social Council, every two years, reports on its activities.

6. States Parties shall make their reports widely available to the public in their own countries.

Article 45

In order to foster the effective implementation of the Convention and to encourage international cooperation in the field covered by the Convention:

(a) The specialized agencies, the United Nations Children's Fund and other United Nations organs shall be entitled to be represented at the consideration of the implementation of such provisions of the present Convention as fall within the scope of their mandate. The Committee may invite the specialized agencies, the United Nations Children's Fund and other competent bodies as it may consider appropriate to provide expert advice on the implementation of the Convention in areas falling within the scope of their respective mandates. The Committee may invite the specialized agencies, the United Nations Children's Fund and other United Nations organs to submit reports on the implementation of the Convention in areas falling within the scope of their activities;

(b) The Committee shall transmit, as it may consider appropriate, to the specialized agencies, the United Nations Children's Fund and other competent bodies, any reports from States Parties that contain a request, or indicate a need, for technical advice or assistance, along with the Committee's observations and suggestions, if any, on these requests or indications;

(c) The Committee may recommend to the General Assembly to request the Secretary-General to undertake on its behalf studies on specific issues relating to the rights of the child;

(d) The Committee may make suggestions and general recommendations based on information received pursuant to articles 44 and 45 of the present Convention. Such suggestions and general recommendations shall be transmitted to any State Party concerned and reported to the General Assembly, together with comments, if any, from States Parties.

Part III: Final Clauses

Article 46

The present Convention shall be open for signature by all States.

Article 47

The present Convention is subject to ratification. Instruments of ratification shall be deposited with the Secretary-General of the United Nations.

Article 48

The present Convention shall remain open for accession by any State. The instruments of accession shall be deposited with the Secretary-General of the United Nations.

Article 49

1. The present Convention shall enter into force on the thirtieth day following the date of deposit with the Secretary-General of the United Nations of the twentieth instrument of ratification or accession.

2. For each State ratifying or acceding to the Convention after the deposit of the twentieth instrument of ratification or accession, the Convention shall enter into force on the thirtieth day after the deposit by such State of its instrument of ratification or accession.

Article 50

1. Any State Party may propose an amendment and file it with the Secretary-General of the United Nations. The Secretary-General shall thereupon communicate the proposed amendment to States Parties, with a request that they indicate whether they favour a conference of States Parties for the purpose of considering and voting upon the proposals. In the event that, within four months from the date of such communication, at least one third of the States Parties favour such a conference, the Secretary-General shall convene the conference under the auspices of the United Nations. Any amendment adopted by a majority of States Parties present and voting at the conference shall be submitted to the General Assembly for approval.

2. An amendment adopted in accordance with paragraph 1 of the present article shall enter into force when it has been approved by the General Assembly of the United Nations and accepted by a two-thirds majority of States Parties.

3. When an amendment enters into force, it shall be binding on those States Parties which have accepted it, other States Parties still being bound by the provisions of the present Convention and any earlier amendments which they have accepted.

Article 51

1. The Secretary-General of the United Nations shall receive and circulate to all States the text of reservations made by States at the time of ratification or accession.

2. A reservation incompatible with the object and purpose of the present Convention shall not be permitted.

3. Reservations may be withdrawn at any time by notification to that effect addressed to the Secretary-General of the United Nations, who shall then inform all States. Such notification shall take effect on the date on which it is received by the Secretary-General.

Article 52

A State Party may denounce the present Convention by written notification to the Secretary-General of the United Nations. Denunciation becomes effective one year after the date of receipt of the notification by the Secretary-General.

Article 53

The Secretary-General of the United Nations is designated as the depositary of the present Convention.

Article 54

The original of the present Convention, of which the Arabic, Chinese, English, French, Russian and Spanish texts are equally authentic, shall be deposited with the Secretary-General of the United Nations.

IN WITNESS THEREOF the undersigned plenipotentiaries, being duly authorized thereto by their respective Governments, have signed the present Convention.

Appendix 2

Optional Protocol to the Convention on the Rights of the Child on the Sale of Children, Child Prostitution and Child Pornography

Adopted and opened for signature, ratification and accession by General Assembly resolution (A/RES/54/263 of 25 May 2000)

**entered into force on 18 January 2002

The States Parties to the present Protocol,

Considering that, in order further to achieve the purposes of the Convention on the Rights of the Child and the implementation of its provisions, especially articles 1, 11, 21, 32, 33, 34, 35 and 36, it would be appropriate to extend the measures that States Parties should undertake in order to guarantee the protection of the child from the sale of children, child prostitution and child pornography,

Considering also that the Convention on the Rights of the Child recognizes the right of the child to be protected from economic exploitation and from performing any work that is likely to be hazardous or to interfere with the child's education, or to be harmful to the child's health or physical, mental, spiritual, moral or social development,

Gravely concerned at the significant and increasing international traffic in children for the purpose of the sale of children, child prostitution and child pornography,

Deeply concerned at the widespread and continuing practice of sex tourism, to which children are especially vulnerable, as it directly promotes the sale of children, child prostitution and child pornography,

Recognizing that a number of particularly vulnerable groups, including girl children, are at greater risk of sexual exploitation and that girl children are disproportionately represented among the sexually exploited,

Concerned about the growing availability of child pornography on the Internet and other evolving technologies, and recalling the International Conference on Combating Child Pornography on the Internet, held in Vienna in 1999, in particular its conclusion calling for the worldwide criminalization of the production, distribution, exportation, transmission, importation, intentional possession and advertising of child pornography, and stressing the importance of closer cooperation and partnership between Governments and the Internet industry,

Believing that the elimination of the sale of children, child prostitution and child pornography will be facilitated by adopting a holistic approach, addressing the contributing factors, including underdevelopment, poverty, economic disparities, inequitable socio-economic structure, dysfunctioning families, lack of education, urban-rural migration, gender discrimination, irresponsible adult sexual behaviour, harmful traditional practices, armed conflicts and trafficking in children,

Believing also that efforts to raise public awareness are needed to reduce consumer demand for the sale of children, child prostitution and child pornography, and believing further in the importance of strengthening global partnership among all actors and of improving law enforcement at the national level,

Noting the provisions of international legal instruments relevant to the protection of children, including the Hague Convention on Protection of Children and Cooperation in Respect of Intercountry Adoption, the Hague Convention on the Civil Aspects of International Child Abduction, the Hague Convention on Jurisdiction, Applicable Law, Recognition, Enforcement and Cooperation in Respect of Parental Responsibility and Measures for the Protection of Children, and International Labour Organization Convention No. 182 on the Prohibition and Immediate Action for the Elimination of the Worst Forms of Child Labour,

Encouraged by the overwhelming support for the Convention on the Rights of the Child, demonstrating the widespread commitment that exists for the promotion and protection of the rights of the child,

Recognizing the importance of the implementation of the provisions of the Programme of Action for the Prevention of the Sale of Children, Child Prostitution and Child Pornography and the Declaration and Agenda for Action adopted at the World Congress against Commercial Sexual Exploitation of Children, held in Stockholm from 27 to 31 August 1996, and the other relevant decisions and recommendations of pertinent international bodies,

Taking due account of the importance of the traditions and cultural values of each people for the protection and harmonious development of the child,

Have agreed as follows:

Article 1

States Parties shall prohibit the sale of children, child prostitution and child pornography as provided for by the present Protocol.

Article 2

For the purposes of the present Protocol:

(a) Sale of children means any act or transaction whereby a child is transferred by any person or group of persons to another for remuneration or any other consideration;

(b) Child prostitution means the use of a child in sexual activities for remuneration or any other form of consideration;

(c) Child pornography means any representation, by whatever means, of a child engaged in real or simulated explicit sexual activities or any representation of the sexual parts of a child for primarily sexual purposes.

Article 3

1. Each State Party shall ensure that, as a minimum, the following acts and activities are fully covered under its criminal or penal law, whether such offences are committed domestically or transnationally or on an individual or organized basis:

(a) In the context of sale of children as defined in article 2:
    (i) Offering, delivering or accepting, by whatever means, a child for the purpose of:
        a. Sexual exploitation of the child;
        b. Transfer of organs of the child for profit;
        c. Engagement of the child in forced labour;
    (ii) Improperly inducing consent, as an intermediary, for the adoption of a child in violation of applicable international legal instruments on adoption;
(b) Offering, obtaining, procuring or providing a child for child prostitution, as defined in article 2;
(c) Producing, distributing, disseminating, importing, exporting, offering, selling or possessing for the above purposes child pornography as defined in article 2.

2. Subject to the provisions of the national law of a State Party, the same shall apply to an attempt to commit any of the said acts and to complicity or participation in any of the said acts.

3. Each State Party shall make such offences punishable by appropriate penalties that take into account their grave nature.

4. Subject to the provisions of its national law, each State Party shall take measures, where appropriate, to establish the liability of legal persons for offences established in paragraph 1 of the present article. Subject to the legal principles of the State Party, such liability of legal persons may be criminal, civil or administrative.

5. States Parties shall take all appropriate legal and administrative measures to ensure that all persons involved in the adoption of a child act in conformity with applicable international legal instruments.

Article 4

1. Each State Party shall take such measures as may be necessary to establish its jurisdiction over the offences referred to in article 3, paragraph 1, when the offences are commited in its territory or on board a ship or aircraft registered in that State.

2. Each State Party may take such measures as may be necessary to establish its jurisdiction over the offences referred to in article 3, paragraph 1, in the following cases:
(a) When the alleged offender is a national of that State or a person who has his habitual residence in its territory;
(b) When the victim is a national of that State.

3. Each State Party shall also take such measures as may be necessary to establish its jurisdiction over the aforementioned offences when the alleged offender is present in its territory and it does not extradite him or her to another State Party on the ground that the offence has been committed by one of its nationals.
4. The present Protocol does not exclude any criminal jurisdiction exercised in accordance with internal law.

Article 5

1. The offences referred to in article 3, paragraph 1, shall be deemed to be included as extraditable offences in any extradition treaty existing between States Parties and shall be included as extraditable offences in every extradition treaty subsequently concluded between them, in accordance with the conditions set forth in such treaties.
2. If a State Party that makes extradition conditional on the existence of a treaty receives a request for extradition from another State Party with which it has no extradition treaty, it may consider the present Protocol to be a legal basis for extradition in respect of such offences. Extradition shall be subject to the conditions provided by the law of the requested State.
3. States Parties that do not make extradition conditional on the existence of a treaty shall recognize such offences as extraditable offences between themselves subject to the conditions provided by the law of the requested State.
4. Such offences shall be treated, for the purpose of extradition between States Parties, as if they had been committed not only in the place in which they occurred but also in the territories of the States required to establish their jurisdiction in accordance with article 4.
5. If an extradition request is made with respect to an offence described in article 3, paragraph 1, and the requested State Party does not or will not extradite on the basis of the nationality of the offender, that State shall take suitable measures to submit the case to its competent authorities for the purpose of prosecution.

Article 6

1. States Parties shall afford one another the greatest measure of assistance in connection with investigations or criminal or extradition proceedings brought in respect of the offences set forth in article 3, paragraph

1, including assistance in obtaining evidence at their disposal necessary for the proceedings.

2. States Parties shall carry out their obligations under paragraph 1 of the present article in conformity with any treaties or other arrangements on mutual legal assistance that may exist between them. In the absence of such treaties or arrangements, States Parties shall afford one another assistance in accordance with their domestic law.

Article 7

States Parties shall, subject to the provisions of their national law:

(a) Take measures to provide for the seizure and confiscation, as appropriate, of:
   (i) Goods, such as materials, assets and other instrumentalities used to commit or facilitate offences under the present protocol;
   (ii) Proceeds derived from such offences;
(b) Execute requests from another State Party for seizure or confiscation of goods or proceeds referred to in subparagraph (a) (i) and (ii);
(c) Take measures aimed at closing, on a temporary or definitive basis, premises used to commit such offences.

Article 8

1. States Parties shall adopt appropriate measures to protect the rights and interests of child victims of the practices prohibited under the present Protocol at all stages of the criminal justice process, in particular by:
   (a) Recognizing the vulnerability of child victims and adapting procedures to recognize their special needs, including their special needs as witnesses;
   (b) Informing child victims of their rights, their role and the scope, timing and progress of the proceedings and of the disposition of their cases;
   (c) Allowing the views, needs and concerns of child victims to be presented and considered in proceedings where their personal interests are affected, in a manner consistent with the procedural rules of national law;
   (d) Providing appropriate support services to child victims throughout the legal process;

(e) Protecting, as appropriate, the privacy and identity of child victims and taking measures in accordance with national law to avoid the inappropriate dissemination of information that could lead to the identification of child victims;

(f) Providing, in appropriate cases, for the safety of child victims, as well as that of their families and witnesses on their behalf, from intimidation and retaliation;

(g) Avoiding unnecessary delay in the disposition of cases and the execution of orders or decrees granting compensation to child victims.

2. States Parties shall ensure that uncertainty as to the actual age of the victim shall not prevent the initiation of criminal investigations, including investigations aimed at establishing the age of the victim.

3. States Parties shall ensure that, in the treatment by the criminal justice system of children who are victims of the offences described in the present Protocol, the best interest of the child shall be a primary consideration.

4. States Parties shall take measures to ensure appropriate training, in particular legal and psychological training, for the persons who work with victims of the offences prohibited under the present Protocol.

5. States Parties shall, in appropriate cases, adopt measures in order to protect the safety and integrity of those persons and/or organizations involved in the prevention and/or protection and rehabilitation of victims of such offences.

6. Nothing in the present article shall be construed to be prejudicial to or inconsistent with the rights of the accused to a fair and impartial trial.

Article 9

1. States Parties shall adopt or strengthen, implement and disseminate laws, administrative measures, social policies and programmes to prevent the offences referred to in the present Protocol. Particular attention shall be given to protect children who are especially vulnerable to such practices.

2. States Parties shall promote awareness in the public at large, including children, through information by all appropriate means, education and training, about the preventive measures and harmful effects of the offences referred to in the present Protocol. In fulfilling their obligations under this article, States Parties shall encourage the participation of the community and, in particular, children and child victims, in such

information and education and training programmes, including at the international level.

3. States Parties shall take all feasible measures with the aim of ensuring all appropriate assistance to victims of such offences, including their full social reintegration and their full physical and psychological recovery.

4. States Parties shall ensure that all child victims of the offences described in the present Protocol have access to adequate procedures to seek, without discrimination, compensation for damages from those legally responsible.

5. States Parties shall take appropriate measures aimed at effectively prohibiting the production and dissemination of material advertising the offences described in the present Protocol.

Article 10

1. States Parties shall take all necessary steps to strengthen international cooperation by multilateral, regional and bilateral arrangements for the prevention, detection, investigation, prosecution and punishment of those responsible for acts involving the sale of children, child prostitution, child pornography and child sex tourism. States Parties shall also promote international cooperation and coordination between their authorities, national and international non-governmental organizations and international organizations.

2. States Parties shall promote international cooperation to assist child victims in their physical and psychological recovery, social reintegration and repatriation.

3. States Parties shall promote the strengthening of international cooperation in order to address the root causes, such as poverty and underdevelopment, contributing to the vulnerability of children to the sale of children, child prostitution, child pornography and child sex tourism.

4. States Parties in a position to do so shall provide financial, technical or other assistance through existing multilateral, regional, bilateral or other programmes.

Article 11

Nothing in the present Protocol shall affect any provisions that are more conducive to the realization of the rights of the child and that may be contained in:

(a) The law of a State Party;
(b) International law in force for that State.

Article 12

1. Each State Party shall, within two years following the entry into force of the present Protocol for that State Party, submit a report to the Committee on the Rights of the Child providing comprehensive information on the measures it has taken to implement the provisions of the Protocol.

2. Following the submission of the comprehensive report, each State Party shall include in the reports they submit to the Committee on the Rights of the Child, in accordance with article 44 of the Convention, any further information with respect to the implementation of the present Protocol. Other States Parties to the Protocol shall submit a report every five years.

3. The Committee on the Rights of the Child may request from States Parties further information relevant to the implementation of the present Protocol.

Article 13

1. The present Protocol is open for signature by any State that is a party to the Convention or has signed it.

2. The present Protocol is subject to ratification and is open to accession by any State that is a party to the Convention or has signed it. Instruments of ratification or accession shall be deposited with the Secretary-General of the United Nations.

Article 14

1. The present Protocol shall enter into force three months after the deposit of the tenth instrument of ratification or accession.

2. For each State ratifying the present Protocol or acceding to it after its entry into force, the Protocol shall enter into force one month after the date of the deposit of its own instrument of ratification or accession.

Article 15

1. Any State Party may denounce the present Protocol at any time by written notification to the Secretary-General of the United Nations, who shall thereafter inform the other States Parties to the Convention and all States that have signed the Convention. The denunciation shall

take effect one year after the date of receipt of the notification by the Secretary-General.

2. Such a denunciation shall not have the effect of releasing the State Party from its obligations under the present Protocol in regard to any offence that occurs prior to the date on which the denunciation becomes effective. Nor shall such a denunciation prejudice in any way the continued consideration of any matter that is already under consideration by the Committee on the Rights of the Child prior to the date on which the denunciation becomes effective.

Article 16

1. Any State Party may propose an amendment and file it with the Secretary-General of the United Nations. The Secretary-General shall thereupon communicate the proposed amendment to States Parties with a request that they indicate whether they favour a conference of States Parties for the purpose of considering and voting upon the proposals. In the event that, within four months from the date of such communication, at least one third of the States Parties favour such a conference, the Secretary-General shall convene the conference under the auspices of the United Nations. Any amendment adopted by a majority of States Parties present and voting at the conference shall be submitted to the General Assembly of the United Nations for approval.

2. An amendment adopted in accordance with paragraph 1 of the present article shall enter into force when it has been approved by the General Assembly and accepted by a two-thirds majority of States Parties.

3. When an amendment enters into force, it shall be binding on those States Parties that have accepted it, other States Parties still being bound by the provisions of the present Protocol and any earlier amendments they have accepted.

Article 17

1. The present Protocol, of which the Arabic, Chinese, English, French, Russian and Spanish texts are equally authentic, shall be deposited in the archives of the United Nations.

2. The Secretary-General of the United Nations shall transmit certified copies of the present Protocol to all States Parties to the Convention and all States that have signed the Convention.

Status as of 1 December 2006

Signatories: 115, Parties: 112.

Participant	Signature	Ratification, Accession (a), Succession (d)
Afghanistan		19 Sep 2002 a
Andorra	7 Sep 2000	30 Apr 2001
Angola		24 Mar 2005 a
Antigua and Barbuda	18 Dec 2001	30 Apr 2002
Argentina	1 Apr 2002	25 Sep 2003
Armenia	24 Sep 2003	30 Jun 2005
Australia	18 Dec 2001	
Austria	6 Sep 2000	6 May 2004
Azerbaijan	8 Sep 2000	3 Jul 2002
Bahrain		21 Sep 2004 a
Bangladesh	6 Sep 2000	6 Sep 2000
Belarus		23 Jan 2002 a
Belgium	6 Sep 2000	17 Mar 2006
Belize	6 Sep 2000	1 Dec 2003
Benin	22 Feb 2001	31 Jan 2005
Bhutan	15 Sep 2005	
Bolivia	10 Nov 2001	3 Jun 2003
Bosnia and Herzegovina	7 Sep 2000	4 Sep 2002
Botswana		24 Sep 2003 a
Brazil	6 Sep 2000	27 Jan 2004
Brunei Darussalam		21 Nov 2006 a
Bulgaria	8 Jun 2001	12 Feb 2002
Burkina Faso	16 Nov 2001	31 Mar 2006
Cambodia	27 Jun 2000	30 May 2002
Cameroon	5 Oct 2001	
Canada	10 Nov 2001	14 Sep 2005
Cape Verde		10 May 2002 a
Chad	3 May 2002	28 Aug 2002
Chile	28 Jun 2000	6 Feb 2003
China	6 Sep 2000	3 Dec 2002
Colombia	6 Sep 2000	11 Nov 2003
Costa Rica	7 Sep 2000	9 Apr 2002
Croatia	8 May 2002	13 May 2002
Cuba	13 Oct 2000	25 Sep 2001

Cyprus	8 Feb 2001	6 Apr 2006
Czech Republic	26 Jan 2005	
Democratic Republic of the Congo		11 Nov 2001 a
Denmark	7 Sep 2000	24 Jul 2003
Djibouti	14 Jun 2006	
Dominica		20 Sep 2002 a
Ecuador	6 Sep 2000	30 Jan 2004
Egypt		12 Jul 2002 a
El Salvador	13 Sep 2002	17 May 2004
Equatorial Guinea		7 Feb 2003 a
Eritrea		16 Feb 2005 a
Estonia	24 Sep 2003	3 Aug 2004
Fiji	16 Sep 2005	
Finland	7 Sep 2000	
France	6 Sep 2000	5 Feb 2003
Gabon	8 Sep 2000	
Gambia	21 Dec 2000	
Georgia		28 Jun 2005 a
Germany	6 Sep 2000	
Ghana	24 Sep 2003	
Greece	7 Sep 2000	
Guatemala	7 Sep 2000	9 May 2002
Guinea-Bissau	8 Sep 2000	
Haiti	15 Aug 2002	
Holy See	10 Oct 2000	24 Oct 2001
Honduras		8 May 2002 a
Hungary	11 Mar 2002	
Iceland	7 Sep 2000	9 Jul 2001
India	15 Nov 2004	16 Aug 2005
Indonesia	24 Sep 2001	
Ireland	7 Sep 2000	
Israel	14 Nov 2001	
Italy	6 Sep 2000	9 May 2002
Jamaica	8 Sep 2000	
Japan	10 May 2002	24 Jan 2005
Jordan	6 Sep 2000	
Kazakhstan	6 Sep 2000	24 Aug 2001
Kenya	8 Sep 2000	
Kuwait		26 Aug 2004 a
Kyrgyzstan		12 Feb 2003 a
Lao People's Democratic Republic		20 Sep 2006 a

Latvia	1 Feb 2002	22 Feb 2006
Lebanon	10 Oct 2001	8 Nov 2004
Lesotho	6 Sep 2000	24 Sep 2003
Liberia	22 Sep 2004	
Libyan Arab Jamahiriya		18 Jun 2004 a
Liechtenstein	8 Sep 2000	
Lithuania		5 Aug 2004 a
Luxembourg	8 Sep 2000	
Madagascar	7 Sep 2000	22 Sep 2004
Malawi	7 Sep 2000	
Maldives	10 May 2002	10 May 2002
Mali		16 May 2002 a
Malta	7 Sep 2000	
Mauritius	11 Nov 2001	
Mexico	7 Sep 2000	15 Mar 2002
Micronesia (Federated States of)	8 May 2002	
Moldova	8 Feb 2002	
Monaco	26 Jun 2000	
Mongolia	12 Nov 2001	27 Jun 2003
Montenegro		23 Oct 2006 d
Morocco	8 Sep 2000	2 Oct 2001
Mozambique		6 Mar 2003 a
Namibia	8 Sep 2000	16 Apr 2002
Nauru	8 Sep 2000	
Nepal	8 Sep 2000	20 Jan 2006
Netherlands	7 Sep 2000	23 Aug 2005
New Zealand	7 Sep 2000	
Nicaragua		2 Dec 2004 a
Niger	27 Mar 2002	26 Oct 2004
Nigeria	8 Sep 2000	
Norway	13 Jun 2000	2 Oct 2001
Oman		17 Sep 2004 a
Pakistan	26 Sep 2001	
Panama	31 Oct 2000	9 Feb 2001
Paraguay	13 Sep 2000	18 Aug 2003
Peru	1 Nov 2000	8 May 2002
Philippines	8 Sep 2000	28 May 2002
Poland	13 Feb 2002	4 Feb 2005
Portugal	6 Sep 2000	16 May 2003
Qatar		14 Dec 2001 a
Republic of Korea	6 Sep 2000	24 Sep 2004

Romania	6 Sep 2000	18 Oct 2001
Rwanda		14 Mar 2002 a
Saint Vincent and the Grenadines		15 Sep 2005 a
San Marino	5 Jun 2000	
Senegal	8 Sep 2000	5 Nov 2003
Serbia	8 Oct 2001	10 Oct 2002
Seychelles	23 Jan 2001	
Sierra Leone	8 Sep 2000	17 Sep 2001
Slovakia	30 Nov 2001	25 Jun 2004
Slovenia	8 Sep 2000	23 Sep 2004
South Africa		30 Jun 2003 a
Spain	6 Sep 2000	18 Dec 2001
Sri Lanka	8 May 2002	22 Sep 2006
Sudan		2 Nov 2004 a
Suriname	10 May 2002	
Sweden	8 Sep 2000	
Switzerland	7 Sep 2000	19 Sep 2006
Syrian Arab Republic		15 May 2003 a
Tajikistan		5 Aug 2002 a
Thailand		11 Jan 2006 a
The Former Yugoslav Republic of Macedonia	17 Jul 2001	17 Oct 2003
Timor-Leste		16 Apr 2003 a
Togo	15 Nov 2001	2 Jul 2004
Tunisia	22 Apr 2002	13 Sep 2002
Turkey	8 Sep 2000	19 Aug 2002
Turkmenistan		28 Mar 2005 a
Uganda		30 Nov 2001 a
Ukraine	7 Sep 2000	3 Jul 2003
United Kingdom of Great Britain and Northern Ireland	7 Sep 2000	
United Republic of Tanzania		24 Apr 2003 a
United States of America	5 Jul 2000	23 Dec 2002
Uruguay	7 Sep 2000	3 Jul 2003
Vanuatu	16 Sep 2005	
Venezuela (Bolivarian Republic of)	7 Sep 2000	8 May 2002
Viet Nam	8 Sep 2000	20 Dec 2001
Yemen		15 Dec 2004 a

Appendix 3

U.S.-Thailand Mutual Legal Assistance Treaty

MUTUAL LEGAL ASSISTANCE TREATIES

THAILAND

TREATY WITH THAILAND ON MUTUAL ASSISTANCE IN CRIMINAL MATTERS

TREATY DOC. 100-18

1986 U.S.T. LEXIS 158

March 19, 1986, Date-Signed

MESSAGE FROM THE PRESIDENT OF THE UNITED STATES

TRANSMITTING THE TREATY BETWEEN THE GOVERNMENT OF THE UNITED STATES OF AMERICA AND THE GOVERNMENT OF THE KINGDOM OF THAILAND ON MUTUAL ASSISTANCE IN CRIMINAL MATTERS, SIGNED AT BANGKOK ON MARCH 19, 1986

TEXT:

100TH CONGRESS

SENATE

LETTER OF TRANSMITTAL

THE WHITE HOUSE, April 22, 1988.

To the Senate of the United States:

With a view to receiving the advice and consent of the Senate to ratification, I transmit herewith the Treaty between the Government of the United States of America and the Government of the Kingdom of Thailand on Mutual Assistance in Criminal Matters, signed at Bangkok on March 19, 1986. I transmit also, for the information of the Senate, the report of the Department of State with respect to the Treaty.

The Treaty is one of a series of modern mutual legal assistance treaties being negotiated by the United States in order to counter more effectively criminal activities. The Treaty should be an effective tool to prosecute a wide variety of modern criminals including members of drug cartels, "white-collar criminals," and terrorists. The Treaty is self-executing and utilizes existing statutory authority.

The Treaty provides for a broad range of cooperation in criminal matters. Mutual assistance available under the Treaty includes: (1) taking testimony or statements of witnesses; (2) providing documents, records, and evidence; (3) serving documents; (4) executing requests for searches and seizures; (5) transferring persons in custody for testimonial purposes; (6) locating persons; (7) initiating proceedings upon request; and (8) assisting in forfeiture proceedings.

I recommend that the Senate give early and favorable consideration to the Treaty and give its advice and consent to ratification.

RONALD REAGAN.

LETTER OF SUBMITTAL

DEPARTMENT OF STATE, Washington, April 18, 1988.

The PRESIDENT,

The White House.

THE PRESIDENT: I have the honor to submit to you the Treaty between the Government of the United States of America and the Government of the Kingdom of Thailand on Mutual Assistance in Criminal Matters, signed at Bangkok on March 19, 1986. I recommend that the Treaty be transmitted to the Senate for its advice and consent to ratification.

The Treaty covers mutual legal assistance in criminal matters. In recent years, similar bilateral treaties have entered into force with Italy, the Netherlands, Switzerland and Turkey; others have been concluded (but not yet entered into force) with the Bahamas, Belgium, Canada, Colombia, Mexico, Morocco, and the United Kingdom on behalf of the Cayman Islands. The Treaty contains many provisions similar to those in the other treaties as well as some innovations.

The Treaty will not require further implementing legislation and will utilize the existing authority of the Federal courts, particularly 28 U.S.C. 1782.

Article 1 provides for assistance in "investigations, prosecutions and other proceedings relating to criminal matters." The Treaty thereby provides for assistance at the investigative stage (such as grand jury proceedings), as well as after formal charges have been filed. Assistance under the Treaty will include: taking testimony or statements of persons; provision of documents, records and evidence; serving documents; executing requests for searches and seizures; transferring persons in custody for testimonial purposes; locating witnesses; and other forms of assistance. The article states that it is not intended to create rights in private parties either to secure assistance or to suppress or exclude evidence obtained under the Treaty. The article also defines military offenses and provides that the Treaty does not apply to such offenses.

Article 2 specifies the limited bases under the Treaty in which assistance may be denied by the Requested State. These bases are when the request would prejudice the sovereignty, security, or other essential public interests of the Requested State, or when the request relates to a political offense. The Requested State may postpone execution of a request if its execution would interfere with an ongoing investigation or prosecution. This article also provides that, before the Central Authority of the Requested State refuses a request, it should try to determine whether there is a way to render the assistance, subject to specified terms and conditions. If the Requesting State accepts the assistance subject to limitations, it must comply with those limitations.

Article 3 provides for the establishment of a Central Authority, which shall be the Attorney General or his designee for the United States and the Minister of Interior or his designee for Thailand. The article also provides that requests for assistance shall be made directly from one Central Authority to the other.

The first paragraph of Article 4 provides that requests shall be submitted in writing in the language of the Requested State. The second paragraph provides that requests shall contain the information required by the Requested State to execute the request, including but not limited to the subject matter and the nature of the investigation or proceeding to which the request relates, a description of the evidence, information or other assistance sought, and the purpose for which it is sought. The third paragraph outlines information that should be provided "when appropriate."

Article 5 obligates each party to execute requests promptly and, to the extent not prohibited by its law, in accordance with the directions of the Requesting State. It also provides that the courts of the Requested State shall have authority to issue all orders necessary to execute a request.

Article 6 provides that the Requested State shall pay all ordinary costs relating to the execution of the request, except for the lawful fees of expert witnesses and the travel and incidental expenses of witnesses traveling between the two States.

Article 7 prohibits the disclosure or use of any information or evidence obtained under the Treaty for purposes other than those stated in the request without the consent of the Requested State. Moreover, the article authorizes the Requested State to require that information or evidence furnished to the Requesting State be kept confidential in accordance with conditions which it may specify, provided that the conditions do not interfere with the use of the evidence in a public trial. In addition, the article permits the Requesting State to request that the application for assistance and the granting of assistance be kept confidential if possible.

Article 8 provides that if compulsory process is necessary the Requested State may complete the taking of testimony or production of documents for the Requesting State by means available under the Requested State's laws.

Article 9 provides that the Requested State shall provide copies of its publicly available government records if such records are requested under the Treaty. In addition, the Requested State may, in its discretion, provide any record or information not publicly available to the same extent that such records or information would be made available to its own law enforcement and judicial authorities.

Article 10 obligates the Requested State to serve any legal documents transmitted by the Central Authority of the Requesting State. The Requesting State must transmit a document relating to a response or appearance in the Requesting State within a reasonable time before the scheduled response or appearance. No person other than a national of the Requesting State can be subjected to any legal sanction for failing to comply with a document that is served pursuant to this article and calls for his appearance in the Requesting State.

Article 11 provides that a request for the search, seizure and delivery of any article shall be carried out if the Requesting State provides sufficient evidence for such action under the laws of the Requested State. In the United States, a Thai request would have to be supported by a showing that probable cause for the search exists, and in Thailand a request by the United States would have to comply with the corresponding Thai evidentiary standard.

Article 12 authorizes the transfer of a person in custody in either State to the other for purposes of providing testimony, subject to the consent of the person and the relevant Party. Authority is also provided to keep such a person in custody unless release is authorized by the sending State. The receiving State is required to send the person back as soon as circumstances permit and is not permitted to condition the person's return on an extradition request by the sending State.

Article 13 requires the Requested State to take "all necessary measures" to locate or identify witnesses, potential defendants, experts, and other persons who are believed to be in its territory and are needed in connection with an investigation, prosecution or proceeding in the Requesting State.

Article 14 provides that one State may request the other to initiate criminal proceedings in certain circumstances.

Article 15 stipulates that a State may notify the other of fruits or instrumentalities of a criminal offense believed to be in the other State. The Parties may, to the extent permitted by their respective laws and this Treaty, assist one another in proceedings regarding forfeiture. "Fruits and instrumentalities" include money, vessels and other property used in perpetrating the crime or acquired as a result of the crime.

This provision expressly authorizes assistance in the execution of penal laws, an area in which countries do not necessarily otherwise assist each other. It is also consistent with a recently enacted U.S. statute, 18 U.S.C. 981(i), which permits equitable sharing of forfeited property with a foreign government pursuant to a treaty in order to reflect that government's contribution in narcotics investigations leading to seizure or forfeiture.

Article 16 provides that if a person in the Requested State is needed to appear in the Requesting State, the Requested State shall upon request invite the person to appear in the Requesting State. The Requesting State is required to pay the expenses of such voluntary appearance in accordance with Article 6.

Article 17 ensures a degree of "safe conduct" for a witness who voluntarily appears in the Requesting State pursuant to Article 16. "Safe conduct" encompasses limited immunity from prosecution, service of civil process, detention or any restriction of personal liberty with regard to acts or convictions that preceded the witness's departure from the Requested State while the witness is present in the Requesting State and for up to fifteen days after notification that his presence in the Requesting State is no longer required.

Article 18 provides that any documents, records or articles of evidence furnished under the Treaty must be returned to the Requested State as soon as possible unless that State waives their return.

Article 19 provides that the Treaty does not preclude either Party from utilizing other international agreements that may offer means of securing assistance or cooperation, such as Interpol, or from using its own internal laws on legal assistance.

Article 20 sets forth standard procedures for ratification and entry into force of the Treaty.

Article 21 provides that either Party may terminate the Treaty by written notice. Termination takes effect six months after such notification.

The United States Delegation, consisting of representatives of the Departments of State and Justice, has also prepared a Technical Section-by-Section Analysis of the Treaty. That Analysis will be transmitted separately to the Senate Committee on Foreign Relations.

The Department of State joins the Department of Justice in favoring approval of this Treaty by the Senate at an early date.

Respectfully submitted,

GEORGE P. SHULTZ.

Treaty between the Government of the Kingdom of Thailand and the Government of the United States of America on Mutual Assistance in Criminal Matters

The Government of the Kingdom of Thailand and the Government of the United States of America,

Desiring to maintain and to strengthen the longstanding bonds which unite the two countries, and to undertake effective mutual assistance in criminal matters,

Have agreed as follows:

Article 1: Obligation to Assist

1. The Contracting States agree, in accordance with the provisions of this Treaty, to provide mutual assistance in connection with investigations, prosecutions, and other proceedings relating to criminal matters.
2. Assistance shall include but not be limited to:
   a. taking the testimony and statement of persons;
   b. providing documents, records, and evidence;
   c. serving documents;
   d. executing requests for searches and seizures;
   e. transferring persons in custody for testimonial purposes;
   f. locating persons;
   g. initiating proceedings upon request; and
   h. assisting in forfeiture proceedings.

3. Assistance shall be provided without regard to whether the acts which are the subject of the investigation, prosecution, or proceeding in the Requesting State are prohibited under the law in the Requested State, or whether the Requested State would have jurisdiction with respect to such acts in corresponding circumstances.
4. This Treaty is intended solely for mutual assistance between the criminal law enforcement authorities of the Contracting States and is not intended or designed to provide such assistance to private parties.
5. A private party may not rely upon any provision of this Treaty to impede the execution of a request, or to exclude or suppress evidence obtained under the Treaty.
6. This Treaty shall not apply to the execution of arrest warrants or to military offenses. For the purposes of this Treaty, military offenses are violations of military laws and regulations which do not constitute offenses under ordinary criminal law.

Article 2: Limitations on Compliance

1. The Requested State may refuse to execute a request to the extent that:
   a. the request would prejudice the sovereignty, security, or other essential public interests of the Requested State; or
   b. the request relates to a political offense.
2. Before refusing the execution of any request pursuant to this Article, the Requested State shall determine whether assistance can be given subject to such conditions as it deems necessary. If the Requesting State accepts the assistance subject to these conditions, it shall comply with the conditions.
3. If the execution of a request would interfere with an ongoing criminal investigation, prosecution or proceeding in the Requested State, execution may be postponed by that State, or made subject to conditions determined to be necessary by the State after consultations with the Requesting State.
4. The Requested State shall promptly inform the Requesting State of the reason for refusing or postponing the execution of a request.

Article 3: Central Authorities

1. A Central Authority shall be established by each Contracting State.
2. For the United States of America, the Central Authority shall be the Attorney General or a person designated by him.
3. For the Kingdom of Thailand, the Central Authority shall be the Minister of Interior or a person designated by him.

4. Requests under this Treaty shall be made by the Central Authority of the Requesting State to the Central Authority of the Requested State.

Article 4: Contents of Requests for Mutual Assistance

1. A request for assistance shall be submitted in writing in the language of the requested State. All accompanying documents shall be translated into the language of the Requested State. Such translations shall be certified by a sworn or approved translator in accordance with the laws or practices of the Requesting State.
2. The request shall include the following:
   a. the name of the authority conducting the investigation, prosecution, or proceeding to which the request relates;
   b. the subject matter and nature of the investigation, prosecution, or proceeding;
   c. a description of the evidence or information sought or the acts of assistance to be performed; and
   d. the purpose for which the evidence, information, or other assistance is sought.
3. When appropriate, a request shall also include:
   a. available information on the identity and whereabouts of a person to be located;
   b. the identity and location of a person to be served, that person's relationship to the investigation, prosecution, or proceeding, and the manner in which service is to be effected;
   c. the identity and location of persons from whom evidence is sought;
   d. a precise description of the place or person to be searched and of the articles to be seized;
   e. a description of the manner in which any testimony or statement is to be taken and recorded;
   f. a list of questions to be answered;
   g. a description of any particular procedure to be followed in executing the request;
   h. information as to the allowances and expenses to which a person appearing in the Requesting State will be entitled; and
   i. any other information which may be brought to the attention of the Requested State to facilitate its execution of the request.

Article 5: Execution of the Request

1. The Central Authority of the Requested State shall promptly comply with the request or, when appropriate, shall transmit it to the authority having jurisdiction to do so. The competent authorities of the Requested

State shall do everything in their power to execute the request, and shall issue subpoenas, search warrants, or other process necessary in the execution of the request.

2. When execution of the request requires judicial or administrative action, the request shall be presented to the appropriate authority by officials of the Requested State at no cost to the Requesting State.

3. Requests shall be executed in accordance with the laws of the Requested State except to the extent that this Treaty provides otherwise. However, the method of execution specified in the request shall be followed except insofar as it would be incompatible with the laws of the Requested State.

Article 6: Costs

The Requested State shall pay all costs relating to the execution of the request, except for the fees of expert witnesses and the allowances and expenses related to travel of persons pursuant to Articles 12 and 16, which fees, allowances, and expenses shall be borne by the Requesting State.

Article 7: Limitations on Use

1. Information and evidence obtained under this Treaty, as well as information derived there from, shall not be used for purposes other than those stated in the request without the prior consent of the Requested State.

2. The Requesting State may require that the application for assistance, its contents and related documents, and the granting of assistance be kept confidential. If the request cannot be executed without breaching the required confidentiality, the Requested State shall so inform the Requesting State which shall then determine whether the request should nevertheless be executed.

3. The Requested State may require that information or evidence furnished, and information derived there from, be kept confidential in accordance with conditions which it shall specify. In that case, the Requesting State shall comply with the conditions, except to the extent that the information or evidence is needed in a public trial resulting from the investigation, prosecution, or proceeding described in the request.

Article 8: Taking Testimony and Statements and Producing Evidence in the Requested State

1. Upon a request that a person be summoned to give testimony, make a statement, or produce documents, records, or articles in the Requested

State, that person shall be compelled to do so in the same manner and to the same extent as in criminal investigations, prosecutions, or proceedings in the Requested State.

2. If the person referred to in paragraph 1 asserts a claim of immunity, incapacity, or privilege under the laws of the Requesting State, the evidence shall nonetheless be taken and the claim made known to the Requesting State for resolution by the authorities of the Requesting State.

3. The Requested State shall furnish information in advance as to the date and place of the taking of the evidence.

4. The Requested State shall authorize the presence of such persons as specified in the request for the taking of testimony or a statement during the execution of the request and allow such persons to question the person whose testimony or statement is sought, insofar as it would not be prohibited by the laws of the Requested State.

5. Business records produced under this Article shall be authenticated by the person in charge of maintaining them through the use of Form A appended to this Treaty. No further certification shall be required. Documents authenticated under this paragraph shall be admitted in evidence as proof of the truth of the matters set forth therein.

Article 9: Providing Records of Government Offices or Agencies

1. The Requested State shall provide copies of publicly available records of a government office or agency.

2. The Requested State may provide any record or information in the possession of a government office or agency, but not publicly available, to the same extent and under the same conditions as it would be available to its own law enforcement or judicial authorities. The Requested State in its discretion may deny the request entirely or in part.

3. Documents provided under this Article shall be attested by the official in charge of maintaining them through the use of Form B appended to this Treaty. No further certification shall be required. Documents attested under this paragraph shall be admitted in evidence as proof of the truth of the matters set forth therein.

Article 10: Serving Documents

1. The Requested State shall effect service of any legal document transmitted for this purpose by the Requesting State.

2. Any request for the service of a document requiring the appearance of a person before an authority in the Requesting State shall be transmitted a reasonable time before the scheduled appearance.

3. The Requested State shall return as proof of service a dated receipt signed by the person served or a declaration signed by the officer effecting service, specifying the form and date of service.
4. A person, other than a national of the Requesting State, who has been served pursuant to this Article with a legal document calling for his appearance in the Requesting State, shall not be subjected to any civil or criminal forfeiture, or other legal sanction or measure of restraint, because of his failure to comply therewith, even if the document contains a notice of penalty.

Article 11: Search and Seizure

1. A request for search, seizure, and delivery of any article to the Requesting State shall be executed if it includes the information justifying that action under the laws of the Requested States.
2. Every official of the Requested State who has custody of a seized article shall certify, through the use of Form C appended to this Treaty, the continuity of custody, the identity of the article, and the integrity of its condition. No further certification shall be required. Such certificate shall be admitted in evidence as proof of the truth of the matters set forth therein.

Article 12: Transferring Persons in Custody for Testimonial Purposes

1. A person in custody in the Requested State who is needed as a witness in the Requesting State shall be transported to that State if the person and the Requested State consent.
2. A person in custody in the Requesting State whose presence in the Requested State is required for the purpose of confrontation may be transported to the Requested State if the person and the Requested State consent.
3. For the purposes of this Article:
   a. the receiving State shall have the authority and obligation to keep the person transferred in custody unless otherwise authorized by the sending State;
   b. the receiving State shall return the person transferred to the custody of the sending State as soon as circumstances permit or as otherwise agreed;
   c. the receiving State shall not require the sending State to initiate extradition proceedings in order to obtain the return of the person transferred; and

d. the person transferred shall receive credit for service of the sentence imposed in the sending State for time served in the custody of the receiving State.

Article 13: Locating Persons

1. The Requested State shall take all necessary measures to locate persons who are believed to be in that State and who are needed in connection with a criminal investigation, prosecution, or proceeding in the Requesting State.
2. The Requested State shall communicate as soon as possible the results of its inquiries to the Requesting State.

Article 14: Initiating Proceedings upon Request

1. When one State is competent to initiate proceedings but wishes the proceedings to be carried out by the other State, the Central Authority of the former shall officially notify the Central Authority of the latter of the facts of the case. If the Requested State has jurisdiction in this regard, it shall submit the case to its competent authorities with a view to imitating criminal proceedings. Those authorities shall issue their decision in accordance with the laws of their country.
2. The Requested State shall report on the action taken regarding the notification and transmit, as appropriate, a copy of the decision issued.

Article 15: Assisting in Forfeiture Proceedings

1. If the Central Authority of one State becomes aware of fruits or instrumentalities of crime located in the other State which may be forfeitable or otherwise subject to seizure under the laws of the other State, it may so inform the Central Authority of that other State. If that other State has jurisdiction in this regard it shall present this information to its competent authorities for a determination whether any action is appropriate. Those authorities shall issue their decision in accordance with the laws of their country, and shall, through their Central Authority, report to the other State on the action taken.
2. The Contracting States may assist each other to the extent permitted by their respective laws and this Treaty, in proceedings relating to the forfeiture of the fruits or instrumentalities of crime.

Article 16: Appearance in the Requesting State

When the appearance of a person who is in the Requested State is needed in the Requesting State, the Central Authority of the Requested State shall invite the person to appear before the appropriate authority in the Requesting State, and shall indicate the extent to which the expenses will be paid. The response of the person shall be communicated promptly to the Requesting State.

Article 17: Safe Conduct

1. No person in the territory of the Requesting State to testify or provide a statement in accordance with the provisions of this Treaty shall be subject to service of process or be detained or subject to any other restriction of personal liberty by reason of any acts which preceded his departure from the Requested State.
2. The safe conduct provided for by this Article shall cease when the person, having had the opportunity to leave the Requesting State within 15 consecutive days after notification that his presence was no longer required by the appropriate authorities, shall have nonetheless stayed in that State or shall have voluntarily returned after having left it.

Article 18: Returning Documents, Records for Articles

The Requesting State shall return any documents, records, or articles furnished in execution of requests as soon as possible unless the Requested State waives their return.

Article 19: Compatibility with Other Treaties and National Laws

Assistance and procedures provided for by this Treaty shall not prevent either of the Contracting States from granting assistance through the provisions of other international agreements to which it may be a party or through the provisions of its national laws.

Article 20: Ratification and Entry into Force

1. This Treaty shall be subject to ratification; the instruments of ratification shall be exchanged at Washington as soon as possible.
2. This Treaty shall enter into force upon the exchange of the instruments of ratification.

Article 21: Termination

Either Contracting State may terminate this Treaty by means of written notice to the other Contracting State at any time. Termination shall take effect six months following the date of notification.

IN WITNESS WHEREOF, the undersigned, being duly authorized thereto by their respective Governments, have signed the present Treaty.

Done at Bangkok, in duplicate, in the Thai and English languages, each text being equally authentic, this nineteenth day of March in the two thousand five hundred and twenty-ninth year of the Buddhist Era, corresponding to the one thousand nine hundred and eighty-sixth year of the Christian Era.

For the Government of the United States of America:

EDWIN MEESE III,

Attorney General of the United States of America.

For the Government of the Kingdom of Thailand:

SIDDHI SAVETSILA,

Air Chief Marshal, Deputy Prime Minister, and Minister of Foreign Affairs of Thailand.

Form A: Certificate of Authenticity of Business Records

I, ___ (Name), attest on penalty of criminal punishment for false statement or attestation that I am employed by ___ (Name of Business from which documents are sought) and that my official title is ___ (Official Title), I further state that each of the records attached hereto is the original or a duplicate of the original of records in the custody of ___ (Name of Business from which Documents are sought)

    A. such records were made at or near the time of the occurrence of the matters set forth, by (or from information transmitted by) a person with knowledge of those matters;

   B. such records were kept in the course of a regularly conducted business activity;

   C. the business activity made such records as a regular practice; and

   D. if such record is not the original, such record is a duplicate of the original.

_____ (Signature)

_____ (Date)

Form B: Attestation of Authenticity of Documents

I, ___ (Name), attest on penalty of criminal punishment for false statement or attestation that my position with the Government of ___ (Country) is ___ (Official Title) and that in that position I am authorized by the law of ___ (Country) to attest that the documents attached and described below are true copies of original official records which are recorded or filed in ___ (Name of Government Office or Agency) which is an office or agency of the Government of ___ (Country)

Description of documents:

_____ (Signature)

_____ (Title)

_____ (Date)

Form C

I, _____ (Name) certify that I am _____ (Title) employed in the _____ (Name of Government Office or Agency). I received custody of the articles listed below from _____ (Name of Person) on _____ (Date), at _____ (Place).

I relinquished custody of those articles to _____ (Name) on _____ (Date), at _____ (Place) in the same condition as when I received them (or if different as noted below).

Description of articles:

Changes in condition while in my custody:

_____ (Signature)

_____ (Title)

OFFICIAL SEAL _____ (Place)

_____ (Date)

Appendix 4
Sample Letter Rogatory

NAME OF COURT IN SENDING STATE REQUESTING JUDICIAL ASSISTANCE

NAME OF PLAINTIFF

DOCKET NUMBER

V.

NAME OF DEFENDANT

REQUEST FOR INTERNATIONAL JUDICIAL ASSISTANCE (LETTER ROGATORY)

(NAME OF THE REQUESTING COURT) PRESENTS ITS COMPLIMENTS TO THE APPROPRIATE JUDICIAL AUTHORITY OF (NAME OF RECEIVING STATE), AND REQUESTS INTERNATIONAL JUDICIAL ASSISTANCE TO (OBTAIN EVIDENCE/EFFECT SERVICE OF PROCESS) TO BE USED IN A (CIVIL, CRIMINAL, ADMINISTRATIVE) PROCEEDING BEFORE THIS COURT IN THE ABOVE CAPTIONED MATTER. A (TRIAL/HEARING) ON THIS MATTER IS SCHEDULED AT PRESENT FOR (DATE) IN (CITY, STATE, COUNTRY).

THIS COURT REQUESTS THE ASSISTANCE DESCRIBED HEREIN AS NECESSARY IN THE INTERESTS OF JUSTICE. THE ASSISTANCE RE-QUESTED IS THAT THE APPROPRIATE JUDICIAL AUTHORITY OF (NAME OF RECEIVING STATE) (COMPEL THE APPEAR OF THE BELOW NAMED INDIVIDUALS TO GIVE EVIDENCE/PRODUCE DOC-UMENTS) (EFFECT SERVICE OF PROCESS UPON THE BELOW NAMED INDIVIDUALS).

(NAMES OF WITNESSES/PERSONS TO BE SERVED)

(NATIONALITY OF WITNESSES/PERSONS TO BE SERVED)

(ADDRESS OF WITNESSES/PERSONS TO BE SERVED)

(DESCRIPTION OF DOCUMENTS OR
OTHER EVIDENCE TO BE PRODUCED)

FACTS

(THE FACTS OF THE CASE PENDING BEFORE THE REQUESTING COURT SHOULD BE STATED BRIEFLY HERE, INCLUDING A LIST OF THOSE LAWS OF THE SENDING STATE WHICH GOVERN THE MAT-TER PENDING BEFORE THE COURT IN THE RECEIVING STATE.)

(QUESTIONS)

(IF THE REQUEST IS FOR EVIDENCE, THE QUESTIONS FOR THE WIT-NESSES SHOULD BE LISTED HERE.)

(LIST ANY SPECIAL RIGHTS OF WITNESSES PURSUANT TO THE LAWS OF THE REQUESTING STATE HERE.)

(LIST ANY SPECIAL METHODS OR PROCEDURES TO BE FOLLOWED.)

(INCLUDE REQUEST FOR NOTIFICATION OF TIME AND PLACE FOR EXAMINATION OF WITNESSES/DOCUMENTS BEFORE THE COURT IN THE RECEIVING STATE HERE.)

RECIPROCITY

THE REQUESTING COURT SHOULD INCLUDE A STATEMENT EX-PRESSING A WILLINGNESS TO PROVIDE SIMILAR ASSISTANCE TO JUDICIAL AUTHORITIES OF THE RECEIVING STATE.

REIMBURSEMENT FOR COSTS

THE REQUESTING COURT SHOULD INCLUDE A STATEMENT EX-PRESSING A WILLINGNESS TO REIMBURSE THE JUDICIAL AUTHORI-TIES OF THE RECEIVING STATE FOR COSTS INCURRED IN EXECUT-ING THE REQUESTING COURT'S LETTER ROGATORY.

SIGNATURE OF REQUESTING JUDGE

TYPED NAME OF REQUESTING JUDGE

NAME OF REQUESTING COURT

CITY, STATE, COUNTRY

DATE

(SEAL OF COURT)

Appendix 5

1992 Inter-American Convention on Mutual Assistance in Criminal Matters

---

Preamble

WHEREAS:

The Charter of the Organization of American States, in Article 2.e, establishes that an essential objective of the American states is "to seek the solution of political, juridical, and economic problems that may arise among them"; and

The adoption of common rules in the field of mutual assistance in criminal matters will contribute to the attainment of this goal,

THE MEMBER STATES OF THE ORGANIZATION OF AMERICAN STATES

Do hereby adopt the following Inter-American Convention on Mutual Assistance in Criminal Matters:

Chapter I: General Provisions

Article 1: Purpose of the Convention

The states parties undertake to render to one another mutual assistance in criminal matters, in accordance with the provisions of this convention.

Article 2: Scope and Application of the Convention

The states parties shall render to one another mutual assistance in investigations, prosecutions, and proceedings that pertain to crimes over which the requesting state has jurisdiction at the time the assistance is requested.

This convention does not authorize any state party to undertake, in the territory of another state party, the exercise of jurisdiction or the performance of functions that are placed within the exclusive purview of the authorities of that other party by its domestic law.

This convention applies solely to the provision of mutual assistance among states parties. Its provisions shall not create any right on the part of any private person to obtain or exclude any evidence or to impede execution of any request for assistance.

Article 3: Central Authority

Each state shall designate a central authority at the time of signature or ratification of this convention or accession hereto.

The central authorities shall be responsible for issuing and receiving requests for assistance.

The central authorities shall communicate directly with one another for all purposes of this convention.

Article 4

In view of the diversity of the legal systems of the states parties, the assistance to which this convention refers shall be based upon requests for cooperation from the authorities responsible for criminal investigation or prosecution in the requesting state.

Article 5: Double Criminality

The assistance shall be rendered even if the act that gives rise to it is not punishable under the legislation of the requested state.

When the request for assistance pertains to the following measures: (a) immobilization and sequestration of property and (b) searches and seizures, including house searches, the requested state may decline to render the assistance if the act that gives rise to the request is not punishable under its legislation.

Article 6

For the purposes of this convention, the act that gives rise to the request must be punishable by one year or more of imprisonment in the requesting state.

Article 7: Scope of Application

The assistance envisaged under this convention shall include the following Procedures, among others:

a. notification of rulings and judgments;
b. taking of testimony or statements from persons;
c. summoning of witnesses and expert witnesses to provide testimony;
d. immobilization and sequestration of property, freezing of assets, and assistance in procedures related to seizures;
e. searches or seizures;
f. examination of objects and places;
g. service of judicial documents;
h. transmittal of documents, reports, information, and evidence;
i. transfer of detained persons for the purpose of this convention; and
j. any other procedure provided there is an agreement between the requesting state and the requested state.

Article 8: Military Crimes

This convention shall not apply to crimes subject exclusively to military legislation.

Article 9: Refusal of Assistance

The requested state may refuse assistance when it determines that:

a. The request for assistance is being used in order to prosecute a person on a charge with respect to which that person has already been sentenced or acquitted in a trial in the requesting or requested state;
b. The investigation has been initiated for the purpose of prosecuting, punishing, or discriminating in any way against an individual or group of persons for reason of sex, race, social status, nationality, religion, or ideology;
c. The request refers to a crime that is political or related to a political crime, or to a common crime prosecuted for political reasons;

d. The request has been issued at the request of a special or ad hoc tribunal;

e. Public policy, sovereignty, security, or basic public interests are prejudiced; and

f. The request pertains to a tax crime. Nevertheless, the assistance shall be granted if the offense is committed by way of an intentionally incorrect statement, whether oral or written, or by way of an intentional failure to declare income derived from any other offense covered by this convention for the Purpose of concealing such income.

Chapter II: Requests for Assistance, Processing and Execution

Article 10: Requests for Assistance

Requests for assistance issued by the requesting state shall be made in writing and shall be executed in accordance with the domestic law of the requested state.

The procedures specified in the request for assistance shall be fulfilled in the manner indicated by the requesting state insofar as the law of the requested state is not violated.

Article 11

The requested state may postpone the execution of any request that has been made to it, with an explanation of its grounds for doing so, if it is necessary to continue an investigation or proceeding in progress in the requested state.

Article 12

Documents and objects delivered in compliance with a request for assistance shall be returned to the requested state as soon as possible, unless the latter decides otherwise.

Article 13: Search, Seizure, Attachment, and Surrender of Property

The requested state shall execute requests for search, seizure, attachment, and surrender of any items, documents, records, or effects, if the competent authority determines that the request contains information that justifies the proposed action. That action shall be subject to the procedural and substantive law of the requested state.

In accordance with the provisions of this convention, the requested state shall determine, according to its law, what requirements must be met to protect the interests held by third parties in the items that are to be transferred.

Article 14: Measures for Securing Assets

The central authority of any party may convey to the central authority of any other party information it has on the existence of proceeds, fruits, or instrumentalities of a crime in the territory of that other party.

Article 15

The parties shall assist each other, to the extent permitted by their respective laws, in precautionary measures and measures for securing the proceeds, fruits, and instrumentalities of the crime.

Article 16: Date, Place and Modality of the Execution of the Request for Assistance

The requested state shall set the date and place for execution of the request for assistance and may so inform the requesting state.

Officials and interested parties of the requesting state or their representatives may, after informing the central authority of the requested state, be present at and participate in the execution of the request for assistance, to the extent not prohibited by the law of the requested state, and provided that the authorities of the requested state have given their express consent thereto.

Chapter III: Service of Judicial Decisions, Judgments, and Verdicts, and Appearance of Witnesses and Expert Witnesses

Article 17

At the request of the requesting state, the requested state shall serve notice of decisions, judgments, or other documents issued by the competent authorities of the requesting state.

Article 18: Testimony in the Requested State

At the request of the requesting state, any person present in the requested state shall be summoned to appear before a competent authority, in accordance with the law of the requested state, to give testimony or to provide documents, records, or evidence.

Article 19: Testimony in the Requesting State

When the requesting state requests that a person appear in its territory to give testimony or a report, the requested state shall invite the witness or expert witness to appear voluntarily, without the use of threats or coercive measures, before the appropriate authority in the requesting state. If deemed necessary, the central authority of the requested state may make a written record of the individual's willingness to appear in the requesting state. The central authority of the requested state shall promptly inform the central authority of the requesting state of the response of the person.

Article 20: Transfer of Persons Subject to Criminal Proceedings

A person subject to criminal proceedings in the requested state whose presence in the requesting state is needed for purposes of assistance under this convention shall be transferred temporarily to the requesting state for that purpose if the person and the requested state consent to the transfer.

A person subject to criminal proceedings in the requesting state whose presence in the requested state is needed for purposes of assistance under this convention shall be transferred temporarily to the requested state if the person consents and both states agree.

The actions set forth above may be denied for the following reasons, among others:

a. the individual in custody or serving a sentence refuses to consent to the transfer;
b. as long as his presence is necessary in an investigation or criminal proceeding that is under way in the jurisdiction to which he is subject at the time;
c. there are other considerations, whether legal or of another nature, as determined by the competent authority of the requested or requesting state.

For purposes of this article:

a. the receiving state shall have the authority and the obligation to keep the transferred person in physical custody unless otherwise indicated by the sending state;

b. the receiving state shall return the transferred person to the sending state as soon as circumstances permit or as otherwise agreed by the central authorities of the two states;

c. the sending state shall not be required to initiate extradition proceedings for the return of the transferred person;

d. the transferred person shall receive credit toward service of the sentence imposed in the sending state for time served in the receiving state; and

e. the length of time spent by the person in the receiving state shall never exceed the period remaining for service of the sentence or 60 days, whichever is less, unless the person and both states agree to an extension of time.

Article 21: Transit

The states parties shall render cooperation, to the extent possible, for travel through their territory of the persons mentioned in the preceding article, provided that the respective central authority has been given due advance notice and that such persons travel in the custody of agents of the requesting state.

Such prior notice shall not be necessary when air transportation is used and no regular landing is scheduled in the territory of the state party or states parties to be overflown.

Article 22: Safe-Conduct

The appearance or transfer of the person who agrees to render a statement or to testify under the provisions of this convention shall require, if the person or the sending state so requests prior to such appearance or transfer, that the receiving state grant safe-conduct under which the person, while in the receiving state, shall not:

a. be detained or prosecuted for offenses committed prior to his departure from the territory of the sending state;

b. be required to make a statement or to give testimony in proceedings not specified in the request; or

c. be detained or prosecuted on the basis of any statement he makes, except in case of contempt of court or perjury.

The safe-conduct specified in the preceding paragraph shall cease when the person voluntarily prolongs his stay in the territory of the receiving state for more than 10 days after his presence is no longer necessary in that state, as communicated to the sending state.

Article 23

In connection with witnesses or expert witnesses, documents containing the relevant questions, interrogatories, or questionnaires shall be forwarded to the extent possible or necessary.

Chapter IV: Transmittal of Information and Records

Article 24

In cases where assistance is carried out under this convention, the requested state, upon request and in accordance with its domestic procedure, shall make available to the requesting state a copy of the public documents, records, or information held by the government agencies or departments of the requested state.

The requested state may make available copies of any document, record, or other information held by a government agency or department of that state that is not public in nature, to the same extent as and subject to the same conditions under which they would be made available to its own judicial authorities or to others responsible for application of the law. The requested state, at its own discretion, may deny, in whole or in part, any request made under the provisions of this paragraph.

Article 25: Limitation on the Use of Information or Evidence

The requesting state may not disclose or use any information or evidence obtained in the course of application of this convention for purposes other than those specified in the request for assistance without prior consent from the central authority of the requested state.

In exceptional cases, if the requesting state needs to disclose and use, in whole or in part, the information or evidence for purposes other than those specified, it shall request authorization therefore from the requested state, which, at its discretion, may accede to or deny that request in whole or in part.

The information or evidence that must be disclosed and used to the extent necessary for proper fulfillment of the procedure or formalities specified in the request shall not be subject to the authorization requirement set forth in this article.

When necessary, the requested state may ask that the information or evidence provided remain confidential according to conditions specified by the central authority. If the requesting party is unable to accede to such request, the central authorities shall confer in order to define mutually acceptable terms of confidentiality.

Chapter V: Procedure

Article 26

Requests for assistance shall contain the following details:

a. the crime to which the procedure refers; a summary description of the essential facts of the crime, investigation, or criminal proceeding in question; and a description of the facts to which the request refers;
b. proceeding giving rise to the request for assistance, with a precise description of such proceeding;
c. where pertinent, a description of any proceeding or other special requirement of the requesting state;
d. a precise description of the assistance requested and any information necessary for the fulfillment of that request.

When the requested state is unable to comply with a request for assistance, it shall return the request to the requesting state with an explanation of the reason therefore.

The requested state may request additional information when necessary for fulfillment of the request under its domestic law or to facilitate such fulfillment.

When necessary, the requesting state shall proceed in accordance with the provisions of the last paragraph of Article 24 of this convention.

Article 27

Documents processed through the central authorities in accordance with this convention shall be exempt from certification or authentication.

Article 28

Requests for assistance and the accompanying documentation must be translated into an official language of the requested state.

Article 29

The requested state shall be responsible for all regular costs of executing a request in its territory, except for those listed below, which shall be borne by the requesting state:

a. fees for expert witnesses; and
b. travel costs and other expenses related to the transportation of persons from the territory of one state to that of the other.

If it appears that the processing of the request might entail unusual costs, the states parties shall confer to determine the terms and conditions under which the assistance could be rendered.

Article 30

To the extent that they find it useful and necessary for furthering the implementation of this convention, the states parties may exchange information on matters related to its application.

Article 31

The domestic law of each party shall govern liability for damages arising from the acts of its authorities in the execution of this Convention.

Neither party shall be liable for damages that may arise from the acts committed by the authorities of the other party in the formulation or execution of a request under this Convention.

Bibliography

Abel, G. G., et al. *Multiple Paraphilic Diagnoses among Sex Offenders.* 16 BULL. OF THE AM. ACAD. OF PSYCHIATRY AND THE L. 153 (1988).

Adelstein, Jake. *This Mob Is Big in Japan.* WASH. POST, May 11, 2008.

Agan, Amanda Y. SEX OFFENDER REGISTRIES: FEAR WITHOUT FUNCTION? (Dec. 2008) (unpublished).

Agbu, Osita. *Corruption and Human Trafficking: The Nigerian Case.* 4 W. AFR. REV. 1 (2003).

Anonymous. *Letter to a Young Boy-Lover.* N. AM. MAN/BOY LOVE ASS'N BULL., Jan/Feb 1993, at 30. *Reprinted in* Wendy Waldron and Michael Yoon. *Obtaining Foreign Evidence in Child Sex Tourism Cases.* U.S. ATT'YS BULL., Nov. 2006.

Asa High, James, Jr. *The Basis for Jurisdiction over U.S. Sex Tourists: An Examination of the Case against Michael Lewis Clark.* 11 U.C. DAVIS 343 (Spring 2005).

Bagnall, Janet. *Sex Trade Blights the Lives of 2 Million Children.* MONTREAL GAZETTE, Oct. 24, 2007.

Baker, James E., and Melanie Krebs-Pilotti. *Internet Pandemic? The Not-So-Secret and Expanding World of Child Pornography.* 53 FED. LAW. 50 (2006).

Bendavid, Naftali. *Huge Child Porn Web Site Broken Up.* CHI. TRIBUNE, Aug. 9, 2001.

Brake, Stephen, and Greig Veeder. RE-OFFENSE RATES OF ADULT SEX OFFENDERS (unpublished literature review) (2007). Available at www.stephenbrakeassociates.com/Reoffense_Rates_for_Website.pdf.

Brown, Geneva. *Woman and Children Last: The Prosecution of Sex Traffickers as Sex Offenders and the Need for a Sex Trafficker Registry.* 31 B.C. THIRD WORLD L.J. 1 (2011).

Carlson, Kristin. *Strong Medicine: Toward Effective Sentencing of Child Pornography Offenders.* MICH. L. REV. FIRST IMPRESSIONS (2010).

Chacón, Jennifer M. *Misery and Myopia: Understanding the Failures of U.S. Efforts to Stop Human Trafficking.* 74 FORDHAM L. R. 2977 (2006).

Children's Exposure to Pornography on Peer-to-Peer Networks. Hearing before the H. Comm. on Oversight and Gov't Reform (2003). Available at http://oversight.house.gov/documents/20040817153704-85383.pdf.

Chuang, Janie. *The United States as Global Sheriff: Using Unilateral Sanctions to Combat Human Trafficking.* 27 MICH. J. INT'L L. 437 (2006).

Citizens Media Law Project. HOW TO MAINTAIN YOUR ANONYMITY ONLINE (undated). Available at www.citmedialaw.org/legal-guide/how-maintain-your-anonymity-online.

Cole, Alison. *Reconceptualizing Female Trafficking: The Inhumane Trade in Women.* 26 WOMEN'S RTS. L. REP. 97 (2005).

Department of Justice, Office of Juvenile Justice and Delinquency Prevention. NATIONAL INCIDENCE STUDIES OF MISSING, ABDUCTED, RUNAWAY, AND THROWNAWAY CHILDREN (October 2002).

Doren, Dennis M. *Recidivism Base Rates, Predictions of Sex Offender Recidivism, and the "Sexual Predator" Commitment Laws.* 16 BEHAV. SCI. LAW 97 (1998).

Doyle, Charles. EXTRATERRITORIAL APPLICATION OF AMERICAN CRIMINAL LAW (Congressional Research Service, March 26, 2010).

Dutch Ministry of Justice. *Appointment of National Rapporteur on Trafficking in Human Beings* (Jan. 27, 2000). Available at http://english.justitie.nl/currenttopics/pressreleases/archives2000/-appointment-of-national-rapporteur-on-trafficking-in-human-beings.aspx.

Ebert, Michael. *Pedophilia Steps into the Daylight.* FOCUS ON THE FAMILY CITIZEN (Nov. 16, 1992).

E.C.B., Jr. *Pedophilia, Exhibitionism, and Voyeurism: Legal Problems in the Deviant Society.* 4 GEORGIA L. REV. 150 (1969).

Economist Intelligence Unit. EUROPEAN POLICY ANALYST 4TH QUARTER 2006 (2006).

Edelson, Daniel. Note, *The Prosecution of Persons Who Sexually Exploit Children in Countries Other Than Their Own: A Model for Amending Existing Legislation.* 25 FORDHAM INT'L L.J. 483 (2001).

Estes, Richard J., and Neil Alan Weiner. *The Commercial Sexual Exploitation of Children in the U.S., Canada and Mexico.* PENN SCHOOL OF SOC. POL'Y & PRAC. 8 (2003). Available at www.sp2.upenn.edu/restes/CSEC_Files/Exec_Sum_020220.pdf.

Council of Europe. CONVENTION ON THE PROTECTION OF CHILDREN AGAINST SEXUAL EXPLOITATION AND SEXUAL ABUSE. Doc. No. 201 (2007).

Exum, Jelani Jefferson. *Making the Punishment Fit the (Computer) Crime: Rebooting Notions of Possession for the Federal Sentencing of Child Pornography Offenses.* 3 RICH. J. L. & TECH. 1 (2010).

Fagan, Patrick. *How U.N. Conventions on Women's and Children's Rights Undermine Family, Religion, and Sovereignty.* HERITAGE FOUND. BACKGROUNDER, Feb. 5, 2001.

Federal Bureau of Investigation. INNOCENT IMAGES: ONLINE CHILD PORNOGRAPHY/CHILD SEXUAL EXPLOITATION INVESTIGATIONS. Available at www.fbi.gov/stats-services/publications/innocent-images-1.

Feltham, Colin, and Windy Dryden. DICTIONARY OF COUNSELING (2004).

Fielding, Nick. *Hackers Caught in Bloomberg E-Sting.* SUNDAY TIMES (London), Aug. 20, 2000.

Fine Collins, Amy. *Sex Trafficking of Americans—the Girl Next Door.* VANITY FAIR (May 24, 2011).

Florida State University Center for the Advancement of Human Rights. FLORIDA RESPONDS TO HUMAN TRAFFICKING (Fall 2003).

Funk, T. Markus. VICTIMS' RIGHTS AND ADVOCACY AT THE INTERNATIONAL COURT (2010).

Gibbons, Patrick J. *Redeeming Peacekeeping: Using the U.N. Security Council to Internationalize the U.S. Military Ban on Prostitution Patronage.* 200 MIL. L. REV. 1 (2009).

Ginsburg, Allen. *The Liberation Is the Word.* THE HARV. GAY AND LESBIAN REV. (Summer 1997).

Government Offices of Sweden. PROSTITUTION AND TRAFFICKING IN HUMAN BEINGS. Available at http://regeringen.se/sb/d/7119.

Hafen, Jonathan O. *International Extradition: Issues Arising under the Dual Criminality Requirement.* 1992 B.Y.U. L. REV. 191 (1992).

Hallett, Carol. *The International Black Market: Coping with Drugs, Thugs, and Fissile Materials.* In GLOBAL ORGANIZED CRIME: THE NEW EMPIRE OF EVIL, edited by Linnea P. Raine and Frank J. Ciluffo (1994).

Hamilton, Melissa. *The Efficacy of Severe Child Pornography Sentencing: Empirical Validity or Political Rhetoric.* 22 STANFORD L. & POL'Y REV. 545 (2011).

Hand 'Em Over: Britain's Tough Extradition Laws Face a Shake-Up. THE ECONOMIST, Sept. 23, 2010. Available at www.economist.com/node/17103867?story_id=17103867.

Hanson, R. Karl, and Kelly E. Morton-Bourgon. *The Accuracy of Recidivism Risk Assessments for Sexual Offenders: A Meta-Analysis of 118 Prediction Studies.* 21 PSYCH. ASSESSMENT 1 (2009).

———. *The Characteristics of Persistent Sexual Offenders: A Meta-Analysis of Recidivism Studies.* 73 J. CONSULTING & CLINICAL PSYCH. 1154 (2005).

Hartzog, Neal. *The "Magic Lantern" Revealed: A Report of the FBI's New "Key Logging" Trojan and Analysis of Its Possible Treatment in a Dynamic Legal Landscape.* 20 J. MARSHALL J. COMPUTER & INFO. L. 287 (2002).

Hepburn, John R., and Marie L. Griffin. AN ANALYSIS OF RISK FACTORS CONTRIBUTING TO THE RECIDIVISM OF SEX OFFENDERS ON PROBATION. Unpublished report submitted to the Maricopa County Adult Probation Dep't and the Nat'l Institute of Justice (Oct. 2002).

Hernandez, Andres E. SELF-REPORTED CONTACT SEXUAL OFFENSES BY PARTICIPANTS IN THE FEDERAL BUREAU OF PRISONS' SEX OFFENDER TREATMENT PROGRAM: IMPLICATIONS FOR INTERNET SEX OFFENDERS (2000). Available at www.kardasz.org/HernandezPrisonStudy.pdf.

Howard, Ty E. *Don't Cache Out Your Case: Prosecuting Child Pornography Possession Laws Based on Images Located in Temporary Internet Files.* 19 BERKELEY TECH. L.J. 1227 (2004).

Human Rights Watch. OWED JUSTICE: THAI WOMEN TRAFFICKED INTO DEBT BONDAGE IN JAPAN (2000). Available at www.hrw.org/reports/2000/japan/.

Hyland, Kelly. *Protecting Human Victims of Trafficking: An American Framework.* 16 BERKELEY WOMEN'S L.J. 29 (2001).

INTEGRATED PLAN OF ACTION TO PREVENT AND COMBAT HUMAN TRAFFICKING WITH SPECIAL FOCUS ON CHILDREN AND WOMEN. Available at http://webapps01.un.org/vawdatabase/uploads/Plan%20of%20ACtion%20to%20Combat%20Trafficking.doc.

International Council of Voluntary Agencies, Inter-Agency Standing Committee Reference Group on Humanitarian Action and Human Rights. FREQUENTLY ASKED QUESTIONS ON INTERNATIONAL HUMANITARIAN, HUMAN RIGHTS, AND REFUGEE LAW (2002). Available at www.icva.ch/doc00001023.html#24 (last visited June 5, 2011).

Ipoque. INTERNET STUDY (2007). Available at www.ipoque.com/.

Kane, Eva J. PROSTITUTION OF CHILDREN AND CHILD-SEX TOURISM: AN ANALYSIS OF DOMESTIC AND INTERNATIONAL RESPONSES (1999).

Kendall-Tackett, Kathleen, et al. *Impact of Sexual Abuse on Children: A Review and Synthesis of Recent Empirical Studies.* 113 PSYCH. BULL. 164 (1993).

Kerr, Kathy. *Returning Home: The Challenge of Repatriating Foreign Born Child.* 16 BUFF. H. RTS. L. REV. 155 (2010).

Kinsey, Alfred, et al. SEXUAL BEHAVIOR IN THE HUMAN FEMALE (1953).

Lally, Conor. *Garda Investigated over Child Porn on Internet.* IRISH TIMES, Dec. 19, 2002.

Lambert, Melissa, and Josh Meyer. *House OKs Crackdown on Trafficking in Sex.* L.A. TIMES, Oct. 7, 2000.

Langevin, R., et al. *Lifetime Sex Offender Recidivism: A 24-Year Follow-Up Study.* 46 CANADIAN J. OF CRIMINOLOGY AND CRIM. JUST. 531 (2004).

Lanning, Kenneth V. CHILD MOLESTERS: A BEHAVIORAL ANALYSIS. 4th ed. Washington, DC: Office of Juvenile Justice and Delinquency Prevention and Department of Justice, 2001.

———. SEX OFFENDER CONTINUUM (2002). Available at www.cac-kent.org/pdfs/Lanning_-_Suspect_Typology.pdf.

Leff, Lisa. *Transcripts Reveal Details about Dugard Kidnapping.* NEWARK STAR-LEDGER, June 4, 2011.

Lehti, Martti, and Kauko Aromaa. *Trafficking for Sexual Exploitation.* 34 CRIME & JUST. 133 (2006).

Levenson, Jill S., and Leo P. Cotter. *The Effect of Megan's Law on Sex Offender Reintegration.* 21 J. CONTEMP. CRIM. JUST. 49 (2005).

LexisNexis and the Polaris Project. U.S. AWARENESS OF HUMAN TRAFFICKING: EXECUTIVE SUMMARY OF SURVEY FINDINGS (2010). Available at www.lexisnexis.com/redlight/lexisnexis-human-trafficking-survey.pdf.

Li, Vickie F. *Child Sex Tourism to Thailand: The Role of the United States as a Consumer Country.* 4 PAC. RIM L. & POL'Y J. 505 (1995).

Linden, Leigh, and J. Rockoff. *There Goes the Neighborhood? Estimates from the Impact of Crime Risk on Property Values from Megan's Laws.* NBER Working Paper 12253 (2006).

Logan, Wayne A. *A Study in "Actuarial Justice": Sex Offender Classification Practice and Procedure.* 3 BUFF. CRIM. L. REV. 593 (2000).

March, James R. *Masha's Law: A Federal Civil Remedy for Child Pornography Victims.* 61 SYRACUSE L. REV. 459 (2011).

Marquis, Christopher. *U.S. Says It Broke Ring That Peddled Child Pornography.* N.Y. TIMES, Aug. 9, 2001.

Marshall, W.L. *Revisiting the Use of Pornography by Sexual Offenders: Implications for Theory and Practice.* 6 J. SEXUAL AGGRESSION 67 (2000).

———. *The Use of Sexually Explicit Stimuli by Rapists, Child Molesters, and Non-Offenders.* 25 J. SEX. RESEARCH 267 (1988).

Massive Online Pedophile Ring Busted by Cops. MSNBC. Available at www.msnbc.msn .com/id/42108748/ns/us_news-crime_and_courts/t/massive-online-pedophile -ring-busted-cops/.

Mattar, Mohamed Y. *Comparative Models of Reporting Mechanisms on the Status of Trafficking in Human Beings.* 41 VAND. J. TRANSNAT'L L. 1355 (2008).

McCullagh, Declan. *Congress: File Sharing Leaks Sensitive Government Data.* July 29, 2009. Available at CBSNews.com.

McIlwaine, Blaine D. INTERROGATING CHILD MOLESTERS. Available at http://investigations helpdesk.com/html/training/le_articles/94JUN001.TXT.

McKinney, Laura. *International Adoption and the Hague Convention: Does Implementation of the Convention Protect the Best Interests of Children?* 6 WHITTIER J. CHILD & FAM. ADVOC. 361 (2007).

McVeigh, Karen. *Police Shut Down Global Paedophile Network in Operation Rescue.* THE GUARDIAN UK, March 16, 2011.

Nelson, Sharon, et al. IN DEFENSE OF THE DEFENSE: THE USE OF COMPUTER FORENSICS IN CHILD PORNOGRAPHY CASES (2009).

O'Briain, Muireann. CHILD SEXUAL EXPLOITATION AND THE LAW: A REPORT ON THE INTERNATIONAL LEGAL FRAMEWORK AND CURRENT NATIONAL LEGISLATIVE AND ENFORCEMENT RESPONSES (submitted to the World Congress against Commercial Sexual Exploitation of Children, Stockholm, Sweden, August 1996). Available at www.csecworld-congress.org/.../ Theme%20paper%20CSEC%20and%20the%20Law.pdf.

Office to Monitor and Combat Trafficking in Persons, U.S. Department of State. TRAFFICKING IN PERSONS REPORT (2008). Available at www.state.gov/documents/ organization/105501.pdf.

———. TRAFFICKING IN PERSONS REPORT (June 2010). Available at www.state.gov/g/tip/ rls/tiprpt/2010/index.htm.

Organisation for Economic Co-operation and Development. ABOUT THE NEW RECOMMENDATION FOR FURTHER COMBATING BRIBERY OF FOREIGN PUBLIC OFFICIALS IN INTERNATIONAL BUSINESS. Available at www.oecd.org/dataoecd/34/15/44281002.pdf.

———. COUNTRY REPORTS ON THE IMPLEMENTATION OF THE OECD ANTI-BRIBERY CONVENTION. Available at www.oecd.org/document/24/0,3343,en_2649_34859_1933144_1_ 1_1_1,00.html.

———. OECD ANTI-BRIBERY CONVENTION: ENTRY INTO FORCE OF THE CONVENTION. Available at www.oecd.org/document/12/0,3343,en_2649_34859_2057484_1_1_1_1,00 .html.

———. OECD ANTI-BRIBERY CONVENTION: NATIONAL IMPLEMENTING LEGISLATION. Available at www.oecd.org/document/30/0,3343,en_2649_34859_2027102_1_1_1_1,00 .html.

————. Ratification Status as of March 2009. Available at www.oecd.org/data oecd/59/13/40272933.pdf.

————. Recommendation of the Council for Further Combating Bribery of Foreign Public Officials in International Business Transactions. Available at www.oecd .org/dataoecd/11/40/44176910.pdf.

Ozalp, Jessica E. Comment, *Halting Modern Slavery in the Midwest: The Potential of Wisconsin Act 116 to Improve the State and Federal Response to Human Trafficking.* 2009 Wis. L. Rev. 1391 (2009).

Pati, Roza. *States' Positive Obligations with Respect to Human Trafficking: The European Court of Human Rights Breaks New Ground in Rantsev v. Cyprus and Russia.* 29 B.U. Int'l L.J. 79 (2011).

Pazuniak, Andriy. *A Better Way to Stop Online Predators: Encouraging a More Appealing Approach to § 2422(B).* 40 Seton Hall L. Rev. 691 (2010).

Plato, Symposium. Oxford: Oxford World Classics, 2009.

Podgor, Ellen S. *New Dimension to the Prosecution of White Collar Crime: Enforcing Extraterritorial Social Harms.* 37 McGeorge L. Rev 83 (2006).

Press Release. *U.S. Customs Service, Russian Police Take Down Global Child Pornography Web Site* (Mar. 26, 2001). http://www.cbp.gov/hot-new/pressrel/2001/0326-00 .htm (last visited October 25, 2011).

Price Cohen, Cynthia. *The Role of the United States in the Drafting of the Convention on the Rights of the Child.* 20 Emory Int'l L. Rev. 185 (2006).

Quayle, Ethel, and Max Taylor. *Child Pornography and the Internet: Perpetuating a Cycle of Abuse.* 23 Deviant Behavior: An Interdisciplinary J. 331 (2002).

Reisman, Dr. Judith A. *Where Have We Been? Where Are We Going?* Nov. 2, 2005, speech to the Utah Council for Crime Prevention.

Richards, James R. Transnational Criminal Organizations, Cybercrime, and Money Laundering (1999).

Rule, Jane. Teaching Sexuality (1979).

Sachs, Aaron. *The Last Commodity, Child Prostitution in the Developing World.* World Watch, Jul./Aug. 1994.

Scalora, Mario, and Calvin Garbin. *A Multivariate Analysis of Sex Offender Recidivism.* 47 Int'l J. Offender Therapy & Comparative Criminology 309 (2003).

Schmidt, Dr. Gunter. *Male Intergenerational Intimacy.* 20 J. of Homosexuality (1990).

Schmitknecht, Douglas A. *Building FBI Computer Forensics Capacity: One Lab at a Time.* 1 Digital Investigation 177 (2004).

Schoettle, Ulrich C. *Child Exploitation: A Study of Child Pornography.* 19 J. Am. Acad. Child Psychiatry 289 (1980).

Scott, Charles L., MD, and Trent Holmberg, MD. *Castration of Sex Offenders: Prisoners' Rights versus Public Safety.* 31 (4) J. Am. Acad. Psychiatry Law 502 (2003).

Select Committee on the European Union. Eu/U.S. Agreement on Extradition and Mutual Legal Assistance, 2002–2003 (House of Lords Session 2002–2003, 38th Report, ordered to be printed 15 July 2003), H.L. 153. Available at www.statewatch .org/news/2003/jul/useuhol.pdf (last visited on June 7, 2011).

Seto, Michael C., and Angela W. Elke. *The Criminal Histories and Later Offending of Child Pornography Offenders.* 17 Sexual Abuse 201 (2005).

Shahidullah, Shadid M. *Federal Laws and Judicial Trends in the Prosecution of Cyber Crime Cases in the United States: First and Fourth Amendment Issues.* 45 CRIM. L. BULL. ART. 2 (2009).

Shannon, Elaine. *Main Street Monsters.* E MAGAZINE, Sept. 14, 1998.

Siegel, Jane, and Linda Williams. *The Relationship between Child Sexual Abuse and Female Delinquency and Crime: A Prospective Study.* 40 J. RES. CRIME & DELINQUENCY 71 (2003).

Skinner, Robyn, and Catherine Maher. CHILD TRAFFICKING AND ORGANIZED CRIME: WHERE HAVE ALL THE CHILDREN GONE (undated). Available at www.yapi.org/rpchildtrafficking.pdf.

Slovenko, Ralph, and C. Phillips. *Psychosexuality and the Criminal Law.* 15 VANDERBILT LAW REVIEW 809 (1962).

Song, Lin, and Roxanne Lieb. ADULT SEX OFFENDER RECIDIVISM: A REVIEW OF STUDIES. Community Protection Research Project, Washington State Institute for Public Policy (1994).

Stabenow, Troy. *Deconstructing the Myth of Careful Study: A Primer on the Flawed Progression of the Child Pornography Guidelines* (2008) (manuscript on file with authors).

Sterling, Claire. CRIME WITHOUT FRONTIERS: THE WORLDWIDE EXPANSION OF ORGANISED CRIME AND THE PAX MAFIOSA (1994).

Stoecker, Sally, and Louise Shelley, eds. HUMAN TRAFFIC AND TRANSNATIONAL CRIME: EURASIAN AND AMERICAN PERSPECTIVES (2005).

Todres, Jonathan. *Law, Otherness, and Human Trafficking.* 49 SANTA CLARA L. REV. 605 (2009).

———. *Moving Upstream: The Merits of a Public Health Law Approach to Human Trafficking.* 89 N.C. L. REV. 447 (2011).

U.N. Economic and Social Commission for Asia and the Pacific. COMMERCIAL SEXUAL EXPLOITATION AND SEXUAL ABUSE OF CHILDREN: DEFINITIONS OF TERMS (1998). Available at www.escap-hrd.org/csec2.htm.

U.N. Global Initiative to Fight Human Trafficking. THE VIENNA REPORT: A WAY FORWARD TO COMBAT HUMAN TRAFFICKING (2008). Available at www.ungift.org/gifts/ungift/pdf/vf/ebook2.pdf.

U.N. Office on Drugs and Crime. HUMAN TRAFFICKING: EVERYBODY'S BUSINESS. Available at www.unglobalcompact.org/docs/news_events/Bulletin/HumanTraffic_Info .pdf.

———. REVISED MANUALS ON THE MODEL TREATY ON EXTRADITION AND ON THE MODEL TREATY ON MUTUAL ASSISTANCE IN CRIMINAL MATTERS (2002). Available at www.unodc .org/pdf/model_treaty_extradition_revised_manual.pdf.

———. THE ROLE OF CORRUPTION IN TRAFFICKING IN PERSONS (Nov. 11, 2009).

UNICEF. CHILD PROTECTION FROM VIOLENCE, EXPLOITATION AND ABUSE (2011). Available at www.unicef.org/protection/index_childlabour.html.

———. COMMERCIAL SEXUAL EXPLOITATION AND SEXUAL ABUSE OF CHILDREN IN SOUTH ASIA (2001). Available at www.unicef.org/rosa/commercial.pdf.

———. PROFITING FROM ABUSE: AN INVESTIGATION INTO SEXUAL EXPLOITATION OF OUR CHILDREN (2001).

United Nations. Optional Protocol to Prevent, Suppress and Punish Trafficking in Persons, Especially Women and Children. G.A. Res. 55/383, U.N. Doc. A/RES/55/383 (Dec. 25, 2003). Available at www.unodc.org/documents/treaties/UNTOC/Publications/TOC%20Convention/TOCebook-e.pdf.

———. Optional Protocol to the Convention on the Rights of the Child on the Sale of Children, Child Prostitution and Child Pornography (Jan. 22, 2010). Available at www.state.gov/documents/organization/136023.pdf.

U.S. Department of Health and Human Services, Administration for Children and Families. Human Trafficking Fact Sheet (2010). Available at www.acf.hhs.gov/trafficking/about/fact_human.html.

———. Fact Sheet: Labor Trafficking. Available at www.acf.hhs.gov/trafficking/about/fact_labor.html.

U.S. Department of Justice. Child Exploitation and Obscenity Section, Sex Tourism (2011).

———. *U.S./EU Agreements on Mutual Legal Assistance and Extradition Enter Into Force* (U.S. Department of Justice, Office of Public Affairs, Feb. 1, 2010). Available at www.justice.gov/opa/pr/2010/February/10-opa-108.html (last visited June 13, 2011).

U.S. Department of State. Trafficking in Persons Report 2010 (2010). Available at www.state.gov/g/tip/rls/tiprpt/2010/index.htm.

U.S. General Accounting Office. Peer-to-Peer Networks Provide Ready Access to Child Pornography (2003). Available at www.gao.gov/new.items/d03351.pdf.

U.S. Sentencing Commission Report. *Sex Offenses against Children—Findings and Recommendations Regarding Federal Penalties* (Official Report to Congress as directed in the Sex Crimes Against Children Prevention Act of 1995, Section 6, Public Law 104–71) (June 1996).

Waisman, Viviana. *Human Trafficking: State Obligations to Protect Victims' Rights.* 33 Hastings Int'l & Comp. L. Rev. 385 (2010).

Wakefield, Hollida. *The Vilification of Sex Offenders: Do Laws Targeting Sex Offenders Increase Recidivism and Sexual Violence?* 1 J. Sexual Offender Civ. Commitment: Sci. & L. 141 (2006).

Waldron, Wendy, and Michael Yoon. *Obtaining Foreign Evidence in Child Sex Tourism Cases.* U.S. Att'ys Bull., Nov. 2006.

Walterbach, Maureen. Comment, *International Illicit Convergence: The Growing Problem of Transnational Organized Crime Groups' Involvement in Intellectual Property Rights Violations.* 34 Fla. St. U. L. Rev. 591 (2007).

Ward, Lucy. *Cook Cracks Down on Child Sex Tourism; Britain Leads Crusade against Paedophiles: International Co-operation to Target Prostitution Trade.* Guardian, Apr. 1, 1999.

Weinrott, M. P., and M. Saylor. *Self-Report of Crimes Committed by Sex Offenders.* 6 J. of Interpersonal Violence 286 (1991).

Willman, Mindy M. Note, *Human Trafficking in Asia: Increasing Individual and State Accountability through Expanded Victims' Rights.* 22 Colum. J. Asian J. 283 (2009).

Wisconsin Office of Justice Assitance. HIDDEN IN PLAIN SIGHT: A BASELINE SURVEY OF HUMAN TRAFFICKING IN WISCONSIN (2008). Available at ftp://doaftp04.doa.state.wi.us/doadocs/Human_Trafficking_Report_Final.pdf.

Working Group on Bribery. DATA ON ENFORCEMENT OF THE ANTI-BRIBERY CONVENTION. Available at www.oecd.org/dataoecd/11/15/45450341.pdf.

Wyre, Ray. *Pornography and Sexual Violence: Working with Sex Offenders.* In PORNOGRAPHY: WOMEN, VIOLENCE AND CIVIL LIBERTIES, ed. Catherine Itzen. Oxford: Oxford University Press, 1992.

Yoder, Henry. *Civil Rights for Victims of Human Trafficking.* 12 U. PA. J. L & SOC. CHANGE 133 (2008–2009).

Yun, Kerry E. *How Japan's Recent Efforts to Reduce Sex Trafficking Can Be Improved through International Human Rights Enforcement Mechanisms: Fulfilling Japan's Global Legal Obligations.* 13 BUFF. HUM. RTS. L. REV. 205 (2007).

Zanahar, Sam. WHY SEX TOURISM (2010). Available at http://sextourism.org.

Zevitz, R. G., et al. *Sex Offender Community Notification: Managing High Risk Criminals or Exacting Further Vengeance?* 18 BEHAV. SCI. & L. 375 (2000).

Zhang, Sheldon X., and Samuel L. Pineda. *Corruption as a Causal Factor in Human Trafficking.* In ORGANIZED CRIME: CULTURE, MARKETS, AND POLICIES, ed. Dina Siegel and Hans Nelson (2008).

Zittler, Jay M. *Propriety of Civil or Criminal Forfeiture of Computer Hardware or Software.* 39 A.L.R.5th 87 (2011).

Index

About the Authors

Virginia M. Kendall was appointed to the federal bench in 2006 after serving over ten years as a federal prosecutor in Chicago. Judge Kendall served as the child exploitation coordinator for the Northern District of Illinois, where she reviewed, coordinated, and supervised the investigation and trials of all child exploitation matters. In 1994, recognizing the significant increase in multi-jurisdictional and international child-exploitation investigations, Judge Kendall urged the initiation of the creation of an advisory committee of senior prosecutors and law enforcement agents to review proposed federal prosecutions impacting multiple jurisdictions. The committee was also designed to provide advice and guidance to law enforcement officers faced with the challenges of protecting victims' and defendants' rights, while at the same time ensuring the efficient collection and processing of evidence. After serving on the Working Committee, which proposed a new protocol in the U.S. Attorney's Manual to effectuate the changes, Judge Kendall was appointed to the Attorney General's Advisory Committee on Child Exploitation Cases, a position she maintained until her appointment to the bench. In her years as a federal prosecutor, Judge Kendall tried numerous cases involving child exploitation, racketeering, fraud, and public corruption. She is recognized for developing a novel inveigling theory to charge a defendant with kidnapping—the defendant had lured his victims over the Internet in this first-of-its-kind case. Judge Kendall has also lectured extensively in the area of Internet investigation, victims' rights, and human trafficking, She has lectured at Cornell University on human trafficking as part of the Avon Global Center for Women and Justice, served as a delegate to the Vital Voices Global Partnership to End Violence against

Women international summit, and spoken at the Inaugural Conference of the
Avon Global Center's Symposium on Post-Conflict Violence against Women.
Judge Kendall has received numerous awards, including the Rape Victim
Advocates Visionary Award in recognition of her work on behalf of survivors
of sexual assault and abuse, DePaul University School of Law's Women and
Gender Right's Leadership Award, Loyola University Law School's Robert
Bellarmine Award for her distinguished legal and service contributions to the
community, and the Chicago Crime Commission's Star of Distinction Award
for her work in law enforcement.

After her appointment to the bench, Judge Kendall continued her work to
educate others about crimes against women and children by partnering with
the Department of Justice and Lawyers Without Borders to teach judges and
lawyers in Kenya, Zambia, and Liberia. Judge Kendall also co-chaired the
American Bar Association's (ABA) Organized Crime and Human Trafficking Committee (together with coauthor T. Markus Funk) and currently co-
chairs the ABA's Jury Innovations Subcommittee. Her publications include
articles in the *Northwestern University Law Journal* and *Cornell University
International Law Journal.* Judge Kendall has taught at the U.S. Department of
Justice's National Advocacy Center, the National Institute for Trial Advocacy,
and the Department of Justice's Office of Overseas Prosecutorial Development, Assistance, and Training, and has also been an instructor for various
international rule-of-law trainings. She continues to teach at Northwestern
University School of Law (since 2005), and at Loyola University School of
Law (since 1994).

In her judicial capacity, Judge Kendall serves on the Judicial Codes of
Conduct Committee and the Seventh Circuit Jury Instruction Committee,
and has also sat by designation with the Seventh, Ninth, and Federal Circuit
Courts of Appeal.

Judge Kendall began her legal career clerking for the Hon. George M. Ma-
rovich in the Northern District of Illinois. She received her undergraduate
and master's degrees from Northwestern University, and her law degree from
Loyola University of Chicago.

T. Markus Funk, now in private practice focusing on the areas of complex
commercial litigation, investigations, and white-collar defense, from 2000 to
2010 served as a federal prosecutor in Chicago. Markus was the lead prosecutor on a wide array of child-exploitation cases, including the notable prosecution of defrocked priest Vincent McCaffrey, who received the then-longest
sentence for possession of child pornography. In 2009, the U.S. attorney
general personally awarded Markus the U.S. Department of Justice's highest
trial performance distinction—a first for a Chicago federal prosecutor—for

his work on the most extensive mob-murder racketeering case of its kind ("Operation Family Secrets").

From 2004 to 2006, Markus served as the Department of Justice's resident legal advisor for Kosovo, helping oversee the United States' multimillion-dollar efforts to fight human trafficking and to bring the rule of law to this war-torn region. In recognition of his service abroad, the U.S. State Department conferred on Markus its prestigious Superior Honor Award, the highest award of its kind bestowed by the State Department. Markus has the distinction of being the only person to have received both the Department of Justice's and the State Department's highest general service awards.

In 2010, the ABA tapped Markus to set up and chair the ABA's Global Anti-corruption Task Force. Markus has also served as a member of the ABA's Haiti and Darfur Task Forces, represented the ABA on the Uniform Law Committee's recent efforts to draft a model human-trafficking statute, and, together with Judge Kendall, co-chaired the ABA's Organized Crime and Human Trafficking Committee. Markus presently serves on the editorial board of the ABA's *Litigation Magazine*, and on the advisory board of the BNA *Criminal Law Reporter*.

Markus, a 1995 graduate of Northwestern University School of Law and a candidate for a PhD in law from Oxford University, started his legal career as a law clerk to the Hon. Morris S. Arnold of the U.S. Court of Appeals for the Eighth Circuit and to Chief U.S. District Judge Catherine Perry in the Eastern District of Missouri (St. Louis). Markus has been a full-time or adjunct professor at, among other places, Oxford University, the University of Chicago Law School, Northwestern University Law School, Denver University School of Law, Loyola University at Chicago, the University of Arkansas at Little Rock School of Law, and the U.S. Department of Justice's National Advocacy Center.

In addition to authoring dozens of criminal law–related articles, as well as book chapters on a wide variety of topics, Markus wrote *Stemming the Suffering: Victims' Rights and the International Criminal Court* (2010) and *The Kosovo Trial Skills Handbook* (2006). His legal work has been featured in publications such as the *Atlantic Monthly, BNA White Collar Crime Report, CNBC, CNN*, the *Economist, Investor's Business Daily*, the *Los Angeles Times*, the *National Law Journal, National Geographic Channel*, the *New York Times*, MSNBC, and the *Wall Street Journal*.

CPSIA information can be obtained at www.ICGtesting.com
Printed in the USA
BVOW041240160212

282953BV00003B/3/P